TIME INC.

TIME INC.

The Intimate History of a
Publishing Enterprise
1923-1941

BY ROBERT T. ELSON

Edited by Duncan Norton-Taylor

New York ATHENEUM *1968*

Acknowledgments

THIS IS the first of two volumes in a history of Time Incorporated done by Time Inc. people. It is, in other words, an "authorized history," enjoying the fullest access to all the company's sources, yet free, one hopes, of the constraints that sometimes surround such projects carried out "on company time."

In 1954 Henry R. Luce assigned Alex Groner and Miss Celia Sugarman to assemble material for a history of Time Inc. Over the span of ten years they interviewed 271 former and present members of Time Inc., whose recollections provided invaluable background and insight into the corporation's past. Their work supplemented that of the archivists, Miss Dorothy Seiler and Miss Lillian Owens, who preserved and catalogued the company papers; during the compilation of the history they have been assisted by Mrs. Elaine Felsher.

In 1964, when Luce decided that the time had come to publish the history of Time Inc., a special editorial staff was assembled consisting of the writer and four researchers: Miss Margaret Quimby, Mrs. Elsa Wardell, Miss Marie McCrum and Miss Sugarman. They had as their guide and mentor Roy Alexander, former Editor of *Time;* then as the date of publication neared, Duncan Norton-Taylor, former Managing Editor of *Fortune,* joined the group as editor.

So many past and present members of Time Inc. contributed in so many ways to this book that it is not possible to mention all by name, but special acknowledgment is due to Manfred Gottfried, *Time*'s first writer and later Managing Editor and Chief of Correspondents, for use of his unpublished memoirs; to John Shaw Billings, the first Managing Editor of *Life* and later Editorial Director of Time Inc., for excerpts from his diary and other contributions; to John S. Martin,

Acknowledgments

Time's first Managing Editor, for excerpts from a family memoir and his speech on the occasion of the dedication of the Briton Hadden Memorial Building at Yale University; to Mary and Daniel Longwell, who played such an important part in the founding of *Life,* for their help and criticism; to Eric Hodgins, former Managing Editor and Publisher of *Fortune,* for his penetrating criticism of an earlier draft; to Roy E. Larsen, Chairman of the Time Inc. Executive Committee, and Charles L. Stillman, Chairman of the Finance Committee, for reading and criticizing various drafts of the manuscript, and for their recollections; to Archibald MacLeish for permission to quote from his personal letters to and about Luce; to David Stech, Associate Art Director of *Life,* who designed the illustrated section; to Mrs. Maurice T. Moore, who edited and made available some of Luce's letters from school; to Mrs. Lila Tyng and Mrs. Henry R. Luce for their gracious assistance.

Noel F. Busch's biography of his cousin, *Briton Hadden,* published in 1949 by Farrar, Straus and Company, is a sprightly account of *Time*'s beginnings. The chapters on Hadden and *Time*'s early days owe much to it and to the research which was done by Miss Lilian Rixey. An important source providing background on the Luce family and the missionary work in China is *One Increasing Purpose: The Life of Henry Winters Luce,* by B. A. Garside (Fleming H. Revell Company, 1948).

Before his death in 1967, Henry Luce had read the first half of this manuscript in preliminary draft; during the compilation of the history he gave a number of long tape-recorded interviews which are the source of many of the quotations. Luce, in assigning the staff to the history, charged it to be candid, truthful, and to suppress nothing relevant or essential to the narrative; in fact, those working on this book have had not only complete access to all the corporation files but freedom in the use of documents without restrictions of any kind.

R.T.E.

Contents

Contents

Illustrations

(FOLLOW PAGE 246)

ix

Illustrations

x

TIME INC.

CHAPTER
I

"To Keep Men Well-Informed"

IMPROBABLE as it may seem, Camp Jackson, South Carolina, a forlorn and sand-swept military post in World War I, is where Time Inc. began. There two Yale sophomores, Briton Hadden and Henry Robinson Luce, were sent for officers' training and there a remarkable partnership was joined between two singular men. Their singularity is attested by affectionate relatives and friends, by colleagues and by critics. Evidence is to be found in their achievement: their joined force altered American journalism. Twenty-five years later, at a dinner celebrating *Time*'s twentieth anniversary, Luce told of that beginning:

"There's a picture in my mind . . . of an army camp in the last war; of two underaged second lieutenants, Brit Hadden and Harry Luce—two shavetails, two second looies doing training duty down in Camp Jackson, South Carolina. It was sickeningly hot that summer, but it cooled off a little at night. One night Brit and I were walking back to our barracks through the vast, sprawling camp. At each step, our feet sank ankle-deep into the sand. But we ploughed on for hours —and talked and talked.

3

"For many months we hadn't either of us talked about anything except artillery, mess, inspection—and Saturday night when we went to town and smoked a cigar. Here we were talking about 'that paper' —about something we would do—cross our hearts—some day. . . . I think it was in that walk that *Time* began. . . .

"Why do I say that *Time* was born during that long talk, of which I cannot remember a single phrase or sentence? On that night there was formed an organization. Two boys decided to work together. Actually that had probably been decided long before then. But that night seemed to settle it. Somehow, despite the greatest difference in temperaments and even in interests—somehow we had to work together. We were an organization. At the center of our lives—our job, our function—at that point everything we had belonged to each other. We were an organization."

"That paper" remained a dream, vague and undefined, for more than three years. After their military service, the two young men completed their education at Yale, then went their separate ways— Luce at first to Europe and Oxford, then to Chicago, where he became a reporter on the Chicago *Daily News,* Hadden to New York, where he broke into newspaper work on the *World.* Then suddenly their paths converged; they both received offers of jobs on the Baltimore *News,* which they accepted eagerly because it meant an opportunity to work together on their long-dreamed-of project. For three months they worked every moment they could spare from their newspaper assignments on a magazine they tentatively dubbed "Facts." Then, deciding that their idea was ripe for trial, they abruptly resigned their jobs in Baltimore on February 6, 1922, and two days later set out for New York. Their confidence was not widely shared; their editor at the *News* told them they could have their jobs back if things didn't work out, which seemed more than likely. Hadden was ten days from his twenty-fourth birthday; Luce was six weeks his junior. They had virtually no capital and were innocent of experience in business or finance. Their towering problem, as they had to admit, was the seeming impracticality of their proposition: to start a magazine that would be self-supporting—nay, profitable—in a nation already engulfed in an ocean of print.

4

Radio and television did not exist as national media, but newspapers and magazines abounded. There were 2,033 dailies (284 more than in 1968)—fourteen of them in New York City alone, ranging from the encyclopedic *Times* to the new tabloid *Daily News,* which shortly would achieve the largest circulation in the United States. Giants of the magazine industry blanketed the country. Every Thursday 2,200,000 American men settled into their easy chairs with the *Saturday Evening Post,* creation of the redoubtable Cyrus H. K. Curtis. As many American women were entertained, instructed and admonished by the *Post*'s sister, the *Ladies' Home Journal.* For those interested in public affairs there were the thirty-year-old *Literary Digest,* a weekly published by Funk & Wagnalls, with a circulation of 1,200,000 and advertising revenues second only to the *Saturday Evening Post,* and the monthlies, *Review of Reviews* and *World's Work.* There were also the periodicals of literary aplomb: the *Atlantic, Harper's, Scribner's,* and the *Century.*

Was there any room for another magazine? Few would have thought so, and yet Hadden and Luce had had some encouragement. Samuel Everitt, treasurer of Doubleday, Page & Company, which published magazines as well as books, had looked over their typewritten dummy, and he and other Doubleday people "saw good possibilities for success"—at least so Luce wrote Culbreth Sudler, a former classmate, adding confidently: "We shall have the constant aid and advice of all these men." He had gone so far as to suggest to Sudler, who was working in his father's outdoor-advertising firm in Chicago, that he abandon that job and throw in his lot with them as their advertising manager. In the letter, designed to inspire Sudler, Luce told how they had discussed the dummy with Henry Seidel Canby, who had been a revered English professor at Yale and was then editor of the literary supplement of the New York *Post:*

All Sunday afternoon with Canby, [who] gave us some great pointers. First as to "style" he said, "You have got to develop the style which will exactly suit your purposes, and when you do that, you will have added an appreciable something to American prose." We have got to get a style which is condensed but not

5

telegraphic. As it is now, people have to think too hard as they read. Canby is all for our spending a year educating ourselves and organizing and then sounding off with a quarter-of-a-million capital, which he thinks can be got. At any rate, Canby says the idea certainly warrants us in tossing our present jobs, marching to New York and finding *tout de suite* what we can do with the idea. Therefore, this very hour we resign our jobs. . . . We gamble now a month's time. When that gamble seems justified, we gamble a few hundred on sample rehearsals of the whole play. Then capital to carry us for three months. Then capital to extend for a year, etc. At any one of these points we can turn back without having ruined our entire lives. . . .

So, presumably, could Sudler, who came on from Chicago. Quite apart from having no investment capital, the enterprise had scarcely enough money for daily expenses. Hadden moved in with his family in Brooklyn. And Luce, along with Sudler, moved into the apartment on West 122nd Street which his family were occupying while Dr. Luce, a missionary in China, was on home leave. Some office space was rented in an old, remodeled house of vaguely Italianate style at 141 East 17th Street; the $55-a-month rent was paid by Hadden.

Sudler has described this unimposing birthplace of Time Inc. To reach the office, he remembered, "You thumped one step down from the street into the windowless dining room on the ground floor and then mounted to the living room which ran across the front of the house. The paint on the woodwork was so thick it was like cheese. Here we set up loft-type tables." The furniture cost $48.70. The most distinctive item was an iron soap kettle which Hadden and Luce planted between their desks as a common ashtray.

Hadden and Luce sat down to write a prospectus. They had thought out their proposition in detail, anticipating, they felt, the argument that there was no room for another magazine. Cocksure as it was, the prospectus contained the unique idea that was to germinate into a publishing empire.

The young men deposed:

Although daily journalism has been more highly developed in the United States than in any other country of the world—

6

Although foreigners marvel at the excellence of our periodicals, *World's Work, Century, Literary Digest, Outlook,* and the rest—

People in America are, for the most part, poorly informed.

This is not the fault of the daily newspapers; they print all the news.

It is not the fault of the weekly "reviews"; they adequately develop and comment on the news.

To say with the facile cynic that it is the fault of the people themselves is to beg the question.

People are uninformed BECAUSE NO PUBLICATION HAS ADAPTED ITSELF TO THE TIME WHICH BUSY MEN ARE ABLE TO SPEND ON SIMPLY KEEPING INFORMED.

It was while they were laboring over the prospectus that Luce hit upon a title. "Facts" they had never liked, and nothing else they had thought of seemed right.[1] One night, riding home dead tired on the subway, Luce glanced at an advertisement with the headline "Time to Retire" or "Time for a Change"—he couldn't afterward remember which. "Time" stayed in his mind. He slept on it, and *Time* it became when he tried it on Hadden in the morning.

Time is a weekly news-magazine,[2] aimed to serve the modern necessity of keeping people informed. . . .

Time is interested—not in how much it includes between its covers—but in HOW MUCH IT GETS OFF ITS PAGES INTO THE MINDS OF ITS READERS. . . .

From virtually every magazine and newspaper of note in the world, *Time* collects all available information on all subjects of importance and general interest. The essence of all this information is reduced to approximately 100 short articles, none of which are over 400 words in length (seven inches of type). Each of these articles will be found in its logical place in the magazine,

---

[1] "Briefs," "Hours," and "such banalities" as "The Weekly News Budget," "The Synthetic Review." They had even tried such fanciful flights as "Destiny," "Chance."

[2] The hyphen was dropped with the cover of January 3, 1927, and *newsmagazine* became one word.

according to a FIXED METHOD OF ARRANGEMENT which constitutes a complete ORGANIZATION of all the news.

The prospectus made clear why *Time* would not be like any other publication:

> *Time,* like all weeklies, differs from the daily papers in what it omits.
>
> It differs from other weeklies in that it deals *briefly* with EVERY HAPPENING OF IMPORTANCE and presents these happenings as NEWS (fact) rather than as "comment." It further differs in that it is from three to fifteen days more up-to-date than they. . . .
>
> The *Literary Digest* treats at great length with a few subjects selected more or less arbitrarily from week to week. *Time* gives *all* the week's news in a *brief, organized* manner. . . .
>
> The *Digest,* in giving both sides of a question, gives little or no hint as to which side it considers to be right. *Time* gives both sides, but clearly indicates which side it believes to have the stronger position. . . .

So *Time,* although it would have no editorial page, would admittedly have some prejudices. Among them:

> 1. A belief that the world is round and an admiration of the statesman's "view of all the world."
> 2. A general distrust of the present tendency toward increasing interference by government.
> 3. A prejudice against the rising cost of government.
> 4. Faith in the things which money cannot buy.
> 5. A respect for the old, particularly in manners.
> 6. An interest in the new, particularly in ideas.
> But this magazine is not founded to promulgate prejudices, liberal or conservative. "To keep men well-informed"—that, first and last, is the only axe this magazine has to grind. The magazine is one of news, not argument, and verges on the

8

controversial only where it is necessary to point out what the news *means*.

And at the end of this document,[3] the founders stated their hopes:

> It is estimated that there are over 1,000,000 people in the United States with a college education. *Time* is aiming at every one of these 1,000,000.
>
> But more than that, there are thousands and tens of thousands of men and women in the country who have not had a college education, but who are intelligent and who want such an organized paper as *Time* to keep them posted on the necessary news. . . .
>
> *Time* should appeal to every man and woman in America who has the slightest interest in the world and its affairs.

Writing and revising the prospectus took several weeks. One of the first persons to whom Hadden and Luce showed an early draft was Everitt at Doubleday, who told them that if they were to sell their magazine, they would have to learn something about direct-mail techniques. He sent them to W. H. ("Doc") Eaton, the head of Doubleday's direct-mail operations and one of the country's most knowledgeable practitioners in this field. "I don't think you have a Chinaman's chance," Eaton told them. But he patiently explained circulation methods, particularly the art of testing direct-mail lists. He pointed out that sample mailing techniques made it possible to project future returns, and suggested they test their idea by mailing a circular on *Time* to 7,000 on the *World's Work* "live list"—i.e., the current subscribers.[4] The mailing, in May, drew the extraordinarily good return of 6½ percent.

So they made progress in a number of areas. People were generous with time and counsel. But money, the commitment they had to have or perish, was something else. Their pursuit of it, while they were also

[3] The first cashbook contains this entry, dated April 26, 1922: "Mimeographing the prospecti [*sic*] $40.85."

[4] *World's Work* was a Doubleday, Page publication. The success of *Time* may have contributed to its demise some years later.

trying to concentrate on production problems, proved to be a harrowing experience.

In an effort to help out, Samuel W. Meek, a young advertising man who had been a managing editor of the Yale *Daily News* when Hadden and Luce were freshmen, introduced them to his brother-in-law, John Wesley Hanes, Yale '15. Hanes was then a member of C. D. Barney & Co. in Wall Street. (Later he was to serve Franklin D. Roosevelt as Under Secretary of the Treasury.) He told them they were "crazy to try to buck the *Literary Digest. . . .* Forget it and save your money."

However, he roughed out a financial plan. "You boys want to keep control of things," he said. This baffled Hadden: "How the hell can we do that if we haven't any money?" Hanes explained how they could sell preferred shares at $25 each, two of these shares to carry a bonus of one share of common, and, as creators of the enterprise, could retain 80 percent of the common stock.

This scheme, somewhat more sophisticated than anything Hadden or Luce had envisaged, became the basis of their money-raising operations. They gave up the idea of a $250,000 capitalization (Canby's suggestion) and decided they would bring the magazine out once they had $100,000 in hand. But their pursuit of that sum was to stretch out through the whole summer. Somewhat naïvely they had thought they might be able to get ten rich classmates from Yale to put up $10,000 each. But "we found that the boys from rich families, even when they had money in their own names," Luce said afterward, "were trying to prove to their fathers that they were good business-men and not taking chances on wildcat schemes."

They found their first investor in a classmate, Henry Pomeroy Davison, Jr., who had gone into J. P. Morgan & Co., where his father was a senior partner. He met Luce and Hadden in the men's bar of the Biltmore, and they laid out their proposition. What did Davison think? He thought the odds against it, against any new publication, were about 100 to 1. But he liked the basic idea of the news-magazine and would subscribe to $4,000 worth of stock. "There and then the news-magazine idea began to become a reality," Luce wrote later.

Davison was helpful in another way. From the beginning, Hadden and Luce were uneasy about Hanes's plan of financing. They won-

10

dered if it was unfair to their investors to retain so much of the common stock. What did Davison think about that? "Well," he said, "let me show this to Dwight Morrow." Morrow, a Morgan partner,[5] assured them that the plan was perfectly proper, because the only chance of success lay in what they contributed in the way of talent. Furthermore, he said, he himself would invest $1,000. Any qualms they had vanished forthwith and they threw themselves into the chase with new exuberance. They made no bones about their proposition being a gamble. They even turned down some would-be investors, among them Hadden's friend Dr. Oswald Jones, a young intern, who volunteered to buy some shares. Hadden told him, "No. We are only taking money from people who can afford to lose it." But anyone they thought could afford the gamble they pursued relentlessly. Hadden had developed a sales talk which he called "the groining iron," and no one who granted them a hearing escaped his treatment. One Yale classmate, Seymour H. Knox, of Buffalo, interrupted them when he had heard half their story: "I'll put up $5,000. Now let's go out and play some golf"—but Hadden insisted first on completing his presentation.

Meek introduced them to William V. Griffin, Yale '12, who was associated with the financier James C. Brady. (Later he became the executive trustee of the Brady Estate, a director of many companies, including Continental Oil, and an organizer of the Chrysler Corporation.) Captivated more by the two young men than by their prospectus, he pledged $2,500. He would become their most important guide and counselor in *Time*'s formative years. He also sent them to see his friend Robert A. Chambers, Yale '17, a wealthy young law student, who apparently was enough impressed by Griffin's gamble to put up $2,500.

Meek was not then in a position to invest any substantial sum of his own, but he continued to be helpful. He suggested that the news-magazine idea would be much easier to sell if they could get important people to become charter subscribers and publicly endorse the proposed magazine. Soliciting such testimonials proved much easier than selling stock; by the time they were ready to launch their first direct-mail campaign, an impressive list had been assembled.

[5] Later U.S. Ambassador to Mexico, father-in-law of Charles A. Lindbergh.

But the arduous hunt for money had to continue. There appeared a fresh and heartening ally: John S. Martin, a cousin of Hadden. He was a junior at Princeton and editor-elect of the *Princetonian*—handsome and bubbling with energy. As a boy he had lost his left arm in a hunting accident, but had nevertheless become a crack shot, could break eighty at golf and had earned his letter on the Princeton soccer team. His ambition was eventually to follow Hadden into journalism; his principal asset at the moment was a maroon Marmon roadster, and he had nothing to do before he went back to Princeton in the fall. He proposed that he drive Hadden to Chicago, stopping and selling stock at various golf clubs on the way.

Hadden's and Martin's friends welcomed them to their country clubs. But alas, they were seldom forthcoming with more than token investments of $100 or $200. The peddlers counted on a sure sale to David Robertson Forgan, founder-president of the National City Bank of Chicago, whose son Russell was a Princeton friend of Martin. Forgan withstood the groining, much to Martin's disgust. (Later, when Martin was managing editor of *Time,* he took a mild revenge. To a story about a speech Forgan made "in accents from which 40 years in the Midwest have not yet rasped the St. Andrews burr," Martin added a footnote: "Seven years ago, while he was still founder-president of the since-merged National City Bank of Chicago, Scot Forgan was approached by two young men about to start a new business. They wanted him to buy some of their stock at $25 a share. Looking down his straight strong nose, Banker Forgan declared he could buy no stock. Said he: 'I'm just a poor mon and I wor-rk for a sollery.' ")

In Cleveland, Hadden called on Newton D. Baker, who had been Secretary of War in Woodrow Wilson's Cabinet, and who offered to buy some stock if the magazine would support the League of Nations. Hadden would make no such commitment. "The magazine will be fair on this and all other issues," he said loftily. Baker did become a charter subscriber and one of the prestigious endorsers Meek had suggested lining up.

Years later, in his McKinsey Foundation Lectures at Columbia University, Luce said: "We had to sell, to peddle stock to our friends and our friends' friends. We did not sell them on an idealistic mission.

12

We sold them—when we did, and our sales were agonizingly few and far between—on a sporting chance." By midsummer they had raised only $35,000, a third of their goal. Even Hadden's exuberance flagged.

The strain told particularly on Sudler. He himself had been able to raise very little money for the cause, and he felt that he was not pulling his weight and that they would be better off without him. He was also under family pressure to find a paying job. In August he told Hadden and Luce he must leave. At the time each of them was putting money from meager personal resources into a common kitty, as needed, each assuming one third of the expenses. Sudler had contributed $569.33, and Hadden and Luce refunded him $476.07, his contribution less one third of the outstanding bills. Sudler never had any doubts about the eventual success of the project, as unpromising as it might look; some forty years later he recalled one of the encouraging moments: "I will never forget the afternoon when Brit and I single-filed down the narrow staircase and there in our rusty black mailbox were three postcards—the first from strangers in Vermont and New Hampshire reserving trial subscriptions. No newborn baby in a hospital delivery room ever looked more incredibly real or made a louder noise than those three postcards."

In August there came a breakthrough. Hadden and Luce had temporarily taken on Wells Root, Yale '22, as a general helper at $15 a week. Root thought that his classmate William Hale Harkness might be interested, and, as it turned out, he was. He not only put up $5,000, but suggested that Hadden and Luce call on his mother and sound her out. They went to Mrs. William L. Harkness' apartment at Fifth Avenue and 66th Street. She had already read the prospectus. "I'll put in $20,000," she said, and the two dumfounded young men realized they were across the halfway mark.

Two other members of the Harkness family also subscribed. One was Mrs. Harkness' daughter, Louise, who was married to David S. Ingalls. Besides being independently wealthy, Ingalls had been a fellow member with Hadden and Luce of Skull and Bones at Yale. His old friends descended on Ingalls at Cambridge, where he was attending Harvard Law School. "Such a magazine already exists," said Ingalls with no Skull and Bones spirit whatever. "The *Literary*

13

Digest is already doing what you propose to do." Louise Ingalls, however, declared: "You keep your opinion. If you don't buy stock, I'll buy some on my own." She signed up for $5,000. The philanthropist Edward S. Harkness, her cousin, put up another $5,000.

By the end of October the two desperate entrepreneurs had $86,975 pledged.[6] They decided then that they could not wait for $100,000 to make their next move. In November, Judge Robert L. Luce, of New York, another Yale man and a distant cousin of Luce, who had been giving them moral support, attended to the legal formalities of organization (without fee) and the company was incorporated.

The capital consisted of 4,000 shares of $25-par-value Preferred, paying 6 percent cumulative; 2,000 shares Class A Common, no par value; and 8,000 shares Class B Common, no par value. The Class A Common was issued to subscribers of the Preferred in the ratio of one share of Common for every two shares of Preferred. The 8,000 Class B Common shares were issued to the management. The Preferred was callable at $27.50 or 110 percent of par value, together with accumulated dividends, after which the Class A and Class B Common were to share equally in the dividends.[7] There were seventy original shareholders, with holdings ranging from a minimum of one share of Preferred to Mrs. Harkness' 800. Forty-six of the shareholders were Yale men, fourteen of them classmates; fourteen were members of Skull and Bones, six of Scroll and Key. The early directors were recruited from the original supporters: Robert A. Chambers, Henry P. Davison, Jr., William V. Griffin, William T. Hincks (a Bridgeport, Connecticut, investment banker and father of Hadden's college roommate John M. Hincks), Samuel W. Meek.

The date on the incorporation papers was November 28, 1922. It was forty-two weeks since Hadden and Luce had departed from Baltimore; now, with some $86,000 of other people's money, they were in business.

[6] A total of $85,675 was finally collected.

[7] As of June 18, 1968, an original investment of $50 in Time Inc. would have returned $74,461. The original two shares of Preferred and one of Common would have become 552 shares with a market value of $57,960, and they would have returned the investor $16,501 in dividends.

From Opposite Sides of the World

T HE DETERMINED young men confidently pushing their project
to the point of publication were children of a confident age.
Hadden and Luce, born in the era of McKinley, grew toward
manhood in the settled days of Theodore Roosevelt, who was a
boyhood hero of both. Those were years when the American horizon
was expanding, times on the whole were good and the outlook was
optimistic. Though the two boys were born on opposite sides of the
world and grew up in far different circumstances, both came from
homes that imparted a sense of security and assurance which came
not from wealth but from place and position, from being a part of the
dominant group. They were raised in an atmosphere in which self-reliance was encouraged, initiative was much admired and duty was
spoken of in terms of unself-conscious patriotism; in Luce's case,
religion was also deeply imbedded in the daily way of life.

They were unusually interesting children; their childhood was relevant to their later careers because, while by no means prodigies, they
early exhibited the journalistic talent that would set them apart. And
both boys had parents who nourished and encouraged it.

Briton Hadden was born in Brooklyn on February 18, 1898, the son of Crowell Hadden, Jr., a young stockbroker whose father was president of the Brooklyn Savings Bank. The Hadden family traced its ancestry to Thomas Hadden, an Englishman who settled in New Jersey in 1736. Briton Hadden's mother was the daughter of Peter Busch, an orphan who had emigrated from the Rhineland to London, where he became a teller in a British bank. There he met Emily Richardson, of Brooklyn, and followed her when she returned home. They were married in 1867 and raised a family of five daughters, one son.

The Busch family lived only a few blocks from the Haddens, and Crowell Hadden, Jr., married Maud Busch in 1893. She died giving birth to a son, Crowell III, and the Busch family stepped in to look after the child. Maud's younger sister Elizabeth did most of the mothering, and married her brother-in-law in 1897. Their first-born was Briton, a frail child, coddled by his mother and a circle of adoring female relatives. He delighted them with his precocious talents, reciting verses from memory at two and composing rhymes of his own long before he could read. These he usually dictated to his mother, who provided him with a little silver bell at his bedside by which to summon her when in the creative mood. "I have a little poem, Mother," he would say to her. "Would you care to take it down?"

She read to him devotedly, ranging into matters rather esoteric for a pre-school-age child: Coleridge's "Rime of the Ancient Mariner," for instance. The length of the poem seems to have been the principal impression left on Briton. On learning that it had 143 verses, and supposing it to be the longest poem in the world, the child versifier announced that he would write a longer one. So he did, thus providing the first evidence of a fiercely competitive nature. A poem entitled "The Mouse's Party" was dictated at the rate of three verses a week and ended at verse 155. No fragments of it survive.

At age eight he was hitting an epic, if not particularly lyric, stride in a composition, "The Fire," which owes something to "A Visit from St. Nicholas" and was no respecter of the margins of paper:

16

The horses were standi
ng all tied in the barn
wen ding a dong ding
went the alarm   The
firemen junped pretty
quick to the seats and
Then in a minute they
were om the streets.
The fire was in a big
hardware store frum
a lighted match
thrown right under the
door. they had put out
the fire went back to the
barn when ding a ding
ding whent another
alarm. they then
turned around and went
out of the door
to a fire don court street
in a big grocery store.

He lived in a wider world of the imagination than most of his playmates, to whom he liked to read his stories—particularly animal stories written in imitation of a favorite author, Ernest Thompson Seton. Some impressive evidence of a future talent for observation and classification, distinguishing marks of his editorship, is provided by these genealogical notes which Hadden compiled at ten on a cherished family of Belgian hares:

Peter II. Bought with Benjamin I at the Long Island Bird Store. When young had a foot which turned in when he hoped but this cured. Almost half the hairs on him black. King and champion jumper of his day. On day ate some meat got very sich for two days at first not blieved to live but was given parsly, at length pulled through. Deid by jumping out 6th story window landing half on curb of yard and half on ground came with great force

17

because some leaves were found where he jumpt flatend out like paper. Mate of Benjamin I, Beljium Hare. 2 month old when bought on April 11, 1908, deid Oct. 1908.

About Peter IV—is greatest fitter. Can lick every rabbit he has ever fought. One day got frozen in yard but did not diy. Can keep cats out of yard and if they come in when he is asleep they get what they are not looking for.

Cottontail II. Bought with Bellee I at Long Island Bird Store Oct. 1908. Can run very fast has white spot under neck and white paws. Has a very big tail. Could chase Peter IV all around when he first came but one day Peter IV got mad and made him squeal after then she left him alone. Was a great friend of Benjiman I, Beljium hare.

Hadden, indulged and encouraged in these childhood enterprises, was deprived of the one thing which was to mean so much to Luce—a father's companionship. Crowell Hadden died suddenly just after Briton's seventh birthday. His mother was only twenty-nine when she was left with the responsibility of Crowell, aged ten, Briton, and his sister Maud, aged four.

Elizabeth Busch Hadden was handsome and vivacious, a woman who enjoyed the social life within the limited circle in which she and her husband moved. Intelligent and witty but without wide intellectual interests, she gave her children a happy home life and sent them to the best schools. They lived singularly uncomplicated lives, and when six years after her husband's death she married Dr. William Pool, a successful Brooklyn physician, he moved into their affectionate circle without in any way disturbing the harmony that had prevailed there. Briton wrote to him as "Dear Bill."

The Hadden family had one thing in common with the Luces: unlimited faith in their offspring. Briton's mother was convinced that he had the talent and ability to achieve whatever goal he sought. She never interfered with any major project, while he in turn was a dutiful son, deferring to her in matters of taste and conduct well into his adult life.

The Haddens, while not wealthy, never lacked means, and the

18

family routine was sedate and seldom varied. The summers were spent on Long Island beaches, either at Quogue or Westhampton, and when their mother altered the pattern one summer by taking the children to Sudbury, Vermont, they were upset. Briton, in a belligerent letter from school, served notice on her that he would not go to "that place" again. As child and boy, he moved in a very small orbit. His early schooling was conventional: Mrs. Jonathan Buckley's select kindergarten, Brooklyn Heights Seminary, then on to Brooklyn Polytechnic Preparatory School.

His mother preserved some copies of a handwritten sheetlet called *The Daily Glonk,* which he produced for his friends at Brooklyn Polytechnic. *Glonk* came from Herriman's famous comic strip, "Krazy Kat." (It was one of the several sounds made by the mouse Ignatz's brick landing on Krazy Kat.) The principal feature of Hadden's *Daily Glonk* was his own comic strip; he had a talent for cartooning which he used, sometimes with ribaldry, later in life, and a lively visual sense. When asked at eight how he was able to draw such a good picture of a horse, he answered, "In my mind I saw a horse and just drew around it."

Hadden contributed to the Brooklyn Poly school paper and tried to sell at least one advertisement for it to his grandfather, the bank president. Grandfather Hadden turned him down cold, explaining that the bank's policy against taking advertisements in school newspapers could not be broken even for a grandson. Hadden suggested that Grandfather could quite well afford to buy it for himself. His grandfather countered by explaining how heavy were his obligations to the family. Briton was still not impressed. "That is what you paid out," he said, "but what did you take in?"

Hadden had deep roots in his birthplace. New York City, it is often said, is nobody's hometown, but Brooklyn Heights, when Hadden was growing up, was all that "hometown" means to most men; it was a quiet, insulated enclave, remote from the turbulence of Manhattan exploding across the river. Families and children had close and cordial relations which would last for lifetimes. Hadden belonged to a group called the "Ponkiesburg Rangers" after a local fort which was famous in the Revolutionary War, a name the boys promptly shortened to "The Porgies." The Porgies were organized by Walter S. Brewster, who had been a close friend of Hadden's father, to keep his own son Rice and other offspring out of mischief and to try to enlarge their horizons. The ties that bound the Porgies in youth survive among those still living, and the careers of its members showed a consistent pattern of professional and business accomplishment.

Hadden parted from childhood more reluctantly than most boys; his childish dream of becoming a professional baseball player was transmuted in adult life into an ambition to one day own a team. He was never parted from a fungo bat, and one of his few escapes from the drill of editing *Time* was to steal away to Central Park, defying the law restricting play to those of sixteen years or under, to bat out flies with one of the writers. His cousin Niven Busch recalls Hadden (who then wore a mustache) arguing with a policeman who told them to move on: "But how do you know I am over sixteen?" and the policeman replying, "Don't give me no trouble, Mister. You can't play baseball here."

As a child he was introduced to baseball at Westhampton, where the sandlot games were important social events on the summer-colony schedule, the teams being made up of varsity men from the Ivy League. His half-brother, Crowell, made the varsity at Princeton, and Hadden, a hero-worshiper, tried hard to follow him. Unfortunately, he lacked the physical coordination to play any game well. Only slowly did he acknowledge this, for even at the age of twenty, in a letter to his mother, he seriously suggested making a career in baseball.

He suffered successive disappointments on the athletic field as a teen-ager. "I realize that I'm not good enough for the first squad, and never will be unless I get lots of practice at Westhampton next summer," he wrote home from Hotchkiss, his prep school. But he had to decide that "Coke [Crowell] is the only ball player in the family, I guess. . . ." To his stepfather, Dr. Pool, he wrote, "Well, Bill, I'm sorry that I am such a poor apology for a ball player."

He had no more success when he turned to other sports. "I have taken to high jumping but I am rotten at it. It is good fun however, and I will keep at it until I am kicked out of the gym." He turned out for hockey, but was cut from the squad. "Class football started yesterday, and I went out, although there isn't much chance for me to make it."

In early childhood Hadden had been introspective, living much within himself and his imagination. In his strenuous efforts to succeed in sports, his dominant character began to emerge. He was born not to a contemplative life, but to one of action and competition.

Luce was born on April 3, 1898, in Tengchow, China, a place of beginning that shaped him to an unusual degree. "You could never guess what I have most missed in my life," he once told his colleagues. "It is the fact that I have never had—and cannot have—a hometown, an American hometown. 'Where do you come from? Where were you born and raised?' These are basic American questions. I would give anything if I could say casually, 'Oskaloosa, Iowa. . . .' " [1]

"Some time after I was born I was baptized in a Christian church in the name of the Father and of the Son and of the Holy Ghost. Then some time after that my parents had a chance to go to Chefoo, fifty miles and two days' journey away. . . . There was an American consul there and as soon as they could my parents went to him to tell him and to tell Uncle Sam the fact that they had a son—me.

"Years later when I got to Hotchkiss School, one of the first charges brought against me by boys of the Lower Middle Form was that I could never be President of the United States. Naturally, it was necessary for me to correct in my fellows their shallow understanding of the American Constitution. That was quickly done. It took somewhat longer to shake off the nickname Chink. This, then, is the prelude to my story: *civis Americanus sum.*"

The Luces traced their ancestry to Henry Luce, who came from England to settle in Martha's Vineyard off the Massachusetts coast in 1643; Luce's mother came from a family founded by John Roote, of Northamptonshire, who emigrated to Connecticut in 1640.[2] Luce's grandfather was a wholesale grocer in Scranton, Pennsylvania; his

---

[1] In 1965 Oskaloosa, Iowa, made him an honorary citizen.

[2] One of the Rootes (later spelled Root) was Elihu Root, Secretary of State under Theodore Roosevelt.

father, Henry Winters Luce, at Yale made a decision to join the Student Volunteer Movement for Foreign Missions, whose objective was "the evangelization of the world in this generation," and was ordained a Presbyterian minister. In Scranton the young evangelist met and, in 1897, married Elizabeth Root, a Y.W.C.A. worker among factory girls.

Henry Winters Luce and his bride were assigned to China, but some months before they were to depart, the Presbyterian Foreign Missions Board, short of funds, said it could not guarantee their maintenance. The intercession of family friends in Scranton enabled them to leave as planned: James A. Linen and his wife pledged the money to maintain them in the Tengchow missionary college. The work was more teaching than preaching. Conditions were primitive and quarters hard to find; for a while they lived in an abandoned temple.

Henry Robinson Luce, their first child, was named after his father and Dr. Charles E. Robinson, pastor of their church in Scranton. The baby was baptized by the head of the mission, one of the great pioneers of the Protestant church in China, Dr. Calvin Mateer, and grew up in a pervasive religious atmosphere that left a deep impression on him. At five he was recording the subjects of sermons he was taken to hear. On Sunday morning American members of the mission attended church with the Chinese; in the afternoon they gathered in one or another of their homes to worship. Luce's sister Elisabeth has an early memory of her brother standing on a stool in the mission compound and preaching a sermon to the assembled amahs and their small charges. In the family's archives is the written text of a sermon he wrote, at six, on II Timothy 1:7: "For God hath not given us the spirit of fear. . . ."

When Chinese resentment at foreign domination exploded in the Boxer Rebellion in 1900, the Luces and other members of the Tengchow mission were evacuated by the sympathetic captain of a Chinese gunboat, and later found refuge in Korea. Henry Winters Luce's closest friend and Yale classmate, Horace Tracy Pitkin,[3] who had joined him in dedicating his life to the missions, was one of the victims of that violence. His mangled body was carried through the

[3] His son, Horace, was to be a classmate of young Henry at Yale.

22

streets of Paotingfu, where he was stationed, by a Boxer mob. The missioners returned to Tengchow to reopen the college six months later, after order had been restored by the expeditionary forces of the foreign powers.

What young Henry knew about America then was what his father and mother told him. His mother read him the Bible and a child's history of America. His father told him about Theodore Roosevelt, then President, and the Declaration of Independence. He first saw the United States at the age of seven, when his father returned for his first year's furlough. The family, grown to five with the birth of two daughters, Emmavail and Elisabeth, planned to spend the year quietly in Scranton. But Henry Winters Luce had persuaded the mission board to move the college from the rather remote site at Tengchow to Weihsien, closer to the capital of Shantung Province. The new campus had been built, but funds had to be raised in the United States if the college was to succeed. The family were together in Scranton for a while, but Dr. Luce had to spend most of the year raising money.[4]

One of Dr. Luce's ports of call was the home of the wealthy and philanthropic Mrs. Cyrus McCormick, of Chicago, matriarch of the International Harvester Company dynasty. She made a handsome donation to the college at Weihsien and offered to adopt young Harry and educate him in the United States. This proposal was declined, but the Luces did accept Mrs. McCormick's offer to build a house for them in the college compound. When he returned to China, Harry wrote a letter to *St. Nicholas* magazine which appeared in the July 8, 1908, issue, no doubt his first published writing:

My dear St. Nicholas,

I am a boy born in China. I live in the country near Weihsien (Way Shen) city, in an enclosed compound or big yard about two blocks large. There are eight dwelling houses, a boys' and

[4] Dr. Luce not only found the money to operate Weihsien, but later was largely instrumental in raising funds to found Shantung Christian University at Tsinan and Yenching University at Peking. "My father's working life didn't turn out at all the way he intended when he decided to do the Lord's work," his son once observed. "The Lord's work, in his case, turned out to be raising money, which is, of all jobs, the worst; so in this sense the Lord was not kind to him."

girls' school, a college, a big church and two hospitals.

A new house is being built (the house we are to live in) by Chinese carpenters and masons.

It will take about eight months to build it. What a long time! The Chinese have no saw-mills, but every log has to be cut and sawed by hand.

I think you are fine.

> Your true friend and reader,
> *Henry R. Luce*

The Luces sent pictures of the house to Mrs. McCormick, who delightedly called it "a Florentine villa." It was hardly that. It had a furnace of sorts, but no running water and no bath. The family loved their home, and the four years they lived in it were the longest period they ever enjoyed under one roof.

"It was a great, big, mysterious world," Luce remembered sentimentally, "filled with a thousand objects, pictures, keys, the frayed edge of the rug, the crack in the window pane, the fly walking, the photograph album exactly placed, the sound of the doorbell—just so, year after year—each of these objects woven with long threads into the pattern of life." There a fourth child was born—a son, Sheldon.

At *Time*'s twentieth-anniversary dinner and on several other occasions Luce described the life of an American boy growing up in a Protestant mission in China. Much of that life was lived with the Chinese. "But there was one day in the year when we Americans, young and old, withdrew from China. That was the Fourth of July. That day we Americans kept to ourselves. I remember a Fourth of July when I was nine or ten. Forty or fifty Americans, old men and children, assembled in the hot afternoon. There were plenty of firecrackers. Dr. Roys kept popping them off, scaring the ladies. Presently came the eats. Ice cream made in freezers brought from America and strawberries and chocolate cake. Then the babies were taken home. It was now time for fancy fireworks. They burst and whirled above us. Again the hush of eventide and we sang our song:

> *My country, 'tis of thee,*
> *Sweet land of liberty. . . .*

Then handclasps all around, and then through the darkness, each to his own home, each with his lantern."

At ten, Luce was sent to a boarding school staffed by British masters, in Chefoo: "I hated it and I loved it. When I didn't have a bloody nose or a skinned knee, my face and hands were swollen with chilblains. The school was very religious and very rough and tough. Yet, after Chefoo, the getting of A's at Hotchkiss and Yale was for me a rather pleasantly soporific pastime. If scholarship in America had not been so soft, I might be an educated man today."

Hating Chefoo and loving it, he wrote home: "I am *going* to get into the fourth form. I do not care if I die for it. I must get inside. I must. I will. And God has, is, and will help me. Just take my 100% in Algebra. It was all God. I prayed He would guide my hand from all careless mistakes and again in the middle of the exam." [5]

There were about 130 boys in residence at the school, one fifth of them American. "We were a strong, conspicuous, successful minority [among which was Thornton Wilder]. The British code—flogging and toadying—violated every American instinct. No wonder that hardly an hour passed that an American did not have to run up the flag. A master insists that Ohio is pronounced O-hee-ho. What are you going to do? Will you agree? The American can't agree; it would betray every other American. So first your knuckles are rapped, then you get your face slapped—by the master—then you are publicly caned. By this time you are crying, but still you can't say O-hee-ho."

The American stubbornly resisted not only his British masters but his British fellows. "I can remember a shameful, futile, endless two hours one Saturday afternoon when I rolled around the unspeakably dirty floor of the main schoolroom with a little British bastard who had insulted my country."

There were some compensations. "Now a surprise," he wrote home, "a school paper has been urged. . . . I am Editor-in-chief (an

---

[5] His sisters have preserved 776 letters of an indefatigable letter writer, sent from Chefoo, Hotchkiss, Yale, Oxford and during other sojourns abroad. One letter they cherish was written from Chefoo when Luce was twelve: "How are my sisters getting on? I was just saying to Hugh how there was nothing I abhorred more than an ignorant woman. But with an abhorrence so there is pride, and that pride I would take in two sisters not necessarily learned but well-read and who knew something."

elephantine title!)" Another was long summer vacations at Tsingtao —"the most beautiful of all places on this earth where the mountains come down to the sea. Kaiser Wilhelm II called it the fairest jewel in his crown. . . . The well-ordered Germans had built a neat little colonial town in a corner of the great bay and were reforesting the surrounding hills and building roads. My father and his friends built the first little summer cottages on a point called Iltus Huk, which later became one of the swank resorts of the China coast. On summer afternoons we could sit on our porch and see way out on the ocean white moving targets and the splashing foam of high-explosive shells as they hit long or short. The shells came right over our cottage from gun emplacements in the hills behind. Early in the morning, we could hear from across a little valley behind us the heavy tramp of German soldiers and the songs they sang, the German *Lieder,* as they marched from barracks to maneuvers: '*O, Wandern, Wandern, meine Lust. . . .*' "

During these relaxed summers at Tsingtao, there were long talks between Dr. Luce and his young son. "The great thing that I owe to my father is that he would talk to me as one adult to another. We would go on walks and he would tell me of the problems of the little college, and then from the problems of the college we would get on to such things as his quest for the historical Jesus, or Teddy Roosevelt and the Bull Moose."

Henry Winters Luce was determined that his son should go to Yale. "Young Harry," his mother wrote a friend in 1911, when he was thirteen, "spends all his free time going over old Yale catalogues trying to figure out what the courses will be like five years from now."

Dr. Luce was to make a second fund-raising trip to the States in 1913, and a scholarship would be open at Hotchkiss that year for Harry. There was one worry—Harry's stammer, which his mother always believed had its origin in a trauma resulting from a tonsillectomy, when the child came out of the anesthetic before the operation had been completed. The family heard that the headmaster of the cathedral grammar school at St. Albans near London had been successful in dealing with such cases. It was decided that Harry should go by himself to England to see what could be done for him before going on to Hotchkiss.

26

He shipped in a German liner from Shanghai, aged fourteen— through the Indian Ocean and the Suez Canal to Southampton, and proceeded to St. Albans. He arrived in October; in February he wrote home that the tutoring was not doing him much good and he was going to Switzerland to learn French. First he went for a week to Paris, where he "just followed the guides around and saw everything."

In Switzerland he settled into a pension in Lausanne and went to his French teacher daily, and then decided on his own to make a trip through Italy. He had $65, which he made last for three weeks, getting as far south as Rome before returning to Switzerland. He spent his fifteenth birthday visiting the Forum in Rome.

His mother, his sisters and his brother met him in Lausanne in June and they spent most of the summer together. A friend of Harry's from Chefoo joined them there, and the two boys took a trip down the Rhine, into Belgium and then on to Hamburg, where Dr. Luce was waiting for them. Thence by steamer to the States in September and, for Harry, Hotchkiss.

Luce felt that of all his childhood experiences the fact that he had grown up in China colored most deeply his own view of the United States. He once said: "In some ways that background endowed me with special qualifications to be editor-in-chief of great American publications. . . . In some ways, it disqualified me. I probably gained a too romantic, too idealistic view of America. The Americans I grew up with—all of them—were good people. Missionaries have their faults, but their faults are comparatively trivial. I had no experience of evil in terms of Americans. . . . Put along with that the idea that America was a wonderful country, with opportunity and freedom and justice for all, and you get not only an idealistic, but a romantic view —a profoundly false romantic view. I do not speak here of disillusionment with America. The fact is I never went through any special period of disillusionment. It marks, I think, some grave fault in me that I did not. I was never disillusioned with or by America, but I was, from my earliest manhood, dissatisfied with America. America was not being as great and as good as I knew she could be, as I believed with every nerve and fiber God Himself had intended her to be."

27

To Hotchkiss, to Yale, and to Arms

HOTCHKISS SCHOOL is magnificently situated on the rolling Berkshire hills overlooking Lake Wononscopomuc at Lakeville, Connecticut. The enrollment when Hadden and Luce arrived there in 1913 was limited to 250 (it is now 375). Presiding over it was Headmaster Huber Gray Buehler, a pious, some thought sanctimonious, man known to the boys as "The King." At the beginning of each school year he told the student body, "There is only one rule in this school: Be a gentleman"; and at least once a year he preached a stern sermon using as his text Matthew Arnold's

> *I sat, obedient, in the fiery prime of youth,*
> *Self-govern'd at the feet of law.*

No great admirers of Buehler in their schooldays, Hadden and Luce, on Buehler's death in 1924, said of him in their fledgling *Time*:

His reign was historic in the development of American public schools. Coming from Gettysburg, an obscure college town in Pennsylvania, achieving his first petty distinction as an author of Buehler's *Modern English Grammar*, he was suddenly elevated

28

20 years ago to be the supreme administrator of a new and comparatively small school. When he died, the Hotchkiss School had equals but no superiors in the land, and was one of a group of schools which boasted a pride of spirit and a social discipline comparable to the ancient schools of England.

And, like the ancient schools of England, Hotchkiss reflected both the aspirations and the prejudices of the governing caste which supported it: the white, Republican, Protestant, upper middle class. In one sense Luce's roots were in this caste. In another he was an outsider: he came from a far country and he was a scholarship boy at a time when that was a mark of discrimination. In lieu of tuition, the scholarship boys were supposed to work their way by waiting on table or sweeping out the classrooms. Luce, well prepared by the Chefoo School, entered the second-year class, or "Lower Mid." He found the academic work all too easy and led his class in the first term. He was immediately into everything, despite his scholarship chores: gymnastics, debating, the literary society, "heeling" the school's weekly newspaper, the *Record,* and writing for the *Literary Monthly.* One of his masters, Walter H. Buell (who had also taught Luce's father in Scranton), reported to Dr. Luce that things were too easy for his son: "He has not met a study yet that has in itself really pushed him." He tended to be "sloppy" and "careless," and Buell prescribed Greek; if young Luce were to complete the school's course, it would mean cramming three years into two. If he did that, Buell predicted, the boy might well win the Greek prize at Yale.

Hadden, also entering as a "Lower Mid" and chafing at the discipline and confinement, was happiest outside the classroom. In midwinter he was "homesickish," he wrote his mother, because there was "not a thing doing up here." The puritan Sabbath imposed by The King irked him because no games were allowed. Hadden, gathering up a few friends, would tuck a deflated football under his jacket and set out on one of the long walks recommended by the faculty to work off energy. Once out of sight, they blew up the ball and played touch football. "I don't think there's any harm in it," he wrote his mother, "but if you don't want me to, I won't."

29

He was having trouble with his studies. He flunked French outright with a 56 and made a resolve "to work harder this quarter. I passed Latin, but didn't think I would." By spring he was doing better and was beginning to enjoy school life: scrub baseball, tennis, cross-country running—he kept on with them all even when he could not make the school teams. Then suddenly in the spring term he found a goal.

Dearest Mother [he wrote]:

Maybe you are wondering whether I'm sick or dead or something. I'm not. I'm only "heeling" the *Record*. Gee, it's *some* job too. Last fall I only went into it half-heartedly, but this spring they have started a new heeling contest for Lower Mids only and I am working hard. One week is over, and there are three more. The guy that is ahead at the end will be taken on the *Record* board and will stand a good chance of being editor in his senior year. That's quite an honor. . . .

One of the other "guys" in the contest was Harry Luce, who in addition was competing for a place on the *Literary Monthly*.

Up to this time, Hadden and Luce knew each other only casually. But in their "Upper Mid" year they had one thing in common: both were members of Dr. Lester Brown's Greek class. Only seventeen boys were permitted to take Greek with "Doc" Brown, a stern, humorless disciplinarian who told each new class, "It is a fact that most recitations at Hotchkiss require an hour's preparation. You will find that Greek requires two hours." Hadden took to Greek with enthusiasm, particularly the *Iliad*. His copy of Homer survives with underlinings—"rolling-eyed Greeks," "far-darting Apollo"—a style which he would later make a distinctive feature of *Time*. He tried to work Greek into everyday speech. Over and over his teacher used the phrases *Oi men* and *Oi de* ("on the one hand" and "on the other"), and Hadden would greet his friends with "Hoy, men!," expecting in return the salutation "Hoy, dee!" Later he referred to editorials in the Yale *Daily News* as "Hoyers."

Luce was top boy in Brown's class (and on matriculating at Yale won the Hugh Chamberlain Prize for Greek as Buell had predicted, making the highest mark in the college's history). "This makes me sound like a mental genius," Luce commented years later. "Actually, of course, it is easier to win the Greek prize if you take three years of Greek in two, because you are concentrating. In my senior year I was taking six hours of Greek a week."

By the end of their second year Hadden and Luce had become rivals in publishing. Hadden was elected editor-in-chief of the weekly *Record,* Luce assistant managing editor and, in addition, editor of the *Lit.* When Hadden returned full of plans in the fall, he announced that the *Record* would henceforth be a semi-weekly, and would carry world as well as school news on its front page: "Beginning with today's issue . . . a special column will be reserved for an article dealing with current events of the week. The purpose [will be] to present a condensed report of the important happenings of the week to those of us who do not find time to read the detailed accounts in the daily papers."

Luce redesigned the cover of the *Lit,* introduced a new illustrated section of fourteen pages and announced that the *Lit* would present articles by prominent Americans. The first contribution was an article he solicited from former President Theodore Roosevelt. He billed the illustrated section, which was financed by advertisements and subscriptions sold to well-heeled alumni, as "First in the Prep School World," and on the new cover flaunted the announcement that the *Lit* was "The 'Better' Magazine."

Hadden hit back in the *Record:* "We are well aware that 'the "better" magazine' means a magazine which aims to be 'better' than itself in each successive issue. At the same time, however, we still fear that the slogan might readily be misinterpreted by an outsider as meaning better than any other magazine. Since this ambiguity does exist, we recommend the use of the blue pencil in this connection. The claim 'First in the Prep School World' is especially uncalled for."

Hadden continued needling as the year progressed: "We believe that in the December *Lit* the literary section has the ascendancy over the pictorial. . . . 'The Star' [a poem which Luce had written] leaves rather a noble but vague impression." Of a one-act verse play, *Candles,* by Luce, Hadden said, "While it contains a remarkable idea, it would certainly appear to better advantage if acted than it does on the written page. The vernacular of Cromwell's time as here presented is more or less unnatural because it is written by an author who is more or less unfamiliar with it." Even more infuriatingly, the *Record* commented, "We notice with pleasure that, upon the advice of last month's criticism . . . 'First in the Prep School World' has been dropped."

By March, Hadden was singling out Luce's contributions in the monthly *Lit* for praise. A poem called "Stanzas" was "by far the best poem that has appeared in the *Lit* this year. . . . *Mediocrity in Scholarship* by the same author is an article which should receive the thoughtful and sincere attention of every fellow in school. More articles by this writer would be desirable."

Their editorships did not bring either of them any particular recognition on the campus. The principal honors of the graduating class of 1916 went to the best athletes. (Luce received ten votes as "brightest" man of the year; Hadden ten votes as the "noisiest.") This galled Luce, who took it on himself to say something on Hadden's behalf (and on his own) in the final issue of the *Lit:*

> To run a semi-weekly, six-page newspaper—outside of study hours—and to have not more than one typographical error a fortnight, and to have a keen, clear, pointed editorial to each issue as we had during 1915–16,—we say that there is no harder job in the entire Hotchkiss School—no football game that ever will demand more "guts" than this. And (casting the convention of modesty to the dust) we say that to publish a monthly magazine with 300 pages of, at least, fairly good attempts at stories, articles and verse, to make these pages have any semblance of an appeal to the fellows in school, and to pay for nearly 200 electrotypes—this we submit is no tea-parlor, silk-sock, poetically temperamental game.

Hadden was chosen to make the class-day oration; delivered at a time when the European war was drawing ever closer to the United States, his speech gives an interesting insight into a developing mind:

> The United States are facing today a situation of utmost gravity, a situation which seems all the more severe in contrast to the

state of care-free abandonment which we are at this moment enjoying. At no previous epoch in the history of our country have politics reached such a state of what may be properly termed "stagnation." . . . We wonder whether such a crisis as confronts Europe today—or another such crisis as faced our own country 55 years ago,—will be necessary to make . . . men forthcoming; or whether the tendency toward a nation-wide awakening now prevalent, will be enough to force us to our senses. Whatever the outcome may be, we, the members of the Class of 1916, should be prepared to leave Hotchkiss determined to do our utmost toward bettering the political conditions of the land we live in. If ours is the power to do this, if we can successfully measure up to the "spirit of service" ideal required of us, then we shall have in some small measure made settlement for that "debt which our lives must repay."

At Hotchkiss, Hadden began to put on the mannerisms which in later life he used as a cloak for his true character. While his letters to his mother reveal him as gay, affectionate, sentimental and, at heart, a conformist, he affected a quite different personality—boisterous, known for his raucous voice and his exaggerated Brooklyn accent: "Youse guys gotta cut that out." He walked with a ballplayer's stance, bent always a little forward with arms swinging free, as if about to field a grounder. His campus nickname was "Cat," conferred on him by the little sister of a friend; struck by his habit of grinning and wrinkling his nose, she told her brother, "That old Brit, he looks just like a pussy cat"—a story which soon got around the campus, inspiring his classmates to greet him with "Meow" or "Here, Pussy." (Hadden described his classmate's sister as "a little girl of about five or six that just sits in a chair with her hands folded and gazes at you like an owl.") Three years at Hotchkiss gave Hadden self-confidence and sharpened his competitive instincts, which were now almost wholly diverted from athletics to journalism.

Luce acquired the hated nickname "Chink." More serious and withdrawn than Hadden, he was somewhat aloof from campus roughhouse; his reputation was that of "a brain." He mastered his

33

childhood stammer, made the debating team and won the oratorical contest as an Upper Mid. He still spoke in sharp, staccato bursts with many sentences left unfinished, as if his tongue could not keep up with a racing mind. No outright rebel, he was nevertheless a campus critic, often impatient with things as he found them.

On graduation neither boy seemed to have thought much beyond Yale; to a question in a class poll about a future career, both had answered "Undecided." Hadden went off to a carefree summer on the beach at Westhampton, Luce to his first job—in the business office of the Springfield (Massachusetts) *Republican,* where he earned $8 a week. He was also permitted to do some reporting on the side, for he wrote home:

> . . . I am learning lots of things that one takes for granted. I never saw a prison cell before. I never spoke to a prisoner. I never saw a brave, tear-stained mother come to bail out her son held on a sure charge of forgery. These things reveal the Christ who said, "I came not to the righteous. . . ." As a matter of fact I believe that I can be of greatest service in journalistic work and can by that way come nearest to the heart of the world. . . .

Yale in 1916, more than now, was the very model of the competitive society. It was the place where, as Harvard philosopher George Santayana wrote in 1892, "American traditions are vigorous, American instincts are unchecked, and young men are trained and made eager for the keen struggles of American life." And something had been added: a literary renaissance that had begun about 1900 was in full swing. "Yale had outgrown its earlier indifference to letters," said Van Wyck Brooks in *New England: Indian Summer.* "The breeze that was blowing over literary Yale was to have its effect on the new generation of writers, brilliant groups of whom were at nurse there." Members of the English faculty in this period, among them Chauncey Tinker, William Lyon Phelps, Henry Seidel Canby and Wilbur Cross (later Governor of Connecticut), were arbiters of the U.S. literary establishment; their pupils included Philip Barry, Sinclair Lewis, Thornton Wilder, Archibald MacLeish, Stephen Vincent Benét.

34

To the excitement of freshman semester there was added the closest Presidential race of a generation, reflecting the tensions of a war in which the U.S. was not yet involved. The election hung in the balance until two days after the polls closed. Then California's ballots for Woodrow Wilson decided the issue against Charles Evans Hughes. Hadden and Luce were both for Hughes, and Hadden wrote to his mother:

> Isn't the election close, though? Up here, you hear shouts of "Hughes elected!" " 'Ray, Hughes!" "Wilson re-elected!" "T'Hell with Wilson!" "T'Hell with Hughes!" every minute. The fellow two doors down the hall has a revolver which he shoots off at each report of a Hughes triumph. For my part, I sincerely hope that Old Whiskers will get it, if only for the fact that it will keep Wilson out of the White House. Perhaps that is only because I have been reading the more or less Wilson-hating [New York] *Tribune*.

By the opening of the second semester, 1917, U.S. entry into the war was imminent, and college patriotic fervor rose. Yale already had a volunteer field-artillery battery. F. Trubee Davison, '18 (later Assistant Secretary of War for Air under Coolidge and Hoover, and brother of Harry Davison, *Time*'s first investor), and a group of Yale undergraduates had learned, at their own expense, to fly seaplanes; they had established the Yale Voluntary Coast Patrol, which, on the U.S. entry into the war, became the first U.S. naval aviation squadron. When the nation's leading pacifist, David Starr Jordan, Chancellor Emeritus of Stanford, came to Yale to plead his cause, the undergraduates gave him a hearing but were solidly against him. "I was an interventionist in the First World War as I was in the Second," Luce said later. Hadden wrote: "After it [Jordan's speech] was all through, the entire student body formed a preparedness parade and marched all around New Haven singing *Bingo* and *My Country, 'Tis of Thee*."

Above all, freshmen Hadden and Luce wanted to make the staff of the Yale *Daily News*. They debated whether they should enter the first freshman competition or wait until the second. Hadden proposed

35

to Luce that only one of them should go into the first competition; the other fellow would help him, and he in turn would help the other fellow in the second competition. Luce was not sure he liked the idea. The first man, he reflected, would have a big head start, and he suspected who the other fellow was going to be. They discussed the idea long into the night, but in the end both entered the first competition.

Twenty-six years later Luce, dining with the British historian Arnold Toynbee, was called to answer the telephone. His son, Henry Luce III, was calling to say he had just made the *News.* "As I returned to the table," said Luce, "I thought that Toynbee would never understand what 'challenge and response' really mean, because it was too late for him to go to Yale and heel the *News.*"

The competition rules vary from year to year, according to the whim of the current board; in the contest in which Hadden and Luce competed, points were awarded for suggesting and writing stories, selling advertisements (which could account for only ten percent of the total lest the rich buy their way in), running errands and performing miscellaneous chores. Heelers could claim priority on a story by dropping a suggestion in the assignment editor's box, although they had to keep to their rooms between midnight and seven a.m.

To Luce, the competition was "awful . . . a blind desperateness," he wrote home. Hadden, determined to win, was not above shaving the rules a little. "I get up at 5:45 each morning and give the papers (N.Y. *Times, Tribune* and New Haven *Journal-Courier*) the once-over," he wrote his mother. "If there's no news I go back to bed again, but if there is, I put on an overcoat and a pair of shoes over my pajamas and beat it across Elm Street to the *News* office . . . where I drop a card for a 'scoop' . . . and then go back to bed again." He discovered that he could pile up extra points by being on duty for errands, and he haunted the *News* office for hours on end. His major scoop was an exclusive interview with the commander of the German merchant submarine *Deutschland,* which had put in unexpectedly at New London.

Just before the end of the competition, according to Luce: "The assignment editor, preparing for the next competition, discovered he had run out of *Daily News* rule books. So he offered 500 points for each and every rule book delivered to him by Sunday night. Five hundred points was big money—as much as you might earn by journalistic effort in a week. Sunday night came; the heelers, ragged and worn, assembled. By dint of having ransacked 200 or 300 college rooms, I had found, I think, three books. The others about the same. Then a tall, saturnine heeler came forward with a suitcase, opened it in front of the assignment editor, and one by one counted out 80 books. The rest of us howled our protests—in vain. Alger Shelden was credited with 40,000 points. How had he done it? Very simple. He had used his brains instead of his feet. He had gone down to the printer's, that drafty plant where we had bicycled so many winter nights in the snow—and up on the rafters under inches of dust Alger Shelden had found his treasure. I have never known tougher competition than that."

Hadden won, despite having some points knocked off for excessive running of errands. The others who made it were Luce, Thayer Hobson and the ingenious Shelden. When Easter came, Shelden treated the other three winners to a house party at his home in Detroit which was climaxed by the biggest news of the year. During the festivities somebody bought a paper. One glance was enough. The U.S. had declared war.

The impact of that news on youth in 1917 will not be understood by a present generation; filled with patriotic fervor, men in 1917 marched to Armageddon with bands playing, voices singing and banners waving. Those too young to enlist responded to their President's plea to undertake humdrum but patriotic chores. Hadden, ever the romantic, drew the line at hoeing potatoes, but considered working in a lumber camp, or on a stock farm or a wheat farm in the West, or selling Liberty Bonds. For a while he dreamed of driving an American ambulance in Paris for three months. What he did do was to go to a junior military camp, run by Harvard, which seems to have been more of a lark than training, much to Hadden's disgust.

Luce's family had returned to China, so he spent that summer with the Linens, working on their farm outside Scranton, pulling himself out of bed at five a.m. and, among other chores, cleaning out the chicken coops. ("If you'll show me any more unhappy labor than cleaning out chicken coops, I'd like to know what it is," he once said.)

In September 1917, when Hadden and Luce returned to Yale, enrollment was down from 3,300 to 2,000. Of these, 1,300 undergraduates, including Hadden and Luce, promptly volunteered for R.O.T.C., which meant that in addition to their studies they had to drill from four to six every afternoon, and each night take an hour's instruction in gunnery, military law and hygiene.

Luce, in a small way, became a war profiteer. He had had a job of sorts in his freshman year: freshmen then fed at various dining tables run by New Haven women, who paid a commission to undergraduates to keep their board filled. Luce had been one of these. In his sophomore year he became a tailor's salesman, taking orders for the uniforms his fellow R.O.T.C. members were required to buy. This all but paid for his sophomore year.

The Yale *Daily News* was one of the extracurricular activities that continued. Just before mid-year examinations, the sophomore members of its board met to elect the officers who would take over publication in the second semester of their junior year. Hadden was chosen as the future chairman, a job for which he thought he would have a year to prepare. The incumbent chairman quit college, and just after Christmas his successor called Hadden and told him, "I am about to enlist, so you are now chairman of the *News*."

Hadden was not in the least intimidated by the prospect. His first move when he got back to the campus after the holidays was to crusade for complete mobilization of the college. He wrote his mother: "You will remember that last week I told you I was going to make it my business to see the Reserve Officers' Training Corps put on its rightful basis in being more generally recognized by the men in it as the most important thing in college. . . . The idea is to make Yale for the duration of the war a second West Point—so good that the Government actually issues commissions direct to Yale men at the end of their training course. When one realizes that the war will last long enough for us all to get into it, the advisability and practicability of such a movement is obvious."

38

Hadden immediately began making the *News* over, subordinating collegiate chatter, playing up the R.O.T.C., boosting Liberty Bond sales and promoting the idea of more military training. When some members of the faculty wanted to drop an academic course to provide more hours of training, Hadden editorialized: "The faculty's action is entirely justifiable. The formation at Yale of what is to be the best artillery school in the land cannot help but be a dominant factor in the Allied cause."

Luce and Hadden were drawing closer to each other; Hadden wrote his mother: "I have to get better acquainted with Chink Luce with whom I will have to work more or less in the next few years [when Luce would be his managing editor]." Luce wrote home: "I have the greatest admiration and affection for Brit which, in some measure at least, is reciprocated."

They agreed on the war effort. A campus issue was whether the junior prom should be held as usual in the spring of 1918. In a column-long letter in the *News,* Henry R. Luce weighed in against the dance:

> . . . a decision not to hold a prom would be a decision to strengthen the cause. We believe that it will be noted to the credit of the so-called plutocrats among the serried ranks of our country's working men and women. We believe the decision will be noted with approbation by the members of the National Army. . . .

Hadden was for the prom at a price—the price being the purchase of a Liberty Bond. "Radical? Jacobin patriotism?" he wrote in an editorial. "Perhaps; but how much worse if the Kaiser 'comes across' instead?" The campus reaction to the idea disappointed him. As he wrote his mother, "Some dumb specimens did not understand that it was aimed more to start people thinking than to give actual suggestions."

The spring semester seemed interminable to two young men eager to get into the Army. Actually, Yale suspended academic work earlier than usual, in May, and the R.O.T.C. went on a full military footing; then in August, in 100° heat, Yale's R.O.T.C. unit was shipped off by

39

day coach to Camp Jackson, South Carolina, to form a cadre of student-officer instructors to the draftees then flooding into the ranks.

That Hadden's and Luce's idea for *Time* should begin to germinate in Camp Jackson was not so implausible. They learned there how poorly informed were most of their fellow Americans in those days when, for example, only one in seven children finished high school, and only one in fifteen went to college. Men going off to fight a war about which they knew so little left a deep impression on Luce. Two or three times a week the student officer had to give a lecture to his platoon on what the war was all about. Luce remembered one night as "one of the greatest successes of my life. I told them the story of the sinking of the *Lusitania,* just what I remembered from my reading of the New York *Times.* They had never heard the story and they were on the edge of their chairs and couldn't wait to get 'over there' and fix the Huns who had sunk the *Lusitania.*"

He marched with one group the eight hard miles to the railroad station, where they were to entrain for embarkation. He was not allowed to go with them because he was not yet commissioned. He said, "Goodbye and good luck," and a few weeks later got word that many of them had been lost when their transport, the *Ticonderoga,* was torpedoed in mid-Atlantic.

It was difficult to be left behind and see the men one had trained go off. "The one thing we wanted to do was to be officers of the Army of the United States, go to the front and fire at the enemy," said Luce. Hadden wrote his mother:

I long to be sent overseas as a Battery Commander or Major General or something, and there to take part in the great 1919 drive, the one that will end the war and smash Kaiser Will. This dreaming and building of air castles is O.K. provided it won't absolutely kill in me any liking that I may have for going back to college. As it is, I shudder at the idea of taking up residence in New Haven, grinding out "hoyer" editorials. . . . I repeat, I shudder at the idea of doing anything other than real war work.

A passionate would-be warrior from the start, Hadden was a first sergeant of one of Yale's four field-artillery batteries ("able to drill a squad in the most ferocious of his Brooklyn vernacular," said the class history). He boasted to his mother that his battery was the best in the regiment. Of course, he could not acknowledge this to the men, for "being the first sergeant, I have to treat them all 'snotty' when on duty and make them do extra fatigue and K.P. and stuff."

"He was a great stylist," Luce recalled. "When he read in the military manual what the perfect military haircut was, he proceeded to lecture his entire battery on the subject, and said he expected them to have all the hair shaved off their heads by reveille the next day. During the day it became apparent that none was going to obey the order. But next morning there was Hadden out in front of his battery, alone, bald as a billiard ball. And before that day was through a song spread through the camp: *That Bald-Headed Sergeant of Battery B.* And from *that* day on, Battery B was the best damn battery this side of Paris. Yes, Sergeant Hadden, I couldn't admit it then, but you were one good soldier." Hadden, for his part, "used to razz the hell out of me," Luce remembered, "because he said I was the sloppiest soldier on the post."

Hadden and Luce were commissioned second lieutenants, but the Armistice, to their absolute disgust, cut short their military careers before they could get overseas. "What are we going to tell our grandsons that we did in the war?" Luce wondered. "Cleaned a horse's hoof at Camp Jackson!" Hadden toyed with the idea of postponing his return to Yale. He might spend the intervening time to better advantage, he wrote his mother, by doping out what he wanted to do with himself. "If I am going to be a journalist, I could read good books. If I am going to be a criminal lawyer or a ward politician, I could take a public-speaking course and hang around courtrooms and saloons." And even after so many setbacks he didn't rule out baseball —"if I am going to be a professional ball player I could watch games at Ebbets Field."

Yale prevailed. In January 1919, when the second semester began, Luce and Hadden were back on a campus dominated by Stateside veterans like themselves and others who had actually seen action. The Yale *Daily News,* suspended in the fall of 1918, began publication again in February 1919, and by April Hadden was not an interim sophomore substitute but in the full glory of the chairmanship in his

41

junior year. Luce, as managing editor, was in charge of the news columns. It was still in very many ways a strange alliance. Hadden's friends were among the athletes and campus politicians, the men of action, and he affected scorn for those whom he called "contemplators." Yet he was pleased when he was elected to the Elizabethan Club, citadel of the literary set. "I am now on equal terms with all these 'smarty high brows,'" he wrote, "and by keeping my mouth shut and looking wise can even pose as an intellectual myself." He enjoyed parading his learning in *News* editorials. "I have taken to reading good literature for pleasure," he reported home, "and have read Barrie's *Auld Licht Idylls* and *Better Dead,* and can quote from them too. I used the phrase 'dead, rotten and forgotten' (from *Better Dead*), in an editorial this week. This gets away big with the college. Folks think I'm literary. This morning I used 'It is my duty, and I will' from Captain Reese's speech in *Bab's Ballads*. The Bible and *Hamlet* are two books which I know *cold* as my writings bear ample testimony."

He took great pains with his editorials, which, by arrangement with Professor John Berdan, were marked as part of the latter's "daily themes" course. In them are some flashes of the style later to brighten *Time*'s pages.

"In the days of Elisha, and Elijah, and Ezekiel of the Chaldeans, there was no football. Today we have football but no prophets," began a *News* editorial on the Princeton game. Under the heading "Tongues Have They," Hadden wrote, "Three-quarters of a century ago—long after the time of John C. Calhoun or the days when Daniel Webster did thunder from the student rostrum at Dartmouth—debating was the biggest collegiate stir." The lead on a plea for contributions to Yale-in-China began: "In days antediluvian men who wanted money, or cattle, or wives got them—with the aid of a big stick or a handy boulder."

Hadden's bias as a college editor was always on the conservative side. He told his successor that a college editor's duty was "to keep cool, keep the boat from rocking." In 1919 the college was divided as to whether or not Yale should continue to sing "Bright College Years," written to the tune of *"Die Wacht am Rhein."* Hadden was against it; as a compromise he suggested that it should remain in the songbook but should not be sung at football games or other public gatherings.

Because Luce was less inclined to the smooth middle way, he and Hadden had frequent differences. "They argued constantly about everything under the sun," a classmate recalled. One row erupted outside Dwight Hall when the football manager, Peavey Heffelfinger, gigged Luce for having put a football story on an inside page. Hadden agreed with Heffelfinger, and the battle was joined. "We thought they would come to blows," an eyewitness reported, "but they never did and afterward the two carried on as if nothing ever happened."

Both of them achieved one ambition held in common: to be tapped for Skull and Bones. Hadden wrote home expressing satisfaction and commented that "most of the fellows I think most of went Bones too . . . Luce, for example. . . ." Luce told his family, "I am sure you understand what perfect satisfaction is mine. . . ."

Luce aimed at certain intellectual and literary goals which did not interest Hadden. He promised his father he would make Phi Beta Kappa, and he did in his junior year. As at Hotchkiss, he was not content merely to make the *News* but went out as well for the *Literary Magazine,* to which he was a frequent contributor of poetry. One Kiplingesque contribution, much admired at the time, had previously seen print in the Hotchkiss *Lit:*

> *Oh give me a Shantung shenzi* [1]
> *And the life of a muleteer,*
> *Oh give me a load*
> *And a mountain road*
> *And the way of a pioneer.*

And the last verse:

> *For, ah, there's a thrill in the long, long way,*
> *And the load brought safe to the end.*

---

[1] The Pullman car and fast freight of North China—a sort of tub of matting on two long poles resting on two mules.

> *—That feeling of pride*
> *Of the true and tried*
> *Is the prize the high gods send.*

His first postwar poem—and one of his last—saluted the returning veterans.

> *What, after a dash in the dark with the rain*
> *Beating like daggers against your face,*
> *You're back—where just a few echoes remain*
> *Peacefully murmuring grace for grace?*
> *What, after you've fought while the summer's sun*
> *Shot through the purplish trees*
> *Fire on the barking and spitting and wind-ripping gun,—*
> *You're with us for afternoon teas? . . .*

He came to the conclusion that he was never going to be a really good poet and confined himself, thereafter, mainly to prose.

Luce was eager to see the intellectual life strengthened at Yale, and in an editorial for the *Lit* he wrote: ". . . to a very large degree, the unifying force in the past year has been common pursuit of intellectual attainment. . . . Those who are entrusted with the guardianship of things of the spirit should . . . see to it that intellectual activity becomes increasingly and notably characteristic of this place."

The class of 1920 had entered college in the midst of a Presidential election; they were leaving it as another began. Yale was caught up in the great debate of the year, when the internationalists fought their losing battle against the isolationism that seized the United States after it counted its World War I dead. "We tried to say our say," Luce remembered. "William Howard Taft, President Arthur Hadley, Henry Stimson, Charles Seymour and all the great men of Yale tried to say it, too. Some of them, like Taft, strove earnestly to get Harding to give us what Wilson had failed to deliver."

There was no doubt where Luce stood. He won the DeForest oratorical contest with an address, "When We Say 'America,' " which said many of the things that he was to say later in *Time*, *Life* and *Fortune*.

When we say "America" twenty years from now may it be that that great name will signify throughout the world at least two things: First, that American interests shall be respected, American citizens entitled to trade and to live in every corner of the globe, American business ideals recognized wherever the trader goes; second, that America may be counted upon to do her share in the solution of every international difficulty, that she will be the great friend of the lame, the halt and the blind among nations, the comrade of all nations that struggle to rise to higher planes of social and political organization, and withal the implacable and the immediate foe of whatever nation shall offer to disturb the peace of the world. . . .

As its contribution to the college's political education, the *News* in 1920 staged a series of lectures by leading politicians and, to cap the year, sponsored a mock Republican Convention, to which the undergraduates elected 1,000 delegates, who packed Woolsey Hall and prematurely (by eight years) nominated the "great humanitarian," Herbert Hoover, 10 to 1.

Hadden on graduation was indisputably the big man on the campus. His classmates voted him "most likely to succeed," "hardest worker" and the man who had "done most for Yale." Luce graduated with "Honors of the first rank"—Yale's *summa cum laude*. On graduation day Hadden took the train to San Francisco and the Democratic Convention. A few weeks later Luce went to the Republican Convention in Chicago. They parted at Yale not to meet again till, more than a year later, the "organization" formed at Camp Jackson came together again in the Baltimore *News* city room.

The Burning of the Ships

HADDEN AND LUCE'S work on the Yale *Daily News* confirmed their choice of career; the 1920 yearbook quotes them as saying they were going into newspaper work, a course which Luce had been warned against.

"It is the end of my senior year at Yale," he once reminisced. "I am determined to be a journalist. At a function at an undergraduate club, an old grad seeks me out. He is Dr. Amos Wilder, father of my classmate, Thornton Wilder. Old Amos is perhaps the most brilliant man on the New Haven campus and certainly the most overpoweringly eloquent. He sits me down in a corner and begins to speak with a deep earnestness. Presently, there are tears in his eyes. He is saying, 'Harry, don't. Don't go into journalism. It will turn you into a cynic.' Amos Wilder had been a long-time newspaper editor himself. 'It will corrupt and corrode you. It will turn your wine into vinegar. You will lose your soul.' So he spoke for nearly an hour, but I went on my way —but never forgetting those words."

Luce was in no hurry to take up his career. On graduation he had $1,500 as his share of the *News* profits and a graduation gift of

$1,000 from the family's benefactor, Mrs. Cyrus McCormick. He decided to use this money for travel on the Continent and a postgraduate year at Oxford. Furthermore, Mrs. McCormick had assured him that on his return he could have a job at International Harvester. Hadden was determined to get into newspaper work as soon as possible.

Their immediate interest centered on the Presidential conventions. Hadden in San Francisco watched the Democrats take forty-four ballots to nominate James M. Cox, and emerged from the experience with a very low opinion of politicians, particularly the New York delegation dominated by Tammany. He wrote home that it was "a terrible organization. . . . I'm not a snob but I frankly don't like its men and its methods, and if I do go into politics by any chance and decide to be a Democrat (I haven't by any means decided yet), I think I'll have to move out of New York State." His opinion of the Democratic nominee was not much better. Cox, he wrote, "represents the low-brow 'boss' interests of the party. . . . As near as I can figure it, there's little to choose from between him and Harding. . . ."

Luce went in style to the Republican Convention that nominated Warren G. Harding. He was a guest on the private railroad car of Rufus L. Patterson, President of the American Machine & Foundry Company, whose son Morehead was going with Luce to Oxford. "Most of our party were for General Leonard Wood, who claimed the mantle of Theodore Roosevelt," Luce wrote. "The man the convention ought to have nominated was probably Governor Frank O. Lowden of Illinois. When, exhausted, we got on the private car to go home we were all thoroughly disgusted with the smoke-filled outcome. The one redeeming factor was the nomination [as Vice President] of Calvin Coolidge, recognized to be a man of character."

In search of a job, Hadden advanced on New York's Park Row, dominated by the *World* building with its golden dome. If you were young, romantic and aspired to be a newspaperman in 1920, the one New York paper you wanted to work on was the *World*. It had a long crusading tradition under the Pulitzers, and its new executive editor, Herbert Bayard Swope, himself one of the most celebrated reporters of the period, was attracting a staff that would become nationally known. In a few years, profits and prestige would slip away and the *World* would cease publication, but when Hadden applied, it was a magnet for young reporters. For Noel Busch's biography of Hadden,[1] Swope wrote his account of how Hadden was hired:

I was sitting at my desk one evening just after the editorial conference on the next day's paper when, suddenly, I became aware of a shadow on my desk. Someone was standing there. I had given strict orders that no one was allowed in my office except one or two of my editors. I took it for granted that it was one of them. When I looked up, I saw a young man I could not recall having seen before.

I said: "Who are you?"

He said: "My name is Briton Hadden and I want a job."

I said: "How did you get in here? My secretary has orders not to let anyone in."

"I waited till she left her desk."

"And how did you get past the managing editor's office?"

"I waited till he went into the city room."

"We don't do things like that. Go out again and send in your name properly tomorrow. I don't talk to young men I have never met before."

"Mr. Swope, you have met me before."

It turned out that he had me there. I had made a talk at some event in New Haven and later met some members of the board of the paper, when he was the editor. Nonetheless, I told him again that he would have to leave.

"Mr. Swope," he said, "you're interfering with my destiny."

Well, that was something new to me. I asked him to explain how I would be interfering with his destiny.

He told me that his destiny required him to work on the *World* for a year in order to get experience to help him start a paper of his own. I asked him why the *World*. His answers seemed to make a lot of sense. By the end of a few minutes I felt

[1] Noel F. Busch: *Briton Hadden* (Farrar, Straus and Company, 1949).

convinced that he had something. We had a rule just then against giving these young college kids jobs on the paper. Most of them expected to be columnists. I could see that whatever Hadden had in mind at the time, it wasn't that. He was serious and sensible in his talk. I said: "All right, you have a job."

There were about fifty reporters in the *World*'s city room, and a new boy put in many discouraging hours waiting for an assignment. On his first day Hadden bustled in and was assigned a desk next to F. Darius Benham. "My name's Hadden," he announced, thrusting out his hand, and then pretended to be very busy. His first assignment was to investigate a robbery in Central Park. "I think they just sent me out to see what I could do," he told his mother, "but I feel like $100." A few days later Benham found Hadden a little dejected. "I am not getting anywhere," he complained. "The city editor won't give me any assignments." Later Hadden brightened and came back to Benham: "Say, I've a scheme. You're ship news reporter, that guy over there covers City Hall. Another man checks hotels. Why shouldn't I meet trains? I'll go and ask if I can be train news reporter."

The city editor agreed to let Hadden try, but it was difficult to interview important people on the run in Grand Central or Penn Station. Eventually Hadden found his first niche as animal reporter, writing stories about dogs that ate their muzzles, cats caught in strange places and the weird strays that find their way into animal shelters—hardly in keeping with Hadden's ambition to publish a paper of his own which would report weekly on the world's work.

He discussed this ambition from time to time with his fellow reporter Benham. As Benham recalled one conversation:

One day, just sitting around, Brit said, "See this [picking up a copy of the New York *Times*]? Full of wonderful news, tells you everything going on in the world, but you haven't got time to read it all every day. You're a rich millionaire. You live at Glen Cove. You get on the train in the morning. You pick up the *Times*. Maybe you get only half-way through by the time you reach Penn Station. I have an idea for a magazine that comes out every Friday with all the news condensed so you and all the

49

other rich millionaires commuting home for the weekend can catch up on the news that they have missed. How's that?"

In August 1921 Hadden took three months' leave from the *World* to ship aboard a British freighter to South America. With two companions—a Yale classmate and a man from Harvard—Hadden worked his way by day but shipped as a first-class passenger at night. "'Arf the time we are gentlemen first-class passengers," he wrote his stepfather, "the other 'arf we are 'bloody deck boys.' . . . All three of us are willing to extend this trip as long as we have fun and our $80 apiece bankrolls hold out. . . ." They put in at Panama City, where, Hadden reported, "one walks for blocks and blocks and every fourth house is a saloon or a dance hall. Beautiful ladies stand in the doorways of the remaining 75% of the houses beseeching everybody to come in and partake of their hospitality. We concluded that these invitations were not exclusive enough to be considered flattering. . . ."

In Ecuador, Hadden interviewed the President, who spoke of opportunities for American investment and mentioned hopefully the possibility of floating a $25 million loan through J. P. Morgan. Wrote Hadden: "We promised to speak to Mr. Morgan about it on our return to the United States." As ex-officers of the Army of the United States, they attended a review of the Ecuadorian army. They went hunting in the interior, were entertained at a party given by a local businessman, where Hadden and his friends gave an exhibition of the "Toddle," New York's latest dance craze. Hadden wrote: "The evening's entertainment closed with a vocal rendition of the *Ecuadorian National Anthem* by our hosts and *Drunk Last Night, Oh, You Beautiful Doll* and *The Eagles in Mobile* by us (loud applause)."

Having had his original $80 bankroll replenished frequently in response to cables home, he returned to his job on the *World* at the end of October.

Luce sailed for Europe on the *Olympic*. After a walking trip in England and Scotland he intended to spend the summer with a French family in a second attempt to master the language. Instead, in Paris he ran into a classmate, Hugh D. Auchincloss, who persuaded Luce to join him on a trip through the Balkans to Istanbul by the Simplon-Orient express. It was something of an adventure, because few tourists penetrated the Balkans in those immediate postwar years when Istanbul (then Constantinople) was still under Allied military occupation. Luce always remembered one of his fellow travelers, a diplomatic courier and Marine sergeant major, whose stories "were an eye-opener even for two worldly Yale seniors." The U.S. Minister in Bucharest could not believe they were mere sightseers. "Tell me," he said, "why you are really here. . . . Who do you represent—Singer Sewing Machine or what big American firm?" Another courier, again a Marine, helped get them across the Rumanian border, which was closed, into Bulgaria. From Sofia they went on to Budapest, a seventy-hour trip by train through Yugoslavia. In Budapest they found every hotel room occupied, although the room clerk at the Ritz offered them the use of a bathroom apiece. A cab driver suggested instead a bordello. "Not necessarily for wholly moral reasons but from an innate conservatism," said Luce, "we eventually returned to the Ritz and slept in the bathtubs."

His year at Oxford was relaxed and a totally new educational experience. He enrolled in Christ Church with the intention of reading history. His tutor asked, "What history?" "A little impatiently," Luce said, "I spelled it out—I intended to read eighteenth- and nineteenth-century European history. Then the don's moment came and he said: 'Luce, I am bound to tell you that here at Oxford we consider that modern history ends with the Glorious Revolution of 1688. After that all is mere hearsay and rumor.' "

At Christmas Luce revisited Italy, and in Rome on New Year's Eve he attended a party at the American Academy as the guest of Thornton Wilder. There he met Miss Lila Hotz of Chicago, whom he was later to marry.

From Florence he wrote home: "A perfectly delightful sojourn. . . . Following my usual plan I read steadily, finishing Lecky's monumental work [a twelve-volume history of eighteenth-century England], Hallam's 'Balance of Power,' Trevelyan, Fox, Strieyenski, Renan's 'Vie de Jésus,' McCarthy's 'Four Georges' and a good bit of

51

Browning's Florentine poetry . . . then every day an hour or so at Pitti or Uffizzi. . . ." He met Miss Hotz again in Paris, and in June she was his guest at the "commen" balls which that year were held at St. John's, Balliol, and Magdalen—three nights, she remembered, when everyone danced till dawn, and three days of festivities ending with the first American-British polo match at Hurlingham.

By midsummer 1921 Luce's funds were running low, and he decided to head for Chicago and take up Mrs. McCormick's offer of a job. "My rather simple-minded notion at the time was that you didn't get anywhere in the newspaper business by starting as a cub reporter and climbing up to be editor. So I thought, 'Well, I'll go out and make some money.' But it so happened that in 1921 when I arrived back in Chicago the country was going through a very sharp depression, one now forgotten in view of the Great Depression of the '30s.

"Madame McCormick's second son, Harold Fowler McCormick, president of the company, drove me in a Rolls-Royce to the offices of the International Harvester Company. I'll never forget the scene in his office. There was an old-fashioned roll-top desk and a swivel chair. Somewhat nervously McCormick sent for Alexander Legge, then vice president of the company, who for the next decade was to be one of the outstanding businessmen of the country. He was a very big, tall fellow and when he came into Harold's office he went right to the couch and stretched himself out full length. Harold seemed even more nervous and began, 'Well, you know Mamma has always hoped Henry would come into the company. . . .'

"Legge just lay there and finally he said, 'Well, of course, if Mrs. McCormick wants us to do it, we'll do it.' Then he turned to me and said, 'But now, Luce, do you want us to do it? If we take you on, you know, we'll have to fire someone else.' So I said—what could I say?—'Of course I don't want you to fire anyone.' Then he said, 'Okay, that's that. Now I'll try to help you get a job somewhere else.' "

Legge gave him two or three introductions. "In a kind of perfunctory way I went around to those places. Then, since I wanted to go into newspapers anyway, I went around to the Chicago *Daily News*. It was the only newspaper in Chicago that I felt I could work for

52

because of the view I had formed in college of Hearst and of McCormick's Chicago *Tribune*. The *News* in those days was a very great paper owned by a fine newspaperman, Victor Lawson, and it had an extraordinary editor in Henry Justin Smith.

"When I asked for a job Mr. Smith said no. As I had read in schoolboy stories, I decided the thing to do was to go back again and say that I would sweep the floor. The third time I tried, Smith said, 'Well, it just happens that Ben Hecht says he's behind in his work and needs an assistant.' "

Ben Hecht was writing a column, "One Thousand and One Afternoons," which consisted of anecdotes about odd Chicago characters. People sent in suggestions, which Luce had to check out. "I remember a woman snake charmer, who lived way out on Halsted Street. My job was to find out if she really existed, really was a snake charmer, and anything else I might pick up. And that is about all Hecht needed to write a 2,000-word column."

The Hecht-Luce association broke up after about five weeks and there is a disagreement as to why. Thirty-seven years later Hecht, who had become a television raconteur after a career as newspaperman, novelist and playwright, gave his version on the air. When he asked Smith for a legman, Hecht said, he told the managing editor, "Don't get me a reporter. A reporter doesn't react to anything but the mangled body of a society leader. Get me a very naïve fellow who will notice everything going on and bring me back tidbits that I can work up into columns.

"About three days later he appeared with a blond, eager-eyed young man about my own age just out of college, looking for his first job. I hired him on sight. I don't remember what he did, but I remember reams of copy coming in about lemonade stands and traffic jams and people who lost suitcases in railroad stations. Finally, I went to Mr. Smith and said, 'Fair is fair, but this fellow is much *too* naïve. Nothing he writes makes any sense. I haven't been able to get a paragraph out of it.' And Henry Smith said, 'He wants to be a journalist very badly.' I said, 'Don't pay any attention to that. He's not going to go anywhere.' So Mr. Smith fired him and I was right. Mr. Luce got nowhere."

Shortly after the Hecht broadcast Luce's editorial assistant sent this memo to the archives:

> HRL agrees that Ben Hecht tells a good story; but for archive purposes he would like to have his own memory given at least equal status with that of Novelist Hecht. . . . It is Luce's impression that Hecht presently said to Smith, "This boy Luce is too good to waste on this errand boy stuff; why don't you give him a real chance in the city room?" And so it was—or at least Luce thinks it was. Which Chicago *Daily News* reporter d'ya read?

As Luce remembered it, after the weeks with Hecht he moved into the city room and was raised from $16 to $20 a week. His few months with the *Daily News* were no more eventful than Hadden's longer apprenticeship on the *World*. He was the cub in a city room of forty much more seasoned reporters. The nearest thing to a real break for him came on a Saturday afternoon when, since the *News* was an afternoon daily, the city room was all but deserted. A student was missing after a particularly savage fraternity initiation and Luce was sent to cover the police search. He was convinced that the boy's body would be found under a pier on Lake Michigan near Evanston, but the police assured him that they had already dragged those waters.

"About a year later I was walking down Broadway with Brit Hadden, who had this habit of picking up newspapers. He couldn't go by a newsstand without buying the latest edition. He was looking at the *Sun* when he said, 'Isn't that the story you were working on?' There was a tiny item reporting that the boy's body had been found under the pier where I thought it was. Maybe if I had had a little more nerve and hired a boat, I might have found that body myself and become a great crime reporter."

Luce's background made him a rather odd figure to some of his fellow workers. This was the era when reporters thought of themselves aggressively as "newspapermen" and repudiated "journalist" as pretentious and a slur on their calling. Luce recalled: "One Saturday I was going out to Lake Forest to call on Lila Hotz. I was dressed to kill in my one Savile Row suit, and I think I still had a mustache and I was carrying a cane. Then I remembered that I had left in the office a book I had promised to lend her. It being Saturday, I thought I could get in and out without anyone seeing me. In the old, ratty elevator in the *Daily News* Building there was room for only two or three people, and coming down, in stepped H. J. Smith. The two of us had, for me, an interminable ride. And as he stepped out, H. J. Smith turned to me, to say with withering scorn, 'Ah, Luce, a journalist, I see.' I have sometimes said to myself that the one thing I was determined to do was to make 'journalist' a good word. And today it *is* a good word."

He was, finally, fired. In September 1921, in an economy drive, the last one in, he became the first one out. But affairs took a happy turn. A Yale classmate, Walter Millis, was working for the Baltimore *News* as an assistant editorial writer. At that time many newspapers were hesitant about taking on college men as beginners, but the *News* management, pleased with Millis, asked him if he could find two more college men like himself. Millis wrote both Hadden and Luce, offering them $40 a week on the *News* and all expenses paid to Baltimore. Luce had hardly put his letter down when he received a telegram from Hadden saying, in effect, "Let's go and at least have a look at it and maybe we can get together there and work on 'the paper.' "

Luce could not resist the temptation to tell his former editor he had landed a new newspaper job. "It will perhaps interest you to know that I had all but accepted the wisdom of your advice to 'get out of newspapers' when along came an offer from the Frank Munsey papers in Baltimore—unasked, unheralded," he wrote Smith. "They want to give two of us $40 a week (with chance to make more on the side, Sunday, etc.) and to put us through all departments with a view to making minor officials of us in the near future—I hope you can restrain any tendency toward Rabelaisian laughter. At any rate, I am afraid I shall be unable to resist the temptation. And what makes it worse is that two of us are showing signs of pernicious insanity and will probably undertake a new publishing venture in a few months. . . ." To this he added a P.S.: "I suppose I am not under any obligation to explain to Mr. F. Munsey's representatives that I was 'fired' from the *News*. If you think I am, will you please let me know?"

The two of them moved in with Millis on the top floor of an old

Baltimore mansion. Because the *News* was an afternoon paper, Hadden and Luce worked early in the morning and generally were through about three o'clock, which gave them plenty of free time to work out their great idea. "We asked ourselves why, with good newspapers and magazines, are people not so well informed?" said Luce. "The idea then was to see if we could organize the news, compartmentalizing it with some sense of continuity. For example, in those days oil was a big news thing. And we thought we could have a regular section in the National Affairs department on oil where you could follow developments.

"But the great thing was simplification—by organization, by condensation, by putting seven days' news into one story. And simplification by just being simple and not being ashamed to say, 'Babe Ruth is a great ball player.' A lot of people might not know Babe Ruth was a great ball player and be ashamed to admit it. This is an extreme example, but it was certainly true when applied to politicians and foreign statesmen. And then you had to add the human bit, the interesting details, to make it all come alive.

"When we began working on 'the paper' people were quite emotional about war debts. Everybody was saying that the foreigners should pay those debts, but if you asked anybody, 'What does France owe us?' they couldn't come within millions of dollars of the amount."

Every afternoon they would rush back from work and cut up that day's New York *Times* and try to classify the clippings by departments. Then they tried writing stories out of the clips, and pasted up dummies based on their first typewritten efforts.

They had been in Baltimore less than three months, and certainly hadn't worked out anything like a prospectus, when Hadden announced in a letter to his mother:

I tendered my resignation to Editor-in-Chief Harwood this afternoon, interviewed City Editor Steuart at his home tonight, and (aided and abetted by his own good rye) succeeded in getting him to agree to the following plan:
   1) Luce and I are to leave Baltimore Wednesday night.
   2) Any time up to April 1 we are privileged to return to

Baltimore and continue at our present jobs on the *News* at $40 per.

3) We can also return to these jobs any time after April 1—provided the *News* is not overmanned.

I am confident that in the seven weeks prior to April 1 we shall be able to determine whether or not the paper, *Facts,* is going to be brought into existence. . . .

Provided *Facts* proves a failure during the seven weeks, I figure that I shall have lost this much:

1) Seven weeks' salary at $40 per ($280).

2) Seven weeks' experience of small-city reporting.

3) Several bucketfuls of respect of my friends and acquaintances, who will know well that I have been without visible means of support for seven weeks and that I have been backing a potential failure.

4) Ten dollars per week from my present capital ($100). (I intend to pay myself that salary while I am living at home; and I swear I can live within its limits.)

To offset these losses, I shall have gained this much, provided *Facts* proves a potential failure:

1) Several cornucopias full of information relative to all the details of the publishing business relative to the organizing of a new paper. (Since there is no doubt but that I shall organize a real paper or magazine some day, the time thus spent on *Facts* can hardly be termed time wasted.)

In the event that *Facts* proves a potential success during the seven weeks, great is my reward and obvious.

Hadden's letter was intended to reassure an anxious parent; he knew he was being over-optimistic as to the time needed to organize the venture. He and Luce, notwithstanding the promises of the Baltimore editor, felt they had burned their ships behind them. With nothing more than an idea, the two young reporters left for New York.

The Hardest Year

T HERE THEN BEGAN what Luce remembered as "the hardest year of my life"—the months of frustrating and discouraging work that made possible the publication of *Time*. The first eight months were taken up with the writing of the prospectus, raising money, learning the business of selling subscriptions, personally soliciting the testimonials and, in odd moments, trying to work out, as Canby suggested, a new writing style. With Mrs. Harkness' pledge of $20,000 the office was moved from East 17th Street to a large room in the Printing Crafts Building, 461 Eighth Avenue, which the partners subdivided with jerry-built partitions. The decision to publish made it necessary to decide who was to be editor and who business manager. The legend is that they flipped a coin. The fact was, Luce knew that Hadden was determined to be the editor, and for the next five years, except for very short intervals, he was. Fortunately Luce, much more than his partner, had an intuitive feel and liking for business.

It was not easy to find men eager to go along with them in their enterprise; and the eager ones were generally as inexperienced as they were themselves. Early in 1922 Manfred Gottfried, a Yale senior taking honors in English and an aspiring novelist, called at the 17th Street office. Canby, to whom he had gone for leads to newspaper jobs, had sent him. Gottfried described the meeting: "The room was rather shabby and bare, but pleasant enough with the morning sun streaming in through the windows, which badly needed washing. At the far end of the room, with their backs to the wall, sat Hadden and Luce with their desks end to end. Between the two small desks there was an iron kettle, perhaps eighteen inches in diameter, half filled with cigarette butts. Luce interviewed me. Hadden obviously could have done little work while the interview was going on, but as I later learned, he was generally embarrassed in dealing with strangers. After fifteen or twenty minutes I walked out of the office, not hired, but having agreed in principle that I would come to work for them. This was the first job I had had offered to me. More important, it was the first prospective job that I wanted to take. Canby had sent me to a series of editors. All their offices were grubby, and, what was worse, their attitudes toward their jobs seemed grubby. One of them gave me a kindly lecture on the foolishness of going into journalism. The office of Hadden and Luce was just as grubby, but their attitude was different. They were two young men who thought they had something useful and profitable to do and intended to do it."

Gottfried met Luce next in June at the Elizabethan Club in New Haven. Luce invited him to walk to a nearby tailor shop, where, while they waited for Luce's pants to be pressed, he offered Gottfried a job at $25 a week commencing August 1, a date postponed several times. Gottfried's faith remained unshaken; with a loan from his father, he bought forty shares of Time Inc. stock. When a new postponement until November 1 was proposed, he showed up in the offices on October 15 and worked the interim weeks without pay, thereby becoming *Time*'s first writer, newspaper clipper and chore boy.

Shortly after Gottfried started work, Roy Edward Larsen, who was to play a role second only to Luce's in the development of Time Inc., joined the staff. Larsen, Boston-born, was Harvard '21; at college, as business manager of the *Advocate,* a literary magazine, he had turned in a profit, a feat almost unprecedented. His collegiate success inclined him to publishing. His father, head of the B. F. Keith theater chain in New England and a former newspaperman, remembered his own discouraging, underpaid years in journalism and persuaded his son to try banking first. Larsen came to New York to take a job promised in the training department of the Guaranty Trust Company, but found his sponsor had been fired and the department eliminated. So he went to work briefly for the International Acceptance Corporation, then switched to the credit department of the New York Trust Company. Soon bored, he began to look again for a job in publishing. A Harvard classmate, John Cowles, wanted Larsen to join him on the family-owned Des Moines *Register* and *Tribune,* but Larsen wanted to stay in New York and work on a magazine. He turned down his first offer, a junior editorial post on *World's Work,* because he felt better qualified for business. Through a mutual friend he heard of Hadden, Luce and their magazine.

He met them first on his ground, the Harvard Club; the three of them agreed then to meet again. At the second meeting Hadden offered to make Larsen advertising manager. Larsen asked the advice of Sam Everitt of Doubleday, who told him, "It will be awfully good experience even if the magazine doesn't work out." But, Everitt added, "Can you take it? Those are awfully strong-minded fellows and they had another fellow who couldn't take it." That decided Larsen. John S. Martin described him as "a grim but smiling terrier" who could never resist a challenge. "I was the champion at one-armed pushups," Martin said. "I could do six or seven. Larsen went home and practiced until he could do twenty." But Larsen wanted to be circulation manager, not advertising manager.

When he telephoned Hadden and indicated his preference, Hadden hung up with a brusque "Sorry." Ten days elapsed; Hadden then called Larsen back and offered him the job he wanted at $40 a week, $15 more than he was making at the New York Trust Company. Larsen reported to work November 15, 1922. "The first back I saw," he remembered, "was that of Gottfried—standing over a table littered with newspapers, clipping the New York *Times.*" There was no desk for him, and temporarily the new circulation manager worked out of the library of the Harvard Club.

Instead of hiring an advertising manager, Hadden and Luce signed a contract with E. R. Crowe, Yale '03, a well-established publishers' representative. His fee was $1,000 a month plus expenses and an overriding commission of 10 percent on all space sold. Crowe was also given a stock option and was made vice president. He agreed to hire, on his own payroll, a salesman to work exclusively for *Time*. For this job he chose still another Yale man, Robert L. Johnson, who had been two years ahead of Hadden and Luce. Johnson left a job as an account executive in a small advertising agency, disregarding the usual cautionary advice about giving up an established position. He had been much impressed with the *Time* prospectus, and he had his wife's enthusiastic backing.

Others, understandably, were unwilling to take the same risks. Walter Millis had talked with them about their magazine and contributed to the typewritten dummies. Luce made a date to meet him for tea at Pennsylvania Station to tell him they were counting on him to be National Affairs editor. Luce offered $40 a week, $10 more than they were paying themselves. He was very disappointed when Millis refused to leave the *News*. Another disappointment followed. Their candidate for Foreign News editor was John Franklin Carter, like Millis a Yale friend who had done some volunteer work in the pre-publication period; among other things, he had tried to solicit a testimonial from Dr. Charles W. Eliot, the sponsor of Harvard's famous Five-Foot Shelf of Books. (Eliot said that the idea of summarizing the news was "disgusting and disgraceful.") Carter had gone to Rome and become a correspondent for the London *Chronicle*. He replied to their cable that he could not accept because of his *Chronicle* contract. Instead, he suggested they hire an English friend, Thomas John Cardell Martyn. On Carter's recommendation, they offered Martyn $60 a week. Martyn, an R.A.F. veteran who had lost a leg in World War I, was completing work for an Oxford degree. He immediately accepted and, though without journalistic experience, he proved an able writer. His counterpart, filling the job which Millis turned down, was Alan Rinehart, a son of Mary Roberts Rinehart, the novelist; he had worked briefly on a Washington paper. To complete the first full-time writing staff they hired John A. Thomas, a

Yale classmate of Gottfried. There was one Girl Friday, Miss Nancy Ford.

At the end of 1922 the expanding staff, too large for the room in the Printing Crafts Building, moved to 9 East 40th Street, into space sublet from E. R. Crowe. "Already we were working Saturday and Sunday," said Gottfried, "and during the winter there was no heat over the weekend, so we did our best in overcoats huddled over electric heaters."

Their trial copy was submitted for criticism to whomever Hadden and Luce could persuade to read it. Hadden did not always like criticism. Gottfried, who was keeping a diary, made this entry early in January 1923: "Down at 9:15. Hadden in ill humor. Could not fathom the cause until I recalled that Walter Lippmann had criticized the copy last night—probably unfavorably. Surmise later shown correct. Assembled this week's copy. Hadden feeling better by evening."

The first budget indicated that it was theoretically possible for *Time* to make a profit in its first year. This unlikely proposition was based on the supposition that the magazine would sell 25,000 paid-in-advance subscriptions at $5 each. In addition to the $125,000 these subscriptions would bring in Luce calculated that they might reasonably expect to sell six pages of advertising plus the back cover each week for $30,000. Against estimated income of $155,000 were these estimated expenditures:

Printing, make-up and mailing	$67,000
Editorial salaries	21,000
Business department salaries	15,000
Operating and Overhead	15,000
Canceled subscriptions	2,500
	$120,500

Newsstand sales—if there were any—would add to the profit. The budget's author did a little wishful thinking; if newsstand sales reached 25,000 an issue, the weekly profit on them would be $660, and "ten such weeks would more than pay the interest on the preferred stock."

The first 25,000 subscribers were to be solicited from a list of a million names. The astonishingly successful test on the live list of *World's Work* produced a 6½-percent return on a 7,000 mailing. Luce and Larsen knew they could not expect a similar return from a larger mailing, but they did think that if they mailed a million circulars they might get a return of 4 percent, or 40,000 trial subscriptions. Prospective subscribers were invited to read three issues before sending in any money; it was estimated that of the 40,000 as many as 37½ percent might drop out, which, by some pat figuring, would give them 25,000 bona-fide subscribers.

The solicitation began:

Dear Sir:

You are one of a limited number of busy men to receive this announcement of America's first news-magazine. . . .

It continued with a brief description of the magazine:

Men are asking: "What is the best way to keep informed?" The practical modern answer is "The News-Magazine . . ."

and concluded:

By returning the enclosed stamped postcard, you become one of the original subscribers to this unique service. But you pay no money unless you are satisfied with the first three issues. Return the card today. It does not obligate you. It does obligate us to give you the magazine that will meet your needs.

The accompanying circular listed the prominent men who had already agreed to become original subscribers. Among them were the presidents of Yale, Columbia, Princeton and Johns Hopkins universities and Williams College; the Episcopal Bishop of Massachusetts and the Roman Catholic Archbishop of Baltimore; the editors of the *Century* and *Harper's* magazines as well as the editors of the Springfield *Republican,* the Hartford *Courant,* the Indianapolis *News,* the Cincinnati *Times-Star* and the executive editor of the New York *World,* Herbert Bayard Swope. The world of finance was heavily represented, two of the most notable names being Thomas W. Lamont, senior partner of J. P. Morgan, and Elbert H. Gary, president of U.S. Steel. Among politicians was Franklin D. Roosevelt. The prospective subscriber could not fail to be impressed.

In the end, somewhat fewer than 500,000 letters were mailed. The response was disappointing; no more than 6,000 subscriptions resulted. As for newsstand sales, the American News Company was, with difficulty, persuaded to accept 5,000 copies.

In the summer of 1922 when Sudler was preparing estimates, he had trouble getting New York printers to submit quotations. One salesman submitted the specifications for a twenty-four-page magazine in quantities from 10,000 to 100,000 to his office and was told that the company preferred not to bid, because the publishers had no credit rating. On December 8, 1922, Luce received confirmation of a contract from the Williams Printing Company at 36th Street and Eleventh Avenue.

> *My dear Mr. Luce:*
>
> Confirming our conversation of yesterday and in reply to your memorandum of December 6, we are willing to print your new magazine *Time* in accordance with our estimate of November 14. Based on your giving us a final O.K. for press at 12 noon on Wednesday, we shall start running as soon as possible and complete make-ready during the run and have 25,000 copies ready for delivery to the post office by 6 p.m. on Thursday. . . .

Williams added the proviso that *Time* would be given a 5-percent discount if the bill were paid on the Monday following publication. It is not altogether clear whether the printers wanted to make sure that they would be paid for one week's issue before starting on the next, or whether this was a result of Luce's canny bargaining.

(At the end of 1923 the Williams Printing Company moved to Albany, and Luce had to find another printer. In 1959 Williams again became a printer for *Time* when a contract was signed for printing the regional editions distributed out of Albany to New York State and New England.)

Just before Christmas 1922, Hadden sent shareholders an optimistic report headed, *"Time* is now well under way":

LOCATION: Offices have been secured at 9 East 40 Street, ninth floor. This is a "Fifth Avenue" location, several jumps more pretentious than a stockholder would naturally expect. It is important to know that, through an arrangement with E. R. Crowe & Co., offices were secured at something less than one-third actual rental.

OFFICE PERSONNEL: A circulation manager and his assistant; an office manager and bookkeeper; three stenographers; an errand boy. Highest weekly salary: $40; lowest weekly salary, $10.

EDITORIAL STAFF: Full time—two Editors; one Assistant; one "National Politics" man; one "Foreign" man; one "Books and Theatre" man. Salaries: $40; $30; $25. Part time—specialists for Music, Art, Religion, Education, Law, Business, Science, Sport, Crime. Salaries—$10 and (in one case) $20. . . .

DATE OF FIRST ISSUE: Feb. 10, Feb. 17 or Feb. 24, depending upon what progress is made by the Advertising, Circulation and Editorial departments during the next five weeks. . . .

PRESENT FUNCTION OF EDITORIAL STAFF: To compile weekly sample or "dummy" issues complete in every way except in that they are not put to press. These typewritten "dummies" are criticized by experts and laymen and even by morons.

HOW STOCKHOLDERS CAN HELP: *Time* knows well that the people that will help it most are those who are best satisfied with it. For that reason it does not desire to antagonize any of its stockholders by asking them to do anything that is distasteful. From time to time summary requests will be made by Johnson, Larsen and others: "Give me a letter to this potential advertiser." "Get me 13 subscriptions."

Please aid us in performance of as many of these requests as you can. But we'd rather you'd write us a brief letter stating: "I've paid my money in and now expect you to produce dividends without further aid from me" than have you function actively for us, the while resenting our envelopes and the request they bring. . . .

If you have in mind any questions regarding the magazine or

its management, either Mr. Luce or myself will be glad to be given an opportunity to answer them.

In January 1923 pressure mounted. "For a couple of months nobody had had any regular days off, and now nobody had any days off whatsoever," Gottfried recalled. "I was the first to weaken. One day I felt tired and just announced that from then on I was going to take every Wednesday off. Neither Hadden nor Luce went that far. At the end of February, when we began actual publication, it was almost a relief because, when we put the paper to bed, you could wash your hands of it and go home and sleep for thirty-six hours."

Two trial issues were written and printed before publication, the second of these bearing the date of February 17, 1923. The format was designed by Gordon Aymar, an art director of the J. Walter Thompson Company, who was paid $500. He also obtained the first cover illustration, a black-and-white drawing of "Uncle Joe" Cannon, Speaker of the House of Representatives, by William Oberhardt, a commercial artist; as a concession Oberhardt reduced his fee, usually between $300 and $500, to $50.

At 12:30 a.m., February 27, 1923, the last copy for the first issue was delivered in person to the Williams press by Hadden and Luce, accompanied by most of the staff. They remained to read proof until dawn before going home exhausted.

Vol. I, No. 1, of *Time,* The Weekly News-Magazine, dated March 3, 1923, consisting of thirty-two pages including the covers, was a thin, unimpressive little magazine selling for the relatively high price of fifteen cents. It was—as the prospectus had promised—a magazine like no other published, compartmentalizing the news into twenty-two departments, written to be read from the first page to the last at one sitting in the span of an hour.

Luce never forgot the warm glow that came over him as he sat down to read the magazine: "I picked it up and began to turn through its meager pages. Half an hour later, I woke up to a surprise: what I had been reading wasn't bad at all. In fact, it was quite good. Somehow it all held together—it made sense, it was interesting." The editors had done more than summarize; they had reported the news with some perception and individuality.

In Vol. I, No. 1, the editors were not dealing with a particularly exciting week in the news. The world was between wars and President Harding's "normalcy" reigned in Washington. Joseph G. Cannon, the first cover subject, was quietly retiring, at eighty-six, after twenty-three terms in Congress. Nevertheless, *Time* was able to find and point to some events of present and future significance. In the first section, National Affairs, which occupied eighteen columns, the editors discerned in the President's request that the Senate approve U.S. membership in the World Court "a growing sense of American discontent with isolation." The second-largest department, Foreign News, with fifteen columns, had items on fourteen countries, plus a column of items on Latin America. A massive sale of Soviet wheat to Western Europe, *Time* predicted (correctly), was "slowly leading 10 or 15 million people—among them 3,000,000 children—toward certain starvation" and was an indication that the Russian government was more concerned with "the propagation of Bolshevik policy than in looking after their own people."

Books and The Theatre were allotted five columns each. The first book reviewed was Gertrude Atherton's novel *Black Oxen,* the subject of which was rejuvenation—then a controversial one—in the setting of "literary New York." Another story reported the current speculation that T. S. Eliot's recently published *The Waste Land* was a hoax, concluding that this was immaterial to the poem's supporters, "literature being concerned not with intentions but results." Another column was a guide to "the best books." The Theatre offered five reviews and a guide to current Broadway hits. Recommended were Galsworthy's *Loyalties,* Jeanne Eagels' performance in *Rain* and Harry Leon Wilson's *Merton of the Movies.* Music, Finance and Education each had three columns. A column and a half in Education was devoted to the question before the Yale Corporation: whether to retain Latin and Greek as requirements for the B.A. degree. Greek scholars Hadden and Luce and/or their Education writer appeared to support the classicists, for *Time* commented: "If the great universities, with their manifold departments and courses and degrees retain no common courses in any way related to the history of the race they will graduate men and women who will have nothing in common but their clothes." Law, The Press and Religion were covered in two columns apiece, while Medicine, Science, Crime, Aeronautics (the news was the proposal to establish dirigible service between Chicago and New York), Art, Cinema, Sport, Miscellany and Milestones had a column each.

The magazine leavened the news with three sections in lighter vein: Imaginary Interviews, two columns about celebrities; Point with Pride; and View with Alarm. These consisted of cryptic but pointed comments followed by page numbers and were intended to send readers riffling back through the pages for a second look. A departure from anonymity was a column of literary notes signed J.F.; the initials were those of John Farrar,[1] the editor of the *Bookman,* who contributed gratis.

Hadden and Luce were listed on the masthead as Editors, followed by the four staff writers, Gottfried, Martyn, Rinehart and Thomas. The contributors followed; these were the part-time writers, Hadden's "specialists." They included Farrar and two men who were becoming known as poets, Stephen Vincent Benét and Archibald MacLeish. Benét reviewed books; MacLeish, who was practicing law by day and teaching it at night in Boston, wrote Education for a fee of $10 a week. What others contributed cannot be identified with any certainty; they were mostly moonlighting Yale college mates and friends. The Religion department was written by Luce, usually on Sunday when he was free of business chores.

After the first issue, Luce wrote his fiancée, Miss Lila Hotz, in Chicago: "Wheels seem to be grinding slowly and smoothly in the production of Vol. I, No. 2. Not until tomorrow can we have any indication of how No. 1 was received, so we have nothing to do but go ahead on the old lines, doing our best to improve."

They had great expectations, were disappointed to see how little note the world took of their magazine. The New York *Times* gave it four paragraphs headed, "TIME A NEW WEEKLY—FIRST ISSUE OF MAGAZINE DEVOTED TO SUMMARIZING PROGRESS." Larsen took heart

[1] Founder in 1929 of the publishing firm Farrar & Rinehart.

because some New York newsstands sold out on the first day of publication. He wrote his father:

> I am really afraid to go on record as saying *Time* has arrived but the newsboys swear it has, and it's their bread and butter. So what else can I believe? When a blind newsdealer almost falls on your neck because you let him have ten copies a day late and tells you two hours later that he could use 50 more—it's a grand and glorious feeling with a bit of awe mixed in. We had only about 1,300 copies in New York City and I know of only 40 or 50 scattered all over that were not sold out this noon.
>
> From the remarks at the No. 1 stand at Grand Central today, they could have sold several hundred copies at that one stand alone.
>
> I am almost afraid to wake up in the morning to hear I have been having hectic dreams for the past 48 hours.

Such euphoria was soon and rudely shattered. When they checked on the subscribers' reaction they discovered many of them had received no copies, others two or three. Larsen had hired several of Hadden's debutante friends to prepare the mailing wrappers for the magazine. These charming but amateur workers had managed to mix up the wrappers. Then the newsstand returns came in: 2,500 out of the first 5,000 were unsold. The circulation of the first issue, so rosily projected at 25,000, turned out to be less than 9,000.

CHAPTER
6

"From an Idea into an Established Institution"

THE NEW MAGAZINE was not, as Hadden put it to the shareholders with masterly understatement, "the fortunate recipient of any overnight popularity." Cancellations of trial subscriptions began arriving shortly after the first issue was delivered. Newsstand sales dropped off sharply once a first slight public curiosity had been satisfied. Many who did not cancel had to be persuaded to pay up. "It was just like pulling teeth to get the $5 bills in," Larsen said. "I settled down and burned the midnight oil writing letters to cajole them into paying. We kept mailing and billing. Lord knows how long we kept on mailing." The magazine's life blood was the trickle of remittances in each morning's mail. Luce often felt like a doctor who has lost his patient's pulse. The circulation receipts tell the story of their ups and downs—$11,486 in March; $17,556 in April; $10,122 in May.

There was trouble on the advertising side. Friction had developed between *Time*'s advertising representative, Crowe, and Luce. To Crowe the *Time* lot seemed rather naïve and penurious. When Luce objected to some of the expenses Crowe charged to the magazine,

70

Crowe told him to mind his own business. But when no advertisement was sold for the back cover of the fourth issue and Crowe was unavailable, they let it run blank. When Crowe saw the magazine, he stormed in to Luce. If they didn't sell a cover, he told him, print a house ad, even give away an advertisement; under no circumstances should a back cover run blank. *Time,* he added, was altogether too amateurish for him; he handed back his contract and his option. At the end of the year, congratulating Hadden and Luce on *Time*'s survival, Crowe wrote, "Good luck to you both in every way—tightwads though you are."

Tightwads they were, of necessity, nursing every cent. Luce's secretary and *de facto* bookkeeper was required to get Hadden's and Luce's signatures on every check. When bills became too pressing she sometimes sent out checks with one signature only, hoping that by the time the omission was discovered there would be enough in the bank account to cover. She remembered Luce looking over the bank statement and saying rather wistfully, "With any luck one day we will have $5,000 on deposit."

Although his employer, Crowe, quit, Bob Johnson did not. He stayed on, transferred to *Time*'s payroll, becoming its first advertising manager, and began building his own sales staff. He and his men had an uphill, discouraging job ahead of them; as the company's first annual report acknowledged, "From the advertising world as a whole *Time* has met with a cold reception. We believe this is due generally to the stolid inertia of human nature. Advertisers are human. It was years before evolution was generally accepted even as a theory. . . ."

There were several upheavals before Hadden found a compatible group of writers. He fired his first National Affairs writer after the fourth issue. He and Luce then cabled a new offer to their friend John Franklin Carter, which he accepted. After Carter had been on the job a month, Hadden insisted that Luce fire him. Carter contended that he had returned on the understanding that his job would be guaranteed and that he would be given stock in the company. He left only after a fearful row—"There was blood on the carpet," Gottfried recalled—and in bitterness. (He subsequently enjoyed a successful career as a Washington columnist and wrote a number of books on

71

politics under his own name and the pseudonym Jay Franklin.) The fourth member of the original writing team, Jack Thomas, shortly thereafter stopped by Gottfried's desk and announced cheerily, "I have been fired." The full-time writing staff was reduced to Gottfried and Martyn, who between them wrote more than half of the magazine; a changing group of "specialists" produced the rest. It was not until 1924 that they were joined full-time by Hadden's cousins John S. Martin and Niven Busch. Hadden called Martin and Busch his "red rovers" because they could be called on to write any section of the magazine.

The first editorial staff also included "secretarial assistants," known informally as "the checkers," whose title some years later was upgraded to the dignity of "researchers." [1] The job began when, in the pre-publication period, Hadden hired Nancy Ford to help him snip interesting items from the papers. Once publication began, the girls were required at the beginning of the week to mark news items, which an office boy then clipped from the papers for the writers; when the *Time* story was written, they verified names, dates and facts. The first reference library consisted of a shelf of Hadden's own books—a dictionary, a thesaurus, a history, a *World Almanac*. For more complicated matters, the girls were expected to use the public library. The girls, like everyone else, were underpaid and overworked to the point of exhaustion. After one closing night Nancy Ford announced she was never coming back. "Holy Grail, Miss Ford," Hadden pleaded, "I think you are making a terrible mistake." But he could not persuade her to return. Another girl went home to bed and did not leave it for a month. On recovery she got a job with J. P. Morgan & Co. Meeting her, Hadden was contrite: "I don't blame you at all. You did quite right." At home that night, remembering Hadden's words, she burst into tears.

[1] At *Time*'s twentieth-anniversary dinner, Luce said that although "the word 'researcher' is now a nation-wide symbol of serious endeavor," the title was originally conceived when he and Hadden were doing some "research" for a drinking club called the Yale Professors. "Little did we realize that in our private jest we were inaugurating a modern female priesthood, the veritable vestal virgins whom levitous writers cajole in vain, and managing editors learn humbly to appease."

72

All of them retained vivid memories of the ordeal of putting the magazine to press. "The staff generally went to the printer's by taxi, in one taxi, that is," said Gottfried. "Brit, Nancy Ford, Martyn and I all went together. We took all our reference material—that is to say, a copy of *Who's Who* and the *World Almanac*. The printing shops were always in grimy parts of town, such as Eleventh Avenue or Vesey Street. We usually located ourselves somewhere near the proofreading area. Every three or four hours we would send out for fried-egg sandwiches and hot coffee. We wrote new stories as successive editions of the morning papers came in. The copy and the fried-egg sandwiches would get covered with printer's ink. There were always more corrections, more holes to be filled in as the evening wore on. In those days I often had fights with Hadden, in the early hours when we were both exhausted. More than once he fired me and more than once I resigned. But nothing was said about it when we started the next week. I remember often going home with the early-morning workers going downtown to Wall Street. The rest of that day we slept. The second day we recuperated and the third day we went back to work." They were young and resilient, never long discouraged.

Four months after the first issue the staff moved from the overcrowded offices on East 40th Street to loft space at 236 East 39th Street, in a building that had once housed Hupfel's brewery. In a report to stockholders, Luce wrote with pride of the new quarters. Hadden, he said, occupied "a spacious room" which he shared with "six secretarial assistants and William, the clipper. William clips out of newspapers and magazines all articles marked by the assistants. These articles he files in bins according to subjects, e.g. 'Congress,' 'Music.' Upon these bins *Time* is built. . . ." He spoke, too, of the writers' "semi-private office"; this cubicle, which had one window and three desks, was so narrow that if the man at the window wanted to leave, the occupant of the middle desk had to pull his chair in to let him pass. Luce, Larsen and Johnson shared their small offices with secretaries. The circulation clerks worked in open space.

In the first six months, expectations continued much higher than incoming subscriptions warranted. But there were some encouraging

73

signs. On completion of Vol. I, the first six months' issues, management sent bound copies to a number of the charter subscribers and received some enthusiastic and promotion-worthy compliments. Colonel E. M. House, Woodrow Wilson's wartime confidant and adviser, wrote that the magazine "filled a long-felt need and I hope you will meet with the encouragement you so well deserve." Newton D. Baker said that *Time* "has taken a place in the very small list of regular periodicals which I have the leisure to read thoroughly. . . . Indeed, I know no other equally adequate and equally brief survey of the weekly news. My effort to discover its partisan bias has failed, and I am beginning to suspect that it has none." Historically, the most interesting of these early letters was from one whose feelings about the magazine would undergo some change:

Dear Mr. Luce:

I am glad that *Time* is proving a success and I feel certain that it will grow in popularity. You ask me various questions—as to which sections of the paper I have found most useful—I think I can say that I have found interesting information in all sections. . . .

I do not think the articles are too brief—they are just about right in length and they are unbiased as far as it is possible for red-blooded Americans to make them so. My only criticism is that occasionally, in the need of being brief, *Time* has made statements in regard to events which are not wholly fact. In other words, you have left out qualifying words which are really essential. . . .

I particularly like the occasional disguised editorial, such as that one . . . the other day which called down the press of the country for extravagant statements in regard to the nation's mourning for the dead President.[2] The more you can hammer

---

[2] In commenting on the death of Warren G. Harding, *Time* described as "falsely sentimental fiction" such headlines as "WHOLE COUNTRY PLUNGED IN GLOOM," adding: "It is no overstatement to say that there was genuine public sorrow at his sudden death," but to 99.9 percent of the people "he was a name, a picture, the holder of a respected office. . . . It was contrary to nature that these people should be 'plunged in gloom.' Nearly all went about their business with undiminished vitality. . . . Many editors [printed] extravagances. . . ."

74

against the tendency of the press to exaggerate simple facts and "dress up" essentially unimportant news the more you will receive applause. It will take courage to laugh at the press of the United States, but I think that you will gain readers by doing so occasionally in a perfectly good-natured way. . . .

May you grow and prosper—

Very sincerely yours,

Franklin D. Roosevelt

There were other readers even more enthusiastic. One phrase recurred so often in the first letters to the editor that it became a central theme in *Time*'s promotion: "I read your magazine from cover to cover."

The first definite pickup in circulation was noted after Labor Day, 1923, and it came after a modest investment in advertising in the *Literary Digest, Harper's,* the *Atlantic,* the *Century* and the literary section of the New York *Post.* It enabled Luce and Larsen to set the circulation guarantee at 30,000 for 1924—the actual circulation in the second half of 1923 averaged 18,500—and in October subscriptions were coming at a rate which encouraged them to increase the guarantee to 35,000. They also joined the Audit Bureau of Circulations. Larsen wrote his father: "There seems little doubt but that *Time* will be at least as valuable a property as the *Outlook* or *Life*—perhaps even reaching the position of the [*Literary*] *Digest.*" His father, who had been doubtful about *Time*'s future, replied that while the magazine often irritated him, he now believed it would survive.

In 1923 *Time* lost $39,454; the annual report listed cash on hand, deposits and investments as $36,533, accounts payable as $9,569. The net assets as of December 31, 1923, were reported as $108,633, a figure which included "no item for good will and, on the other hand, no item for subscription reserve." As president of the company, Hadden was cautious but optimistic:

. . . *Time* has grown from an idea into an established institution . . . has gradually been accepted by an increasing number of people as part of their weekly reading. On December 31,

75

1923 *Time* was on a small paying basis, able to look forward with reasonable optimism to greater earning power.

Time pays, on a 30,000 circulation, because of the strictest economy, including an unprecedented low scale of salaries. This low scale cannot be maintained indefinitely. The object, therefore, in 1924, must be to place *Time* in a position to pay on a bigger scale.

The chief factor will be the degree to which subscriptions are renewed. Present indications point to a renewal percentage higher than any other national weekly.

Hadden's reference to the salaries was pertinent to himself, Luce and Larsen, who in December 1923 were each drawing $40 a week. (So tight were *Time*'s finances that at first the founders kept their salaries at a subsistence level; a friend remembers walking around New York's Bryant Park with Luce one evening when *Time* was nearly three years old while Luce debated whether he and Hadden could afford to give themselves a $10 raise.) In Luce's case there was real hardship because he was now a married man. Martyn was a little better off, for he was paid $60 a week. Johnson had a contract that called for a salary of $4,000 a year plus 10 percent of the advertising sold. In lieu of higher salaries Hadden and Luce had retained for themselves 2,775 shares each of the first issue of 8,000 shares of Class B Common. For the nominal price of $2 a share they had allocated to their associates the remaining 2,450 shares. Johnson, Larsen and Martyn received 500 shares each and Gottfried 450 shares, but these were subject to resale to the company if they left or were fired. In 1924 John S. Martin received 500 shares under the same terms. However, the Class B Common remained subordinate to the Preferred shares and the Class A Common until all arrears on the Preferred were paid. For the time being, the market value of both Class A and Class B Common was negligible, but some other members of the staff were nevertheless eager to buy some. Hadden circularized the Class A shareholders:

We have had several applications for Common Stock from men in the employ of this company who wish to have an interest in

76

the business. It is absolutely impossible for me to advise you what your Common Stock is worth. Its face value is probably not 50 cents. Its speculative value may be $50. I can only report to you that bids of $2 and $4 per share have been made for the Common Stock, Class A. Kindly advise me whether you desire to sell any of your stock (and if so, how much) at either or both of these prices.

No shares were offered; the shareholders, it would seem, were finding *Time* an interesting speculation.

The critical period was, as Hadden indicated, February 1924, when the original subscriptions ran out. The magazine met the test with ease, not only renewing a very large percentage but steadily continuing to add new ones.

In May 1924—surprisingly, for *Time* was little more than a year old— the youthful publishers undertook to publish a new magazine, the *Saturday Review of Literature.* This was more because of sentiment than by design. Thomas W. Lamont, senior partner of J. P. Morgan & Co., tired of underwriting the losses of the New York *Post,* sold that paper to Cyrus H. K. Curtis, who published the Philadelphia *Ledger* as well as the *Saturday Evening Post* and *Ladies' Home Journal.* With the *Post* went its Saturday *Literary Review,* which had a circulation of 8,000 to 10,000 apart from the *Post* and had much prestige in bookish circles. It was edited by Hadden's and Luce's friend Henry Seidel Canby, who also enjoyed the friendship and patronage of Lamont. Canby, absent when the sale took place, returned to find "a brisk managerial person in charge, who was unimpressed by our practical idealism (for our section of the paper had made money) and our national circulation and influence. We seemed to him a string quartet proposing to play in a corner of his two-ring circus. And soon I was writing what I knew to be a farewell editorial, summarizing what we had tried to do. I entitled it 'And Twitched His Mantle Blue,' feeling sure that the new proprietors would not recognize the quotation from Milton or know that the next line in *Lycidas* reads: 'Tomorrow to fresh woods, and pastures new.' " [3] Canby re-

[3] Henry Seidel Canby: *American Memoir* (Houghton Mifflin Company, 1947).

signed, along with his whole staff—Amy Loveman, William Rose Benét, the poet-critic, and Christopher Morley, the *Review*'s columnist.

Lamont was upset; an admirer of the *Review* and its editors, he offered to help them publish an independent literary magazine. Larsen, who was a classmate of Lamont's son at Harvard and had obtained a charter subscription and endorsement from the senior Lamont for *Time,* was the one to whom the first approach was made. At Lamont's instance, the circulation manager of the New York *Post* called to tell him that if *Time* would publish such a literary magazine he would deliver the circulation list of the *Post*'s supplement. "Can you do that and keep us out of jail?" Larsen asked. Reassured, he took the proposition to Hadden and Luce: Lamont to put up $50,000, Time Inc. to publish the magazine, Canby and his associates to have editorial control. Hadden and Luce accepted enthusiastically. They admired Canby and his publication and they had a score to settle with Curtis. When they were soliciting testimonials, he had refused to see them and hear their story.

"And so," Canby wrote, "we migrated—editors, columnists, poets, reviewers—carrying a baggage of morale, enough money for a new start, and a draft of our subscription list which we personally had built with great care. We left Vesey Street [where the *Post* was published] for the noisy [third] floor of an East Side factory where *Time* had its headquarters, and there launched the *Saturday Review of Literature,* which was the *Literary Review* come of age, more humorous, wiser, more literary, better printed, but with the same will to further the cause of good thinking, good feeling, good writing and good books." The first issue appeared August 2, 1924.

Canby and his associates brought a raffish, Bohemian touch to the Time Inc. offices. The editors occupied a single room next to Hadden and his girls, where they were often joined by the exuberant Christopher Morley. One afternoon the *Time* staff was startled by a series of heavy thumps coming from the *Saturday Review* quarters. Morley was opening a bottle of whiskey by thumping it on the table until the cork popped out.

"It was seldom dull . . . ," Canby admitted. "We could count upon at least one paranoiac a week. I do not mean paranoiacs in the strict medical sense, though a few of them were definitely crazy. Our would-be reviewers of this kind were obsessed creatures of one idea. . . . The modernist critics invaded our office . . . with lightning in their eyes and grenades in either hand."

The *Review*'s visitors were on the noisy side: poets who liked to declaim, convivial raconteurs who told stories at the top of their voices. The commotion upset Hadden, a stickler for the proprieties —in the office. He was moved to issue an indignant memorandum: "Unseemly hilarity in one office causes disturbance in all. In future will all editors receiving visitors in their offices bear that in mind." On the whole, however, the two editorial staffs worked in mutual respect and harmony.

Larsen got the *Review* off to a good start: on a trip to the Midwest in June 1924 he managed to get 10,000 orders from bookstores; he was equally successful in a direct-mail solicitation. By the end of the year the *Saturday Review* had a circulation of 23,000, more than twice its independent circulation as the *Post*'s literary section. In advertising sales it jumped ahead of the New York *Herald Tribune* book supplement and the *Bookman,* a long-established literary monthly.

Though Hadden and Luce did not, as they had planned, alternate as editor, they did alternate as president of the company. It was Luce, as president, who had the satisfaction of telling the shareholders that in 1924 the company, after "an exhaustive audit," made a profit of $674.15. Minuscule as it was, this was cause for satisfaction. He also announced that in 1924 *Time* had doubled its circulation—from 35,000 to 70,000—and that the magazine was beginning to attract advertisers. Luce noted that "in professional advertising circles . . . *Time* is given the highest praise because of the tangible results achieved in the short space of 22 months. Professional ad-men now look through *Time* and find many an advertisement which signifies (1) that *Time* is a good and potentially a great advertising medium; (2) that this fact has been ably set forth by the advertising manager and his assistants." He listed some of the major companies—General

Motors, Western Electric, Colgate, etc.—which had taken advertising, and concluded: "This significant list indicates that professional approval has been obtained from many and that many more will follow."

In 1925 the remainder of the original stock offering was sold, realizing the founders' goal of $100,000. It was decided at this time to raise additional capital to finance the *Saturday Review* and permit a more rapid expansion of the company. To do this the authorized capital of 14,000 shares was increased by 4,000 Preferred and 1,000 Class A Common. Half this new issue was held in reserve and half offered to the original shareholders on the basis of four shares of Preferred and one Common for $100, eventually raising an additional $50,000.

Breaking the Canons of Journalism

A FRIEND OF Hadden's calling at his office found him engrossed in the mail, murmuring, "Wonderful, wonderful." "What is wonderful?" he asked. "These people," said Hadden. "They're beginning to take this thing seriously."

Hadden and Luce worked desperately to that end, scarcely dared hope that it might be true; they knew the odds against a rewrite sheet produced with no more editorial resources than a pile of yesterday's newspapers, some well-thumbed reference books and their own wits. Slowly through the first hard year of publication they had shaped *Time* into a breezy little magazine that provided an effective if somewhat superficial summary of the week's news in a manner that commanded reader attention. *Time* strove hard to be clever, sometimes too hard. But it could be epigrammatic and often offered shrewd, fresh comment on current affairs. It was candid, often to the point of rudeness. It was certainly provocative. The readers were usually delighted or infuriated; seldom, if ever, bored.

Hadden took a highly individual view of his readers; his cousin Noel Busch [1] said that he regarded them as members of a club, a

[1] *Briton Hadden* (Farrar, Straus and Company, 1949).

81

circle of initiates. He never conceived of a circulation in the millions; he had in mind an audience of about 250,000—an elite group which he hoped would include the most important people and young men and women on the way up. Luce put his ceiling a little higher—about 300,000. *Time* readers did develop a club-like feeling, looking on one another as kindred spirits. "One reader on a train would see someone else reading *Time*," said Luce, "and that would often be enough to serve as an introduction."

For the first five years *Time* reflected Hadden's outlook more than it did Luce's, because Hadden was the editor. He was very much a man of his day and generation. He was self-assured; *Time* was cocky. He wanted to make a million dollars before he was thirty, not because he was interested in money itself but because a million was the mark of success; *Time* accepted the materialistic outlook of the day. ("The bitch goddess sat in our outer office," said Luce years later.) Hadden extravagantly admired the satiric novels of Sinclair Lewis, the criticism of H. L. Mencken, who derided "the booboisie"; *Time* did its share of "debunking," made a determined effort to show up fools, vulgarians and crooks, deflate the pompous. Hadden was a man of style, in journalism as in military manners; above all else, *Time* developed a style all its own.

When Hadden elected himself editor he announced that he would write no more, and never did. John Martin [2] has given a vivid picture of him at work:

> With . . . astonishing ease Brit would edit copy to eliminate unnecessary verbiage. He had boasted that the whole of *Time* would be read by one proofreader whose sole duty would be to save words. It was. He was that proofreader. If you wrote something like "in the nick of time," five words, he might change it to "in time's nick," three words, or knock the phrase out entirely as trite and superfluous: if the rescue was made, obviously the hero was in time. Observations about the weather

[2] In a speech at the dedication of the Hadden Memorial on the Yale Campus, 1932.

such as "one fine day" or unnecessary conjunctives like "on the other hand," "and also," "nevertheless," he pounced upon fiercely. In *The Flying Inn,* G. K. Chesterton has a magnificently boresome newspaperman called However Hibbs. Brit would have fired However Hibbs instanter. Sitting behind his rolltop desk, in shirt sleeves and old trousers, green eyeshade cocked over his nose, big *Time* pencil [3] firmly grasped and ready for action—he always followed that pencil's sharp digs and dashes with a jutting movement of the lower lip and jaw, sometimes accompanied by a grinding of teeth and a snort—he suggested a large and determined snapping turtle lying in wait for foolhardy small fry. I have never seen anyone throw himself into a job with such energetic concentration, such patience over the minutest detail, such enthusiasm for the elaboration of a useful or original point. At all times he had by him a carefully annotated translation of the *Iliad.* In the back cover he had listed hundreds of words, especially verbs and the compound adjectives, which had seemed to him fresh and forceful. The classic ring of this vocabulary, which he frequently reviewed, served him as a tuning fork for the language that he wanted in *Time.* He carried with him everywhere a little black looseleaf notebook into which he popped words or ideas with startling plunges of his big pencil, often in hurried hieroglyphics which none but he understood. . . .

Hadden struck from *Time*'s lexicon such current journalese as "one hears," "on high authority," "informed sources." If *Time* could not make a statement directly attributable to a person, it made it on its own authority. Men were not famous but "famed," not powerful but "potent," and if they were "famed" and "potent" they were also "able."

Hadden moved cautiously in the new form of journalism. In the first issue there was only a slight foretaste of what was to come. But Danzig was described as "many-towered," Charlie Chaplin's *The Pilgrim* as "a gorgeously funny example of custard-piety," the readers

---

[3] *Time* created its own big, thick lead pencils, still used by some writers.

of the New York *Daily News* as "gum-chewers." Hadden's liking for Homer was reflected in an item under Press:

"A little man with an angry face and a repulsive manner, who sought to make no man his friend, who never made an interesting speech and never talked less than four hours." That is a description (in the current issue of *The Forum*) of a prominent United States Senator who would like to be President.

"He was bandy-legged and lame of one foot; his shoulders were crooked and contracted towards his chest; his head was peaked towards the top and then wool was scattered over it. . . . And on this occasion, shouting out shrilly, he uttered bitter taunts."—That is the description of Theristes, "reckless babbler" of Homer's *Iliad.*[4]

At first Hadden kept his writers reined in rather tightly, and the sentences moved from subject to predicate unadorned by adjective or adverb. The emphasis was on summary, paring every item to the marrow. The form began to change; as Gottfried described the process: "The original prospectus said that no story would occupy more than about seven inches of type. We tried to write it this way, but gradually we found our medium changing under our hands. Writing a story, particularly a complicated story, in seven inches of type could only be done by adopting a style that was like dropping stones into a bucket of water. It was plunk, plunk, plunk, and there you are. This contributed to the magnificent deadpan quality of the early issues. . . . What one could do (in the very limited space) was limited. To give more information and to get other literary effects, it was necessary to have more space, and we gradually took it. *Time* style became not a formula of words, but a kind of mental discipline."

Soon, in imitation of Xenophon, *Time*'s account of President Harding's journey to Alaska, entitled "Anabasis," began: "Forth from the White House followed by innumerable attendants, Mr. and Mrs. Warren G. Harding set out. . . ." When the party turned homeward the head was changed to "Katabasis." Homeric epithets became

[4] The passage contained two typographical errors, much to Hadden's annoyance: the description was of Thersites, and "then" should have read "thin."

84

frequent—President Francisco Madero of Mexico was "wild-eyed," the World War I German Admiral Alfred von Tirpitz, "long-whiskered."

Time began using the middle names of prominent people to satisfy reader curiosity, but, surprisingly, said John Martin, the effect was something like "undressing them in Macy's window."

. . . Grover A. Whalen and James A. Farley, for example, turned out to be delightfully embellished by "Aloysius." Everyone knew about the Mannes in Bernard M. Baruch, but what a surprise was the Percy in Walter P. Chrysler! To the rugged Mr. Chrysler, ex-mechanic, it came as such a shock that he threatened to cancel all his advertising, until a deal was made whereby the Percy was suppressed save for one time a year, to save *Time*'s face. Men like John Llewellyn Lewis and Leonor Fresnel Loree rose to their full stature when given their due from *Who's Who,* but something else happened—something like a pin in the pants—when the same was done consistently for Warren Gamaliel Harding, Heber Jedediah Grant or Cyrus Hermann Kotzschmar Curtis.

Nicknames in parentheses were also used—e.g., the tennis champion Helen ("Poker Face") Wills; the publisher of *Physical Culture Magazine,* Bernarr ("Body Love") Macfadden. Then came the reiteration of identifying phrases; the senior Senator from Alabama was always "James Thomas ("Tom Tom") Heflin, who mortally hates and fears the Roman Pope," and Senator Henrik Shipstead of Minnesota was "the duck-hunting dentist."

Descriptive adjectives multiplied. George Bernard Shaw was "mocking, mordant, misanthropic"; General Erich von Ludendorff, as he "sallied forth into the streets of Munich," was "flagitious, inscrutable, unrelenting." Wolcott Gibbs wrote that no mother could ever be pleased with the description of her son in *Time*—*viz.,* this one of the young Harry Emerson Fosdick: "His face was paunchy, his black knitted hair gave an unkempt appearance. His voice, too, retained the flat tones, the slightly nasal twang of upstate New York." Fosdick's hair was one of his most distinguishing features and often a subject of

85

comment, for the magazine, which had then adopted the practice of using footnotes, put an asterisk after "knitted" and recalled that "at a great banquet, a bald-headed toastmaster referred to this personal feature. Replying to the introduction, Dr. Fosdick pleaded that hair that was knitted was better than hair that was nit."

Behind this insistence on physical description was a method, as Luce described: "No idea exists outside a human skull—and no human skull exists without hair and a face and a voice—in fact the flesh and blood attributes of a human personality. *Time* journalism began by being deeply interested in people, as individuals who were making history, or a small part of it, from week to week. We tried to make our readers see and hear and even smell these people as part of a better understanding of their ideas—or lack of them."

Hadden became bolder in his experiments, had his writers delving into dictionary and thesaurus for words to intrigue his readers. From his beloved Greek came "kudos" for honorary degrees; from the Japanese, "tycoon," [5] perhaps the most famous of all *Time* words. "Pundit" for learned man was an echo of his days at Yale, where he had been a member of a literary club known as "The Pundits." Coined words were introduced: "omnivendorous" described the U.S. drugstore; "eel-hipped runagade," football star Red Grange; "paradoxhund," G. K. Chesterton. Cornelius Vanderbilt, Jr., an aspiring young newspaper publisher, was introduced as the "able, active scion of an

---

[5] The title, meaning "great lord," used by the Japanese in describing the shogun to foreigners. For some reason the word irritated many readers, one of whom wrote:

> *Time*'s editor is tall and thin.
> He and Roget are next of kin,
> Thesaurus is his middle name,
> Terseness his very end and aim.
>
> He stalks the shy, uncommon word,
> To give the inarticulate herd
> Vocabularies wide and weird
> And potent as the Prophet's beard.
>
> He passes by 'galloon,' 'simoon,'
> He scorns 'monsoon,' 'baboon,' and 'loon,'
> But he's married himself to the word 'tycoon,'
> God help the poor buffoon—and soon!

able, active line, whilom Hearstling."

The writing drew a long way from the plunk-plunk-plunk narrative of the first issues. An item reporting the illness of Trotsky began: "Criticism to the left of him, enmity to the right of him, jealousy in front of him, the Red Army behind him, a high fever within him, all tried to blight him. He resolved to take a trip to the Caucasus." An article on the New Society of Artists show in New York began: "Met a group of solemn judges, their faces reflective of the well-nigh sinister gravity of their office. They were the Hanging Committee. . . ." Janáček's opera *Jenufa* was summarized cryptically: "In a Moravian village lived Jenufa, the prettiest girl in the countryside, in whose grey glance lodged witchery. She was loved by Stewa, village stew, and by his brother Laca, an honorable gaffer, who deplored the low-lived ways of Stewa. Without virtue himself, Stewa appropriates Jenufa's. Months go by. She gives birth to a difficulty. . . ." The writers strained to arrest the reader's eye with such sentences as "Slowly the ribbon of his voice unrolled, with here and there a knot," or "Bells altoed. Morning classes were over at Harvard University." Sometimes they overdid it, hence: "A ghastly ghoul prowled around a cemetery not far from Paris. Into family chapels went he, robbery of the dead intent upon."

One of *Time*'s important innovations was the use of historical background. Hadden is said to have pinned to a report of the death of the last Crimean War general a note, "Great story." The writer was puzzled, said, "I don't get it." "It ain't duh General," said Hadden, "it's duh war." The writer still didn't get the point. Hadden snapped, "Tell 'em all about it—tell 'em what duh Crime was." He sometimes exhibited strange gaps in his own background. He passed for publication an item about the illness of the Japanese Emperor in which the writer speculated on the dilemma confronting a doctor called upon to give a deity an enema. A checker objected that it was in bad taste. "What's wrong with it?" asked Hadden. When she explained, he said: "My God, I thought it was a kind of medicine." The checkers and writers felt free, at all times, to challenge him on either fact or opinion. "We all had squawking rights," said Gottfried.

Hadden was capable of working up a high head of indignation and of using *Time* as his famous "groining iron" to punish those who he felt deserved it. As John Martin recalled:

It was the day of Sinclair Lewis's *Babbitt* and Henry L. Mencken's angry iteration in his new *Mercury* of the epithet "moron." To vent his dislike for all that was stupid and pompous in those racy '20s, Hadden gave these words prominence in his private and public vocabulary, and to them added "crook," "quitter," "louse," "bum," "simp," "clown," and many more to express his feelings about people with other failings. None of these words, of course, was actually printed in direct application, but at least half of the duty of a *Time* writer under Hadden was to find ways and means of calling nonfactors, misfactors or malefactors such names without literally doing so, and to help vent B.H.'s impatience with human folly and fraud. When (as often happened) the belabored party felt maligned and complained about it, Hadden was all apologies, but always armed with his facts and seldom in real retreat. . . . It was his idea, and a right one, that no editor ever became great by being, in his young days, overly polite.

No one called *Time* overly polite; it once described Mayor John F. Hylan of New York as "a partial illiterate."

Hadden's reaction to the snobbery explicit in *The New Yorker*'s pre-publication announcement that it would not be "edited for the old lady in Dubuque" is a case in point. Hadden called over Niven Busch —whose nickname was "Bullet Joe" after Bullet Joe Busch, Hadden's favorite baseball hero—and handed him the first issue. "Bullet Joe," he said, "just look at this damned magazine. 'Not for the old lady in Dubuque.' Damn it, the old lady in Dubuque is smarter than they are. Dubuque is a great place and just as sophisticated as New York. That's your angle, and make it plain that the magazine won't last." Busch turned in a mocking review which concluded by quoting the opinion of a fictitious old lady in Dubuque. According to *Time,* she said:

The editors of the periodical you forwarded are, I understand, members of a literary clique. They should learn that there is no provincialism so blatant as that of the metropolitan who lacks urbanity. They were quite correct, however, in their original assertion. *The New Yorker* is not for the the old lady in Dubuque.

Busch later contributed to *The New Yorker* occasionally, and Harold Ross, its founder, once asked him who had written *Time*'s review. "I did," said Busch. Ross forgave Busch but not *Time*.

Under Hadden *Time* followed no consistent editorial line; his judgments were *ad hoc* and *ad hominem*. He did not flatter himself that the magazine was in any way influential. The attitudes reflected in the magazine could not be characterized as liberal or conservative in the present meaning of the words. There was one characteristic attitude of which Luce was proud. "We were what would be called pro civil rights for Negroes from the beginning," he said. "One of the things in which we may have been useful is the fact that we tried to report every single lynching. We tried to print the exact story, without moralizing." By so doing, *Time* sought to arouse a sense of outrage. The first of these stories appeared in the issue of May 5, 1923. It told of the arrest of a Negro in Columbia, Missouri, on the charge that he had accosted the daughter of a university professor. That night a mob had gathered, taken another Negro from the jail and hanged him from a bridge. *Time*'s story concluded:

James Scott is dead. He was put to death by the premeditated violence of yokels who believed in their gross way that they were maintaining the honor of the race that bred them. What they did, some people call murder; others, lynching.

Once a year *Time* tabulated the number of lynchings in the U.S.

So long as *Time* made a practice of using the title "Mr.," it was applied to black and white alike; whenever a Negro was so termed, a spate of letters from bigoted Southern readers made Hadden ever more determined to continue the practice. On the other hand, he used the terms "blackamoron" or "blackamoor" in writing about Negro delinquents.

* * *

Time readers proved to be lively correspondents. The Letters column, introduced on November 10, 1924, remained one of the magazine's best-read departments. The first letters were selected for publication, said the editors, "primarily for the information they contain either supplementary to, or corrective of, news previously published in *Time*." Hadden was ever ready to print correspondence calling attention to *Time* itself. In the first column a Methodist complained of his church being referred to as "a sect." The editor replied that Webster found "sect" and "denomination" synonymous and *Time* preferred sect because it contained only four letters.

Another reader protested: "Back in the School of Journalism at the University of Missouri, we were taught that it is not good newspaper style to make a title of an occupation. Yet in *Time* . . . I read 'Teacher Scopes,' 'Evolutionist Scopes.' . . ." Said *Time:* "Brevity, accuracy, significance moved *Time* to the adoption of such titles as Teacher, Evolutionist, Philosopher, Publisher, Ditch-digger, Bootlegger, Undertaker, Politician, etc. before last names. The teaching [at Missouri] is standard in the newspaper world. *Time,* to be concise and to the point, breaks this and other canons of journalism."

Time's inverted sentences drew criticism too: "I doubt if the majority of your readers enjoy so constant an inversion of phrases or so much adjectival alliteration. . . . Presumably the purpose of such a style is humorous—but there are still those who enjoy the English language." The editors made no comment on this one.

The Religion section had said of Sherwood Eddy [6]: "Preeminent among the exhorters of Americans and others, [he] speaks always with clenched fist, contracted brow, tight-drawn lips. He bullies men's consciences. . . ." A reader called this "a baleful charge." The editors replied: " 'Bullies' was doubtless an unfortunate word; it was intended to convey an impression of the moral strenuousness for which Mr. Eddy is justly famous. 'Jolts' would have been better—or 'prods,' 'pounds,' 'lambasts,' 'whacks,' 'scourges,' 'belts.' "

As editor of the Yale *Daily News,* Hadden had occasionally planted letters written by himself and others to arouse controversy. In *Time* he

[6] Eddy, who had been at Yale with Luce's father, had also elected a missionary career.

90

and his writers created a cast of characters who were soon prodding readers to indignation. One was a mysterious Mary Elizabeth Robinn, who appeared November 16, 1925, and at intervals until 1929, when she finally fell silent. Usually she was exposing or relaying rumors about the Prince of Wales—"Edward of Wales," *Time* called him. Her first letter, titled "Wales Flayed" ("flayed" was a favorite editorial reproof), condemned the Prince's appearance in girl's clothes in a ship's concert: "I wish to protest and protest strongly against such antics on the part of the Prince of Wales as you describe. . . . I visited England last year and I want to say that a great many people in London *know him for what he is.* Too many Americans think he is a sweet, baby-faced, 'innocent,' 'embarrassed' young man! That is perfect nonsense, and anyone with half an eye should know it. I only hope [this] will open people's eyes in this country. In England everyone knows the truth." Late in 1926 she chided *Time* for having failed "to expose or even mention the 'exploits'—not to use a cruder term—of the Prince of Wales at Biarritz and Paris. . . . When I was in London, I found that the Court considers the situation *extremely grave.* Whenever possible, attempts are made to keep photographers from snapping the Prince, so that the pouches under his eyes and his general run-down appearance will not come to public notice. . . ." "Mary Elizabeth Robinn" was a plant; but there was nothing phony about the replies her letters provoked from readers. "I am not clear as to whether this lady is a disappointed old maid or a designing widow. . . ." "Any itinerant may pick up salacious gossip. . . . Would it be possible to let us know how old Mary Elizabeth Robinn may be?" "That disappointed virgin Robinn must need a mate to soften her perennial ire against the Prince of Wales. . . . You need no humorous column as long as you sow your Letters with such luscious tidbits of outraged virginity."

To which she came back (her letter was datelined Monte Carlo): "The detestable, foul-minded men and women whose letters about me you printed are slanderers and slanderesses. The noun 'virgin' is not one which gentlemen or ladies employ, in any other than a religious connection. I shall inquire from my attorneys whether its use in the letters to which I refer is or is not libelous. You may rest

91

assured that my married or unmarried state, as the case may be, is not a subject upon which I shall stoop to satisfy curious vulgarians."

An example of well-tended reader-baiting was the episode of "the black grey rat" in December 1925. Miscellany reported the ghastly adventure of Rachael Galpern, who was taking a "hot soap-bath" before a party: "Hearing a slight scratching in the ceiling above her, she raised her eyes in time to see a pointed grey face peer at her from a hole in the plaster. The hole widened, the thin mortar crumbled and an enormous black rat fell into the water with her, splashed about, caressed her with its clammy paws and insolently ogled her. . . ." (Rachael sued, got $1,700 from her landlord.)

Just a week later (suspiciously soon) a Henry R. Travers of Patchogue, New York, wrote: *"Time's* inaccuracies are chronic, flagrant and even self-evident. . . . A rat with a 'pointed *grey* face' fell into Miss Rachael Galpern's 'hot soap-bath'; yet a moment later you speak of the animal as 'an enormous *black* rat!' Squirm out of that, if you can! I suppose you will say that a black rat can have a grey face." The editors retorted: "A wet grey rat is black."

A few weeks later a reader commented on the original letter: "When one reads some of the letters which you publish, it is evident that some people expect a piece of letter-perfect literature for fifteen cents. Take, for example, the masterpiece which Mr. H. R. Travers offered for publication in your issue of Dec. 21. Exactly what difference does it make to Mr. Travers what the color of the rat was which fell into a certain lady's bath? It seems to me that a grey rat would be just as disagreeable as a black one. . . . It is evident that these small-time critics have missed the whole point of *Time's* aims, to get the news across in a brief, snappy way. . . ." The editors thanked the subscriber for "his kindness, his courtesy," but also hoped that his "vigorous defense of their shortcomings will not discourage the honest critics who locate errata and write letters that speak out so eloquently. *Time* must not tolerate mis-statements. Writers and lexicographers who commit them merit thorough-going rebukes. If a grey rat falls into the hot soap-bath of Miss Rachael Galpern, then 'grey rat' (not black rat) must be the phrase used in *Time*. If a news-magazine is not scrupulously accurate even in little things, what faith will its subscribers have in any of its reporting?"

Hadden frequently handed out "thorough-going rebukes" to writers and proofreaders for errors spotted by readers. He even invented a scapegoat, Peter Mathews, a fictitious character whose name first appeared on the masthead on February 25, 1924, and was not finally dropped until April 18, 1960. Mathews was frequently fired or rebuked for errors; a little later he became the subject, sometimes the source, of *Time* articles. He once had the misfortune to be arrested for annoying an old lady; the incident, reported in the February 29, 1932, issue, reflected well on his resourcefulness—in order to gain his release from a locked room, he had lowered an ink bottle on a string and banged it on the lady's window. As *Time*'s correspondent in Lower Slobbovia, he reported (with by-line) that Lena the Hyena had been chosen to fill that country's U.S. immigration quota of one per hundred years. He traveled about the Baltic Sea area and was quoted by the magazine as the source for the fact that policemen guarded nude bathers, making sure no men (morning hours) remained when it was time for the women (afternoon). Peter had observed the policemen, the editors informed a questioning reader. Even after his disappearance from the masthead Israel Shenker, *Time*'s Moscow correspondent in 1964, found that references to Mathews were useful in helping the editors interpret his cables. In *Time*'s editorial reference department there remains a special file: "Mathews, Peter—Writer, Editor."

Hadden believed in having all the fun he could get away with, consistent with a serious purpose. The present-day *Time* editors and writers can envy the free-wheeling, independent ways of the magazine's first editor. But Hadden and Luce enforced a discipline on their writers as well. As John Martin said, "We were weekly historians, not just journalists, and Hadden and Luce saw to it that we took ourselves much more seriously than is generally realized."

Westward to Cleveland

E ARLY IN 1925, with *Time*'s circulation moving past the 70,000 mark, Luce began planning for the day when it would reach 100,000. To handle it would require improved press facilities and a more central mailing point. He was receiving complaints of late delivery; the aim was to have the magazine in the readers' hands not later than Friday, but it seldom reached Western readers before Monday. At first there had been little effort to get much circulation west of the Mississippi; now the West offered attractive possibilities. On his trip for the *Saturday Review,* Larsen discovered that interest and enthusiasm for *Time* seemed to increase with the distance from New York and its metropolitan press.

With decisions on these important business matters pending, Hadden, who like the rest of the staff had hitherto not permitted himself the luxury of a vacation, announced impulsively that he was taking off for Europe and Larsen would go with him. Luce was not happy about the decision ("But that was Hadden").

Hadden and Larsen sailed on the *Paris* at the end of March, second class, hoping that what they saved on passage money would stretch their budget of $1,500 and permit more extended travel on the

Continent. Hadden found that a number of his friends were in first class, and he and Larsen spent much time there as guests. On the last night, to repay that hospitality, Hadden threw a lively and expensive party that continued as the group moved on to Paris. There the travelers had to cable Luce for another $1,500. Hadden and Larsen then parted, Hadden to spend six weeks roaming Europe, Larsen to take a leisurely and restorative bicycle tour.

Hadden left the editing of the magazine to Gottfried, who also continued to write the National Affairs section. "I knew bloody little about editing," said Gottfried, "and I merely went through the motions." He was being excessively modest; quite on his own he made at least one important decision. Hadden's and Luce's old friend John Farrar had been writing his literary column ever since Vol. I, No. 1, and it was beginning to run down. "One week his copy came to me," said Gottfried, "and it concerned some third-rate female writer nobody wanted to hear about. So I telephoned him and asked whether he couldn't find somebody more interesting. Could I suggest anybody that he hadn't already written about? I suggested Norman Douglas, and to this he replied that Douglas' private life was altogether too disgusting and he didn't want to have anything to do with it. Exercising an editor's prerogative, I did not run the column, nor the following week's, which was equally dull. He stopped sending in copy. When Hadden returned I reported on what had happened. A slow grin formed and he said, 'Well, that's O.K.' "

In Hadden's absence Luce settled on Cleveland as the future base of operations; the Penton Press there offered excellent facilities, including office space adjacent to the composing room, which made for convenience in closing the magazine. Hadden had never envisioned leaving New York and was upset to find preparations for the move past the point of no return. This led to the first serious quarrel. They withdrew to the Allerton House to argue the issue out of earshot of the staff. Luce had the better of it. Altogether, he estimated that the company would save $20,000 a year in operating expenses. The move was announced to readers in the August 3 issue:

To insure more rapid delivery to subscribers and newsstand buyers, *Time,* the Weekly News-Magazine, will be edited, printed and mailed from Cleveland, Ohio, commencing with the issue to be dated August 31, 1925.

After August 20, communications to the Editorial or Circulation Departments should be addressed to the Penton Building, Cleveland, Ohio.

Subsequently the magazine printed a letter from a reader:

While it is your business exclusively, of course, if you desire to locate in "the sticks" . . . you should give an address other than Penton Building, Cleveland, Ohio. I have been going to that burg occasionally for many years, and have a fairly good knowledge of the streets and avenues, and I assure you that I don't know where the Penton Building is. And I presume there are many more in the same fix.

"The sticks" reflected Hadden's view of Cleveland and suggests that he might well have written the letter. He was not alone in his objections. Robert Johnson and his salesmen argued, successfully, that they must remain in New York, and the editors of the *Saturday Review* refused to be uprooted. The move led to a parting of the two magazines. The *Saturday Review* complained of the inconvenience of editing in New York and printing in Cleveland, and were upset by errors in proofreading. "We probably should have made a greater effort to satisfy Canby and company," said Luce, "but we did not have enough strength morally or financially to press the matter. They were unhappy, so we said, 'Let's have an amicable divorce.' " Early in 1926 the *Saturday Review* was reorganized as a separate corporation, in which Time Inc. retained no financial interest.

The staff learned of the move informally, for it was bruited about many weeks in advance. The official announcement was abrupt. A notice was posted on the bulletin board telling the staff they were dismissed as of Monday, August 17, and would be rehired on August 19 in Cleveland if they applied. This was one way of saying that the company assumed no responsibility for moving expenses. There were exceptions: the checkers and secretaries had their train fare paid and hotel accommodation for several nights, Gottfried got transportation for himself, wife and furniture. Hadden and Luce refused expenses to T. J. C. Martyn, arguing that as the highest-paid man on the staff ($100 a week) he should bear these costs himself. He was married, had two children, and had just bought a house on Long Island. Not unreasonably, he thought Hadden and Luce were being unfair. They were adamant. He resigned, surrendering his stock as required by the agreement.

Niven Busch, who worked Tuesday, Wednesday and Thursday for the *Boardwalk News* in Atlantic City and the other four days for *Time,* was not enthusiastic about losing moonlighting pay. Hadden persuaded his cousin to move by promising that he could share Hadden's Cleveland apartment at one fourth of the rent. He also raised Busch from $45 to $50 a week. John S. Martin remained behind in New York to write Sports, Press and Miscellany and act as metropolitan reporter, but he too moved to Cleveland within a short time.

Time reaped a very substantial benefit from the move to Cleveland. In New York the publishers had applied to the Post Office to have the magazine classified as a weekly newspaper, which would have given it priority handling. The application was rejected and the adverse decision was upheld on appeal to Washington. From Cleveland, delivery was much improved, but there were still complaints about lateness. In solving this problem, Luce received a lesson in practical politics. The company's attorney in Cleveland suggested that the magazine renew its application to the Post Office. The Chamber of Commerce, which welcomed the new little enterprise to its city, endorsed it. "Then I learned what was true in those days—and still is: that a place like Cleveland is a lot closer to Washington than New York City is. People are more aware of their Congressman and he is more willing to help them," said Luce. Together with their attorney and a representative of the Chamber, he called on Representative Theodore E. Burton in Washington. Burton arranged for an immediate hearing on the application and it was approved. Understandably jubilant, management reported to the directors: "In theory, this means that *Time* will travel

97

as fast as first-class mail. Thus from Maine to the North of Texas, from Colorado to New York, *Time* will be received every week by subscribers on Friday or Saturday. This is the greatest single piece of good fortune that has ever come *Time*'s way."

The good news was encouraging at a time when the financial squeeze was still very tight. Apart from the original capital and the addition in 1925, *Time* operated within its income without recourse to borrowing. It was able to do so because *Time* charged a relatively high price for subscriptions, which were solicited by mail and paid in advance. This revenue financed publication. There was, moreover, another important advantage. Under provisions of the Internal Revenue Code, a publisher has the choice of method of accounting for such revenue. *Time* chose to charge the cost of obtaining the subscriptions to expense in the year incurred and report the revenue received over the period during which the subscriptions were serviced. This unearned portion of paid subscriptions was the most critical plus factor in the financial affairs of Time Inc. from the day it started. It not only sustained *Time* in the days before there was any substantial volume of advertising, but it was to be the principal source of financing for the expansion of the company for many years to come.

In the 1920s the cult of self-improvement reached an apex. The advantage of dinner-table knowledgeability was an oft-recurring theme of advertising; the reward for buying *Elbert Hubbard's Scrap Book* was advertised with the headline "He's the most interesting man I know." It was also one of the basic promotion appeals of *Time*—"To Keep Men and Women Well Informed." It was reflected too in the crossword-puzzle craze and the popularity of quiz games. Hadden and Luce were both addicts of the quiz; in fact, Hadden was an inveterate quizzer, using questionnaires as a method of selecting checkers and office boys. The boys were expected to answer such questions as *What is the quickest route to City Hall? Name five brands of chewing gum. What is the percentage standing of the first four teams in the National League? Where are police headquarters?*

Hadden and Luce were soon using quizzes to promote *Time*. Early in 1924 Larsen wangled free time on radio station WJZ, New York, for a program presented by *Time: The Pop Question Game*. Hadden would read a question and Larsen would strike a musical chime similar to the later famous NBC signature. As the last note faded, the listener was expected to have guessed the answer before Hadden read the correct one. A few months after *Time* moved to Cleveland the Chamber of Commerce invited Hadden and Luce to address a luncheon meeting. They suggested that instead they stage a variant of *The Pop Question Game* which they called a "skull test." The audience was furnished with thick *Time* pencils and pads. Hadden and/or Luce then read out twenty-five questions based on the current issue of the magazine. Anyone who answered twenty questions correctly received a year's subscription free. In the first test only five of the 350 present won subscriptions, but the program was a huge success. Hadden and Luce were asked to repeat it before twenty other Chambers of Commerce ranging from Hadden's home borough of Brooklyn to New Orleans.

In the issue of March 1, 1926, the Letters page of the magazine carried the following box:

QUIZ

Can you answer the questions? Are you well informed? Read *Time* from p. 5 to p. 32. Then look on p. 33. Did the facts go in one eye, and out the other?

QUIZ YOURSELF

And if you do not like the quiz and feel that valuable space in *Time* should not be "wasted" on future quizzes, write so stating.

A column and a half on page 33 carried twenty-five questions. They included: *"This is scandalous," said George V. What was scandalous? How many Gutenberg Bibles are known to exist? What country has for its dictator "a short, cynical, perpetually sneering soldier?" Why is Nevada the middle name of whom? Name any doctor or any dentist in the House or Senate.*[1]

The Quiz ran as a regular feature until the fall of 1926, when it disappeared. There was some reason to believe that it had started a

[1] (1) That typewriters used in British government offices were of U.S. manufacture. (2) 45. (3) Greece—Pangalos. (4) Marion Talley, who had just made her debut at the Metropolitan Opera, was born in Nevada, Missouri. (5) There were five doctors and two dentists in the House, one doctor and one dentist in the Senate.

craze—at least, the editors gave themselves a kind of wry credit for it and in a later issue ran a feature which lampooned the whole thing. A box read:

AN EVENING NEXT WEEK

Time has been giving "pop question games" (i.e. questions and answers) over the radio since 1924. *Time* has presented "skull tests" (i.e. questions and answers) to the Chambers of Commerce of leading U.S. cities.

Perceptible now, throughout the land, is a craze: Questions, Questions. Let subscribers who wish to see potent questions, ably put, turn to page 41 of next week's issue. There they will find eight games that will well warrant their calling in their shrewdest friends, appointing an umpire and making an evening of it.

Who will be the champion at your party? Who State champion? Who champion of the U.S.?

In the event of a tie, the editors suggested the matter be settled "as becomes ladies and gentlemen." A footnote explained:

Lady and a gentleman tied, gentleman will discover a mistake in his score, withdraw. Two ladies tied will "draw lots." Two gentlemen will dice. Two boors, louts or bounders will duel with fists or canes.

The Pop Question Game was played out, but *Time* continued to intrigue its readers with provocative questionnaires, using them to ferret out marketing information. Readers seemed to enjoy answering questionnaires as to their incomes, property and possessions. One of the most successful began with the question "Do you own a horse?" A surprising number of readers did—testimony to the over-all affluence of the magazine's audience. Later the Quiz was reintroduced in the form of *Time*'s well-known current-affairs test, still used extensively in schools.

There was a moment just at Christmas 1925 when Time Inc. was "technically busted," as Luce put it; the survival of the magazine hinged on whether or not the drive for Christmas gift subscriptions

100

succeeded. The returns that year were slow in coming in, and day by day the cash balance dwindled until it touched a low of $1,976.16. *Time*'s Cleveland bank, the Central National,[2] offered to come to the rescue of the struggling enterprise with an overdraft. Then in January the checks for the new subscriptions began to come in and once more there was money in the bank. In 1925 the circulation rose from 69,500 to 107,000; revenue was $450,000—$107,800 from advertising—but the loss on the year's operations was $23,829, which, in part, was due to the expense of moving. The annual report took note of the smallness of the bank deposits and the extent of accounts receivable. Stockholders were told they should not take alarm, for by February 1, 1926, when the report was prepared, 90 percent of those accounts had been received and the $38,000 on hand was "ample for present needs."

The strain on the Hadden-Luce relationship imposed by the decision to move to Cleveland continued during their residence there. Hadden was never reconciled to the move. He put the best face he could on the situation, writing an article for the Chamber of Commerce magazine in which he said, *"Time* is here to stay. We like Cleveland." But his real feelings were expressed when in May 1926 he wrote to Director William Griffin that he and Luce were exchanging jobs for six weeks: "Luce is pleased because he considers himself a journalist at heart. Hadden is delighted because he sees a possible avenue of escape from Cleveland." To another friend, who asked him how he liked Cleveland, he growled, "I have been here forty-four weeks and have been to New York thirty-six times."

Hadden's pleasures in Cleveland reflected his restlessness. While he partially achieved one boyhood ambition—to own a baseball team— by organizing a sandlot team, the Crescent Athletic Club, his boisterous spirits sought other outlets; one of them was the rather cruel game, duly publicized in the columns of the magazine, which he called

---

[2] The Central National Bank is still the depository for Time Inc. circulation receipts, an operation which in 1967 required the handling of 15,500,000 items and the full-time attention of from 30 to 35 persons at peak periods. The bank maintains a complete list of U.S. banks through which it must clear the items, but also clears thousands of them through banks in Canada.

101

"Babbitt." The object of it was to spot "Babbitts"—a Babbitt being "any person who by his muddled features, raucous costume, attitude or gesture defines himself as inescapably belonging to that type of native American popularized in the novel of Sinclair Lewis." Hadden's method of spotting Babbitts was to drive the streets in his battered second-hand Chevrolet looking for the victim; having spotted one, he would shout "Babbitt!" at the top of his voice and wheel away, leaving his quarry unnerved and baffled. As an eligible young bachelor, Hadden did not lack invitations; he had the habit of accepting them but then backing out at the last minute. He preferred the speak-easy to the formality of local society. In Niven Busch and Larsen, Hadden at first had two bachelor companions. But Larsen deserted the ranks there, for it was in Cleveland that he met and married Miss Margaret Zerbe.

Luce, now with a newborn son, liked the familial, hometown atmosphere of Cleveland and the sense of being part of an American community which had been denied him by his boyhood in exile. He and his wife joined a country club and settled comfortably into the round of the young married set. But he could not help being aware of the attitude of his partner. It was not the only source of friction; he was often upset by Hadden's impulsiveness. On one occasion he wrote to his wife, who was visiting her mother in Chicago: "This Hadden-Luce yoke is certainly galling. His intentions are okay—but the differences between us are so great. However, I don't see any way out which seems better than struggling through with it. Perhaps if I made up my mind to include mentally in our budget, 'Hadden nonsense, $50,000—or $100,000—per annum,' it might be conducive to peace of mind!" Luce suspected that at times Hadden went out of his way to annoy advertisers. A case in point occurred shortly after *Time* acquired the Fisher Body Co. account. This was in the days when fine car bodies were made of wood. In an account of the New York automobile show the magazine extravagantly praised the all-steel body built by the Budd Manufacturing Co. and pointed out that in wooden bodies "it's the splinters that kill." The Fisher account was canceled.[3]

[3] Two and a half years later Luce wrote to his wife at their summer home: "Great milestone . . . Fisher Body has signed up for back covers in color."

On the whole, the *Time* group were not noticeably diplomatic or sparing of one another's feelings. Gottfried recorded this episode in his diary:

Harry suggested lunch of Brit, J.S.M., himself and me. J.S.: "Let's go to the little Hungarian place across the street—if Brit will promise not to disgrace himself as he did yesterday—pounding with his spoons on the china till the proprietor said, 'This is a restaurant, not a quick lunch!' " Brit: "Grr!" So we went there. Brit very glum—did not pound on the china even though no waiter took our order for five minutes and Harry finally got the headwaiter (quietly). Brit ate spareribs in an excess of martyrdom, thinking he had ordered roast beef. Really he had ordered pot roast. Afterwards half an hour's conclave in criticism of *Time;* Brit very resentful of all remarks.

The deepest wound was inflicted on the Hadden-Luce friendship by their Alma Mater, Yale. In June 1926 the university conferred on Luce an honorary M.A. "in recognition of distinguished accomplishments in a novel and worthy field of journalism" as co-founder of *Time,* making no mention of Hadden by name. Luce, either embarrassed at being singled out for the honor or too scrupulously observant of the secrecy imposed on all recipients of honorary degrees, did not tell his partner in advance. Gottfried guessed that Hadden was not similarly honored because "the lowbrow manners which he affected did not sit well with the scholars at Yale." A subsequent unofficial explanation was that Luce was chosen, and not Hadden, because of his brilliant academic record and because he had been on the editorial boards of both the *News* and the *Lit*. Hadden was resentful and hurt; the sense of injury passed and the partnership survived because of the deep mutual respect in which they held each other.

Editorially Hadden still ran a tight ship. When T. J. C. Martyn resigned, his place as Foreign News editor [4] was taken by a young Yale

---

[4] Writers thought of themselves as department editors and called themselves editors. Not until 1937 did *Time*'s masthead designate writers as "associate" and "contributing" editors.

man, Laird S. Goldsborough, who almost singlehanded would write Foreign News for the next thirteen years. Another long-time writer, hired in Cleveland, was Myron Weiss. Hadden wrote the directors that Weiss was "a Jew and a Clevelander. He probably is an atheist. He is an expert on all matters pertaining to printing. In addition to his writing duties he makes up (pastes up) the paper. He owns and operates his own reference library, has a vast acquaintance among medical and religious men, does all his own research and all in all is a very useful member." Weiss, a Harvard man who had been a medical corpsman in World War I, wrote Medicine and Religion. He was given Religion, said Weiss, because "I was Jewish and therefore must know something about it."

In the spring of 1926 *Time* lost its first editorial employee, Manfred Gottfried. "For me, journalism was not a romance," said Gottfried, "but a marriage of convenience; my romance was with fiction. Henry Canby, who first sent me to *Time,* had advised me not to spend more than a year in journalism. By the spring of 1926 I had at least three and a half years and, after thinking it over, I told Luce and Hadden that I was going abroad, and not just for the summer; I was going to stay and write a novel." It was a decision that cost him the fortune he might have made if he had held on to his original Time Inc. stock; by leaving he was obliged to sell it back to the company. Gottfried's diary entry for June 21 reads: "Drew my last pay check and with $600 in my pocket said goodbye to all the boys in the office."

Time made considerable progress as it moved through 1926. There was a substantial upturn in the company's business; the size of an average issue was 44 pages (v. 36 pages in 1924) and there were five issues of 52 pages. The cover was now printed on coated stock, which permitted the sale of four-color advertisements on the inside and back covers; on the cover itself, tests were made of color, and the *"Time* red" border was first used on the issue of January 3, 1927. In the annual report for 1926 Luce, as president that year, thought it necessary to assure stockholders that they "need not fear that *Time* will become 'too bulky.' There is a natural limit to the amount of space that can be devoted legitimately to printing news of the week.

This natural limit would be about 32 pages; and, since it is generally admitted that it would be unsightly in a magazine of the calibre of *Time* to print much more than 50 percent advertising, the limit in bulkiness would seem to be about 64 pages, exclusive of covers." On revenues of $684,362—of which $240,590 came from the sale of advertising—*Time* showed a profit of $8,541. Circulation had averaged 111,000 for the year, and it was announced that in 1927 the circulation guarantee would be raised to 135,000.

On the strength of a substantially increased volume of business in the first quarter of 1927 Hadden and Luce felt justified in asking the directors to approve an increase in their salaries and that of Larsen to $10,000 a year retroactive to January 1. Luce thought it was time for him to take a vacation; he announced to Hadden that he and his wife were going to Europe. They sailed in June.

Now it was Hadden's turn; he decided to move *Time* back to New York. He explained his reasons to the directors:

> (A) because Cleveland is all but void of news sources, and (B) because *Time* has reached a point where it is possible for us to consider entering some other publishing venture. Our public of 135,000 or more is willing and ready to buy something from us beside *Time*. . . . No new venture can well be entered into, however, unless both the editor and the general manager are on the job in New York.

Hadden estimated that the additional cost of operating in New York and printing in Cleveland would not be more than $10,000 a year. On July 16 the Board passed a somewhat tentative resolution:

> Resolved that the management of Time Inc. be empowered to move the chief editorial offices of *Time* to New York for an experimental period not to exceed five months, the cost of the experiment not to exceed $5,000 unless further authorization is granted.

Hadden had other reasons. "They think we're hot stuff here—big frogs in a small puddle," he told John Martin's wife, Mimi. "But what

105

are we? A bunch of kids deafened by adulation. We sit at dinner parties with people twice our age and they listen to us. We must get back to New York where we have some competition. . . ."

Luce returned from Europe in July. The editorial department moved back to New York on August 1, with circulation and production temporarily remaining in Cleveland. "Hadden was so determined to get back to New York," Luce said later, "that there was no use arguing."

Once the major decision was made, other changes followed. The growing circulation required a still more central distribution center in the Midwest. Chicago, the hub of the U.S. rail network, offered many advantages.

"We began to think that it might be possible to split our operation— to edit in New York and print in Chicago," said Luce. "The next thing I knew, a very distinguished gentleman, Mr. T. E. Donnelley [of R. R. Donnelley & Sons, Chicago], was knocking on my door. Over a period of six or eight weeks, Mr. Donnelley spent many days and nights in Cleveland working with me on the minute details of a contract. The contract couldn't have been worth much to him and I was a very penny-pinching bargainer—yet Mr. Donnelley treated the contract— and me—as if it were the biggest deal of the century. Well, it did indeed turn out to be something of the sort—certainly one of the world's biggest and longest-playing printing contracts." [5]

The parting from Cleveland was not an easy one. Returning there fourteen years later to address the Cleveland Advertising Club, Luce summed up how he felt:

> To return here is to return to a hometown and also to the scene of an important part of my education. For it was here that I took my post-graduate course in the facts of life—and many of my instructors are in this room. Here, under Professor Allen Billings-

[5] Appended to Time Inc.'s copy of the contract is an astrological forecast appearing that day in a Cleveland newspaper. It reads: "Thursday, September 1, 1927. This is pre-eminently a day for signing contracts and entering into business agreements of importance. There is a sign read as auspicious for publicity, especially for that which is connected with new contracts or enterprises. Newspapers and magazines will prosper greatly and it is foretold that literary folk will benefit. . . ."

ley [of the advertising agency Fuller & Smith], I unlearned logic
and learned about advertising. Here, when we almost needed a
loan to meet the payroll, Professor McHannan [of the Central
National Bank] . . . taught me how near you can come to going
busted and not quite do so—a very exciting course. Here Doctors Ernst & Ernst [*Time*'s auditors] demonstrated that there is
no such thing as being a little bit crooked, just as in China I had
learned that there is no such thing as a little garlic. I learned a
good many other things . . . about the unspoken friendships
which grow up between those who live and work together in an
honorable community.

"The day we signed the Donnelley contract and definitely told John
Penton we were leaving," Larsen recalled, "he called Harry and me
up to his office—we thought to wish us godspeed—but the whole
purpose was to try to unsell us on our decision. John Penton was
about six-foot-three. He came around to the front of his desk with a
very sad and worried look on his face. He was worried for us, he said.
'I've been in the publishing business for many years. I know that these
publications and the confidence of your audience depend on many
intangible things. One of the great things you have is the affection and
confidence of this area, of the people that know you here. You leave
here and you may lose that. It is just like ash in the hand. Some
publications just blow on it and it disappears.' We didn't disappear,
but we were damned scared when we left his office."

A New Editor—
An Election Year

ADDEN WAS obviously right in his decision to return to New
York. To the editors and publishers of a magazine becoming national in scope, the big city offered a stimulus
that Cleveland could never match. From Wall Street, which controlled
U.S. business, to Broadway, with its "naked, profane and salacious"
theater (as the Methodist Board of Temperance, Prohibition and Public Morals described it), New York was the center of power and the
fountainhead of new ideas. Even Luce, who throughout his life continued to have reservations about New York as the headquarters for
Time, had to concede that the city, which he called "the great work-
shop," offered certain advantages.

Hadden and Luce, believing that *Time* was reaching its ceiling in
circulation, were thinking about a new magazine, and New York was
the logical base from which to launch it. For the moment, however,
they put aside ideas for a new publication as they resettled in the big
city. The editorial staff moved in temporarily with the salesmen at 25
West 45th Street, a building that also housed *The New Yorker.*
Beginning in January 1928, the magazine was printed in Chicago, but

the circulation department did not move there until July. Larsen remained behind in Cleveland until that move; he then returned to New York, leaving his assistant Nicholas L. Wallace in charge of all Chicago operations.

Wallace, an early fan of *Time,* was working for Doubleday, Page & Co. in New York when he decided it would be fun to work for his favorite magazine and wrote asking for a job. To his own surprise, his application was accepted and he moved to Cleveland, becoming Larsen's assistant. The work of circulation fulfillment is a demanding but unglamorous part of magazine publishing; in this, and in printing and production, Wallace played a vital role in the growth of Time Inc.

The move to New York, separating the editors from the printers, made for complications. They could not afford to send the copy by wire, so delivery was made by mail packets entrusted to railroad crewmen; telegraph and telephone were used only in the last hours before closing. When printing in Chicago started, copy sent on the Twentieth Century Limited was delivered into the printer's hands the next morning. But, inevitably, there came the Monday afternoon when Chicago telephoned at five to ask, blandly, where was the copy for the closing forms? It later turned out that the copy had landed in Omaha. In due course, as finances permitted, these arrangements were superseded by the lease of wires for the transmission of copy and pictures.

At the beginning of 1928 Hadden changed jobs with Luce, promising to devote himself to business management for a whole year. His intentions were good, but it went against his grain to subordinate editorial instincts to business judgment. For example, in the fall of 1927, just before giving up the editorship, he had agreed with Larsen as to the desirability of a special subscription drive directed to schoolteachers and promised to assist it by devoting special attention to the Education section. When the September 26 issue appeared with only three items under Education—two of them reporting assaults on schoolteachers by pupils—Larsen wrote indignantly:

> The art of fishing consists of making the poor fish think you have
> a banquet for him. He bites, you yank him out of his nice fresh

109

or salt water and once you have him inside the boat you sock him with an oar, later skin him and serve.

We have adapted this art to our handling of schoolteachers, only we do it on a much more expensive scale. We spend $2,000 for bait which evidently looks sweet to teachers, then we spend $2,000 more for printing issues of *Time* which literally sock the teachers over the head with insults.

And there the simile ends because the teachers are able to get up and walk away. . . . It's discouraging. 15,000 school sample copies gone to pot.

Were there no *new* schools opening? . . .

No *new* teaching systems starting this fall? . . .

Schoolteachers' conventions? . . .

What about infantile paralysis' effect on openings? . . .

The memorandum came back with Hadden's scrawl: "Lar—you are quite right. See October 3. B.H." But the October 3 issue covered only one Education story. It began: "One-sixth of the college population should be sacked. . . ."

As business manager, Hadden contrived to remain a part-time editor by taking over a company house organ called *Tide* and converting it into an advertising trade journal. In 1927, as part of the general advertising-promotion campaign, *Time*'s agency, Fuller & Smith, had written a monthly digest of advertising news which was distributed free to the trade and called *Tide*. In October *Tide* announced that it would become a full-fledged trade journal and solicit advertising; the first issue in its new role, January 1928, carried a *Time*-style cover but with a blue instead of a red border. Subscriptions were offered at $1 a year. Among the first advertisers were *Liberty,* a national weekly, the *Literary Digest* and the New York *Times*. *Tide* imitated *Time* in style and in organization: one section was called Controversy. The magazine was highly controversial; Hadden's irrepressible mischievous bent was evident and *Tide* was even more irreverent than *Time*.

When a Marlboro cigarette advertisement, "What Famous People Would Have Said About Marlboro," quoted Napoleon, "Always before a famous battle I calm my nerves with a Marlboro," *Tide* produced historical evidence that Napoleon loathed tobacco. The magazine poked fun at those advertisements which asked people to "buy more," calling the sales approach "Oliver Twisting." Said *Tide:*

> Anticipating other "Oliver Twisted" ads, readers wondered . . . watched for a soap campaign urging people to "take *two* baths per day." . . . The renewal idea is another approach for Oliver Twisters. Let the consumer not be content with his old razor or clock or lampshade. Let him trade the old one in periodically for a new one. This selling angle can be made to fit almost anything from Ford cars to puppy-dogs. For puppy-dogs the argument should be: "Nothing is more unsightly and unsatisfactory than an old dog. People who *know* do not keep their dogs more than two years at most. Real dog lovers turn their dogs in for puppies after the first year. Write for Booklet B, which outlines our unique Puppy-a-Year plan. Enjoy your dog during his puppy-hood, when he is fuzzy, wuzzy, uzzy and adorable. Then, before he grows up to be just a plain dog, send him to us and receive in exchange a new puppy, exactly the same. Modest prices! Perpetual puppy-love! New dogs for old!"

The story was illustrated by a forlorn picture of Hadden's sister's aging pooch.

With such antics *Tide,* in Larsen's words, got Time Inc. into "a lot of hot water." Nevertheless, it continued to be a lively, uninhibited and often perceptive critic of advertising practices. In 1930 management decided that there was a fundamental conflict of interest between *Tide* and *Time,* and *Tide* was sold to a group headed by Raymond Rubicam, one of the founders of Young & Rubicam. After passing through several ownerships *Tide* ceased publication in 1959.

The change in the editorship from Hadden to Luce at the beginning of 1928 made no immediate discernible difference to the cover-to-cover reader. Luce was content to leave the impress of Hadden's style, even though his approach to editing was different. Writers who worked under both men believed that Luce had a wider range of interests;

111

John Martin found him "more aware of cultural values, more conscious of public opinion"; Gottfried thought Luce's "literary tastes were a good deal more catholic. [He was] a man of ideas, even an intellectual. If you argued with him he might bring up St. Augustine or Pareto." One researcher described him as "the best of all editors because of his temperamental ability to be constantly surprised and delighted by what he didn't know before. Plus his curiosity . . . Luce's questions were always the kind you should have known the answers to, because they were right in line with the story." It was this curiosity which contributed as much to the liveliness of the early *Time* as did Hadden's sense of word and style. Luce prized the nugget of information, the snippet of gossip, which would stop a reader in the middle of an item and cause him to exclaim, "Now *that* was something I didn't know before." Luce was quick to pounce on and point up a fact that would make good dinner-table conversation.

Luce was fascinated by politics and 1928 was the year of a Presidential election. In March he made one of his first speeches, to the Rochester (New York) Chamber of Commerce, in which he set forth his ideas on the men and issues long before the choice of Hoover and Smith as candidates was obvious. "America needs at this moment a moral leader," said the thirty-year-old editor. In discussing eighteen men who had been mentioned as possible candidates, he made it clear that his personal choice lay between the Democrat Alfred E. Smith, New York's four-time governor, and the Republican General Charles G. ("Hell 'n' Maria") Dawes of Chicago.

Luce said of Dawes, "I am inclined to believe that the General is pretty fully loaded with moral 'It.' Will Rogers said he got the Nobel Peace Prize because he could smoke a pipe upside down without setting his clothes on fire. I think he might smoke out a lot of vermin from the national parlor without setting the national storehouse on fire."

Smith, he said, "unlike most politicians in high places . . . does not weary you with descriptions of the infinite beatitude of God. He is a practical politician, and he has had his moments of magnificent moral leadership."

Luce also discussed Hoover, then emerging as a Republican favor-

112

ite, in words that were somewhat prophetic: "The bigger the job, the better he is. But the bigger the issue, the worse is Mr. Hoover. Politically indifferent, he asks for the highest office of political leadership in the world. Mr. Hoover deserves the Presidency. But it is almost the ultimate in degradation of politics to make a man President simply because he deserves it. The White House ought not to be regarded as a mausoleum. Mr. Hoover's nomination would represent a widespread popular preference. Here the paradox reaches its climax. So despairing are we of finding great politicians that we feel forced to oppose bad politicians by clamoring for a poor one."

The nomination of Hoover and Smith posed an interesting choice for the co-editors of *Time*. In 1920, because Hoover towered so high above the political hacks competing for the G.O.P. nomination, Hadden and Luce had led the drive to nominate him at the mock convention they had organized at Yale. In the election of 1924 the odds had been so stacked in favor of Calvin Coolidge and against John W. Davis that the campaign had generated little emotion. The atmosphere in 1928 was highly charged. For one thing, there was Prohibition and both editors of *Time* were against Prohibition; Hoover defended "the noble experiment." The magazine never explicitly declared its position on Prohibition, but the effect of its week-to-week coverage was to emphasize the unworkability of the law. The other issue was Smith's Catholicism. Although there was distrust of Smith in liberal circles because of the Democratic candidate's religion, there was also disgust and repugnance against fundamentalist extremists and the Ku Klux Klan, the forces of prejudice arrayed against Smith.

As for Luce's personal attitude, he recalled his own differences with his father on these subjects. "There were two subjects which we could not discuss in reason and in amicableness. One was Roman Catholicism and the other was Prohibition. The Roman Catholic Church had not yet become 'the anti-Semitism of the intellectuals.' Still, in the '20s, people who were very liberal-minded—and my father tended to be theologically liberal, and certainly was globally liberal and humanly charitable—characteristically shared a deep and old American sentiment that there was something wrong about the Catholic Church; they were worried about the Catholic Church in-

113

creasing in power and influence in this country. About Prohibition my father's argument was a pragmatic one. He was thirty years older, and he would say to me, 'You don't know the amount of anguish, trouble, pain and sorrow caused by alcohol.' My reply was on the abstract constitutional thing. I simply said that this is not the kind of thing we should have in the Constitution. I also argued that Prohibition was working out very badly. It was not decreasing alcohol consumption but increasing it. . . . . And let me put in a big parenthesis. One of the worst things about the '20s, maybe the worst damage done by Prohibition, was the way it pre-empted conversation. You didn't have to be an intellectual, you could be a real nitwit, but still hold attention by the latest news about the new bootlegger. Then later, when I was in my thirties, I began to see what my father meant about alcohol, not from personal experience, but from seeing what happened to some of my friends and colleagues."

Hadden shared Luce's general attitude up to a point. They were both attracted by the frank vulgarity of Alfred E. Smith with his brown derby and cigar, and by his debonair manner and his skill as an administrator. Hoover, the great engineer, compelled admiration, but his high stiff collars and his aloofness did not sit well with youth—and, indeed, not too well with the party that nominated him. The editors of *Time* set out to walk the high wire of impartiality; there were times, inevitably, when the readers were sure they had fallen off.

The political coverage began with a laudatory cover story on Hoover, naming him "Beaver-Man," the pertinence of which *Time* explained this way:

> Most people know that he was born in Iowa, son of a Quaker blacksmith; that he is chunky, round-faced, about six feet high, with beaverish shoulders and neck and with greying hair, much thinner and less brushed down than it used to be, and with his teeth chewed down to a peculiar slant on the left side, where he keeps his cigars. This feature repeats his beaverish aspect which is, of course, enhanced most of all by his well-earned reputation for patient industry and again, perhaps, by his familiarity with rivers and dams and husbanding food through lean seasons. Any

114

man of distinctive personality and appearance resembles some animal. Senator Borah is a bear; Secretary Mellon, an aging horse of fine blood; Senator Heflin, an astounding whale calf. . . . Herbert Clark Hoover is a beaver-man, aged 53, in his prime.

The cover on Al Smith that followed some weeks later revealed no partiality, though one sentence in it suggests political naïveté on the part of the writer: "Unless the U.S. is at heart intolerant, bigots of the Heflin type will have eliminated Roman Catholicism as a consideration" in the nomination and election.

Very early in the campaign Smith's opponents started a rumor that he was a drunkard. *Time* picked up the issue and reported candidly on the Governor's drinking habits:

> In the first place, Drys and Wets seldom agree on what constitutes a "drunkard." The official Brown Derby reply to this whisper is (in effect): "Yes, of course Nominee Smith takes an occasional drink. Who doesn't? But he never drinks beyond self-control, never drinks on duty, has not got the Habit." The popular observation is that the Nominee, when seen off duty, often has had, before evening, enough drinks to be visibly stimulated thereby. To the friendly eye the effect is one of good-fellowship. To the unfriendly, on whom the Nominee's high office may have the effect of a magnifying glass, it looks like rank intoxication.

But it was Smith's Catholicism that became the target of the worst smear tactics and a major factor in his defeat. Early in September *Time* printed this news story:

> Unauthorized by the Republican National Committee but undeterred, civil servants of the U.S. handed out campaign cards in the Capital. A sample:
>
> > *When the bullfrog learns to sing tenor,*
> > *When the rattlesnake walks on legs,*
> > *When the razor-back hog grows feathers,*
> > *And the old muley cow lays eggs;*

> *When the fountain is both sweet and bitter,*
> *When figs on the thistle shall grow,*
> *Then Al Smith will be President;*
> *And we'll all kiss the Pope's big toe.*

A few weeks later a letter to the editors gave another, even more offensive version then circulating in Texas. This provoked Sister Mary Basil, O.P., of Watertown, Massachusetts, to cancel her subscription because "the tone of your magazine is not only hostile but insulting to members of the Catholic Church." In an act of questionable taste, the editors then reprinted the offending lines. This brought further reproof. Mary Burchard Pryor, of Worcester, Massachusetts, wrote: "If the Presidency of the United States were being contested by a Buddhist and a Mohammedan, I should wish *Time* to print no shocking, versified allusion to the sacred Beard of the Prophet." The editors' answer shows them definitely on the defensive.

> If the Presidency of the United States were being contested by a
> Buddhist and a Mohammedan, *Time* would observe due rever-
> ence in mentioning the "Beard of the Prophet." But if hundreds
> of Buddhist verses ridiculing the "Beard" should appear, in such
> scurrilous myriads as to violently affect the campaign, then *Time*
> would print a very few significant specimens of such doggerel.
>
> If these typical verses were of a self-evidently odious and
> detestable nature, *Time* would expect both Mohammedans and
> Buddhists to join with *Time* in holding them up to general odium
> and detestation. . . .

Part of *Time*'s coverage of the campaign was an eight-page special section which reproduced outstanding newspaper cartoons of the campaign. The center spread of this was a double-page drawing, commissioned by *Time* from H. S. Barbour, depicting personalities and issues of the campaign, and one segment drew protests from some readers: the Reverend Dr. John Roach Straton, a New York Baptist minister, a fundamentalist and a vehement opponent of Smith because of his Catholicism and his attitude toward Prohibition, was pictured as a cockroach.

Which candidate was *Time* really for in the election? In a post-election answer to a reader's suspicion that *Time* was Republican, the editors answered: "Erroneous . . . is [the reader's] dogmatic information that the editors of *Time* are Republican: one voted for Hoover, one for Smith. During the campaign no subscriber successfully demonstrated that *Time* favored either candidate." Actually Hadden, who had been for Smith earlier in the campaign, switched to Hoover, while Luce voted for Smith.

On election night the editors of *Time* held the presses one day, and by working through the night managed to put to press by Wednesday morning an issue that, delivered to most of the readers Friday morning, contained a complete summary of the results—a remarkable performance then, considering the size of the staff and the limited facilities. Today the operation is routine.

In 1927, notwithstanding an increase of 72 percent in advertising revenue, *Time* made only a nominal profit of $3,861. In submitting *Time*'s budget for 1928 to the directors, Luce, as treasurer and business manager, had committed management to a definite course of action. He wrote: "Time Inc. has entered into its sixth year. It has had five years in which to talk futures rather than presents. The time has come to consider the present equally with the future. If the habit of postponing profits is permitted to continue, it may well become chronic, and there may be white beards on the chins of the Directors before satisfactory profit is actually shown. Before then Time Inc. may set into a decline. It is in any case a speculative business. Speculative businesses should take their profits when they can get them." He estimated that the company should make a 15-percent profit on total revenues of $1,275,000.

When the books for 1928 were closed, the company's revenue from all sources was $1,308,539, with a net profit after taxes of $125,788. The magazine had published 1,095 pages of advertising; the circulation guarantee for 1929 was announced as 220,000, and management said it would be 300,000 in 1930—which promised an increase twice as big as *Time* had ever made in a single year.

During the year, said the annual report, there occurred "the following 'firsts' ":

The first 60 page issue, the first 68 page issue.

The first portrait in color on the cover [the Emperor of Japan].

The first maps.

The first aeronautical advertisement [a page from Command-Aire].

The first notable jump in newsstand sales: from 1923 through 1927 the highest newsstand sale was 12,000 copies; in 1928 the average for the last three months was 23,000.

The directors, on the basis of the profit and prospects, initiated the payment of back dividends on the Cumulative Preferred Stock during the year and, added the report, "if current rate of earnings is maintained, Directors will be in a position to complete the payments of back dividends between now and early in 1930."

But in writing this glowing report Luce had to add a somber concluding paragraph:

This report will close with a personal word about Briton Hadden, with whom most stockholders are personally acquainted. As many of you already know, he has been seriously ill with a streptococcus infection of the blood stream. Early in December he contracted flu. After several weeks came the more serious development. He has had the best medical attention and at the moment of writing there is reason to hope that his condition will steadily improve. The disease has caused him the greatest discomfort. More than that, he has had to make a strenuous fight against the spread of the infection. Through it all, his concern for the welfare of *Time* has been equalled only by the personal concern which the members of *Time*'s organization have felt for him.

CHAPTER

10

The End of a Partnership

T HE HOPED-FOR improvement did not occur. Hadden's illness was attributed to *Streptococcus viridans,* which infected the blood stream and also affected the heart.[1] Undoubtedly the six years of effort which he had poured into *Time* had weakened him physically and made him more vulnerable. He had made enormous demands on his nervous system, working, in the beginning, seven days a week. When this was no longer necessary he still drove himself without stint; he played as hard as he worked.

Back in New York, he was in his element. With his friend and former Foreign News editor T. J. C. Martyn (now divorced) and William J. Carr, a rising young lawyer, he set up bachelor quarters at 25 East End Avenue, a spacious apartment where the three of them lived in considerable style attended by a Chinese butler and a maid. He was often to be found, late after deadlines, at P. J. Moriarty's speakeasy on Third Avenue. It was the heyday of the Cotton Club in

[1] Hadden was fond of animals, and one legend is that the infection was due to a scratch by a mangy stray cat that he had rescued on a rainy night. His doctors denied any connection.

119

Harlem, and Hadden enjoyed making forays there.

But *Time*'s success, and his own, seemed to bring him little satisfaction. Many new ideas for publishing projects were simmering in his mind. Jotted down in a notebook: "Bus. Mag; Fiction Mag; *Time* monthly; School *Time.*" Toward the end of 1928, in November, his colleagues and friends noted that his spirits seemed to flag; some weeks he would come into the office only a few days. He would call in to say that he was ill. Katherine Abrams, the bookkeeper, warned Luce, "You had better look after Hadden. . . . He really must be sick." Hadden's friend Dr. Oswald Jones, a frequent visitor at the East End Avenue apartment, was struck by the change which had come over him: "He walked up and down the living room saying how bored he was." His old friend from the *World* days, Darius Benham, called one day. "What's the matter, boy?" asked Benham. Hadden answered: "I'm not well. I don't know what's the matter with me."

He came down with influenza. His stepfather, Dr. Pool, took him back home to Brooklyn, where Hadden's mother and he could look after him. When Hadden's condition did not improve, he was moved to Brooklyn Hospital. The doctors could do little for him. The infection in the blood stream spread. The only known treatment, before sulfa drugs or antibiotics, was to try to halt the infection by repeated blood transfusions, for which Hadden's colleagues in the office volunteered.

In January Luce wrote to Gottfried, who had returned from Europe, asking him to give a hand for six months. The January 30 entry in Gottfried's diary read: "An hour late getting in to New York. . . . To *Time* and had a long palaver with Harry. Brit is ill unto death with streptococcus." On January 31 he wrote: "Took Lexington Avenue subway two stations beyond Borough Hall and walked to Brooklyn Hospital. Harry there and we had our blood tested. . . ." When Hadden's secretary called at the hospital with a $20 gold piece which the directors had sent him as fee for a directors' meeting which he could not attend, Hadden turned her hand away. "Take it back," he said. "I wasn't there. . . . Anyhow, I won't get well." She remembered him looking like a frightened little boy.

Luce, who tried to rally him with news of the office, was startled

120

and depressed when Hadden was confused by Luce's reference to "President Hoover," who had been elected in November. When Luce talked about an advertising campaign which *Time* proposed to launch in the New York *Times,* Hadden brightened, asked how much it would cost.

"Oh, about $15,000," Luce replied.

"My God, Harry," said Hadden, "have we got that kind of money?"

The illness could not be checked. He died at four a.m. on February 27, 1929, six years to the day after he put the first issue to press.

Hadden's death staggered his colleagues, Luce in particular. "I do not know what I shall do without him," he told Gottfried. A few days later he called a meeting of the staff in his office and outlined how he proposed to carry on. Hadden's cousin John Martin said that Luce had their confidence, and they adjourned to get on with the next issue.

The emotion under which they worked is reflected in an unsuccessful attempt to write Hadden's obituary, a fragment of which survives in the archives. It is in Martin's handwriting and is headed "The Late Gargantuan Man." It begins: "In Chicago at three o'clock one Wednesday morning blue lights shone through the windows of a vast printing plant upon deserted streets. Through the windows an idling gunman might have seen two presses bigger than elephants. Each gave forth noise as of a distant aeroplane. . . . Whir, tick-tock, whir, whir, tick-tock—a thousand miles distant, a young man died." It never appeared, of course; the kind of editorial discipline that Hadden himself had imposed on the staff reasserted itself and what finally appeared was an item in Milestones, characteristically concise. It concluded, "To Briton Hadden success came steadily, satisfaction never."

Hadden died, at thirty-one, too young to realize the promise of his years. *Time* was only just emerging as an influence in the American community. He had won the public's attention for it by the force of his own personality, which had endowed the magazine with its style. He was an innovator, at the same time profoundly conservative; a

121

man who could be irreverent, mocking of all pretense and pomposity, and yet enormously respectful of what he thought worthwhile. He early conceived, and held until his death, respect for three men whom he considered the great editors of his age: Herbert Bayard Swope, his mentor and first editor; Arthur Brisbane, the Hearst columnist and editor (he liked Brisbane's writing style); and the late Lord Northcliffe (he was impressed by Northcliffe's success). In every sense Hadden was more creative than any of them and his contribution to journalism far more eloquent.

Noel Busch concluded his cousin's biography by explaining why he had been impelled to write it. At the Hotel Scribe in Paris, while serving as a war correspondent in World War II, he met a fellow reporter from *Time* who was new to the magazine and asked Old Hand Busch how the magazine had begun.

"Well," said Busch, "it seems that Harry Luce and Briton Hadden—"

"Wait," the new man interrupted, "I've heard about Luce, but who was Briton Hadden?"

Busch ended his book: "This seemed to me to be a fair question; and one that deserved an answer."

It was a question few reporters would have asked some fifteen years before. The men of Hadden's generation were very much aware of him and his achievement. On the morning after his death the New York *Times* saluted him on its editorial page for his "determination, his organizing ability, his frankness and great personal charm," and added: "His life, in its achievements, remains as an example of the fruits that can be plucked by youth; his industry, his touch of genius and his character have added a novel chapter to the book of journalism."

The extraordinary stream of messages to *Time*'s office, some of which *Time* printed in the March 11 issue, reflected the mark which he had made as an editor on the 1920s. Three years later his family, colleagues and friends put up as a memorial to him the building which now houses the Yale *Daily News*. His portrait hangs in the board room. A plaque reads: "His genius invented a new form of journalism."

122

CHAPTER

II

"The Largest of the Planets"

FOUR WEEKS before Hadden died, already too weak to sign his
name, he put his "X" to a last will and testament, directing
that his stock in Time Inc. not be sold for forty-nine years.
Hadden's heir was his mother, Mrs. Pool; the trustee and executor
was his half-brother, Crowell Hadden III, who was elected to the
Time Inc. Board after Hadden's death. The estate consisted almost
entirely of shares in the company. A final gesture of Briton Hadden's
faith in Time Inc., his will presented practical difficulties. Legally,
Crowell Hadden, as executor, could do almost anything he judged
prudent; sentimentally, he was bound to consider his half-brother's
wishes. He also had to think of his stepmother's needs and future. His
decision was that in order to diversify its holdings the estate would sell
some of its shares.

But how many and at what price? At his death Hadden owned
3,361 shares for which no market had been established. As Luce put
the problem of price to his friend and director Harry Davison: "If
you can figure out a way of figuring the value of Time stock so that
both buyer and seller are happy you are *indeed* a financier!"

The solution was found by twenty-five-year-old Charles L. Stillman,

123

the assistant treasurer of the company. Stillman (Yale '26) had been hired as business manager on the recommendation of William Griffin, who, while Stillman was still an undergraduate, had discovered his gift for management in the course of a fund-raising drive for their fraternity, DKE. On Stillman's graduation Griffin hired him to manage the James C. Brady properties in Georgia; the job involved such diverse matters as company stores and the launching of a reforestation program. When Stillman wanted to return to New York, Griffin found him the job at *Time*. One of Stillman's first assignments from Hadden was to mix a bathtubful of gin to celebrate the move in October 1928 from the quarters on 45th Street to new offices in the Bartholomew Building on East 42nd Street.

Slight in build, a man of few words, Stillman had a quick and powerful mind which would make an inestimable contribution to the company's future growth. In the impasse over the will he evidenced a sophistication in finance: he told Luce the only way to establish an independent valuation of the Hadden shares was to solicit a bid for them from interests outside the organization. He approached friends in the First Boston Corporation, who were prepared to pay $360 a share. At this figure and on terms, as Luce put it, requiring "cash on the barrelhead," the Hadden estate was prepared to sell 2,828½ shares to Luce and a syndicate he organized.

Luce acquired 625 of the shares, Larsen 550, and three other members of the Time Inc. staff 100 shares each—Martin, Stillman and F. J. Dusossoit, a salesman. Four directors also participated: Davison bought 300 shares; Griffin, 303½ shares; William H. Harkness (who had become a director in 1926), 100 shares; and Robert A. Chambers, 50 shares. The other two members of the group were friends: John Hanes, who had devised the original financial plan, took 100 shares, and Wilton Lloyd-Smith, whose brother was a member of the editorial staff (of whom more later), took 500. The company also acquired 158½ shares from the estate, the nucleus of the first employee stock-purchase plan.

Luce borrowed the money to purchase his shares, using as collateral his original holdings. He was surprised at the ease with which this was arranged. "I am pretty sure," wrote Gottfried, with whom Luce discussed the transaction, "that it was this event that made Luce realize for the first time that he was a rich man." Larsen, in order to buy his shares, sold RKO stock inherited from his father—a seemingly improvident action taken against the advice of his broker. He sold RKO at $35 a share. Within two years Time Inc. reached $1,000 and was split 20-to-1; on December 21, 1931, RKO hit a low of 75 cents.

The acquisition of the Hadden stock was a decisive turning point in Time Inc.'s history. It confirmed the control and direction of the company in Luce, giving him freedom of action which he would not have had if such a substantial interest had remained vested in an estate or had been dispersed and sold to outside interests.

The sale of the Hadden stock took place in September 1929, when plans were well advanced for the publication of a new magazine, news of which aroused public curiosity about the single figure now heading Time Inc. What was he like, this Henry Luce who had operated more or less in the shadow of his brilliant partner?

Garland Smith wrote in the Brooklyn *Eagle:* "[He] is just as brilliant and just as dynamic. 'A most interesting young man'—'Phenomenal energy'—'Remarkable mental ability'—'Astonishing absorption in his work for one so young'—so the rumors and adjectives fly about."

Smith found his subject cooperative but not self-revealing. "The trouble with me is that I work nearly all the time," Luce told him. "I'm sorry that I've never done anything exciting. Never killed an Indian [1] or rescued anybody from drowning. . . . I'm married and have two sons, Henry 3rd and Peter Paul. That's about all." Luce admitted that he sometimes played tennis and that his hobby was "conversing with somebody who knows something."

Smith was not the only journalist to find Luce a frustrating subject. *Vanity Fair's* Mrs. Clare Boothe Brokaw, assigned to do an item on him for its "Hall of Fame," could not get to talk to him, but wrote

---

[1] On re-reading the interview years later, Luce commented, "It's probably what I said, but maybe it ought to be edited into 'a lion.' It sounds as if one of the sports of the times was to kill Indians. It was a clumsy remark on my part."

her piece anyhow. Apparently she could find nothing more interesting to say than: "... He claims that he has no other interests outside of his work, and that this work fills his waking hours." She remembered thinking, "What a dull fellow that must be." Condé Nast, *Vanity Fair*'s publisher, held a different view. In mid-1929 Luce received an unexpected offer from Nast, who also published *Vogue* and *House & Garden*. Nast, then fifty-five and riding the crest of the great bull market, wanted to take things easier and enjoy the profits of his speculations, which on paper were in the millions. He suggested merging Condé Nast Publications with Time Inc., and invited Luce to take on the management of their combined properties. "I told him that I was enormously flattered," Luce recalled, "but that I was working very hard on a new magazine to be called *Fortune*." [2]

With an intuitive sense of the way the current of society ran—a sense that marked his career—Luce's mind turned to American business as a field for journalistic enterprise. The American people in the late 1920s were enjoying very good times. True, the farmers were having a tough time, and millions of others were trapped in hopeless poverty, but more people were comfortably off or rich than ever before. Amazing technological advances had nearly doubled industrial production between 1921 and 1929. Employment was high, and although wages had not risen in proportion to the tremendous increase in profits and dividends, prices were stable. The general consensus was that the credit for the soaring prosperity must be given to American business.

This was Luce's view; in a speech in March 1929 he said:

... Business is, essentially, our civilization; for it is the essential characteristic of our times. That which controls our lives and which it is necessary for us to control is the science and technology and the development of credit and the circumnavigability of

---

[2] After the crash Nast, whose wealth had been all but wiped out, again approached Time Inc., suggesting that it buy out the Nast publications. Luce and Larsen, after careful consideration, turned down the offer because "we didn't want to go into the fashion business. That wasn't our métier."

126

the globe—in short, modern business. Long since has business ceased to be a low and private and only regrettably necessary affair to be escaped when possible. Business is our life. It is the life of the artist, the clergyman, the philosopher, the doctor, because it determines the conditions and problems of life with which either artist or philosopher, let alone ordinary mortals, have to deal.

At the same time Luce felt that American businessmen—the "tycoons," he called them, in *Time* style—seemed to deny their primacy. He criticized them for shying from the press, for pretending to hate publicity and for being "kittenish as a Victorian subdeb or boorish as a lion sickening in captivity" when caught in the public eye. But he also criticized the press for its ignorance of business, saying, "The average reporter knows much more about astronomy than he does about industry. The reason this has been so is fundamentally that the public as public has never taken much interest in business as business. And the reason that is so is because business as the prime determinant of society began only day before yesterday. But now all this . . . has changed. . . . The significant change is the incipient public curiosity as to the modes and objectives and processes and personalities of industry and commerce and finance."

In this curiosity Luce had perceived an opportunity—for a magazine that would cater to the men who managed the nation's business. It would be a magazine that would treat in a sophisticated way industrial civilization in all its aspects. He had discussed all this with Hadden, who was not convinced but had agreed (in September 1928) to detach *Time*'s Business writer and a researcher from their regular jobs in order to explore the idea.

The writer was Parker Lloyd-Smith, whom Martin had known at Princeton and had recommended on the argument that, since Scottish banks recruited classicists, a student of the classics would make a good Business writer. The son of a judge, Lloyd-Smith had gone to The Hill School and Princeton, spent a year at Oxford (Magdalen), and had worked briefly for the Albany *Evening News* and the *Knickerbocker Press*. He was a friendly, brilliant and witty young man.

Margaret Bourke-White, the photographer, remembered him as having "a headful of tight, short black curls and a profile of almost Grecian regularity." [3] His researcher was Florence Horn, who had come to *Time* after a short stint with Lee, Higginson & Co. in Wall Street and a period with a Bridgeport, Connecticut, newspaper as a society editor.

The two of them had been "packed upstairs in the West 45th Street building," as Miss Horn recalled, "in a little sound-proof room just big enough for two desks." Luce was the driving force behind this modest Experimental Department; the lists of subjects he drew up for the new magazine were to supply *Fortune* in the first years of publication with many of its articles: "The Rothschilds"; "Household budgets for incomes of $5,000 to $100,000"; "Who is now making money out of munitions"; "The Meat Business—range to eater." Lists of possible writers to be assigned to these subjects included Ernest Hemingway, Philip Guedalla, Joseph Hergesheimer, President Calvin Coolidge. One idea was to have John D. Rockefeller, Jr., write on the topic "I Retire from Business" and his son John D. 3d on "I Enter Business." Hadden held himself aloof from all this. Miss Horn recalled, "When the Experimental Department started he took the absurd position that Lloyd-Smith and I did not exist."

As a test, they researched an article on International Telephone & Telegraph, controlled by the secretive brothers Behn, Sosthenes and Hernand. The Behns refused to be interviewed, and neither would even supply a *curriculum vitae*. In spite of this, Lloyd-Smith and Miss Horn produced an article with considerable detail. Lloyd-Smith wrote Luce, ". . . There is no real competition. Established business magazines will not or cannot handle stories as we think they should be handled." Their experiment was the precursor of the *Fortune* corporation story, a journalistic innovation that has been an important feature of the magazine for thirty-eight years.

Five months of such experimenting convinced Luce that further development of his idea was warranted. In February 1929, shortly before Hadden died, he submitted to the directors a remarkable

[3] *Portrait of Myself* (Simon and Schuster, 1963).

128

blueprint of the magazine he wanted to publish, complete even to the name: *Fortune* was chosen from many suggestions because it appealed most to Luce's wife, Lila. He described the opportunity for the new magazine:

Business, the smartest, most universal of all American occupations, has no medium of expression except the financial pages of newspapers and the cheapest, least distinguished of magazines. In kindness to the *Nation's Business,* the *Magazine of Business,* the *Magazine of Wall Street, Forbes* and *System,* it may be said that they have made some effort to be presentable. . . .

[But] unless we are prepared to believe that America's industrialists are chiefly concerned with the technique of sales departments, with the stale Get-Rich-Maxims of onetime errand boys, the subject matter of such a magazine as *Forbes* must be thought piddling and inexpressibly dull. Even the *Nation's Business* . . . is enslaved by the idea that any article by a great name (Ford, Schwab, Hoover, Farrell) is *per se* entertaining reading no matter what the Great Name may tell his ghost writer to say.

We conceive that the failure of business magazines to realize the dignity and the beauty, the smartness and excitement of modern industry, leaves a unique publishing opportunity. . . .

We propose to become a national institution, perhaps the greatest of all institutions which are concerned with criticism and interpretation. The field which lies open is as immense and as rich as was ever offered to journalistic enterprise. We have wars to record, strategy to admire, biographies to write. The 20th Century trend in merchandising, the growth of the chain store system, is no less significant in the century's development than the decline of the theory of states' rights. Industry is a world in itself, for which we must be critics, historians, biographers and secretaries. And this World is more macrocosm than microcosm, is in fact the largest of the planets which make up our system.

After describing plans for the magazine's appearance and contents in rough outline (some articles already written were submitted as illustration), the presentation concluded:

129

Fortune is primarily a conception. The conception is revealed in the material herewith presented plus assumptions which cannot yet be proved but which may be summarized as follows:

1. It will be as beautiful a magazine as exists in the United States. If possible, the undisputed most beautiful.

2. It will be authoritative to the last letter.

3. It will be brilliantly written. It will have *Time*'s bursting-with-fact, economical, objective merits, but the language will be smoother, more sophisticated, which combination of virtues can be obtained because there will be far more time to assemble the facts, write, edit.

4. It will attempt, subtly, to "take a position," particularly as regards what may be called the ethics of business. Of course, business is *not* a profession, and so one cannot set up a definite professional code. Nor is it desired blasphemously to equate business with religion. But in a general way, the line can be drawn between the gentleman and the money-grubber, between the responsible and the irresponsible citizen. *Fortune* is written for those who have a sizable stake in the country and who ought, therefore, to yield to no other class in either the degree or the intelligence of their patriotism.

It is much more difficult to describe *Fortune* than to describe *Time*.

An investment of only $50,000 was asked at this time to continue development work; in event of publication a total investment of $400,000 was envisaged. Of this, $300,000 was budgeted for pre-publication work, $100,000 for the first year's operating loss. The circulation goal for the first year was set at 30,000; subscribers would be asked to pay the high price—even for those boom years—of $10 a year, or $1 a copy. The first 100 advertisers who contracted for six pages or more and who at the end of 1930 were not completely satisfied were to be guaranteed a 100-percent refund. Luce forecast that after the initial investment *Fortune* might produce a profit of not less than $400,000 a year. But he observed that even if an investment of $800,000 were eventually required and profits were only $200,000

130

a year, the new magazine could be expected to repay the initial investment in ten years plus the equivalent of 6-percent interest compounded for fifteen years.

Luce had to overcome an obstacle to win the Board's approval. Hadden's opposition was well known. He had argued earlier that 1929 might be a critical year and *Time* should have the undivided attention of Luce and himself; his illness made it impossible for him to reassess the project on the basis of current developments. On February 7, 1929, the day before the directors' meeting, Luce wrote Harry Davison:

> In view of Brit's expressed wish I am willing to withdraw my recommendation to the Board even though it represents my best judgment and conviction in the matter. But I would prefer to have it done this way: Let the Board, if it please, make the authorization as recommended. Let me review the whole situation. . . . Let me then, if I have any reasonable doubt as to the security and progress of *Time,* notify the Board that work on *Fortune* has been indefinitely postponed.
>
> I am certain that, if Brit had not been taken ill, he would be in agreement with me on this course. . . . The recommendation makes it emphatically clear that if Brit should disapprove, the whole venture can be and will be promptly and easily dropped.

With this assurance the Board approved further work on *Fortune,* subject to the provision that no more than $50,000 be spent until further notice, and that Time Inc. should not be publicly or privately committed to publication of the new magazine—conditions that Luce willingly accepted.

The death of Hadden just nineteen days after this decision temporarily set the work back. At the end of May, Luce wrote the directors:

> Progress on *Fortune* during this period has been made under difficult circumstances. . . . More than any detail were the doubts which Hadden's loss occasioned, especially in the mind of

131

the writer—doubts as to whether *Time* would continue equally strong, and, even if so, whether the organization could manage a big expansion. These doubts have by no means vanished, but they have been diminished by circumstances. Superficially, we have enjoyed remarkable and unexpected prosperity, in the face of which it would seem querulous to worry. But the writer well realizes that prosperity can sometimes be deceiving. If *Time* declines editorially, it will soon decline financially. However, there is no reason for believing that it has declined. Recent issues have perhaps lacked the unique Hadden touch. But something of this may be regained. Meanwhile, to make up for this loss, there has been a definite advance along the line of complete and accurate material. . . .

He closed by recommending that the company go ahead with *Fortune* because it "has a 50–50 chance" and it "is a worthwhile thing to do and a *Time*-like."

Crowell Hadden voted against the new magazine, explaining that, while he considered it a good gamble, it would tend to defer dividends on the common stock. William Hale Harkness also voted no, saying he was not against Time Inc. undertaking new ventures, but that he did not like the particular one proposed. Hadden's and Luce's college friend Sam Meek, who had been a director since 1923, said, "If it had not been for our confidence in Harry Luce, probably none of us would have voted to go ahead." A majority of the Board gave their approval.

Fortune: Vol. I, No. 1

> Almost on the eve of *Fortune*'s publication, the
> whole economy of the United States clapped a hand
> over its heart, uttered a piercing scream, and
> slipped on the largest banana peel since Adam
> Smith wrote *The Wealth of Nations.*
>
> ERIC HODGINS
> *addressing the twentieth-anniversary dinner*
> *of Time Inc.*

LUCE WAS NOT going completely off the deep end when, with
the Board's lukewarm blessing, he set out on his "50–50"
gamble. *Fortune* was a venture carefully planned and thoroughly researched—on the editorial side by Luce, Lloyd-Smith and
Miss Horn; on the business side by Luce and Larsen (who at Hadden's
death had become general manager and Luce's deputy for business).
They had solicited the reactions of corporation executives and their
advertising agencies. They had sent confidential inquiries to a representative group of leading businessmen, potential subscribers, as to

their interest in the proposed publication. The encouraging, even enthusiastic, reaction of these men was a decisive factor in the decision to publish.

A sales staff was recruited to sell advertising in advance of publication. Florimond J. Dusossoit, who was shortly to change his name to F. Du Sossoit Duke (at the behest of his wife), was appointed advertising manager. He told Luce he wanted a free hand to hire his men and that every member of the sales staff would be at least six feet tall. He himself was a six-footer, captain of the Dartmouth football team, a pilot in World War I, and had once played professional football for the New York Giants. He hired seven men, who began work about July 1. Each got a list of prime prospects, a short memorandum describing the projected magazine, some sample pages of trial articles, and a dummy of heavy, glazed pages with penciled ruled lines and some lettering to suggest the format and content. In August a printed dummy, Vol. I, No. 0, was produced. In the pre-publication prospectus the editors promised: *"Fortune* will make its discoveries clear, coherent, vivid, so that the reading of it may be one of the keenest pleasures in the life of every subscriber." In an extraordinary gesture the money-back guarantee to advertisers was broadened: *"Fortune,* confident of the success ahead of it, pledges . . . *Should any Original Advertiser feel (after using* Fortune *for six months) that he has made a bad bargain, he may cancel his contract and have all his money back."* (Only two advertisers—with contracts for quarter-pages—asked for the rebate.) *Fortune* was an instant success as an advertising medium; of the 779 pages of advertising which the magazine published in its first year, Duke's men had signed contracts for 763½ pages (at a basic black-and-white rate of $500) before the first issue went to press.

To Thomas M. Cleland, an artist and one of America's distinguished typographers, was assigned the job of making *Fortune* "the most beautiful" magazine. He aimed at a format classical in style and elegant in appearance. He specified 18th Century Baskerville as the body type; it was reproduced especially for *Fortune* by the English Monotype Company. The text matter was to be printed by letterpress

134

and illustrations by sheet-fed gravure. The paper chosen was "wild wove antique," designed to eliminate the eye-disturbing glare of coated stock. The cover, 125-pound weight, was almost the thickness of cardboard; the magazine had to be gathered and sewn by hand.

Charles Stillman, assigned to *Fortune*'s business management, said later, "We were willing to take chances which we would have better sense than to take now. I decided the only thing to do was to follow Cleland slavishly." Only one company in the U.S. could produce the gravure specified by Cleland, the Osborne Chromatic Gravure Company in East Orange, New Jersey. There, many of the forms had to go through a three-color, sheet-fed gravure press and then pass through another press to take care of the monotone pictures. These presses averaged only 8,000 copies in an eight-hour shift, because each side of a sheet had to be run separately. Because the antique stock had a tendency to warp and shrink, the presses were stopped frequently to make adjustments. Once the gravure forms were run, the pages were trucked to the Cuneo Eastern Press in Brooklyn, where letterpress borders, text and cover were printed. The covers often required seven different press runs. It was only in 1932, after the Jersey City Printing Company took over the entire printing operation, that *Fortune* was produced in a single shop.

In one of his calls at the J. Walter Thompson Company office in New York, Luce came across some photographs taken for the Otis Steel Company of Cleveland. He immediately telegraphed the photographer, Margaret Bourke-White, in Cleveland: "Can you come to New York within week at our expense?" She very nearly did not answer; his name meant nothing to her, and a look at *Time*'s illustrations did not suggest that Time Inc. offered much opportunity for her kind of photography.

But a trip to New York was a trip to New York. Portfolio under her arm, she called at *Time*'s offices in the Bartholomew Building and there met Luce and Lloyd-Smith. Luce began questioning her with machine-gun rapidity. She described their first meeting: [1]

[1] *Portrait of Myself* (Simon and Schuster, 1963).

His words tumbled out with such haste and emphasis that I had the feeling he was thinking ten words for every one that managed to emerge. . . . Who was I and what was I? Why was I taking these industrial pictures? Was it just for fun? Was it my vocation? Or was it my profession? I solemnly assured Mr. Luce it was my profession, and a very serious one.

Then his idea came into focus:

The camera should explore every corner of industry, showing everything, Mr. Luce explained, from the steam shovel to the board of directors. The camera would act as interpreter, recording what modern industrial civilization is, how it looks, how it meshes. . . .

It seemed miraculous to me that these editors and I should meet and join our forces at just this time—I with my dream of portraying industry in photographs, and they with their new magazine designed to hold just such photographs.

Within two months the twenty-four-year-old Bourke-White was hard at work for *Fortune* and was busy all that summer with various writers as the editors began to build a bank of articles—photographing orchid-growing in New Jersey, glassmaking in Corning, New York, and Midwestern industry in South Bend, Indiana. On the South Bend assignment Luce himself accompanied her as reporter, carrying her heavy and cumbersome 5 × 7 Corona View camera. Their reception was on the cool side; *Time* was little known in South Bend, and no one had yet heard of *Fortune*. One of the few persons who took a friendly interest and seemed to understand what they were trying to do was Paul Hoffman, vice-president of the Studebaker Corporation (later to become a director of Time Inc.).

From South Bend, Bourke-White went on to Chicago to work with Lloyd-Smith on an article on Swift & Company and the stockyards. A game reporter, he followed her into every nook and cranny of the yards until they came to one particularly malodorous building. She wrote:

136

Countless times we had heard the well-worn adage that the Swifts used all of the pig but the squeal. The sight that faced us proved it. Before us were pungent macabre mountains—rich tones of ochre in the yellow light—mountains of the finest pig dust. . . .

Parker Lloyd-Smith took one sniff, bolted for the car and put up the windows tight while I took the photographs. He had a long wait, for the yellow light had low actinic value and I had to make time exposures. When it was over, I left my camera cloth and light cords behind to be burned.

Her photography was one of the distinguished features of the first issue of *Fortune* and of many issues thereafter.

The original concept of having *Fortune* written by authors of established reputation proved impracticable and it was decided that the new magazine, like *Time,* would be largely staff-written. Neither Luce nor Lloyd-Smith anticipated any difficulty in staffing it. They assumed that newspapermen working on the business and financial sections of the New York newspapers would be interested in writing for their magazine, and so they invited the number-two men from these sections to a dinner at the Princeton Club. The newspapermen showed little interest; their hosts were disappointed in their guests' seeming lack of imagination.

Luce wanted writers who could see beyond the balance sheets and describe the lights and shadows of factories and the personalities of the men who ruled them. "There are men who can write poetry, and there are men who can read balance sheets," Luce decided. "The men who can read balance sheets cannot write. That, happily with some exceptions, is the general rule. Of necessity, we made the discovery that it is easier to turn poets into business journalists than to turn bookkeepers into writers."

The roster of *Fortune* writers abounds in proof of Luce's dictum. One of these unique business journalists was Archibald MacLeish. He had fled to Paris from the practice of law and the writing of *Time's* Education section and had devoted himself to writing poetry. But Paris, after five and a half years, had proved too expensive for a

137

literary man with a growing family, and he returned to the U.S. "When Luce asked me to go to work for *Fortune*," said MacLeish, "the stock which paid me the only income I had (such as it was) had suspended dividends and I literally didn't know how my wife and my three children, to say nothing of myself, were going to eat. At the same time, however, I was working on a long poem (*Conquistador*) which had to get written if it killed me. I told Harry my situation. He replied that I could work for *Fortune* as long in any year as I needed to to pay my bills and then go back to my own chores. And that is precisely what happened for the next eight years. Some years I worked twelve months; some I worked three or four, depending on doctor's bills and the like. I have never heard of comparable generosity or understanding in a publisher; certainly Ross [2] was a skinflint by comparison." MacLeish proved to be the magazine's most consistent producer, reporting on almost every phase of American life from the building of New York skyscrapers to the dust bowls of the West and the changing climate of world politics. "My essential education as an American began on *Fortune*," he said.

Another poet who played a decisive role in shaping *Fortune* was Russell Davenport. His father had been an eminent metallurgist who had produced at Bethlehem Iron Company the first heavy armor plate for the U.S. Navy and was a descendant of the John Davenport who founded the Colony of New Haven; his mother, a Philadelphia beauty, was a member of one of that city's great families. On his father's death, his mother had taken her two sons west (Russell's brother John was also to work for *Fortune*); after graduation from the Thacher School in California at seventeen, Russell went to France as an ambulance driver and twice won the Croix de Guerre. He then went to Yale; graduating in 1923, he did a brief stint of writing on infant *Time,* followed by some reporting for the Spokane *Spokesman-Review.* Then Paris and poetry claimed him from journalism; he spent a year or so there working on a long poem, *The California Spring,* and moving on the fringes of the American émigré circles. In 1930 he was back in New York and, looking for a job, called on his fellow member of Skull and Bones, Harry Luce. Here in Davenport's own words is what happened:

[2] Harold Ross of *The New Yorker.*

138

Harry called up something called the research department and asked someone called Miss Horn if she had that material on the A & P Company. He then called *Fortune*'s managing editor; and presently Lloyd-Smith and the A & P joined us. It devolved that there was an article to be written on the A & P and there were left exactly three weeks before it had to be closed. It was a huge article in three parts. One section was to be a description of an A & P store, another an analysis of the corporation, and a third, a summary of the world situation in coffee. Almost immediately after Harry had introduced me, Lloyd-Smith suggested that I take over this little job. Even Harry recoiled from that. "My God, Parker, don't you know that Russ doesn't even know how to read a Standard Statistics card?" Lloyd-Smith's answer was that the cards were not very hard to read and that anyway somebody else could read the cards. So I got the story.

One equally devoid of expertise in business when he came to *Fortune* was Dwight Macdonald. He had been chairman of the Yale *Record,* and had written a column for the *News* called "The Inquisitor." On graduation he joined Macy's Executive Training Squad; his plan was "to make a lot of money rapidly and retire to write literary criticism." Soon disillusioned with the retail trade, he got a job on *Fortune.*

An exception to the rule of poets and Ivy Leaguers with literary ambitions was tough little Edward E. Kennedy, who had been denied a degree from the University of Cincinnati because he failed to show up for commencement. He found his way into the Time Inc. organization by way of advertising. As a copywriter for Fuller & Smith, he was the first writer on *Tide* and, after moving with it to Time Inc., wrote in *Time*'s Business section before joining *Fortune.* He was a prodigious producer who, according to Luce, "wrote more good copy than anyone else in the first few years." He was an equally prodigious drinker. Sometimes he would disappear, and then the *Fortune* office boy was summoned, handed $5 and told to search the nearby speakeasies; when found, Kennedy was locked in an office overnight to be sure he was on hand for the next day's stint. Kennedy wrote clean, crisp prose with great dispatch and during his service with *Fortune* produced some eighty articles on leading American corporations.

Fortune was first announced to *Time*'s readers in the issue of October 21, 1929, an issue that was still on sale on "Black Thursday," the day that marked the beginning of the Great Wall Street Panic. On that morning, October 24, shares were dumped on the New York Stock Exchange in blind, mindless fear, and billions in paper profits were swept away in minutes. At noon that day, in an effort to check the panic, a consortium of bankers met at 23 Wall Street, the offices of J. P. Morgan, and decided on measures to support the market; the mere news that they were meeting steadied it, and when, at 1:30, Richard Whitney moved to the Steel post to bid $205 for 10,000 shares of U.S. Steel, confidence returned. On Friday and Saturday the market held its own, and over the weekend business leaders issued comforting statements intended to reassure the nervous public. But on Monday the panic started afresh, and on Tuesday, October 29, the New York Stock Exchange was inundated with selling orders; according to the official statistics, 16,410,030 shares were, in *Time*'s phrase, "dumped as if they were so much junk." However, in the same issue (November 4, 1929), reporting the situation as of the close of business on that horrendous day, *Time* said, ". . . It seemed again that the worst was passed. . . . Hysteria, it was hoped, had met its master in the Banking Power of the U.S., which appeared to have bought a good proportion of U.S. Industry."

And for a brief time it did so appear. In the following issue *Time*, which had Thomas W. Lamont, senior partner of J. P. Morgan, on the cover (the caption: "He felt the helm respond"), reported that "Confidence" had won "its subtle race against Panic." In the November 25 issue the editors, again reporting on the market, concluded: "To all things must come an end. Last week there came an end to the almost uninterrupted panic of selling that has fermented U.S. stock markets . . . ." In effect, *Time* was right; the stock-market panic was ended. What the editors did not foresee was that the Great Depression was taking over.

Through these hectic weeks *Fortune* was still being readied for publication. On November 8 Larsen wrote to Luce reporting that of the $300,000 earmarked for the magazine's development, $200,000 had been committed. He summarized what had been accomplished:

. . . design and general layout of the magazine's pages; the contents of at least two issues practically complete . . . contracts secured for 75 pages of advertising . . . approximately 30,000 subscribers, of whom 500 are paid . . . a list of 150,000 best prospects for *Fortune,* a list which does not duplicate *Time*'s own subscription list. We hope to have 50,000 provisional subscribers to start with the first issue and to convert at least 30,000 into paid subscribers . . . 2,000 dummy copies . . .

With approximately $200,000 invested in the magazine on January 1st, with 30,000 paid subscribers, printing a 174-page magazine carrying an average of 87 pages of advertising, *Fortune* should break even for the year 1930 (11 issues).

The prospect was pleasing but some account had to be taken of the Crash. "We will go ahead and publish," Luce and Larsen decided, "but we shall be realistic." And, with what they considered great farsightedness, added: "We shall recognize that this slump may last as long as one year." Luce thought there might even be an advantage in starting out in poor rather than boom times: "We didn't want *Fortune* thought of as a stock market fluff. . . . In starting out in a slump we had a more solid base."

Vol. I, No. 1, of *Fortune* appeared in February 1930, impressive in its black-and-bronze cover of a wheel of fortune, its large pages (11¼″ × 14″) providing magnificent display for Bourke-White's photographs, with heft enough to justify the price of one dollar a copy. In the advertising pages there was reflected the afterglow of a great age of prosperity, pages in color glorifying long, sleek, classic automobiles, ocean-going yachts, holidays in Hawaii, a resort in Banff. The editorial frontispiece was a schematic drawing of a hog, showing the various cuts of pork. "The reason we put that pig there," said Luce, "was that we wanted to establish that we were not talking about abstractions but real things, like 'here's a damn pig.' " This was the opening illustration for Parker Lloyd-Smith's article on Swift & Company, the first published corporation story; the title, "Tsaa-a Tsaa-a

Tsaa-a." Bourke-White always thought the subject was "a wonderful choice. Certainly most of our readers would not expect to find beauty in the Chicago stockyards. But to Parker and me, the interior of the Swift meat-packing plant . . . had a Dantesque magnificence." Later *Fortune* would develop a distinct and literary style of its own; in the first issue many articles echoed *Time* in such tortured syntax as "Beautifully certain are the ministrations of the killing room to the rows of carcasses which were hogs," or "In mammoth dust-heaps ends the pig." The article was very bullish on Swift & Company: ". . . Nothing but an unimaginable outbreak of vegetarianism can interfere with Swift's basic structure and basic prosperity."

Turning from this exhaustive survey of meat-packing, the reader was confronted with an article written by Luce in quite a different, matter-of-fact style, and so headlined as to deter all but the most dedicated reader: "Banking, Group and Branch: A 10,000-word survey of the chief current problem in American finance." To this, Secretary of the Treasury Andrew Mellon contributed a brief, non-committal introduction. Luce's thesis was that bigger banks were needed to provide better credit service and branch banking was a natural outgrowth of the new industrial society. "The Machine has despatched us," he wrote, "upon an adventure in consolidation and organization. . . . On the whole, we like extraordinarily well the huge neighborhood into which our lives are cast." Moreover, he argued, extension of branch banking would help to offset the "disgraceful record of bank failures in the United States."

Variety was added to all this weight: an article on the Radio Corporation of America, in which David Sarnoff was called "Puck of Radio"; a study of the Biltmore Hotel profit-and-loss account; a discussion of the economics of orchid-growing. For human interest there was a profile of "A Gentleman Funded Proprietor," Arthur Curtiss James ("America's greatest railroad stockholder"), whose life revolved around a Park Avenue mansion, a palace at Newport and the world's largest square-rigged yacht. Luce's sister Elisabeth was then living in France. Parker Lloyd-Smith called on her to go to Paris, Vienna and London to assemble a family album of the Rothschilds. Items of business news were summed up in a department entitled

142

Transactions, and a column, Off the Record, added such gossipy bits as "Professor Irving Fisher, Yale's great economist, sleeps in an electric bed" and "To Mr. James N. Gamble, of Procter & Gamble Co., is served each day one special dish. It is called 'graveyard stew,' and consists of a bowl of applesauce, into which graham crackers are broken, and upon which is poured a pint of milk."

A sense of anticipation, however premature, was reflected in the annual report for 1929, issued in March 1930:

> . . . It is hoped to have the venture on a profitable basis before the end of the year. . . . Confident of success, *Fortune*'s guaranteed circulation for 1930 is 30,000. It went to press at the close of the year with 110 pages of advertising in its first issue, most of the accounts on a monthly basis.

The ability of the Company to produce a full-fledged magazine in advance of publication of the first issue is in marked contrast to the early beginnings of *Time*. It was possible only because of a strong financial position and a tremendous goodwill among subscribers and advertising customers.

The first issue was very well received. The New York *Times* called it "sumptuous to the point of rivaling the pearly gates"; Owen D. Young of General Electric said he was "overwhelmed"; Walter Teagle of the Standard Oil Company of New Jersey thought it "exceedingly well done," and George Verity of American Rolling Mill said it was "a very unusual magazine."

Russell Davenport wrote in retrospect, "The most notable fact about the early *Fortune* was its daring; and this was a product, chiefly, of two lines of force—Luce's journalistic experience and Parker Lloyd-Smith's journalistic inexperience. *Fortune* could never have been founded by professionals alone. Luce was a professional all right, but Lloyd-Smith was the precise contrary."

Throughout 1930 *Fortune* had to make its way against the enveloping Depression. A generation steeped in a decade of prosperity was at first incredulous, then determined to conjure away hard times with a plucky optimism. "Forward America! Nothing can stop U.S.," proclaimed the nation's billboards; a song hit of the year was "Happy Days Are Here Again" from a movie appropriately entitled *Chasing Rainbows*. Neither the confidence of the country in American business nor that of businessmen in themselves was immediately shaken. An arrogance still pervading board room and management dictated that shareholder and public knowledge of corporate matters be limited to whatever management graciously chose to disclose—this and no more. *Fortune*'s determination to "inquire with unbridled curiosity" into all phases of business ran head-on into this attitude. Luce's view was that all business was invested with a public interest, but he soon discovered that in 1930 this was a radical and unacceptable proposition to many managements.

In putting the first issue together, the editors ran up against this attitude in the management of the Biltmore Hotel. The editors expected the hotel to provide figures illustrating just what determined profit and loss. The Biltmore management refused. Luce set Stillman to work; he solved the problem by going to the New York Public Library, borrowing *Hotel Management* by Lucius Boomer, hotel impresario and operator of the Waldorf-Astoria, and from that manual estimating the Biltmore operations. "Our results were so accurate," Stillman wrote, "that the Biltmore executives chose to confirm the figures in substantially the same form rather than to have us give credit to the great Lucius Boomer." The published figures revealed few secrets to Biltmore rivals; the article explained: "These figures contain in as complete detail as space permits, the essentials of high-grade innkeeping in the Twentieth Century. . . . They are given in round numbers and some detail may be off by 10% or perhaps even 20%."

Officials of the Great Atlantic & Pacific Tea Company were equally uncooperative. When Lloyd-Smith told them that *Fortune* would publish an article, with or without cooperation, they agreed reluctantly to see the researcher, Florence Horn. The vice-president detailed to receive her was not informative. For Miss Horn it was an agonizingly frustrating experience, made more difficult for her because of a personal crisis—her father was dying. On one occasion, after a particularly unrewarding interview had brought her to the

144

point of tears, John Hartford, one of the two brothers who controlled the company, came into view and the vice-president offered to introduce her. He was taken aback when Miss Horn broke down: "I don't want to meet Mr. Hartford. Now that you've made me cry, *now* you want to introduce me."

The article was scheduled for the July 1930 issue. Then, at the very point of publication, an unwitting error turned A & P's stony attitude into contrition. The article contained a picture of Mr. and Mrs. Hartford which *Fortune* perforce had bought from a picture agency. When the page proof was submitted to the company, as was *Fortune*'s custom then, an enormous flap followed. "The picture must be killed," said A & P. Years earlier Mr. John Hartford had divorced his wife and married her seamstress; he had then divorced the seamstress and remarried the first Mrs. Hartford. The picture was of the wrong Mrs. Hartford. Luce, of course, killed the picture but took a certain satisfaction in refusing A & P's offer to pay the expense involved. John Hartford sent for Miss Horn, apologized for the company's treatment, and promised future cooperation if *Fortune* ever again chose to do an article on his company (which *Fortune* did in March 1933 and again in April 1938, November 1947, March 1963).

Some businessmen went to extraordinary lengths to preserve their anonymity. Orlando Weber, head of Allied Chemical & Dye, *Fortune* reported, "has never given an interview nor made a speech, and under only one document—the 1929 annual report—has he signed his name. . . . This impenetrable reticence has irritated a good many people. . . . Mr. Weber is the complete autocrat, a dictator as absolute as Mr. Ford, and rather less approachable." But *Fortune* had discovered that Weber had an Achilles' heel. He was the son of a Socialist labor leader in Wisconsin and had once been a bicycle racer known as "The Pride of Milwaukee." *Fortune* found a picture of Weber crouched over his racing bike in a striped jersey. Weber desperately wanted the picture killed; he therefore proposed a bargain which Luce and Lloyd-Smith accepted. If *Fortune* would promise not to print the picture, he would open the doors of the I. G. Farbenindustrie in Germany to Lloyd-Smith and Margaret Bourke-White. "He bought himself off," said Luce—for the moment; in 1935 and again in

1938 *Time* would refer to Weber's sporting past. By then Weber was reconciled to it and he and Luce had become friends.

Fortune's difficulties in getting corporations to open up with facts and figures were compounded by the use of women "researchers." In the first years *Fortune* writers had little or no time to do their own reporting because they were often called upon to write as many as two long articles a month. This meant that they relied heavily on the women for the facts, figures and interviews.

The roster of *Fortune* researchers had grown rapidly and numbered close to a dozen by the time the first issue went to press. They were hired in extraordinary ways and for odd reasons. One of the early recruits owed her job to the fact that she and Parker Lloyd-Smith had been members of the same wedding party. No experience or expertise was required; the theory was that what would interest the girls would interest the reader. Debutantes were hired in some cases because it was thought that *whom* their fathers knew was more important than what *they* knew. A *Time* writer remembered "the cold fury which used to fill the *Time* researchers' hearts when they would see a *Fortune* researcher walking around with her hat on. The *Time* girls used to feel that the *Fortune* girls wanted to pretend that they were just dropping in for a few hours now and then to occupy themselves with something useful in the midst of their busy social rounds."

Management bristled at questions asked by females; business executives were uneasy in their presence. When Florence Horn telephoned Westinghouse Air Brake to say she was coming to research a *Fortune* article, the incredulous reaction was, "Did you say *Fortune* is sending down a *woman?*" The unhappiness of the Westinghouse people increased when they had to let Miss Horn eat in the directors' dining room because there were no other restaurant facilities in the factory.

Patricia Divver, arriving in Boston to research a story on the shoe business, was treated with gallant condescension. However, a few days of her relentless questioning changed the climate, and some time later she received the following letter:

When Mr. Schwarcz [executive of one of the companies involved] first heard that a mere woman had been assigned to the

146

shoe machinery story, I think he had some misgivings, or at least was a bit surprised. He rather expected that the conversation would be similar to that of Gracie Allen at the baseball game. How completely you have overcome that first prejudice! Very early we both developed a tremendous admiration for the way you approached the job, and your knack of sensing what it was all about.

Miss Divver, who some years later was elected to *Fortune*'s Board of Editors, owed part of her success to the fact that she, like Miss Horn, had had some experience in the *Time* Business News department. Most of the girls, however, had to learn their jobs on the job. Those who survived the rigorous demands made on them became a corps of capable business journalists who more and more came to command the respect of the various managements. In a letter to Director William Griffin written some three years after *Fortune* started, the managing editor of *Fortune* spoke with pride of the professionalism of his research staff and the stiff qualifications a newcomer was required to meet:

A girl is not much use to us unless she has had a college education, majored in economics and had a high scholastic record. In addition to which we now require at least two years' work elsewhere. You can readily understand how important it is to us to have people we can entirely rely on when we send them into new companies whose everlasting impression of the magazine will be based on research interviews. You may or may not remember the unhappy repercussions of the first two years of *Fortune* when we were accused of basing our interpretation of business on the opinions of flighty young ladies who popped in asking stupid questions. If we put these ugly rumors down it is because our research staff has become professional.

The pre-publication planning for *Fortune* had not fully anticipated the staff needs; in its first year the magazine was undermanned and, as the small bank of articles accumulated against the first months of publication dwindled, writers and researchers found themselves hard pressed to meet deadlines. There was little system. "Sometimes Luce used to

147

take Lloyd-Smith's place and managing-edit a whole issue," said Russell Davenport. "On one of these occasions, late at night, with the printer, the proofroom and the research department in a dither, he exclaimed: 'My God, if *Fortune* had a system it would have broken down tonight!' "

The *Fortune* staff had to be strengthened; the magazine needed both a full-time business manager and an experienced editor capable of assisting Lloyd-Smith. Luce found his business manager when an old friend and fellow member of the Yale *Daily News* called on him with an interesting proposition. Pierrepont Isham Prentice believed that the New Bedford (Massachusetts) *Times,* of which he had been managing editor, was for sale and he hoped Luce would buy it and restore him to his old post. Prentice at this time was the news editor of the Philadelphia *Record,* a job which he thought had a limited future. Luce was not interested in buying a newspaper, but he did offer to make Prentice business manager of *Fortune.* Prentice would have preferred a place on the editorial staff, but the offer had more promise than his current post and he signed on.

For the post of associate editor William Griffin recommended Ralph McAllister Ingersoll, then managing editor of *The New Yorker.* Griffin knew Ingersoll because they were married to half-sisters. Like Luce and Hadden, Ingersoll had gone to Hotchkiss but was several classes behind them and neither knew him in school; he matriculated at Yale's Sheffield Scientific School and so the three men had little contact at the University; however, as managing editor of the *News,* Luce published a letter by Ingersoll that stirred up a campus row of brief notoriety. Graduating in 1921, Ingersoll worked as a mining engineer in California, Arizona and Mexico, wrote a book, *In and Under Mexico,* that led him into journalism as a reporter for the New York *Morning American.* He was hired by *The New Yorker* in its early struggling days because in the course of his interview for a job, Harold Ross, the editor, had accidentally knocked over a bottle of ink, spoiling Ingersoll's new Palm Beach suit. "Okay, you're on," said Ross in embarrassment; as Ingersoll closed the door in leaving he heard Ross shouting, "Hell, I hire *anybody!*" After five years on the magazine, Ingersoll felt that ". . . the excitement of its creation was

148

over and the leadership I had felt in Ross had evaporated. It was about that time, and in that state of mind, that I received my first overture from Harry Luce's organization." [3]

Luce was impressed by Ingersoll's journalistic background, and Ingersoll was impressed by Luce. His steady rise in Luce's confidence from their first encounter gave him briefly a commanding and important position in the company. His personality did not always endear him to his colleagues. One of them has described him not too amiably as "a tall, stooping man, bald except for an encircling fringe, with a compensating moustache; fleshy nose, full lips, protuberant and mournful eyes that could freeze into a choleric stare." [4] Another, recalling a hypochondria strange in so positive a character, remarked that his desk was littered with "drops, salves, sprays, ointments and unguents." Somewhat maliciously, he was once described as "twelve yards of quivering mucous membrane."

Ingersoll responded enthusiastically to the fresh journalistic challenge in *Fortune*. The magazine was exploring an exciting new field that hitherto had been largely neglected or at best superficially reported by the press at large. Some of the subjects covered in the first year of publication show how wide and far the magazine ventured: oil; nitrogen; the revolution in Hollywood brought about by talking pictures; the House of Mitsui in Japan; Gandhi's independence movement and the prospect it promised for the economic betterment of India; the gold standard; the story of the Turksib Railway in the U.S.S.R., just completed under the direction of "Big Bill" Shatov, a former I.W.W. agitator in the United States; and an article by Henry Cabot Lodge arguing that the U.S. should maintain a strong navy (v. advocates of naval disarmament). Luce had reason to feel well pleased with his venture into "the largest of the planets which make up our system."

Luce was not so pleased by some troublesome rumors that presently reached his ears: that companies were buying their way into *Fortune*'s pages. These rumors were probably inevitable in view of the publicity

[3] *Point of Departure* (Harcourt, Brace & World, 1961).
[4] T. S. Matthews: *Name and Address* (Simon and Schuster, 1960).

derived from an article. The president of Gulf Oil told his daughter that Texaco had paid $50,000 for an article on that corporation. She was a friend of Mrs. Luce, and *Fortune*'s editor soon heard the story. At a dinner party Luce was startled when a young woman solemnly assured him that she had it on the best authority that *Fortune*'s rate for editorial matter was $100 a page. "I don't know which annoyed or insulted me worse," said Luce, "the story that we charged $50,000 an article or only $100 a page." When Luce received a letter implying that payment was necessary to get into *Fortune* he told Parker Lloyd-Smith that he was going to sue for slander. Lloyd-Smith laughed: "Harry, you've got it all wrong. They're not insulting you, they're paying you a compliment. They think you have a good racket going!"

Fortune was to have a last, short word on the matter in January 1931. In a letter to advertisers, F. Du Sossoit Duke, reporting on the magazine's first year of operation, said:

> Not so long ago *Fortune*'s publisher was asked how much it would cost to get a story about a certain company into *Fortune*.
>
> His reply was: "$5,000,000—and along with the article we would throw in the whole magazine, lock, stock and barrel."

By the end of 1930 *Fortune* was a promising and thriving property; its circulation guarantee had been increased by 10,000 after eleven issues. According to the annual report, written in February 1931, "For the first twelve months of publication . . . its receipts exceeded expenditures, although it did not contribute to the earnings of the Corporation . . . after charging off all expenses and setting up of customary reserves. *Fortune* is expected to contribute to the Company's profits in 1931."

Even with the ebbing tide of business, the company as a whole had made phenomenal progress: "The most successful and fortunate year in the history of Time, Incorporated . . ." *Time* had a striking gain of 17.2 percent in advertising, publishing 2,353 pages. This placed it third among all general magazines in number of advertising pages published, behind only the venerable *Saturday Evening Post* (which

150

of course had a tremendous lead in over-all revenue) and *The New Yorker*.[5] *Time*'s circulation exceeded 300,000, and the guarantee announced for 1931 was 350,000. Time Inc.'s revenues rose from $2,334,692 in 1929 to $4,008,810 in 1930; profit after taxes was $818,936, out of which the company paid $258,342 in dividends. And at the beginning of 1931 there was on hand $1,516,288 in cash and marketable securities.

To the story of *Fortune*'s beginning must be added a sad epitaph. Next to Luce, the man who had most to do with the conception of *Fortune* and its development and success was its managing editor, Parker Lloyd-Smith. By all accounts, he was not only a brilliant editor but also a blithe young man with a gift for making friends. At twenty-nine, Lloyd-Smith seemed secure, confident and successful.

Toward the end of the summer of 1931 his manner changed; he appeared tired and troubled. Usually confident and decisive, he suddenly became vague, detached and unable to address himself to his work; his colleagues attributed this to overwork. On September 15 he announced he would take the afternoon off to go flying; an amateur pilot, he was negotiating the purchase of a private plane. When weather canceled the flight, he worked all day, then dined and went to the theater with a Princeton friend. After midnight he returned to the apartment in the East Eighties where he lived with his widowed mother. The next morning his naked body was found on the eighth-floor extension of the Hotel Croydon, fifteen floors below his bedroom. He left a note:

> *Mother Charm:*
> Heat is frightful—but this is a farewell—if this is waiting—I shall wait for you. My love and gratitude always.
>
> *Parker*

"His act," the obituary in *Time* reported, "dumbfounded his associates." Luce's tribute read: ". . . Parker Lloyd-Smith possessed one of the most brilliant minds of his generation. He had a wide back-

[5] *The New Yorker*'s black-and-white page rate was $850 v. *Time*'s $1,200. The *Post*'s was $8,000.

ground of knowledge. His ability to master new facts was phenomenal. With this he combined a keen artistic taste. And as managing editor of *Fortune* in its first and formative years, he not only displayed an extraordinary executive talent, but gained the devotion of all who worked with him."

Prospering in a Depression

IN JANUARY 1931 *Time* reported the raid of 500 half-starved, drought-ruined farmers on the grocery stores of England, Arkansas (pop. 2,408). When someone tried to stop them, he was greeted with shouts of: "We want food and we want it now! We're not beggars, we're not going to let our children starve." This little item was only one incident symptomatic of the economic sickness wasting the countryside and the Hoover Administration's seeming inability to remedy it. Twelve months later, in its January 1932 issue, *Fortune* drew a somber if less dramatic picture of New York City in the grip of the Depression: 750,000 unemployed out of a city of 7,200,000—"160,000 of them at the end of their tether." But the writer [1] observed, "Wandering about the city looking for Disaster, the visitor from out of town will very likely find no more than he would have found in New York in any other winter—the kind of Disaster, that is, which impinges on the eye." Instead it was the kind of catastrophe that corroded the soul, and the depths of it had not yet been plumbed.

[1] James Thurber. The article was unsigned.

153

The Depression was beginning to have a sobering effect on U.S. journalism. One characteristic of the press in the 1920s—"the era of wonderful nonsense"—was the lengths to which mass media went to cater to public taste; in newspapers politics, foreign affairs and solid economic news were relegated to second place while enormous space was devoted to the new stars of the screen and the heroes of the great age of sport; in magazines the emphasis was almost wholly on entertainment. In fact, Hadden and Luce had been told by the Sunday editor of the New York *World* that their magazine would almost surely fail because readers did not want to be instructed but to be entertained. As conditions worsened, the definition of news changed; the demand for facts and explanations of what was happening increased. This was a trend which benefited *Time* and *Fortune,* as was evidenced by their rising circulations.

The position of Time Inc. versus the general state of the publishing business was strikingly stated in the annual report for 1931:

> The progress of the year just passed cannot be summarized adequately by the simple statement that a new record consolidated net profit of $847,447 has resulted from operations. [Time Inc.'s revenues that year: $4,501,486.] Rather it is to be found in the fact that the appeal both of *Time* and of *Fortune* to their readers has increased to a marked degree during the year. During a time when magazine circulation declined, the increase in the number of persons who regard *Time* and/or *Fortune* as worthy of their regular attention, is deeply significant.

Director William Griffin regarded the Time Inc. board room as the only cheerful one in town. "The men at *Time*'s meetings were young, aggressive and alert," he said. "They were even making money. Everyone else was breathing hard."

The company was continuing to expand. A radio program, *The March of Time,* launched over the Columbia Broadcasting System in March 1931, was bringing the magazine to the attention of millions previously unaware of its existence. Time Inc. was also actively experimenting with a publication in the field of building, a venture which would lead, in 1932, to the acquisition of an old and much

154

respected professional journal, the *Architectural Forum*. The story of these two enterprises is told in the next two chapters.

To accommodate the expanding staff, Time Inc. in August 1931 signed a lease for the fiftieth and fifty-first floors of the recently opened Chrysler Building, the most prestigious new address in midtown Manhattan. Against the possibility of too great expectations on the part of the staff, the announcement of the forthcoming move was accompanied by a reminder that "no money will be spent for anything but bare necessities. . . . If a desk is actually coming to pieces it will be replaced. Any piece of equipment that has any service left in it will be taken over and used. . . . Private offices will be, as now, of Spartan simplicity." Luce followed up with a warning to the staff against "extravagance and extravagant ideas," concluding, "We haven't got a cent to waste." To the directors he said, "I regret the Chrysler lease at a time when 'overhead' ought to be kept in a flexible and reducible condition. Directors are, however, invited to enjoy the view as often as possible."

The company continued to be run by a small informal group who worked collegially, with no hierarchical distinctions and with freedom for personal initiative. The driving force was Luce, who was into everything. At his right hand was Larsen; his direct responsibility was circulation, but he was forever experimenting, as with the radio program, in publicity and promotion. Stillman, who became treasurer in November 1930, looked after the money, but from time to time he would emerge from what he called "the countinghouse" to venture into special projects. In 1931, for example, he launched and carried out a pioneering market-research study in Appleton, Wisconsin, demonstrating that *Time*'s readership was concentrated in the income classes whose buying habits were least affected by the Depression, a study which was of tremendous assistance to the advertising salesmen. The sales staff was headed by Robert Johnson, but he had delegated direct management of the men to Duke of *Fortune* and a rapidly rising power, Howard Black of *Time*. A red-haired, Brooklyn-born Irishman, Black had sold classified advertising for the old New York *Telegram* before becoming one of *Time*'s earliest salesmen. He won

155

his place in the nest of Ivy Leaguers through sheer ability. A man of burning ambition cloaked under an air of genial cynicism, he was also a shrewd intuitive salesman whose fund of common sense and good judgment of men made him an excellent manager.

On the editorial side, after the death of Lloyd-Smith, Ingersoll had taken over as managing editor of *Fortune;* on *Time* John S. Martin, as he had since the death of his cousin Briton Hadden, presided as managing editor. It was a job that was becoming ever more demanding.

Time had changed since Hadden's death, but in ways that were not necessarily perceptible to the casual reader. Luce thought of it as "more complete," by which he meant a degree more serious, responsible and informative. This reflected his bent and influence. At the same time Martin was determined to perpetuate the Hadden style. Martin revered his cousin; in personality and outlook he was very much like him. Before he became managing editor he had written in every department of the magazine, was a master of the art of condensation and a literary stylist in his own right. He developed into an able editor. He was also mercurial and dominating, a merciless critic without the boyish qualities that had endeared Hadden to the staff. It was said that "half the writers wanted to kill Martin, the other half made allowances"; on the other hand, the girls liked him because he respected their function as checkers and enhanced their status. Outside the office Martin was gay, gregarious and a fine sportsman who played as hard as he worked. One writer recalled that after closing the magazine Martin would take him home and they would play ping-pong until they dropped exhausted. He spent every hour he could spare from work in field or stream, once shot a peregrine falcon from his fiftieth-floor office window in the Chrysler Building.

Martin believed that a *Time* writer's point of view should be that of "the man in the moon at the end of the current century." He cultivated a detached, benevolently cynical view of men and events. This was well suited to the editorial policy—or, rather, lack of it, for, as Martin recalled, the attitude was mugwump: "We said things were right or wrong according to our personal reaction. There were few

156

debates about what should be said. In fact, there was a surprising unanimity."

There is no record of a clash of opinion between Luce and Martin during his period as managing editor. This is rather remarkable in view of the delicate relationship between the two men. Hadden and Luce had been partners; Martin had inherited Hadden's editorial mantle, but was clearly subordinate. While he respected Luce's ability, there was between them no personal bond such as had prevailed between the two founders. Luce, mindful of Martin's feeling about Hadden, was also in a difficult position; colleagues recalled that he often treated Martin with more consideration than he extended to them.

Martin continued to work with a very small staff of writers. On becoming managing editor, to succeed himself as National Affairs editor he hired John Shaw Billings of the Brooklyn *Eagle*'s Washington staff. Billings had been acting as *Time*'s "stringer correspondent" in the capital for eight months.

The "stringer correspondent," forerunner of staff reporters who today form a worldwide corps, had been no part of *Time*'s original plan of operation. Hadden and Luce had believed that all the raw material could be found in newspapers and reference books. As the magazine grew, the newspaper accounts, particularly those from Washington, left more and more questions unanswered. In 1924 *Time* hired Henry Cabot Lodge, Jr., a member of the New York *Herald Tribune*'s Washington bureau, on a part-time basis to answer queries. He left in 1925 to join the *Tribune*'s New York staff, and was not replaced until 1928, at which time Billings was hired, together with stringers in Boston and San Francisco. Billings was recommended to Martin by Congressman Loring Black, Howard Black's brother. The son of a New York physician and the grandson of the first director of the New York Public Library, Billings was born on the South Carolina plantation of his maternal great-grandfather Senator James Henry Hammond. He spent a year at Harvard, then enlisted in the French army, serving as an ammunition-truck driver on the Aisne front, transferred to the American army as a flying cadet, and ended his service as a lieutenant and flying instructor in Texas. After a post-war year at Harvard, he went to work for the Bridgeport (Connecticut) *Telegram,* from which he was fired (so he wrote in his Time Inc. office autobiography) "for writing too goddam much purple prose." He had been seven years with the *Eagle* and had scarcely heard of *Time* when Martin made his offer. "It isn't anything very much," Billings noted in his diary, "and the time it takes is brief, but it does represent six percent return on $5,000." (His pay—$25 a month.) He hoped the job would lead to the writing staff in New York, and it did. In January 1929 Martin offered him a three-week trial writing National Affairs. If successful, Billings was to be paid $6,500 a year. Because the *Eagle* had just been sold to Frank Gannett and Billings was "anxious to get out before I was let out for economy reasons," he accepted on two days' notice.

He was installed in a cubbyhole with window, desk and bookcase, behind a glass partition and a sign, NATIONAL AFFAIRS. His three-week trial was the ordeal new *Time* writers still live through. "That first week was really rough," he said. "Martin was dissatisfied with everything I wrote, and rewrote most of it." His second week he worked from 9:30 in the morning to 11:30 every night. He wrote a piece about Elihu Root, and Martin said, "You're learning!" At the end of the third week Martin said he had made the grade—and talked expansively of a glowing future in which Billings might make $20,000 a year and be permitted to buy some Time Inc. stock.

Billings was, incidentally, the only person with solid newspaper experience to join the staff until Albert L. Furth, who had worked for Hearst, was hired in 1930. Until the late 1930s *Time* continued to hire most of its writers fresh from Eastern universities and on the basis of academic background. One of them was startled when Luce began his job interview: "I want to know what's in your mind, what you carry around with you. What do you know, for instance, about Palmerston?" Fortunately, the applicant had done a term paper on the British statesman.

Billings suffered through a long period of readjustment and insecurity. He was acutely aware that Martin, encouraging though he sounded, regarded his style as pedestrian. "It took me almost a year

158

to learn to write to Martin's general satisfaction," Billings recalled. "By 'satisfaction' I mean that three quarters of my stories passed his desk without major change." He found Luce a much more sympathetic editor; on an occasion when Luce temporarily took over Martin's desk, Billings noted in his diary: "At first I was frightened, but soon found he was much better than Martin. He gave me a free hand and made fewer changes and corrections. I like him a lot and only wish that I could work under him more."

As it had from the beginning, the *Time* work week started on Thursday; writers would select from the piles of newspaper clippings the most likely items, which were then offered as suggestions for Martin's scrutiny. When he approved the departmental lists, the checkers were sent off to dig out additional facts and fill in backgrounds.

Stories written on Friday were often discarded. On Saturday there was a further culling and writers wrote from morning to midnight in order to have copy on the managing editor's desk Sunday morning. Late Sunday afternoon the first copy, mostly for the back-of-the-book departments, went to Chicago by packet. The last copy—for the Foreign News and National Affairs departments—would clear the managing editor's desk by nine or ten Monday evening.

Writers suffered over every sentence. There was always the necessity to condense. Luce once wrote a memo to his staff on the need of sweating over copy:

> The other day a fairly interesting item was written in 50 lines. I got fussing with it. Fuss. Fuss. Fuss. I fussed for an hour. At the hour's end I had in 30 lines every single fact which was in the 50 lines—plus one or two extra facts. . . .
>
> This particular story was interesting enough for 30 lines; in 50 lines it was dull. . . . [Writers] are supposed to have time enough and to be just as willing as the M.E. to sweat and swink until they have reduced 50 lines to 30—without losing a single fact. . . .

At the end of a day wastebaskets overflowed with discarded first versions. Writers spent hours in and out of the office discussing ways

and means of writing the perfect *Time* story. They played with words
and style. One began an item: "Pantophagous is the shark." He was
asked why "omnivorous" would not do instead. "Oh, omnivorous is
just too commonplace," he said. Their preoccupation with trying to
say things differently, their determined effort to be detached and
uncommitted, inclined many of these young men to a somewhat
supercilious point of view which was all too often reflected in the
magazine. Ed Kennedy was provoked into writing this contemporary
lampoon of his colleagues, whom he called "The Genii."

> Who writes for *Time* a genius is,
> No rule controls his acts,
> He's bored by punctuation
> And superior to facts,
> One-finger type, two-finger brain,
> Six sneers and one suggestion—
> Simple the formula and plain
> For reader-indigestion.

> His deadly pen he takes in hand,
> His weapon well he primes,
> With wealth of information which
> He snitches from the *Times,*
> A phoney fact, a cock-eyed guess,
> And ethics grown elastic
> Are all the Genii ever need
> To wax iconoclastic.

> To see a head, to throw a brick,
> To wield a verbal hammer
> Involves no great acquaintance with
> Intricacies of grammar;
> If substance fails, if fact eludes,
> Out of the air he picks it—
> If obviously foolish, why
> The girls will probably fix it.

With tortured style, with coinings vile
(Tycoon, example recent)
He builds the theme that none are great
And very few are decent.
The sappy Cal, the nit-wit Herb,
Sc—Mabel, naughty Greta—
He looks upon the world, but not
As once looked its Creator.*

Well, blessed be the Genii,
With all sophistications,
Contributing immensely to
The gayety of nations,
From college campuses they come
With many a college caper,
And, unsuspecting, still they write
Their college comic paper.

* "And God looked upon the world and found it good."—Genesis, maybe, but get research.

Between the writers and the readers there was the valiant and embattled corps of checkers, who not only supplied the information required but also tried to make sure that the final product was accurate to the last decimal point. Their part was described in another, blasphemous verse by Kennedy, entitled "Research Wanted—J.S.M."

There's a rumor that the world is almost over,
The Redeemer's Second Coming is proclaimed.
As Catastrophe we'll do it, and Researchers should see to it
That their Research shall be able, potent, famed.
Call up God and ask if we can get a picture,
But for Christ's sake try to make them give it free,
There's a History of Creation in the February _Nation_—
Let Researchers get their Research and See Me.[2]

[2] "See me," scrawled on a piece of copy paper, is still a favorite way with _Time_ editors of summoning writers or researchers to discuss a point.

161

Is Christ Episcopalian, as is rumored,
Did the Holy Ghost matriculate at Yale?
God the Father, to my knowledge, never went to any college,
But call Vassar on the Virgin, without fail.
See if Judas isn't working with the Warburgs,
Ananias on the *Times* is bound to be,
The Disciples, I should guess, now are writing *Sport* and *Press*—
Let Researchers get their Research and See Me.

Tell Production to take Hoover off the cover,
We will run the Angel Gabriel instead.
And the caption, *Time*-like, witty, will be "Welcome to our city,"
But we'll make the border black instead of red.
From what bakery came the loaves in loaves and fishes?
When the water changed to wine, the vintage see;
For the Virgin Birth however there is need for small endeavor—
Let Researchers drop their Research and See Me.

At the end of the week, checkers were deep in a painful and long-drawn-out process—dotting every verified word in the copy, a red pencil dot for every incontrovertible historical fact, name, place and date. As deadlines approached, the tired writer would be faced with the dogged and equally tired researcher. He was irritated if points had to be altered, but she—not he—was disgraced if the story found its way into the weekly "errors report." The writer's cherished but inaccurate adjective, the quotation out of context, the physical description not borne out by the photograph—over these matters the battle was joined. Martin recalled how one of his favorite researchers would stand before him, politely holding her ground, pointing to the offending sentence and saying quietly, "It isn't that way; let's get it right." The girls, he said, "were the most long-suffering group of people I ever knew."

Life, a magazine of humor, in 1932 published a cartoon depicting *Time*'s editorial offices hung with portraits captioned: ". . . achieved kudos"; ". . . he blushed"; ". . . outargued." At desks sat a "Trick

162

Word Editor" playing with alphabet blocks; a "Middle Name Editor" studying *Who's Who*. An office boy opening the door to Luce's office shouted: "Short, stocky, pig-eyed tycoon Otto Drinkwater Bottomly sits, waits . . ." It was an amusing, not unfair summary of the current impression conveyed by *Time*.

Longest-lasting of *Time*'s early stylistic trademarks is the cryptic caption. It serves now, as in the beginning, to hook the reader and draw him into the text. A *Time* promotion piece once asked: "What one thing about *Time* do its critics pick on most? What one thing about *Time* calls forth the merriest favorable comment from admirers?" The answer to both questions: "Those flip captions under the pictures." Typical of the Martin period was one beneath the picture of the Queen Mother of Spain, just deceased: "They took her to the Dump." *Time* explained that the Escorial, where she was buried, means literally "The Dump."

Under Martin, *Time* continued to coin words, sometimes successfully, sometimes straining too hard for the effect achieved—i.e., the whole family of words compounded from cinema: "cinemactor," "cinemactress," "cinemaddict." The stress on physical characteristics continued. *The New Yorker* carried a cartoon showing a seedy, pot-bellied politician standing at his desk, arms flailing, shouting: "Me run for public office? Nothing doing! Think how *Time* would describe me!" Any *Time* reader could imagine. *The New Yorker*'s politician could never hope to be "intense, eloquent, bushy-headed" (as was Wisconsin's Philip La Follette); or "six feet tall, broad-shouldered, big-faced, genial" (as was Supreme Court Justice Owen J. Roberts); or "button-nosed, pugnacious, curly-headed, loose-jawed, incredible" (as was Huey Long). He could, however, come out as "buzzard-bald," like Mayor Thomas Walmsley of New Orleans; or "long-legged, large-paunched, small-eyed," like Senator James Watson. He was probably closest of all to Senator David Walsh of Massachusetts: "Tall and stout. A double chin tends to get out over his tight-fitting collar. His stomach bulges over his belt." He would never walk through *Time*'s columns, though he might "strut," "bob along," "lumber." He could be, like Treasury Secretary Morgenthau, "a bald-browed beagle baying on the trail." If he risked it, ran for

163

office, served for years, he could then count on becoming, after "as it must to all men, Death came," the "late great" with no comma.

When a reader protested: "It matters not at all that Capone is sleek and fat, that Chiang is wasp-waisted. . . . These persons' importance is in their relationship and effect on humanity [and] . . . does not arise out of physical characteristics," the editors did not agree. Appended to the letter was this comment: "Physical characteristics are an inevitable concomitant of personality. And personalities are the stuff of which history is made. *Time,* historian, must continue to notice noses large and small, waists wasp or fat." But when *Time* described Dr. S. Parkes Cadman as "a bag-jowled, voluble Congregational clergyman," the *Christian Leader* huffed: "Except that the article ignores the main facts . . . and everything pertinent, it is useful in using up space which might be filled with other Smart Aleck witticisms and cynicisms, which are the main stock in trade of the publication."

The magazine ran into a storm of criticism when it referred to Franklin D. Roosevelt's "shriveled legs." This description came as a double shock because newspapers did not picture him in a wheelchair and refrained from reference to the aftereffects of poliomyelitis. Leo M. Brown of Mobile, Alabama, wrote, "How can you justify the utter cruelty?" Another reader demanded to know "who is your editorial writer so completely lacking in a sense of common decency and good taste?" The editors attempted to justify their description by arguing that by not ignoring his infirmity

> . . . *Time* conveys the full significance of a man, paralyzed in the prime of life, rising above what to another man might have been an insuperable hindrance and going on to high national destiny. It was of historic interest that one of England's greatest Chancellors of the Exchequer, Viscount Snowden of Ickornshaw, is a cripple. *Time* never unduly stressed that circumstance, but *Time* never glossed it over. . . .[3] Were Mr. Roosevelt sensi-

[3] A moot point. Among *Time*'s references to Snowden: "His deep-lined face white as a handkerchief, wizened [Snowden] hoisted himself to his feet and, leaning heavily on his two canes, advanced . . ." "Philip Snowden, the crippled Chancellor . . . more gnome-like than ever as he stumped on his canes . . ."

164

tive on the subject, the case might be altered. But his whole attitude is one of gallant unconcern.

Without stressing the subject, and certainly never with malice or disrespect, *Time* will continue to regard Mr. Roosevelt's legs as mentionable—unless a great majority of *Time* readers commands otherwise.

The controversy continued for some weeks, until it was terminated with this curt editorial note: "No clear majority of readers 'commands otherwise.' Score of letters through last week: 238 *con,* 252 *pro.* This *Time* construes as a firm mandate to continue mirroring Nature. . . ." Nevertheless, over the next few years there were fewer and fewer references to Mr. Roosevelt's infirmity.

It was Luce who finally decided that his writers and editors had gone far enough, if indeed they hadn't overreached themselves, and he issued the following dictum:

No more cracks please about Mr. Gielgud's nose.[4] Long experience has taught us that what hurts people most is a reference to some physical characteristic—and this is also what readers most resent our saying about people in whom they have no personal interest. . . . Any reference to any characteristic is peculiarly the responsibility of the M.E. This means that any writer who says a man has a nose as big as a hockey puck is putting the M.E. on a spot—because if the M.E. doesn't catch it, it is the M.E. who is peculiarly at fault—and the M.E. is apt to become annoyed with a writer who pitches him too many sour balls. Obviously this does not mean a ban on physical characterizations. What it does mean is that physical characterizations are to be given the first call on our best journalistic skill, sensitivity and sense of responsibility. Hereafter if a king is to look like a dentist [5] or if anybody is to have a nose as big as a hockey puck, he will have it for *Time*'s best considered reasons. . . .

[4] John Gielgud had been described as "a sensitive and intelligent Englishman of 32 with a nose the size of a hockey puck."

[5] King Alexander of Yugoslavia was regularly termed "dentist-like." To a dentist reader who wrote asking the meaning of the description, *Time* replied: "[He] has about him an air, not quite clinical, of cleanly meticulousness commonly found in dentists. He also, on occasion, wears a white coat."

165

It is clear that *Time* went overboard on physical characterizations; some were offensive, all too often they were merely clumsy. But it is no apologia to say that physical description is often as essential to journalism as it is to history.

One small but significant new indication of the increasing seriousness with which *Time* readers were taking their magazine was the letters protesting the appearance of Al Capone on the cover when he was released from prison. Hadden and Luce had always taken care in choosing covers; for many years the artist S. J. Woolf, who drew many of the early black-and-white covers, was listed on the masthead among the weekly contributors. It was not for some years that the cover was linked with a long article which, in addition to sketching the personality of the cover subject, would attempt to add background on an important situation. However, the cover article became such a distinctive feature that many readers felt that by selecting Capone *Time* had inferentially honored the man identified as Public Enemy No. 1. *Time* published three columns of their protests with this comment:

> If it is considered an honor to be pictured on *Time*'s cover, *Time* is glad that is so. But in selecting national figures for its cover, *Time* does not presume to be "honoring" those figures. If they are outstanding nationally or internationally, that is solely and definitely to their own and to society's credit and not by virtue of anything *Time* has done for them. . . . *Time* was aware in advance of the day upon which Gangster Capone would once more be at large in the land. Recognizing him as the personification of an "underworld" which continues [to be] a national phenomenon, *Time* estimated [him] to be easily man-of-the-week and acted accordingly. Let objectors quarrel, not with *Time* but with those conditions—whatever they may be—which bring forth objectionable national "monsters."

It was an issue that would rise again later in connection with the choice of a "Man of the Year." This practice began with the first issue of 1928, when Charles A. Lindbergh was selected; the editors named

166

him 1927's "Man of the Year" to justify their selection of him for a cover months after his flight to Paris. This was done because they regretted that *Time* had not printed more on the man and his feat at the time, and it was a way to justify a reprise of the biggest news story of the year.

At various times the magazine drew cries of rage from almost every religious bloc for flippant or irreverent treatment of matters considered sacred. When relics of saints were referred to as "teeth, bits of jaw, tibia, femur," *Our Sunday Visitor,* a Roman Catholic publication, retorted, *"Time* tries to serve up the weekly platter of news in a form pleasing to the appetite. . . . The dinner expected to please sometimes disgusts." *Time* also freely identified persons by race or religion—Jew, Catholic, Protestant—even when the identification had little significance. *Time*'s description of George Gershwin as "a young Jew" brought a protest—which Rabbi Felix Mendelsohn, of Chicago, dismissed, however, as "Jewish hypersensitiveness." After the Nazi persecution of the Jews began, this practice, always questionable, was deemed by many Jews to be an indication of prejudice. When *Time,* in reporting the closing of the banks in New York and Illinois, gratuitously identified Governors Henry Horner of Illinois and Herbert Lehman as Jews, a reader directly raised the question in such a way that Luce himself felt compelled to answer:

> . . . if the pages of *Time* were scanned for the past ten years it would be found that the reference to a man as a Jew occurs far, far more often to the praise and honor of the race or religion than to the contrary. Many prominent Jews have been pictured on the cover of *Time.* To name but a few: Adolph Ochs, Einstein, Eugene Meyer, the Marquis of Reading, the late Mr. Rosenwald, etc., etc. . . . *Time* does hold as a matter of plain observation that whether a man is a Jew is often of more intrinsic interest than whether he is a Baptist. It perhaps ought not to be so. It is perhaps a sad reflection on the Baptists that their religious connection is a point of such minor interest. . . . But the point is, that to say a man is a Jew *usually* conveys more

information than to say he is a Baptist. . . . I believe you mainly want a categorical answer to a categorical question. And the categorical answer is that *Time* harbors no racial or religious prejudices and that its influence is decidedly on the side of breaking down prejudices of whatever sort.

Luce was sincere in stating this to be *Time*'s policy, and he was to restate it before the decade was out. Thereafter in its coverage of domestic news *Time* was more careful to have a tenable reason for identifying a person as a Jew.

Evidence of *Time*'s rising influence was its marked effect on journalism, both at home and abroad. Some newspapers, notably the Oregon *Journal* and the Des Moines *Register* and *Tribune,* for a time published *Time*'s Foreign News section as a special Sunday feature. But syndication was dropped because Larsen felt it detrimental to *Time*'s own growth. Newspapers emulated *Time*'s methods in various ways. In 1932 *Editor & Publisher* quoted George Olds, managing editor of the Springfield (Missouri) *News & Leader:* "*Time* is not only a threatening competitor but a worthwhile style book. . . . For thoroughness of detail, vividness of description and the graphic simplicity of its literary style *Time* is as far ahead of most newspapers as the radio is behind them." *Variety* reported that *Time* was replacing the *American Mercury* "in its influence upon young newspaper reporters and budding writers in the great open spaces. Where a few years ago city desks, and other depositories for the written word, were inundated by pseudo-Menckens and conscious or unconscious imitations of the *Mercury*'s style, today the pattern seems to be the short, crisp, comma-studded phraseology typical of *Time*. . . . But editors avow it is the biggest nuisance in journalism today."

Not all editors agreed; Frank Gannett, of the Gannett newspapers, enjoined his editors and writers to read *Time* and write in the same manner. *Time* had a direct influence on Fleet Street. Lord Beaverbrook, a diligent reader, put the magazine on the "must" list for editors of the *Daily Express* and the *Evening Standard*. Imitations of *Time* proliferated abroad: *Today* in Australia, *Hoy* in Chile, *Cavalcade* in Britain.

168

Attempts to copy *Time*'s style often produced a ludicrous parody of the original. When this happened it was not the imitator, but *Time,* that was held to account—viz. this editorial in the Ottawa *Journal:*

> The magazine *Time* has set a style for writing in the news weeklies which we do not count as one of our blessings.
>
> Thus *Cavalcade,* published in London, copies *Time* very frankly, even to the use of sentence construction which is supposed to be "smart" and sharp but actually is confused and obscure.
>
> *Cavalcade,* as an example, reports a visit to South Africa of Sir Leslie Frederic Scott, Lord Justice of Appeal, and says:
>
> "Chief Scott delight-giver is unspoilt countryside, well-planned towns. . . ."
>
> This sort of thing may be extremely smart, but it is bad writing. "Chief Scott" might be the head of an Indian tribe. On second or third reading one realizes that this is what the writer was trying to convey:
>
> "Sir Leslie's greatest delight is in unspoilt countryside, well-planned towns."
>
> Why he did not say it that way is one of the mysteries of the style for which *Time* more than any other publication is responsible.

Criticism of *Time* was one reason cited for launching a direct competitor in the U.S. Rather remarkably, in the depression year 1932 *Time*'s first Foreign News editor, T. J. C. Martyn, succeeded in raising substantial capital for such a venture from an impressive list of backers which included the Cheney family, John Hay Whitney and Paul Mellon. Martyn's prospectus argued that "some people feel *Time* is too inaccurate, too superficial, too flippant and imitative" and promised that his magazine would be "written in simple, unaffected English [in] a more significant format [with] a fundamentally sober attitude on all matters involving taste and ethics." Obviously this was a very minor reason cited primarily for promotion purposes. The success of *Time* had revealed a fertile new field of publishing which the promoters of *Newsweek* were eager to exploit.

On publication of the first issue (February 17, 1933) Martyn sent a copy of his magazine to Luce with a note saying that he hoped "you will take some degree of satisfaction from the knowledge that a former *Time* man is competing with you . . . on the friendliest possible basis." Luce responded with best wishes for "a long and useful life"; *Time* noted the appearance of *News-Week* (with a hyphen at birth) with a thirty-seven-line item under Press. Martyn underestimated the amount of capital needed to enable his magazine to compete with *Time,* and in order to survive, *Newsweek* required several transfusions of new money. In the course of reorganization Martyn lost both his original investment and his position.

Luce was confident enough of his organization and its business prospects by May 1932 to take off on a three-month trip around the world. He went west by train to Seattle and Vancouver to sail for Japan on the *Empress of Canada,* a journey which made him conscious of some of *Time*'s failures; from Seattle he fired off a letter to Larsen and John Martin complaining, "We *do* muff news from the *U.S.A.* I *never* leave New York that I don't hear a great story which *Time* should have had."

He was particularly upset over one *Time* stringer, a part-time circulation agent who on occasion answered questions from the editors and who, Luce thought, was "a sap." Luce felt that

> . . . We ought to set out to get 30 *right* editorial contacts in 30 key cities from Pittsburgh west. . . .
>
> I don't think *Time* can afford to be represented by inferior people, editorially. . . . From now on we've got to have some standards. . . . The only reason we haven't felt this more is that we haven't given much of a damn about news not appearing East of the Hudson. . . .
>
> I feel pretty strongly about this and am terribly ashamed of my laxity in letting the matter slide these several years. . . .
>
> There's a huge opportunity here—an opportunity to *really* be the national paper. If I and Martin and Billings and all the rest of the staff don't get out to the Mississippi Valley and West more, we ought to be shot.

170

He concluded, "If you want to lynch me in absentia for writing this kind of a letter as a parting shot, don't know as I could blame you. Take what comfort there is in the thought that there's so much to do you couldn't possibly do it in 48-hour *days!* And then, for a great space, forget, yours very appreciatively, Harry."

In Japan Luce was profoundly shocked by the hold that the military terrorists had on that country and its people. By contrast, he was delighted and enthusiastic about the change he found in China. He said, "In 1932 the biggest example of progress that I had ever seen was the difference between the China which I had left as a child and what I saw twenty years later. . . ." He visited Tsingtao in Shantung Province, where the Luces had spent so many happy vacations.[6] From there he wrote Larsen in a euphoric mood:

> If Tsingtao were within even seven days of New York I would no longer debate the matter of a summer home. . . . The cares of the world have almost (not quite!) slipped behind the mountains. The newspapers from Tientsin and Shanghai carry abbreviated N.Y. stock quotations. I learn that Steel on Wednesday was 24. Good Lord! Isn't that damned depression over yet?

In two and a half pages of typewritten notes Luce reported the news and gossip he had picked up in Nanking, Shanghai and Hankow. Among the items:

> Wide and far among the Chinese is the belief that Chiang is reincarnation of a great sea beast which used to live in the waters and sun himself in the sands near Ningpo, Chiang's birthplace. (Check birthplace.) Dictionary gives iguana as translation of Chinese word for this beast but Pearl Buck says it really isn't the iguana (a giant lizard?) but more like a great shellback turtle. Nevertheless, I think we could nickname Chiang "Iguana"— Chiang ("Iguana") Kai-shek. Belief that all great men are rein-

---

[6] Dr. and Mrs. Luce had been called back to the U.S. again in 1925 to raise funds for Yenching University, and had not returned to China. Nearing retirement, Dr. Luce was teaching in the Chinese Department of the Kennedy School of Missions at the Hartford Seminary in Hartford, Connecticut.

carnation of *great* beasts or of stars is very common among the people. . . .

One of Chiang's numerous political enemies had criticized him for having "a medieval mind." "I rather think there is something in this," Luce wrote. "The nickname 'Iguana' might be a neat way of suggesting it."

Luce took the Trans-Siberian Railway to Moscow, spent four days there, and moved on to Poland, again by train. *Fortune* in March had published a special section on the Soviet Union; his notes from the Soviet Union, Luce wrote to his colleagues, were "set down as addenda and, in part, corrections to *Fortune*'s March opus." But, he added:

> I saw no more than any lazy tourist might see, and I have little faith in my observations and overhearings. . . . First of all, I was amazed to find that Russia is, as advertised, 100 percent proletarian in appearance. Somehow this picture had never quite fixed itself in my imagination. Of course, there are no well-dressed people—but what astounded me was that there are no *neatly* dressed people. They are all sloppy and boorish. . . . Thus it becomes apparent that your correspondent took a violent dislike to the U.S.S.R. I think it is a thoroughly disgusting place. It is, what I saw of it, a place completely without charm. Since boyhood I have been traveling in many countries, and I think never before have first impressions caused me to dislike a country. . . .
>
> Undoubtedly these notes overemphasize the sourness of the bread in the mouths of the Russians. To give a sweeter picture I would have to repeat most of *Fortune*'s article . . . a great performance. . . . But I do think that it omitted the stink and the sourness of Russia.

The notes concluded with the startling contrast Luce felt in passing from Russia into Poland. When he left the Russian *wagon-lit* at the border and stepped onto the Polish train, he said, "It seemed to be the

172

most beautiful railroad car in the world. Clean, glistening, all steel, immaculate. A waiter came running up, bowed. Would we have some ice cream and cake? A few minutes later I sat, content, looking out the window. My God! Where were we? In England? In France? Look at the velvety fields, all neat in their patterns of green and gold. The perfectly cylindrical haystacks. . . . And people—girls waving at us gaily. And two buxom *Hausfrauen* positively stylish in black dresses trimmed with white lace, each under a parasol. And still the fields and a great abundance of dustless air. Paradise! . . . Never in all my tens of thousands of miles of travel has a border seemed to signify so much."

In Paris a letter awaited him from Larsen. The Democrats had nominated Franklin D. Roosevelt and the result, according to Larsen, was that "Bob [Johnson] has changed his outlook on *Time*'s advertising. . . . There is no question but that that nomination did help depress us all, at least in the East."

Luce had no particular reaction to the nomination of Roosevelt. He personally supported (and voted for) Hoover, but had no strong partisan feeling against the Democratic candidate. Except on the tariff issue, the platforms of the two major parties were virtually interchangeable, and Roosevelt waged a conventional campaign, promising to balance the budget and reduce taxes. Walter Lippmann failed to see in Roosevelt the qualities of a dynamic leader, but concluded that he was the better choice because he had a better chance of being able to deal with Congress and the Republicans were economic isolationists. Many of the nation's intellectuals (e.g., Elmer Davis, Stuart Chase, Reinhold Niebuhr) felt that the only honest vote in 1932 was one for Socialist Norman Thomas.

Time reported the campaign with no bias that was discernible to any but uncompromising partisans. *Fortune,* which then had no editorial page, presented one article by the President's friend and confidant, the commentator-historian Mark Sullivan, defending the Hoover record. But this was more than offset by an article entitled " 'No One Has Starved' . . . which is not true . . . ," a devastating attack on Hoover's "diffuse, unrelated and unplanned relief program" before the passage of the Federal Relief Act, written, but not signed, by Archibald MacLeish. It accepted as accurate an estimate by University of Chicago Professor Paul H. Douglas that there were 10,000,000 unemployed in the U.S. and that 34,000,000 Americans were living without adequate incomes. (There were at the time no official statistics of unemployment.) The article was illustrated with paintings by Reginald Marsh, one of which depicted "Outpost of a Hundred Cities: Hooverville." The filthy and horrifying shacks that had sprung up outside the cities, homes of thousands of the unemployed, were to haunt Hoover's campaign. They were the symbols of a failure and portended Hoover's defeat.

After the election Luce felt personally relieved by Roosevelt's victory. "The country will feel better and that's fine," he said. *Time* commented:

> . . . In his campaign President-elect Roosevelt exhibited himself as a smart politician and no smart politician who wants to stay in power suddenly and violently revolutionizes the game's rules on his first deal.
>
> The Thirty-Second President emerged from the campaign fog as a vigorous well-intentioned gentleman of good birth and breeding who had large hopes for improving his country by ordinary political processes. If he lacked crusading convictions, he was at least free from his predecessor's stubborn pride of opinion. One week after his election he seemed destined to give the U.S. the kind of administration it thought it wanted rather than the kind he thought it ought to have. . . . The country seemed ready and waiting for him to lead. . . .

Roosevelt was named Man of the Year for 1932, and *Time* asked, "Will he make good in the White House? The country is only too ready to hope so. . . ."

Time Marches On the Air

I N THE LATE TWENTIES and early thirties, adapting its editorial
material and technique to the new and burgeoning medium of
radio, *Time* had a far-reaching influence on the presentation of
news on the air and was a factor in bringing to its listeners greater
coverage of news and public affairs.

Roy Larsen's primary reason for going into radio was to promote
Time; the program that resulted may fairly claim to have been a precursor of the radio and television documentary. *Time*'s involvement
with radio began in 1928, when Larsen received a request from Fred
Smith of station WLW in Cincinnati for permission to use material
from *Time* in a news broadcast, an inducement being that the magazine could buy an announcement on the same program for $25 a
week. Larsen gave Smith permission and bought the announcements.

Smith came back with a new suggestion: that *Time* develop its own
radio program. Larsen then decided to hire Smith, and together they
worked out a format which Larsen named *Newscasting,* a title copy-
righted by Time Inc. It consisted of a radio script containing items of
about 100 words each, drawn from the current issue of *Time* and

175

offered free to stations in return for credit to the magazine. It was first broadcast over thirty-three stations. *Tide* described the program as "in no way designed to compete with . . . 'spot news.' . . . It either carries material not usually found in newspapers, or gives a new interpretation of occurrences already reported." *Newscasting* tried to avoid the impression that it was competing in spot news reporting, which at that time was largely sponsored by newspapers and strictly limited by most of them to brief bulletins. But some newspaper editors took exception; Larsen reported to Hadden and Luce that they thought the program was "unethical." The program continued, but the criticism was a portent of the press-radio friction that continued in the 1930s and still finds an echo in current press criticism of radio and TV reporting.

Successful as was *Newscasting,* Smith believed that he could reach still more listeners by rewriting *Time* material in the form of dramatic sketches. He had written what he believed was the first original play for radio, as well as a number of other early radio dramas. His experiments were so promising that Larsen decided to launch a new program called *NewsActing.* It employed a small cast of actors, plus sound effects, and was recorded. Because recording techniques of the time limited such transcriptions to five minutes, the program lasted ten minutes—two records. These were offered free to radio stations in exchange for mention of *Time.* The rather rudimentary sketches had novelty and more than 100 radio stations agreed to broadcast the program. But the resulting publicity playback was not very good. Larsen said, "We weren't hearing about it—we couldn't tell anybody when it was coming on the air and we couldn't promote the magazine directly."

NewsActing, like *Newscasting,* pointed up the radio public's avid appetite for news and public-affairs programs. Radio, with programming largely dictated by advertisers and overweighted with entertainment, much of it vapid, was best described by one of its pioneer performers, Fred Allen, as a medium in which "oleaginous-voiced announcers smoothly purred their commercial copy into the microphones, enunciating each lubricated syllable." [1]

[1] Fred Allen: *Treadmill to Oblivion* (Atlantic–Little, Brown, 1954).

Some industry leaders, notably Lee de Forest, the inventor whose work in electronics contributed much to its development, believed radio was killing its audience. "The present all too marked tendency of the broadcast chains and of many individual stations to lower their bars to the greed of direct advertising will rapidly work to sap the life-blood . . . of this magnificent new means of contact . . . ," he said in a speech in 1930. "The radio public is, I believe, becoming nauseated by the quality of many of the present programs." De Forest was wrong; the quality of programming did not improve and the audience kept on growing. In this situation lay Time Inc.'s opportunity.

Smith, like Larsen dissatisfied with *NewsActing,* proposed that it be supplanted by a network program produced live with the "ten best radio actors," an "announcer extraordinary," a "splendid orchestra" and a "clever director." Thus *Time,* he argued, "could take its proper place at the head of Magazines-on-the-Air," a reference to the fact that the *Literary Digest* was then sponsoring Lowell Thomas on NBC. This was an ambitious and expensive proposal involving the possible expenditure of several hundred thousand dollars. Larsen warmed to the opportunity of bringing the magazine to the attention of a wider audience and of impressing advertisers with *Time*'s importance.

Luce was reluctant because he did not think *Time,* as a magazine, would appeal to the radio audience; he was impressed, however, by the success of *Newscasting* and *NewsActing.* At first he was unhappy because neither Smith nor Larsen could come up with a prospectus for their enlarged show. Luce was always wary of new ideas that could not be outlined on paper. But Larsen persisted: "I would try to explain . . . that this was journalism and *showmanship,* and showmanship threw out the possibility of having any pattern. So he threw up his hands and said, 'I don't understand any part of it, but I like it.' "

Five months of experimentation preceded the first broadcast of the new program. During this period Larsen and Smith had the help and encouragement of the Columbia Broadcasting System. On Friday, February 6, 1931, a test program was produced in a CBS studio and piped by telephone wire to a small, select audience in Larsen's home. Among those present were Luce; the managing editors of *Time* and

177

Fortune, John Martin and Lloyd-Smith; William S. Paley, president of CBS; Fred Smith; Larsen; and Bruce Bromley, a partner in Cravath, de Gersdorff, Swaine & Wood, Time Inc.'s counsel. Most listeners were critical: the show was "unworthy of the magazine," "too sensational," "inaccurate," etc., etc. But Bromley overcame the objections by declaring that it was "the greatest thing I have ever heard on radio."

The program was scheduled for a thirteen-week cycle over twenty stations of the Columbia network. Batten, Barton, Durstine & Osborn, the advertising agency, was selected to handle the show, and Arthur Pryor, Jr., son of a famous bandmaster and head of the agency's radio department, became its producer.

The title was suggested by the musical theme chosen for the show, Harold Arlen's "The March of Time," originally written for the eighth edition of Earl Carroll's *Vanities.* The first broadcast was preceded by the first closed-circuit preview in radio history, a special dress rehearsal staged by CBS for the stations in its basic network, where radio editors of newspapers listened to the program. The show was broadcast on Fridays at 10:30 p.m. The first program, March 6, began with a fanfare followed by bars from "The March of Time." Then as the music faded a voice intoned:

On a thousand fronts the history of the world moves swiftly forward—

(Music up and end)

Tonight the Editors of *Time,* The Weekly Newsmagazine, attempt a new kind of reporting of the news—the re-enacting as clearly and dramatically as the medium of radio will permit of some memorable scenes from the news of the week—from *The March of Time!*

(Music Up)

A thousand new details, new facts in the world's history, come into being every hour. In India, at midnight, nut-brown Mahatma Gandhi comes out of conference with Viceroy Lord

178

Irwin, tells his followers that peace with England is approaching.

In Peru, three men . . . all have been president within the past week.

From every corner of the world come news facts about politics, and science, people, crime and religion, art and economics. There is one publication which watches, analyzes and every seven days reports the march of human history on all its fronts. It is the weekly newsmagazine—*Time*.

Tonight with *The March of Time,* a new kind of reporting of the news, let's review some of the dramatic events of the week.

(Orchestra—Fanfare)

Chicago! In the executive offices on the fifth floor of the City Hall, adherents of the Mayor have gathered, to celebrate with their chief his victory at the polls. . . .

So began the re-enactment of the victory celebration of "Big Bill" Thompson, the mayor of Chicago who gained some notoriety in the 1920s by promising to "punch King George in the snoot." There were six other episodes, of which the most interesting was the dramatization of the death of the New York *World,* which had just suspended publication as an independent newspaper. The introduction and setting for each episode was read by an actor designated as "The Voice of *Time.*" His voice was the element that, along with the music, unified the program, which invariably concluded with the line "TIME MARCHES ON!" The only commercials—brief promotional announcements for *Time*—came at the beginning and end and were also read by "The Voice of *Time.*" The first two "Voices" were Columbia's star announcers, Ted Husing and Harry Von Zell. In 1935 a young actor who had been a member of the cast since the earliest broadcasts became "The Voice of *Time.*" On the air and in the movies, the basso and portentous voice of Cornelius Westbrook Van Voorhis reverberated throughout the land reminding all men that "TIME MARCHES ON!"

All episodes were based on articles that appeared in the current issue of *Time,* which went on sale the day of the broadcast. Writing was on

179

a very tight schedule, as the author, in most cases, was preparing his first draft as the magazine was going to press; he had to have his copy finished not later than Tuesday afternoon. The sketches were checked for accuracy and wherever possible the dialogue was based on verified quotations. If direct quotations were not available, the writer was permitted to invent dialogue consistent with the facts. Announcements at the beginning and end of each program clearly labeled the program a re-enactment.

When the first draft was ready, casting began and preliminary musical scores were prepared for Thursday rehearsal. Larsen was an exacting editor. "Roy was obsessed with the idea that nothing could be right the first time," said Smith. There were changes and additions even after Friday's final rehearsal, right up to performance time. At which moment, when the red light signaling ON THE AIR flashed, *Redbook* magazine reported: "Those involved in the production who are neither in the grave nor the madhouse . . . bring you the dramatized news of the week. . . ."

Though the cast was large, actors were required to double in roles and shift accents during the program in impersonating different characters and nationalities. "Hitler" always spoke in German-accented English. The directors were unsuccessful in getting Chinese and Japanese actors to speak "pidgin" English; a Jamaican, Juano Hernandez, usually played Oriental roles. The impersonations were often uncannily close to reality. The Count de Covadonga, hearing an impersonation of his father, King Alfonso XIII, speaking to the Spanish people, said, "It is the very voice of my father." Among members of the cast who later attained star status were Kenny Delmar, who became "Senator Claghorn" on Fred Allen's show; Agnes Moorehead; Ted de Corsia; and Orson Welles, who later startled the nation with his own *March-of-Time*-like version of H. G. Wells's *The War of the Worlds*.

Sound effects played an enormously important part, and *The March of Time* made extraordinary demands on ingenuity and skill. CBS boasted that Mrs. Ora Nichols, their sound-effects expert, was equal to any demand. One of them was that she reproduce the sound of a decapitation. She obliged, after some experimentation, by slicing

180

a cantaloupe in front of the microphone and allowing one half to fall into a box of sawdust. Donald D. Stauffer,[2] who succeeded Pryor as director, recalled that "The sound engineers were always complaining that *The March of Time* made too much noise. We often blew the needle clear off the column gauge, but we never actually blew the station off the air." Two sound engineers had to quit the program to avoid nervous breakdowns.

Music was provided by Howard Barlow's versatile twenty-three-man studio orchestra. In one typical program, that of September 25, 1931, there were twenty-five separate musical cues. An episode involving the American Legion was supported by Weber's overture to *Der Freischütz* and Sousa's "The Stars and Stripes Forever," the Japanese invasion of Manchuria by Becce's "In a Critical Situation." Other music on the program ranged from snatches of Strauss's "Death and Transfiguration" to Bruch's "Kol Nidrei" and the Good Friday music from Wagner's *Parsifal*. The "Internationale" appeared frequently on the cue sheets; later, excerpts from Alban Berg's atonal opera *Lulu* were first heard on the U.S. air on *The March of Time*.

To hear recordings of those old programs is to be lifted back into American political history. Listeners to the September 25, 1931, program heard President Hoover (impersonated) addressing the American Legion Convention in Detroit. The Legionnaires, that year, were pushing two causes: a soldier's bonus based on World War I service, and the legalization of 4-percent beer.

> The world is passing through a great depression fraught with grueling daily emergencies alike to men and to governments [came the voice of the "President"]. This depression today flows largely from Europe from economic and political forces caused by the Great War, in which your service brought bloodshed to an end and gave hope of reconstruction to the world. Recovery of the world today rests and awaits in no small degree upon our country, the United States of America. Some individuals may have lost their nerve and faith, but the real American people are

[2] Later a founder of the advertising agency Sullivan, Stauffer, Colwell & Bayles.

181

digging themselves out with industry and courage. We have the resources, the manhood, the intelligence, and by united action we will lead the world in recovery. . . .

Delayed applause rumbled, cut short by "The Voice of *Time*":

In the moment of silence which follows President Hoover's last words, his audience feels that its bonus hopes have vanished, shamed away. The President turns to leave the platform. Suddenly there is a cry from the gallery:

A voice: We want beer!

Other voices: We want beer!—We want beer!

A few bars of music, then once again "The Voice of *Time*":

The President leaves Detroit with the word beer still ringing in his ears. He has killed the bonus. But the Legion votes to demand of Congress an out-and-out showdown on Prohibition by a National Referendum. . . .

TIME MARCHES ON!

The program quickly won a very large audience. In its second week, the New York *Times* listed it among the "outstanding" broadcasts; Walter Winchell, an inveterate critic of *Time,* was enthusiastic: "The mag *Time*'s broadcast is a thrill." The trade paper *Variety* judged the program "the apex in radio showmanship. It is provocative in form and potent in listener interest."

The first series of broadcasts was extended from thirteen to sixteen weeks and the second series was scheduled to run until February 1932. But as the end of 1931 approached, Luce proposed dropping the program when the second series was completed. It had cost $211,-000, a substantial sum in a Depression year. Luce wrote the directors, "I do not believe we will ever know whether this large expenditure was worthwhile. About all that can be said is (1) that the idea of radio promotion was adopted for fundamentally good reasons; (2) that as a radio program *The March of Time* has been a success. *Time* needed

182

some form of introduction to a very wide public, and this introduction has been accomplished about as effectively by *The March of Time* as it could have been by any other method for the same money." He proposed to limit the next year's general promotion budget to $80,-000 on the theory that *Time*'s advertising "should make up in brain-work what it may lack in ballyhoo."

But on the basis of the year-end figures, *The March of Time* had paid off handsomely in circulation, for, as Larsen pointed out, it had "converted what has been a disastrous circulation year for most magazines into an excellent one for *Time*. . . . For the first time in our history we will enter the new year with that year's guaranteed circulation already achieved."

In line with Luce's decision, an announcement was made on the air February 19, 1932, that the next program would be the last. Promptly, 22,231 listeners wrote in protesting this summary execution—letters which Larsen seized upon as splendid promotion; one listener threatened to throw his radio out the window. Excerpts from the letters were printed in a two-page spread in *Time*. To one fan who called the decision "regrettable," the editors replied: "It would not be so regrettable if there were many another program equally good." And in a footnote to the double page *Time* commented:

> *The March of Time* is, of course, an advertising campaign. Its specific purpose having been accomplished, *Time*'s Business Department sees no need to continue to spend some $6,000 a week on this particular form of advertising. But it now appears that the advertising is considered by many to be a public service. Whose the responsibility to continue it—*Time*'s? *Time*-subscribers'? the radio chains'? a philanthropist's? the government's? *Time* will gladly cooperate in producing *The March of Time*. But *Time* will pay for radio advertising only when it desires such advertising. Obviously *Time* cannot be expected to buy advertising when it does not want it, in order to perform public service.

This self-serving challenge understandably nettled the Columbia Broadcasting System's president, William S. Paley. "We must answer 'no' to *Time* magazine's editorial board when it asks rhetorically whether it should 'continue paying for radio advertising it does not want in order to provide radio with something worthwhile,' " he said. "We must also deny the inference thus raised."

In the fall of 1932 *Time* bowed to public demand and restored the program, signing a new contract to run from November to March. In view of the upcoming Presidential election, CBS asked *Time* to begin the series in September, and carried it for two months as a sustaining feature.

In succeeding years *The March of Time* was sometimes produced under a unique arrangement: various advertisers sponsored the program, but the editors of *Time* retained editorial control. *The March of Time* continued over the CBS network until 1937, when Larsen transferred the program to NBC. It had built an audience of millions from coast to coast, and was one of the most elaborate productions on the air; some 75 people and 1,000 man-hours of labor were required to prepare and produce it.[3]

The program had one inherent problem. The impersonation of voices without permission of the individuals impersonated worried Time Inc. lawyers from the beginning, lest this be considered an invasion of privacy. The practice was challenged in 1933, when White House Press Secretary Stephen Early requested that *The March of Time* cease simulating President Roosevelt's voice. Luce foresaw a threat to the program if others made similar requests. He argued, in a letter to the President, that the program represented "people whose affairs become matters of public interest. For while its technique is that of the theater, its validity lies in its journalistic freedom to present whatever matters may be properly deemed to interest its audience."

The White House was not moved; Early replied that if *The March of Time* continued to imitate the President's voice on the air, other programs would do it, and "the time would not be far distant when his voice would be so continuously on the air that it would be a bore to those listening in." Moreover, Early added, "We have had reports of

---

[3] Recurring series were broadcast until *The March of Time* was suspended in April 1939; it was revived in October 1941 and in somewhat different format lasted until 1945.

many individuals who tuned in while your program was on the air and thought they were listening to the President." During the election campaign of 1936 the White House did permit the program to simulate the President's voice. But in February 1937, when the President's controversy with the Supreme Court began heating up, Roosevelt, after hearing his voice imitated on a *March of Time* broadcast, asked that the program not do so any more. The producers complied.

In spite of Luce's argument, *The March of Time* was founded on a theatrical technique which would become less and less defensible as journalism. When the program was first conceived, impersonation and re-enactment were the only methods available to cover certain subjects. At the time these techniques were not only accepted but were soon widely imitated. They were also soon outmoded; with improved broadcasting facilities the technique of the theater could not rival the drama of the news itself. No actor speaking in accented English could surpass the sense of dread and menace conveyed by hearing Hitler scream into an open microphone and the roar of his massed Nazi followers as they shouted *"Sieg Heil!"*

185

Adventure in Architecture

IN EXPLAINING WHY Time Inc. acquired the *Architectural Forum,* Luce once wrote, "To influence architecture is to influence life." In its thirty-two years of publication by Time Inc., the *Architectural Forum* had a salutary influence on American architecture and an influence on American life out of all proportion to its limited circulation.

Luce's personal interest in architecture was of long standing; his interest in publishing in the professional field antedated the purchase of the *Architectural Forum* by at least a year. In fact, he intended, not to buy a magazine already long established, but to create a new one. As businessmen sought a way out of the steadily worsening Depression, many came to the conclusion that what was needed was a new industrial effort on the same scale as the automobile industry, which had given such an impetus to the 1920s. The most obvious field of opportunity lay in housing; the techniques of the building industry were outmoded and the need for better homes was everywhere manifest. In an undated memo written sometime in 1931 Luce wrote, "I have been deluged during the past few months . . . with letters,

186

plans, prospectuses on the construction problem, buildings, housing, architecture of the future, real-estate financing, building materials, etc. *ad infinitum*. All tending to confirm what I have been increasingly conscious of for some time—that the next great industrial effort which this country will witness will be in building and all affiliated trades. I have received many suggestions to participate from a publisher's standpoint. . . . None of the proposed magazines quite hit the mark. . . . Finally, the novel idea has been brought in—a weekly newspaper for architects." The weekly, proposed by George P. Shutt, an unemployed salesman formerly of the *Architectural Forum,* was to aim at an initial circulation of 5,000, confined to architects; once established, the paper was to widen its audience to include members of other trades dependent on architects; an ultimate circulation of 20,000 to 25,000 was envisaged. The Board appropriated $10,000 for exploratory work and Luce turned the project over to his newly hired assistant, Charles Douglas Jackson.

Jackson, who in the next thirty years of his career would have widely varied responsibilities in Time Inc., in government, politics and diplomacy, was a close friend and classmate of *Fortune's* Parker Lloyd-Smith. On graduation from Princeton, Jackson, an accomplished linguist, intended to teach French at the college level. But his father's death obliged him to take over the family business, the importation of marble. The Depression and the subsequent collapse of the building industry wiped it out, forcing Jackson to seek a job. On Lloyd-Smith's recommendation Luce hired him as his personal assistant.

Along with Jackson, Luce assigned a writer, Washington Dodge II, from *Time's* Business section to prepare a dummy which was called *Skyline*—The Weekly Newspaper for Architects. Its columns bear sad witness to the fact that the time was not propitious for such a venture. To cite only one example: on the first page of *Skyline* the President of the American Institute of Architects warned out-of-town members to stay out of New York because there were no jobs. The last line of a column of gossip entitled "In the Loggia" read, "We wonder if there will ever be any building again."

The established architectural magazines were in the same straits as

187

the industry. In 1928 the *Architectural Forum,* which had been founded nearly forty years before as the *Brickbuilder,* had reported a profit of $150,000 and been sold to the newly organized National Trade Journals for $1,000,000. In 1931 National Trade Journals was bankrupt and the *Architectural Forum* was purchased out of receivership by Gordon W. Reed for $75,000. Reed, now Chairman of the Finance Committee of American Metal Climax, Inc., had investments in brick manufacturing and hence some interest in the building business. As publisher he brought back to the magazine Howard Myers, who had been in the same position at the time of its sale to National Trade Journals. Myers, educated in the New York public schools and the New York School of Fine and Applied Arts, had begun his career as a salesman for *Vogue.* As publisher of the *Forum* he had established a wide circle of friends in advertising and the building industry.

Reed also hired Miss Ruth Goodhue, a friend of his wife. A University of Michigan graduate who had done postgraduate work in child psychology in Vienna and Munich, she had become interested in European architecture. Though she had taught school and also practiced as a child psychologist, she had no experience in publishing. When Reed suggested she join the *Forum* she was at first hesitant, but her developed interest in architecture had deepened and the job was an interesting new challenge.

However, Reed was not interested in publishing the *Architectural Forum* as a long-term investment and wanted to sell it. Miss Goodhue, who had known Briton Hadden slightly, suggested that Time Inc. might be a possible purchaser. She made a personal call on Luce, who did not commit himself immediately. The actual sale was negotiated between Reed and Time Inc.'s Charles Stillman. For $80,500 Time Inc. acquired a 75-percent interest and a year later the rest of the stock. The total price was $111,000.

Time announced the acquisition in the issue of April 11, 1932, in its Press section under the headline "Organ of Integration":

Not largest in circulation but the richest, most expensive, most comprehensive journal of the building profession is *Architectural Forum.* Last week Time Inc., publishers of *Time* and *Fortune,*

188

announced it had bought a majority interest in *Architectural Forum*. Reasons: the several elements of the building world— architects, engineers, contractors, workmen, investors—are at last integrating a great single industry. Early advocate of that integration, *Architectural Forum* promises to be the leading chronicler of a revolution in Construction in the next decade. . . . One of the first to recognize that there is much more than esthetics to architecture, *Architectural Forum* gave emphasis to the social, economic, structural and financial aspects of the profession. . . .

As the article indicates, the *Architectural Forum,* of the professional journals then published, came closest to the idea behind *Skyline*. The magazine *Sales Management* attributed Time Inc.'s purchase to its "acutely developed sense of timeliness" and surmised that the new publishers would not have made the investment unless there was already in sight a definite improvement in building. Luce, in a letter to the trade, said this gave the new publishers "too much credit for shrewdness and too little for faith in an idea. . . . We believe that the architect, as he has been in days past, will again be the decisive factor in the rate and character of building progress." In this case Luce and Time Inc. were not gifted with prophetic vision; there was no improvement in the building business. Indeed, as Miss Goodhue said, in the months following the purchase "a trip along the graph line of building activity was like a descent into the Grand Canyon."

It was a year before any *Time*-like innovations were introduced into the *Architectural Forum,* which remained a separate organization, publishing from its own offices in the *Daily News* building with its same small staff. The first new feature was a department entitled "Building Money," a news section covering the building industry in the manner of *Skyline*. At about the same time the *Architectural Forum* became a staff-written magazine like *Time* and *Fortune*. Ruth Goodhue, who became managing editor not long after Time Inc. purchased the magazine, some years later described how the magazine began to change:

"Architectural and building magazines of five years ago [she was

189

speaking in 1936] . . . were all profusely illustrated textbooks. We were all of us then handling pictures as though they were postage stamps to be pasted into a collector's album. . . . [Now] we use pictures to provide the visual image. We use words to answer all the reasonable questions which the picture might provoke. . . . In presenting a case study of a building, we begin with a statement of the problem to be solved; we show plans and photographs of the solution, point out why it merits publication, dare to criticize what we consider to be its flaws . . . particularize on the building's distinguishing features and its relation to the general trend. All of these things were publishing innovations." Architectural journalism was entering a new phase.

However, even before these changes, the *Forum* in its first year under Time Inc. auspices scored a notable coup. Miss Goodhue persuaded Luce to give her a small sum in addition to the regular editorial budget to commission a series of portfolios of the work of European architects, written by them and printed abroad. European architecture at that period was more innovative than that in the U.S. but little known to Americans. The 1932 exhibition of the Museum of Modern Art introduced modern European architecture to the U.S. public in the work of Gropius, Mies van der Rohe, Le Corbusier. The *Forum* portfolios, running at intervals for nearly three years, provided readers with an opportunity to study it in greater depth. Miss Goodhue wanted the portfolios printed abroad because she felt that if the European architects supervised the work personally they would better project the architectural language of their own country.

It was an enormously complicated project, managed mainly by correspondence on a very slim budget. When the German portfolio ran into production problems, the business manager relented and allowed Miss Goodhue to go to Europe. This portfolio, printed in Vienna, used a new "flash dry" ink, a product that a few years later was to play an important part in the development of another Time Inc. magazine.

The portfolios, covering a dozen European countries, were not only beautifully printed but are still of some historical interest. When they were published, the concept of shelter as involving something more than a roof over the head was quite new to the U.S.; the government as planner and supplier of great units of housing was a concept still as new and unfamiliar as economic planning. The *Architectural Forum* portfolios reflect the contemporary framework of economic, political and social thinking as well as the actual building and decoration of the period.

In June 1933, with the passage of the New Deal's first major public-works bill making $3,300,000,000 available for a wide variety of construction projects, the *Architectural Forum* seized an opportunity to be of service to the building industry. In the short space of a month the staff produced an eighteen-page comprehensive guide to the new legislation, showing architects, builders and contractors how to qualify and bid on the new projects.

In quite another way the *Forum* had ingratiated itself with a hard-pressed profession. Howard Myers and his small staff personally cultivated friendship with young architects and were instrumental in sponsoring a number of competitions which provided money prizes at a time when commissions were scarce. In his autobiography [1] Edward Durell Stone wrote appreciatively of Myers' efforts: "[Myers] was sympathetic with our problems and tried to find work for us. In effect, he established his own architectural WPA. To provide us with bread and butter, he arranged competitions, got us jobs designing houses for advertising campaigns and other projects. One was a competition for a Magic Chef range. He invited several architects from all over the country to be on the jury and thoughtfully arranged to have the judgment take place in Phoenix, Arizona, in the middle of the winter. So we came, an impoverished and bedraggled group, to that beautiful resort to judge the competition. Frank Lloyd Wright lived nearby and came down to see us. When we sheepishly admitted that we were judging a cookstove competition, he said, 'Having all you fellows out here to decide about a cookstove is like aiming a howitzer at a hummingbird.' "

In 1935 Myers took over the title of editor as well as publisher.

[1] *The Evolution of an Architect* (Horizon Press, 1962).

After he became editor, the magazine became an even more aggressive champion of the new school of American architecture, presenting the work of such men as Stone, Richard J. Neutra, William Wurster and the Pereira brothers. In defending, for instance, Stone's precedent-breaking Mandel and Kowalski houses in Mount Kisco, New York, which raised such a storm that the town changed its zoning regulations to forestall any more of them, the *Forum* attacked the "unbalanced scholarship, prejudice, [and] arrogant desire for respectability" which had inhibited U.S. architecture in the past. Such outright espousal of the new men incurred the wrath of many traditionalists, brought many cancellations of subscriptions; Myers defended his editors, and the magazine remained fast in its allegiance.

This was evidenced in two very special issues. In 1934 the *Forum* commissioned four American architects—Neutra, William Lescaze, Wallace K. Harrison and W. Pope Barney—to produce designs for new schoolhouses. In proposing the project to Luce, Myers wrote: "Whether education in the U.S. is getting better or worse, little is happening to improve the buildings in which it is carried on. Inspection of the material available for our next school number disclosed the appalling fact that we could reprint the School Issue of 1922 with scarcely anyone being the wiser. From cupola to cupboard, the inevitable Roosevelt High School today is identical with its prototype of twelve years ago." The ideal designs that the *Forum*'s architects presented offered a sharp break with the past, featured open and functional arrangements of classrooms, labs, study and play areas in spreading multi-winged buildings that made use of much glass and open space and aimed at the integration of school and community activities. The issue featuring the new designs (January 1935) was a tremendous success, evoking nation-wide response; the *Forum* published an eighteen-page supplement of letters pro and con.

The other issue, stimulating wide comment and discussion, was a single-subject number on the work of Frank Lloyd Wright in January 1938. At the time Miss Goodhue approached Wright to write and supervise this issue, the famous architect was temporarily somewhat in eclipse. His work had been included in the Museum of Modern Art architectural exhibition of 1932, but he was not represented at the Chicago Century of Progress Exposition. Wright agreed to come to New York at his own expense to produce the issue, with one proviso: that he have a room in which to rest for two hours after luncheon. The issue was placed in jeopardy by Wright at one point when he told the engravers that they did not know their business and proceeded to the engraving room to improve a plate. The union served notice that if he again touched so much as one tool they would make no more engravings. This issue was the first of three special issues on Wright's work published by the *Forum*.

One of the most useful services that the *Forum* provided for the housing industry in the pre-war years was the publication of plans for small houses. By selecting and circulating the best of the new designs, the *Forum* provided builders and prospective house-owners with a wide variety of choice, including many houses in the low-cost field. Though these designs were intended primarily for the industry, collections of the *Forum*'s small-house plans published in book form by Simon and Schuster in 1936, 1938 and 1940 became best-sellers when offered to the general public.

As the U.S. rearmed, Miss Goodhue and her staff shifted emphasis once again. In November 1940 the *Forum* produced a notable "Building for Defense" issue. It provided a guide to industry on the problems and requirements of military construction ranging from reception centers for draftees to housing for civilians in defense plants.

The *Architectural Forum* was edited by a small group working informally on a strictly limited budget. They were sustained by their enthusiasm for a chosen field and the causes which the *Forum* championed: better design and modern architecture. Luce's relations with the magazine were never as close as he would have liked. The field fascinated him, and in the 1930s he was convinced that the country must be rebuilt and that the *Forum* would have an important part to play in that rebuilding. In 1935 he expressed that conviction in a new prospectus for the magazine in which he wrote:

To influence architecture is to influence life. The most widely accepted concept about architecture is that architecture is above

193

all arts *the social art.* "Design for living" is a phrase which cannot be escaped. And perhaps never before in the history of the world has it been so imperative and so possible to do something, by conscious thought and effort, about "designs for living." The reason why it is imperative to do something is that, by general agreement, the old order, that is to say the only existing order of life and thought, is passing or has already passed—and unless chaos is to intervene, a new order must be more or less consciously created—and, in terms of decades, soon. ("Either you will have architecture or you will have revolution" is the famed phrase of Corbusier.)

The building boom came not in the form that Luce anticipated but in building for defense; he continued to believe that the magazine had an important journalistic role to play in spite of the fact that events made it impossible for him to devote much time to its operation. In his prospectus Luce posed a question: Did Time Inc. have a conviction and a plan by which it could publish an architectural magazine of outstanding excellence and vigor? The answer, he wrote, "after considerable incubation, is Yes."

From 1932, when Time Inc. purchased the *Architectural Forum,* until 1941 the circulation continued to expand: from 5,500 to nearly 40,000, a remarkable growth in view of the fact that, because it was a professional magazine, subscriptions had to be limited to architects and those in related fields. Unfortunately, the *Forum* in those pre-war days only once returned a profit—$15,116 in 1937. Though the deficits were small and easily carried, the fact that the magazine continued to lose money cast a shadow over the relations between the *Forum* and central management. There was always pressure on Luce to sell the *Forum.* He was reluctant to part with it, but finally agreed that it should be sold. When a buyer was found, Luce at the last moment vetoed the sale. He based his decision not on the profit-and-loss statement but on his belief that the *Forum*'s prestige was an intangible asset valuable to the company.

Another consideration entered into his decision. He would not part with the magazine without the approval and consent of its staff.

Reluctantly the staff acquiesced in the decision to sell, but made it so plain that they preferred to remain with Time Inc. that Luce decided that, lacking their wholehearted approval, he could not go along with the deal.

Ten Years Old

WITH THE ISSUE of March 6, 1933, *Time* passed its tenth birthday; the magazine made no mention of the milestone in its own columns. Some months earlier, as part of the subscription-renewal campaign, Luce wrote a letter to subscribers referring to the coming anniversary. The circulation letters were written in a personal, almost confidential tone. In this one Luce discussed the magazine's progress, and it indicates that his view of the magazine's function had changed very little:

> *Time* was, it now appears, a sort of invention. But the invention lay not, as we perhaps thought, in its format or in its "principle of organization," or in its brevity-notion or in any other item or "formula." The invention lay in [the prospectus's] clumsy emphasis on the *instructive role of journalism.*
>
> Instruction does not arise from the mere publication of a fact. Instruction does not arise from the mere existence of brilliant or profound comment on the fact. Instruction arises only when something happens *in a reader's head.*

196

Time has devoted itself exclusively to the job of causing facts and association of facts and correlation of facts to happen in people's heads. It has been dazzled by no other purpose. It has not sought, though it has received, the acclaim of the literati. It has not sought to become, though perhaps unwittingly it is, a moulder of public opinion. It has just one axe to grind—again quoting from that prospectus: "To keep busy men and women well-informed, that is the only axe *Time* has to grind."

Thought ten years ago to be a laudable but impractical because utterly unprecedented project, *Time* today is accepted by perhaps a million people as one of the perfectly normal and obvious services of the modern world.

Some months later Luce showed the staff that he was equally unchanging as to the magazine's basic function. Over the first ten years the editorial services provided for the writers greatly expanded. The reference and newspaper-clipping library were rapidly built up, the network of stringers was expanded and was supplemented by a special query-answering service provided by the United Press. Some of the writers apparently began to feel that *Time* was now in a position to originate its own news. Luce swiftly deflated any such notions with this memorandum:

Since a good many . . . people on *Time* bridle at the suggestion that *Time* is a re-write sheet or that it gets its news out of the newspapers . . . I want to take this opportunity to make my biannual noise on this subject.

Time is a re-write sheet. *Time* does get most of its news and information from the newspapers. *Time* is not only proud of the fact, but, in fact, the genius of *Time* lies in that fact. . . .

Nothing affects my digestion so badly as to find that I am telling a *Time* writer a fact which I have read in the newspapers. . . .

It takes *brains and work* to master all the facts dug up by the world's 10,000 journalists and to put them together in a little magazine.

197

At the nadir of the Depression, the interregnum between Roosevelt's election and his inauguration, the U.S. was almost in a state of economic paralysis. Roosevelt would not take responsibility until sworn into office; without the President-elect's cooperation Hoover felt himself unable to cope with the enveloping crisis. It was symptomatic of the widespread fear that Time Inc., like many other corporations, felt obliged to take steps to preserve its liquidity. Luce and Stillman invested $150,000 in gold on the London market and withdrew another $50,000 in cash to ensure compliance with postal regulations requiring payment in advance of mailing. Luce was somewhat apologetic about these measures, assuring the directors, "Considerations of patriotism have been properly balanced with my specific obligations as Publisher of *Time* and of *Fortune*. . . . The steps taken . . . are concerned only with carrying the business through a temporary crisis." Luce reminded the directors that this was only a small portion of "some $2,500,000 of assets tied to the gold standard."

With the Executive Order of April 5, 1933, making it illegal for U.S. corporations and citizens to hold gold, Time Inc. sold its holdings. An inflationary trend was now evident, enabling Luce to carry a point in a disagreement with the directors that had simmered on and off for two years. Luce was not normally a man to quarrel with his directors; he was mindful of the great benefit the company had derived from having men of the stature of Davison and Griffin on the Board. When in 1929 Davison felt that he must resign on becoming a partner of J. P. Morgan & Co., his interest continued undiminished. In 1931, at the suggestion of Davison, Time Inc. added to its Board his brother-in-law, Artemus L. Gates, the president of the New York Trust Company. As a small company, Time Inc. was again fortunate in acquiring a director of Gates's prestige and financial knowledge.

His presence was soon felt. It was agreed that Time Inc. would follow a more conservative course, a fortunate decision: Time Inc. sold out Kreuger & Toll bonds before the Swedish financier's suicide, and a number of other securities before they collapsed. Gates opposed the company's practice of investing some of its surplus funds in common stocks, but Luce felt that unnecessary restrictions were imposed on

198

Stillman, and that his treasurer should have a freer hand. "It was Harry Luce's idea especially that a good treasurer ought to be a good speculator," said Stillman.

Just before his world trip in the spring of 1932 Luce had argued that "a certain amount of trading must be done. We dislike trading. We realize its dangers. We want to get out of the investment business entirely. But to paraphrase the words of a great President [Grover Cleveland], let us deal with a condition and postpone our theories to happier days." Gates objected and wrote Luce en route to the West Coast; he received this reply from Vancouver:

> I feel duty bound to record my unqualified disagreement with your views! . . . You oppose purchase of common stocks. I believe that purchase of common stocks *may be under certain circumstances* essential to a successful investment policy for Time Inc. So what do we do? . . .
>
> I only know one answer: pick a good man and let him do his best. . . . If you know somebody better than Stillman who is available to devote himself to *Time*'s investments (*and to no other master*) by all means let the Executive Committee appoint him. He'll have my support. But if you have no alternative to Stillman, I do hope that you can conscientiously . . . give Stillman his head.

When Luce returned in September the discussion was renewed, Gates holding his ground. The minutes note: "Mr. Gates stated his opposition to the general policy of a corporation owning common stocks at any time as a part of its investment fund. . . ." Then in April 1933, anticipating the abandonment of the gold standard and its inflationary effect, Luce and Stillman bought additional common stocks. In a letter to Larsen,[1] Luce exulted in a coup: "Week before the inflation announcement Charlie and I had sense enough to buy a few common stocks. (Thank God, the Finance Committee was out of town. . . .) The result is that we have more than made up now for the book loss

[1] Larsen was vacationing in Italy. On his return he was elected to the Board of Directors.

199

on the stocks held over from 1930 and 1931 purchases. But of course I'm kicking myself that I didn't quadruple the ante!"

Shortly thereafter the Board, which had hitherto restricted common-stock purchases to $300,000, lifted the ceiling to $500,000, provided that the treasurer maintained at least $1,300,000 in cash, government securities or highest-grade bonds; later the restriction was relaxed still further. Under Stillman's management the portfolio went through a complete transformation in 1933. At the beginning of the year, in addition to cash and government bonds, the company held long-term corporate bonds worth $1,312,000 and stocks valued at $85,000. At the end of the year it had no high-grade bonds, $750,000 in stocks and $250,000 in second- and third-grade bonds. In the new inflationary situation the position taken in common stocks had forestalled what would have been an even greater loss in bonds. In presenting this picture to the Executive Committee, Stillman wrote, "If it is to bear fruit at all, our speculative position must do so in the year 1934. . . . Now that we have a speculative position, let us hope we will be quicker to abandon it at the proper time than we were to build it up. There can be no conflict of principles involved in that happy procedure."

By now, however, even conservative counselors had conceded the necessity for a new investment policy. "No member," said the minutes, "felt that he could criticize the action of the Corporation under the present highly unsettled conditions." The annual report for 1933 noted that the "most difficult financial problem which had to be faced during the year was the question of the investment of the company's funds," and reported that they were held "one-third in cash, one-third in government bonds and short-term obligations, one-third in equities."

When the company was originally incorporated, the legal document establishing the corporation had inserted a comma between Time and Incorporated. On July 31, 1933, the comma was suppressed in a famous edict reading:

Re: Comma

From this date forth the comma between TIME and INCORPORATED is taboo. Let it never be used by any person for any reason at any time. Let it nowhere appear in print—on promotion or circulation matter, letterheads, bills, checks. Even your best friends should not use it. . . .

Henceforth let no person who puts pen, pencil or typewriter to paper forget to eschew that comma.

The management has spoken.

The memo was incorporated in the Board minutes, and a comma excised from a rubber stamp was preserved for the archives. As part of the vigorous extermination effort the company secretary wrote Luce, "Want to spend $25 to amend the Certificate of Incorporation to take the comma out legally?" Luce replied, "If that's all it costs, yes." [2]

From 1932 to 1933 the company had passed through a crisis of the economy, the bank holiday and other hazards. It had moved in a very satisfactory manner from the depths of deflation into a new period of inflation, with the help of a little speculation. In 1932 the company's profits had fallen back to $650,000. In 1933 for the first time the profit after taxes exceeded a million dollars: $1,009,628. In submitting the 1934 budget to the Board, Luce forecast another record profit of $1,625,000, adding, "I do so with mixed feelings of surprise and doubt—but mostly of surprise since I have been unable to find good reasons for translating my doubts into a lower estimate." The stage was set once more for new ventures.

Luce had already started a search for possible new projects into which the company might channel its energy. In November 1933 the staff learned, as usual by one of his memoranda, that he was thinking of new publications: "For years there have hung on the hook such ideas as *Time* in England, a new women's magazine, a children's magazine, a picture magazine, an all sports magazine, a daily newspaper," he wrote, announcing the establishment of a new Experimental Department to be headed by John S. Martin, who thereby ceased to be managing editor of *Time*. To assist Martin, Luce assigned a writer

---

[2] It was never done. On documents requiring the company to state its name "as specified in the charter," Time Incorporated inserts the comma.

and a researcher from *Fortune,* Dwight Macdonald and Miss Natasha von Hoershelman. The memo continued, "It will be the purpose of the Experimental Department to study these ideas one by one and to settle finally which of them, if any, are practicable . . . and then to undertake one or more of them. The net result . . . may be to prove that each and every one of the above ideas is 'out.' Or it may be that three or four new publications will result. Or maybe only one . . . Now is the time for . . . people to send to the Experimental Department any ideas or fractions of ideas which they may have in regard to magazine journalism. The daily newspaper is 'out' until we are satisfied that no new magazine makes enough sense."

The Experimental Department served a secondary purpose in that it removed Martin from *Time.* Martin, as Gottfried put it, "had kept the show on the road since Hadden's death and it was a back-breaking job." As managing editor of *Time,* he was becoming a problem; he was drinking heavily, not attending to his job as Luce thought he should. For more than a year Luce had been troubled by Martin's behavior but unwilling to do anything about it. "The more rope Luce gave Martin," Billings observed, "the worse Martin seemed to behave." Billings had by this time become Martin's understudy. After Hadden's death, Luce had relieved Martin whenever he was absent or on vacation, but because this was not always feasible Billings was more and more often called on to fill the breach. His apprenticeship as managing editor was almost as difficult as his initiation as a writer. The first time he acted as managing editor, Billings said, "I worked like the devil and put in extra-long hours. My one fear was that I would turn out a dull, stodgy issue, and that is just what Luce, a few days later, said I did turn out."

In June 1933 when Billings was again filling in for Martin, who was in London, Luce gave him a hint that he was thinking of making a change. He told him of Martin's troubles and said: "Martin must make a decision soon whether he's going to be editor of *Time* or not. It's a man-sized job." When Luce made his decision to create an Experimental Department, Billings was in South Carolina, halfway through a long-delayed, long-promised eight-week vacation; he cut it short to take over the job of managing editor.

202

Martin had been a brilliant managing editor; Billings was steady and predictable. He was quiet, restrained, reticent in discussing his personal affairs, rigorously separating his home life from that of the office. He deprecated his writing skill, yet the article he wrote on Calvin Coolidge's death and funeral was widely reprinted in contemporary anthologies as a model of journalistic narrative. He had an encyclopedic knowledge of U.S. history and politics. His genial exterior masked an unyielding will, but the writers liked him and, more important, they respected him. Elizabeth Armstrong, the Music writer, thought he gave the organization a sense of balance and his genius lay in "getting the best out of everybody." Robert Cantwell, one of his book reviewers, discovered that he had a literary background though he never mentioned it: "He posed as the average reader of *Time* and his attitude was that if I could interest him in a particular book, the chances were I could interest some of the readers as well." He did not change *Time*'s style, but he curbed some of the more exuberant writers. One of them observed that "he had a narrower field of fire [than Martin] and nothing would move him to widen it—as I learned when I tried some of my fancier bits on him."

Billings did not inherit a uniformly strong staff. As he recalled his early months as managing editor, "Nobody but a managing editor will ever know the agony of bad writing by staff. If he stops to rewrite, he falls far behind in his schedule. If he tosses the story back to the writer, he rarely gets anything better on the second go-around. Luce, during this initial period, was constantly critical, as was to be expected." But Luce found Billings to be an excellent collaborator and Billings looked to Luce as "a critical gadfly to keep me and the staff from getting soft and flabby. *Time* needed his running comments to keep it jacked up and taut. He had a habit of coming into the office on Sunday afternoons, reading copy, then pointing out what he called 'sour spots' to me. Now and then he would edit a whole issue and run the staff nearly ragged. Afterward he would have a session with me as to who was good and who was bad among the writers. His phrase was 'those who had interesting minds and those who did not.' He was all for discharging the latter. Once he handed me a piece of very poor copy and remarked that no managing editor ought to be bothered with a writer who turned in such a bad story. But if he did not pay lots of attention to *Time,* I'd feel that something was wrong."

Billings was never one to inflate his own importance, as managing editor or as journalist. He looked on journalism, he said, as "an honorable trade with a certain discipline, but it was certainly not a profession. It always griped me to hear fatheads inflate the importance of journalism and attribute all sorts of highfalutin qualities to it I never felt it possessed." After a visit from a Canadian publisher (Robert Cromie of the Vancouver *Sun*) who called on him with "pompous talk" about *Time*'s "responsibility," Billings noted in his diary: "Lord! As Managing Editor I make it a point never to consider public opinion or civic duty or any of that kind of twaddle invented to make journalism seem more important than it really is." With this workaday attitude Billings kept *Time* in its well-grooved routine; his complaints about the lack of a strong staff notwithstanding, his firm hand on the editorial department made, on the whole, for a smooth and relatively trouble-free operation. The discerning cover-to-cover reader saw no change in his favorite magazine and the circulation continued to grow.

The only publication directly attributed to the Martin Experimental Department was the little magazine *Letters,* which appeared in January 1934. It began as a fortnightly eight-page supplement to *Time,* accommodating the overflow of letters to the editors—"controversy, correction and information on *Time* subjects ranging from Oklahoma's Chief Justice to Prize Lies, from Andrew Jackson's pipe-smoking wife to the Loch Ness monster." It was offered free to all who asked to be put on its mailing list. When circulation reached 25,000 and publication was costing $35,000 a year, readers were asked to pay a subscription price of fifty cents a year, later raised to one dollar. Expanded from eight to twenty pages, the magazine solicited advertising.

Once *Letters* began using material other than letters to the editors of *Time* it lost some of its vitality and became a ragbag of historical curiosa, antiquarian notes and answers to such questions as "Can the pronghorn antelope outrun the cheetah and all other living crea-

204

tures?" *Letters* was always the neglected child of *Time*'s editorial department, "handed around," as one of its many editors observed, "from lap to lap like a baby with a wet bottom." Though at times expectations for *Letters* were inflated by the seeming ease with which it picked up subscribers, the circulation never exceeded 35,000 and the magazine was not a viable proposition. It was finally suspended in 1937.

The project on which the Experimental Department concentrated was the one that had top priority with Luce—the picture magazine. Obviously there was a great potential in such a publication; they had only to look to Europe for examples—the *Illustrated London News, L'Illustration,* the *Berliner Illustrirte Zeitung.* The experience with *Fortune,* which owed much of its success to pictures, also inspired experimentation. Over a six-month period half a dozen dummies were prepared; an option on the name *Parade* was acquired from a short-lived publication founded in Cleveland, but there were many seemingly insuperable problems in production. In any case, by June of 1934 Luce said he felt that "the thinking and creative imagination had run into a dead end. Not only was I dissatisfied but thought we had got off on the wrong track and that the best thing would be just to forget the whole thing for the time being."

"Telling Them What the Hell's What"

WHEN ANDREW MELLON, Secretary of the Treasury under Harding, Coolidge and Hoover, was haled into court under the Roosevelt Administration and charged with tax evasion, *Fortune* observed, "The plain fact of the matter was that Mr. Mellon had made out his tax return in one economic era and was being prosecuted for it in another." The editors of *Fortune,* in no such embarrassing situation, also had to adjust editorial sights from Mr. Hoover's era, which held business in high public favor, to the new age of Roosevelt, which found business in disrepute, the scapegoat for the Depression. The center of action was no longer in Wall Street but in Washington. By 1933 there was a marked change in *Fortune*'s emphasis; much more space was devoted to economics and politics, a journalistic consequence of the legislative revolution under way in the capital.

In his first Hundred Days, President Roosevelt proposed and Congress enacted fifteen far-reaching measures that touched every phase of the nation's economy. Just before Mr. Roosevelt's inauguration the nation had seemed on the verge of economic collapse. After the

206

Hundred Days, Walter Lippmann wrote, "At the end of February we were a congeries of disorderly panic-stricken mobs and factions. . . . From March to June we became again an organized nation confident of our power to provide for our own security and to control our own destiny." With surprising unanimity the American people supported the President in this first phase of his administration, and *Fortune's* articles of the period reflect the same feeling. Even on such questionable legislation as the National Industrial Recovery Act, which *Fortune* termed "pure socialism," the magazine was willing to go along because General Hugh Johnson and his lieutenants were no socialists. The result of the paradox, *Fortune* wrote hopefully, "may be not only the salvation of American industry but the rejuvenation in America of the now decayed and outmoded ideal of democracy itself." On such experiments as TVA the editors were equally open-minded: "Such is the laboratory for a great experiment. Such are the raw materials good and ill from which TVA prepares to fashion a civilization which, in a certain important way, is new and is significant to all the U.S."

Even when the New Deal Honeymoon ended and mutterings about the President taking the country down the road to Socialism became audible, *Fortune*—and Luce—were willing to play along. An article in the December 1933 issue was headed "What's to Become of Us?" and the lengthy subhead gave a hint of *Fortune's* answer: "Roosevelt only knows. Who is Roosevelt? The American tradition. But *does* Roosevelt know? He knows what he wants. What does he want? Industrial democracy. What is industrial democracy? Neither Wall Street in 1929 nor the Kremlin in 1934 but . . ." The article was reassuring; the writer, Archibald MacLeish, confidently told the readers:

> Both in the furniture of his mind . . . and in the background of his training the President is a product of the American tradition. . . .
>
> Any competent observer plotting Mr. Roosevelt's probable course would expect him to hold to individualism and the profit system but to insist that no man should be able to exploit the profit system to the injury of others. . . .

Granted that Mr. Roosevelt, shaped as he is by nature and tradition . . . will attempt to preserve a profit system operating under the eye of a kind of public conscience, the regulations which he is obliged to impose to enforce that end will irk only those who are irked by any limitation upon sheer industrial banditry.

Luce and MacLeish, after the article was drafted but before it went to press, had an off-the-record meeting with Roosevelt. The President made a tremendous impression on Luce. "As we came down the stairs," MacLeish recalled, "Harry grabbed me by the arm, stopped me, faced me and said, his face young and open as a boy's, 'What a man! What a *man!*'" His opinion would change, but in a memo to *Fortune*'s managing editor, Luce took a tempered satisfaction in the magazine's sympathetic coverage of the New Deal's first year:

On the whole *Fortune* did a good (though by no means systematic) job on it. We pricked the Gergesenes [1] swine idea of Inflation and we are, to date, right. We made an American out of F.D.R.—and to date we are right. We missed the practical success of CCC. We covered (though a bit late) the personalities of the New Deal. We rather fumbled the NRA codes and I think perhaps there is more code work for us to do. (General Johnson and the NRA boys are more fully covered in *Time* than in *Fortune*). We have a pretty good position in Cotton but we muffed AAA. (We should have published Secretary Wallace's "America Must Choose.")

He added that he thought that two articles were "potent scoops": one by James M. Beck, which anticipated the Supreme Court decision invalidating the NRA; the other a legal opinion of the Federal Securities Act, by Arthur H. Dean, a partner in Sullivan & Cromwell.

Fortune was still uniquely Luce's magazine. He took a great interest in the scheduling of articles, read most of the manuscripts at one time or another before publication, and frequently edited important stories. He was in on illustrations and layouts and passed on the

[1] Matthew 8.

208

covers, all of which involved the closest kind of collaboration with Ralph Ingersoll.

Ingersoll had not been particularly close to Luce until after Lloyd-Smith's death, when he became, so he said, Luce's "pupil in the Aristotelian sense. We talked about everything under the sun." Ingersoll certainly had the friendship and favor of Luce, who thought of him as a forceful and effective editor. He gave an impression of brisk efficiency, but not everyone appreciated his style. His former boss, Harold Ross, recalled Ingersoll as "a great man for system. If I gave him a thousand dollars a week just to sit in an empty room, before you know it he'd have six people helping him." One thing that appealed to Luce was Ingersoll's abrasiveness. He reacted fiercely to any threat, direct or implied, to *Fortune*'s editorial independence. When the Matson Navigation Company canceled its own and the Hawaiian Tourist Bureau's advertising because *Fortune* referred to its ship *Malolo* as "Maloler the Roller," Ingersoll wrote to Matson's vice-president:

> The Matson Line's policy on advertising is obviously no concern of the editorial department of *Fortune*. . . .
> *Fortune*'s editorial department has neither the right nor the disposition to concern itself with whether the advertising executives of American industry consider its columns worthy of advertising or unworthy.

He had the full support of Luce, who, when he heard of Matson's action, commented: "Good! Good! Ought to lose an account every month."

Fortune's operations continued to be chaotic and harrowing. In April 1933 Luce wrote a memo to the harassed researchers: "There has undoubtedly been too much wasted effort—too much unnecessary strain. . . . Mr. Ingersoll and I hope to make radical improvement during this year." A beginning had been made, Luce said, by centering the responsibility for research and the entire research organization in Allen Grover.

209

A tall spare handsome man with a gracious manner, James Allen Grover was the son of the president of the St. Louis Union Trust Company; he had graduated from Yale two years after Hadden and Luce and spent five years with the United American Lines. Injured in a plane crash of which he was the only survivor, he spent a year convalescing and then worked as a statistician in Wall Street; he was with the firm of Pynchon & Co. when it failed in 1931. Grover, unemployed, was summering in East Hampton with his wife when a friend chided him for indolence.

"What do you suggest?" Grover asked.

"Come into town some night next week," she said, "and have dinner with me and a friend of mine, John Martin, the managing editor of *Time.*"

The dinner was a success; Grover took Martin back to his mother-in-law's apartment to sleep off the celebration. In the morning Martin told him, "I'll see you Thursday."

Grover remembered some talk of his coming to work for *Time.* He showed up on Thursday, uncertain of Martin's offer. "Give me your hat," Martin said. "You're going to work this afternoon." Grover was shown into an office, handed a batch of newspaper clippings and told to write a story. He had never used a typewriter, and some time later a fellow writer found him puzzling over the keyboard. "If you are looking for the number one," he said, "you will find we use the small el." Grover wrote for several departments but primarily for Business. In 1932, at Stillman's suggestion, Grover was transferred to *Fortune* because of his Wall Street experience. At that time *Fortune* was paying J. & W. Seligman's Tri-Continental Corporation to supply a business advisory service. That was canceled and Grover took over the job. Late in 1932 Luce sent him overseas to research the Ivar Kreuger scandal. The two-part story, written by MacLeish, has often been cited as a classic example of how *Fortune* made business journalism come alive. Here is how *Fortune* described Kreuger's last hours:

The morning was Saturday, twelve March, a sunless, white-skied, pale spring day. In the Salle de l'Horloge over at the Quai d'Orsay, Aristide Briand, unembarrassed in death, exposed his

210

ironic face to the long stares of his countrymen. The Seine, swollen with a springtime flood, sucked at the arches of the Pont Royal. There was a cold wind with the smell of the charcoal stoves blown thin and gusty past the stale cafés. From the salon *au troisième* at Numéro Cinq Avenue Victor-Emmanuel you could see the raw light on the roof of the Grand Palais and the open ground with its gravel and its plane trees and the new buds swelling on the trees. By nine o'clock the hum of the taxi wheels had started on the asphalt and Mr. Kreuger, writing at the salon desk, writing three letters, two in Swedish, one in English to Krister Littorin his friend, could hear the wagons on the Cours la Reine. He ended the letter to Littorin—"Goodby now and thanks. I.K."

But Luce was not completely satisfied; his memo on Part I is a good example of the inquisitive editor at work:

The MacLeish Kreuger missed, just missed for one reason: Arch was not edited into enough plain explicitness. One intelligent reader never did get with certainty the point that Briand was buried the day Kreuger died. I was totally mystified (and disgruntled) by the paragraphs concerning the rumors about Kreuger. I don't know yet whether he had 28 women or only one. I don't know yet whether he drank himself stupid or scarcely a drop. Of course, the whole effect was swell but us literally-minded Americans—we who take *Fortune*—want to know!

Grover's impressive job of sorting out the tangled story of Kreuger's finances commended him to Luce as capable of overseeing *Fortune's* research.

Ingersoll, who had a talent for counterattack, disagreed with Luce about the urgency of reorganizing editorial procedures; it was the magazine's contents that needed the fresh approach, he argued. In his judgment, *Fortune* had been covering its field like "a slightly crack-brained and hysterical reporter." He thought the current problem was "not how to get a story but what story to get." Luce, nevertheless,

211

proceeded with his plans to improve the editorial organization. He thought that its trouble stemmed from the fact that *Fortune*'s organization was patterned after *Time*'s, although "the technique is entirely different."

The two staffs had very different attitudes. Although there had been frequent interchanges in personnel, *"Fortune*'s staff, not unnaturally, considered itself the intellectually superior," said Ingersoll, "and presumably the *Time* staff thought us nuts." In any case, Luce believed that his *Fortune* writers were not taking enough responsibility for getting the facts, meeting deadlines and suggesting illustrations. Because of *Fortune*'s elaborate and complicated production schedule, which required illustrations to go to press before the article, it was important for the writer to select the proper pictures. If pictures did not square with the text, costly substitutions had to be made.

Luce produced a memorandum:

I have come, much too slowly, to the conclusion that our form of editorial organization of *Fortune* is all cockeyed. . . .

The following is the ideal editorial organization for *Fortune:*
(1) *A Staff Writer*
Responsibility for one story each month will be entirely on this staff writer.
Responsibility for pictures as well as text.
Responsibility for facts as well as literature. Fundamentally we don't give a damn how he gets the story—whether it's written out of his head or after months of scholarship. We don't care much how it's written: it could be written sixteen different ways and still be a good *Fortune* story. Furthermore it can be about most anything—from an essay on the Gold Standard to a description of the method of making tomato juice in Alaska. All we care is that it should be a knockout *Fortune* story. What a *Fortune* story is, may or may not need definition. (I hope not!)
Now, this Staff Writer should ideally be able to write a knock-out *Fortune* story literally unaided. Actually he can't. Therefore we provide him with certain forms of assistance.
In the first place we provide him, if necessary, with an Idea—

212

which comes usually from the Managing Editor.

Second, we provide him with an Art Department. The function of the Art Department is:

(a) To help him locate and produce pictures which, owing to his ignorance of the source of pictures, he could not otherwise locate or cause to be produced.

(b) To exercise a moderate degree of artistic taste in selection and arrangement of illustrations, since the writer has little or no taste or expertness in this matter.

Third, we provide him with an Assistant. This Assistant may be male or female. He or she is responsible to no one on earth except the Writer. He runs his errands, does his dirty work, and, if necessary, repairs his typewriter and commits arson for him. But this Assistant also does some of the Writer's thinking for him.

Fourth, we provide the Writer and his Assistant with a sophisticated journalistic Economic Adviser & Critic [Grover]—for although the writer must absolutely be a considerable Economist himself, his approach to economics is through the emotional world of the imagination rather than through the cynical market place. . . .

The Staff Writer is assigned an Idea—it happens to be on May 1st and the article is wanted in the August issue. On *May 8th* he reports either:

(a) The story idea is lousy for a variety of reasons or that he has no confidence that he can get it for the August issue.

or

(b) That the story has possibilities; he doesn't guarantee it; but he proposes to attack it as follows.

Let us say he reports "b" and let us say the story is International Harvester. Managing Editor discusses his plan of attack. Responsibility for getting *into* Harvester is the Writer's. M.E. may or may not help with introductions. Writer may have certain wild notions about illustrations which M.E. turns down. M.E. sells him alternative notions.

About *May 22nd,* Writer advises M.E. that he has *got* the

story. Maybe many a missing link, many a looming quarrel, but there *is* a story. Writer has seen Economic Adviser Grover and is told Grover checks there *is* a story. This moment is the guarantee. M.E.'s peace of mind rests entirely on these guarantees. M.E. takes dreadful responsibility—if he finally schedules Harvester story for August before getting this guarantee.

From here on course of pictorial make-up and writing proceed together—Writer knows what's going on about his story *every minute*. If portrait is being painted of Legge [Alexander Legge, the man who discouraged Luce from going to work for International Harvester in 1921], Writer knows all about it. At some point, Writer & Treacy [Eleanor Treacy, the art editor] make up the pages. Writer naturally wants *twice* as many pages as M.E. can give him. Writer will battle for it. M.E. may step in and completely remake the pages. M.E. is final judge. But what he does must every step of the way be sold to Writer.

At some later point, Draft One is finished. M.E. criticizes. Draft Two. *There are no more drafts.* Either M.E. likes or doesn't like. If he likes he "edits" and that's that. If he doesn't like, he rejects and Writer's name is MUD. Here the theory breaks down. But the point is—the theory has broken down. It is a collapse. The red light goes up. I am told about it. It is all very, very sad and dreadful. There is a crisis. We recognize it as such. Probably the Writer isn't going to be fired. He has done excellent work before. Somehow we pick up the pieces—of the story and of the utterly and quite properly heartbroken writer. It is a dreadful situation. But, my God, it isn't the *normal* situation.

Normality: the M.E. accepts the story, edits it, hands it back to the Writer, tells him to deliver proof complete with headlines, captions, boxes, etc.

The story is then checked *by* the Writer! *He is personally responsible for every single statement and implication.* In his checking process he is, of course, enormously aided by his Assistant. He tells his Assistant to verify every name and date and figure. He asks himself critically where he got this fact or that notion. He has, of course, faith in Grover; anything Grover tells him is the same as from God. But the Writer, trusting here and trusting there, is completely responsible. And, among other things, we pay him to be. . . .

But the nut of the whole thing is this: No story is scheduled, no story is anything more than an "ideer" until the M.E. has a Writer's guarantee, and after the guarantee the M.E. doesn't have to do a damn thing except watch the wheels go round. . . .

The writers were sent an abbreviated version of Luce's memorandum edited and signed by Ingersoll. The researchers were startled by an abrupt note from him: "It is proposed to scrap entirely our present setup. . . . (1) Instead of a staff of writers we shall create a staff of editors. Each editor will have *complete* responsibility for articles assigned to him. . . . (2) The present research staff will be abolished. (3) From the personnel of the present research staff ex-researchers will be chosen as assistants to the newly created editors."

The Luce memorandum was an idealized rendering of something that, in the practical nature of things, could not take place, then or later. Few *Fortune* stories ever stopped at second drafts. Managing editors continued to be held finally responsible and exercised more influence over manuscripts than Luce thought should be necessary. Although the responsibilities of writers were enhanced, researchers continued to be "researchers" and were held accountable for any errors that slipped by. But the method of attack on the subject and the technique of getting an article in the magazine to this day generally follow the *modus operandi* that Luce laid down (with reservations for the "dreadful situation" which continued to be more "normal" than Luce was ready to allow). No *Fortune* M.E. would ever know a time when he didn't have to "do a damn thing except watch the wheels go round."

Fortune's editorial organization was strengthened in 1934 when Eric Hodgins joined the staff as associate editor and deputy to Ingersoll. On graduating from the Massachusetts Institute of Technology in chemical engineering, Hodgins swore "never to use as much as a Flit gun without professional assistance." He was born to be a journalist and writer, not an engineer. He edited M.I.T.'s *Technological Review,* then was successively managing editor and editor-in-chief of the *Youth's Companion* until it was sold to *American Boy.* Hodgins came to New York, sold advertising for *Redbook* before becoming its associate editor. Luce hired him on the recommendation of a mutual friend, Daniel Longwell of Doubleday, Doran and Company.

Hodgins was impressed for work at *Fortune* before leaving *Redbook.* A good month before, Ingersoll called and asked him to do a fast rewrite on a *Fortune* article. Hodgins did it on his own time, finished the job at 10:30 one evening and, on impulse, called the Time Inc. number and asked for Ingersoll. "He answered and I asked him when I should bring the manuscript over. 'Instantly,' was the reply." Hodgins was surprised to find all the lights burning in the *Fortune* office, the research girls hard at work at their desks in "the bullpen." He and Ingersoll worked on the manuscript until 3:30 a.m. He found that this was not unusual.

Hodgins had told Luce that he wanted a little time off to go abroad before taking on *Fortune.* "Well, since it's winter time," said Luce, "I should think you'd be taking the Southern route—and that would be fine because we're planning a single-subject issue on Italy. You can be the advance man for it." So Hodgins devoted most of his holiday working for a special issue on Italy, planned for the following year. He ruefully recalled that not only was he not paid for his holiday chores but that he also almost missed a bonus because he had not been on the payroll in 1933.

His first major staff assignment led to one of the most widely quoted and controversial articles *Fortune* ever published, "Arms and the Men" in March 1934. Norman Hezekiah Davis, a former Under Secretary of State and Roosevelt's ambassador-at-large, told Luce that there was a vast Middle European arms scandal that should be exposed. With researcher Katharine Hamill, Hodgins dug into it; their principal sources were a single-subject issue of a radical French magazine, *Crapouillot* (*Trench Mortar*); the galleys of a forthcoming book, *Merchants of Death,* by Helmuth C. Engelbrecht and Frank C. Hanighen; and additional documentation supplied by the Union of Democratic Control in London. When the advance proofs were read by Allen Dulles, a partner in Sullivan & Cromwell, his comment on

216

the exposé was, "I hope you're right. If you're right, it's wonderful."

The article was described in its subhead as: "A primer on Europe's armament makers; their mines, their smelters, their banks, their holding companies, their ability to supply everything you need for a war from cannons to the *casus belli;* their axioms, which are (a) prolong war, (b) disturb peace." Hodgins poured into his lead paragraph a shocking indictment of European munitions makers; it still stands as a surpassing exhibit of vivid journalistic style:

> According to the best accountancy figures, it cost about $25,000 to kill a soldier during the World War. There is one class of Big Business Men in Europe that never rose up to denounce the extravagance of its governments in this regard—to point out that when death is left unhampered as an enterprise for the individual initiative of gangsters the cost of a single killing seldom exceeds $100. The reason for the silence of these Big Business Men is quite simple: the killing is their business. Armaments are their stock in trade; governments are their customers; the ultimate consumers of their products are, historically, almost as often their compatriots as their enemies. That does not matter. The important point is that every time a burst shell fragment finds its way into the brain, the heart, or the intestines of a man in the front line, a great part of the $25,000, much of it profit, finds its way into the pocket of the armament maker.

Neither Luce nor Hodgins foresaw the repercussions. However, when business manager Pierrie Prentice read the proof, his news sense told him he had a very hot property. Edward L. Bernays, *Fortune*'s public-relations counselor, suggested that he send a marked copy to Senator William E. Borah, who had supported Senator Gerald P. Nye's resolution calling for an investigation into the munitions industry, an investigation which up to then the Senate had been reluctant to approve. Borah made a notable speech; Nye entered *Fortune*'s article in the *Congressional Record*. Together with the publication of the Engelbrecht-Hanighen book, the article helped carry the day for Nye. The publicity came flooding in and with it endorsements such as that by one of America's foremost internationalists, Nicholas Murray But-

217

ler, then President of Columbia University and head of the Carnegie Endowment for International Peace, who called the article "the greatest sensation since the World War." *The New Yorker* added this comment:

> Today, for radical reading, turn not to the *New Masses,* or to the *Daily Worker,* or to the *Nation*; turn to *Fortune,* that well-groomed organ of Big Business which sells for a dollar and to which we award the 1934 Pulitzer Prize for its article, "Arms and the Men." It is something when *Fortune,* born into the lap of capitalism and nurtured at the breast of salesmanship, begins taking the profit system apart. . . .

Much of the comment on "Arms and the Men" missed an important point. *Fortune* was exposing a situation in Europe that had very little relevance to the United States; as Hodgins had pointed out, the American munitions business was very small potatoes.

In working on "Arms and the Men," Hodgins got an insight into Luce's own journalistic attitude. After approving the final proofs, he handed them to Hodgins with the comment, "Now don't get me wrong about any of this. It doesn't mean that *Fortune* might not want to turn around next month and publish one hell of a fine story whooping it up for the biggest navy in the world!" As the *Fortune* article continued to be ever more widely quoted in support of current pacifist propaganda, Luce decided to restate the magazine's position. In his view, "Arms and the Men" was "not about the making of war. It was about the making of armaments"; the August issue published this editorial note:

> *Fortune* did not say, did not imply:
> (1) That armament makers are the sole cause of war.
> (2) That if they were eliminated, war would be eliminated.
> (3) That the situation it revealed in Europe had an exact parallel in the U.S.
> (4) That this country should spend less—or more—upon national defense. . . .
> *Fortune* does not know the answer to the armament question. But if the article stimulated the world in its search for the

solution, that is encouraging. Meanwhile *Fortune* restates its own position as that of a reporter, not a crusader.

Fortune brought out its first single-subject issue, the one Hodgins had explored, on Mussolini's Italy, in July 1934. Hodgins, by Luce's direction, was its editor. In 1932 *Fortune* had published a special section on the Soviet Union and Communism; it was Luce's idea that the magazine should now examine Fascism *in extenso*. He did not accept the widely held view that Fascism could be equated with Communism as an economic and political system. In a speech at Scranton in April 1934, he anticipated some of *Fortune*'s findings: ". . . The more you examine Italian Fascism, the more you will feel that it is not so much a system as it is a moral force. . . . The moral force of Fascism . . . may be the inspiration for the next general march of mankind. But the plan and order of march does not exist in any concrete terms. By Mussolini's own acknowledgment his Corporative State does not exist—it is in process of invention."

The Italian issue was one of the first major journalistic examinations of Fascism, its ideology, the Corporative State, Fascist finances, agriculture and industry, the relations between Party and Church, and the old aristocracy. The purpose, as *Fortune* put it in the lead article, was to discover how, under Mussolini, "the wops are unwopping themselves." *Fortune* disclaimed an over-all bias toward Fascism, explaining in a foreword: "No 100 per cent journalist can be more than a few per cent Fascist, which is to say, he is by definition non-Fascist. But the good journalist must recognize in Fascism certain ancient virtues of the race, whether or not they happen to be momentarily fashionable in his own country. Among these are Discipline, Duty, Courage, Glory, Sacrifice."

Notwithstanding the editors' disclaimer, the magazine was later criticized as having been too favorable to the Italian regime. In the light of subsequent developments, it seems that the editors might have been even more qualified in their assessment, but it is interesting that the issue was not well received in Italy. In part this was because the Fascists thought *Fortune* failed to glorify Il Duce, and in part because *Fortune* touched on the amorous exploits of Mussolini and the scan-

219

dals prevalent in Rome. *Time*'s Foreign News editor, Laird Goldsborough, who was a contributor to the issue, had ferreted out much previously unprinted gossip. In 1933 Goldsborough and Larsen had been received by Mussolini. On his way to Italy, Goldsborough had stopped off in Berlin, where Hitler's aide, Harvard man "Putzy" Hanfstaengl, had introduced him to Hitler; knowing that the Foreign News editor of *Time* would be *persona non grata* to Hitler, Hanfstaengl described him as "the architect of the Chrysler Building." When Goldsborough told Mussolini he had met Hitler, the Italian dictator exclaimed: "That *papier-mâché* buffoon. He has copied everything I have done in eleven years in three weeks! Where is he going to go from here?"

Goldsborough was apparently identified in Rome as the author of the articles to which the Fascists took greatest exception. Wallace R. Deuel, Rome correspondent of the Chicago *Daily News,* who had helped on the issue, wrote to Hodgins that it was "a damned good job. . . . You have offended the finest sensibilities of not only all good Fascists but also of several not-so-good Americans. The secret police, with that sagacity and promptness which I believe characterize secret police the world over, have been asking penetrating questions of various persons with whom Goldsborough came in contact, such as 'Who is this man Gullsboorough? What is his New York address?' and the like. The few Americans I know who frequent what is called Roman society say the number is in what they describe as bad taste. Anything which refers to the venereal exploits of the chief of government and speaks out in meeting is included under this heading. . . .[2] You undoubtedly know that the Embassy quarantined the copies you sent for us. The delicacy of American diplomats would be more impressive if accompanied by equal comprehension in other respects."

By February 1935 *Fortune* had attained a circulation of more than 100,000. Such an increase, as in the case of *Time,* seemed to surprise

[2] *Fortune* quoted Mussolini as saying: "What do I do first when I wake up? Jump straight out of bed! No matter how beautiful the head beside me on the pillow." Of the Roman aristocracy, the magazine wrote, ". . . Concupiscence is epidemic among the better beds of the town."

Luce; Hodgins remembered an occasion when he had been called into Luce's office with business manager Pierrie Prentice. As Hodgins told it: " 'What are you guys doing?' Luce inquired. We assured him we had not been doing anything. The accusation in his tone was because he had seen a circulation projection carrying *Fortune* above 100,000. 'I don't understand it. *Fortune* with a circulation of 100,000? I don't understand it at all and I don't think I like it.' With that he dismissed us." Nevertheless, Luce showed himself well aware of and anxious to please *Fortune*'s enlarged constituency, particularly when he thought the writers were not paying enough attention to it.

In describing how *Fortune* should report the political scene, Ingersoll had once said that *Fortune*'s function should

> neither be that of prophet nor expounder but that of the stern, complete factual authority, giving the reader the material with which to answer the questions the politicians will be batting back and forth over his head. They will be talking about "liberty lost" and "the forgotten man"—we will be telling them what the hell's what.

But the poets who had become economists and business writers were disinclined to confine themselves to the factual reporting of political and business news.

In the spring of 1935 Ingersoll wrote the staff that the May issue had been exceptionally good-looking, set a fine standard of research and presentation, but "Journalistically it reaches not a new high, but a new low," because of failure "to think in terms of News." To this Luce added his Amen and voiced some qualms about his writers:

> Ingersoll has clearly articulated an unhappy feeling which I have had lately about *Fortune*. . . .
>
> By way of echo, I can only cry: "For God's sake, let us have some ragged, jagged rocks of *contemporary* facts. Generalizations are exciting, too, but let them be crude generalizations, crudely stated—and the hell with the professors."
>
> Footnote: it occurs to me that paradoxically the *Fortune* editors become too interested in their work. Editors become so interested themselves in a subject that they lose all interest in

221

their readers. We are playing to an audience of 1,000,000 people. Let us therefore try to propel our jokes at least as far as the first row of the gallery.

Two months later he reverted to this theme in a memo to MacLeish, who objected to *Fortune*'s advertising promotion; MacLeish felt the advertising overstressed its readers' wealth and should concentrate more on *Fortune*'s appeal to those who truly understood, and were active in, modern industry. Luce did not agree, writing:

At 100,000 circulation, *Fortune* is far from being any millionaires' club—but the presence of the millionaires has a lot to do with paying our bills.

Fortune writers should not, I think, resent their presence.

We want to publish an unsubsidized magazine. A certain "formula" (hateful though the word is) was found in this case.

Maybe we would like to publish a magazine for intellectuals only, but I don't know how you do that except by getting *one* millionaire to pay the deficits!

Finally, it has seemed to me that it was eminently worthwhile to inform millionaires (especially the active ones).

Therefore, I think *Fortune* writers (1) ought not to resent the millionaires in the audience, and (2) should cheerfully remember that *that* happens to be the audience to which they were invited to lecture.

Remembering what the audience is that they happen to be addressing, the lecturers can use jokes and facts appropriate thereto.

There is no question involved of Truth. To use another illustration, a professor who would rather lecture in a post-graduate seminar ought not to let a class of Yale Seniors feel that he resents having to waste his time on them.

And that, I think, comes as near as I can come to stating the difference which sometimes arises between me and the staff as to "journalistic attitude."

In July 1935 *Fortune* introduced to journalism an innovation of far-reaching significance, the *Fortune* Survey, the first published pub-

222

lic-opinion poll. *Fortune*'s editors were not aware of the work which Dr. George Gallup, research director of the Young & Rubicam advertising agency, was already doing in this field; his first surveys did not appear in the newspapers until the fall. The idea of adapting the techniques of market research to the sampling of public opinion was brought to *Fortune* by Richardson Wood, who as a free-lance had written some *Fortune* articles and, while working for J. Walter Thompson, had become a "survey bug." Wood was at that time a member of the market-research firm of Cherington, Roper & Wood. His partners were Paul T. Cherington, first professor of marketing at the Harvard School of Business, later market-research director of the J. Walter Thompson Company, and Elmo Roper, who had developed an interest in analyzing consumer preferences while holding various sales positions with manufacturing companies connected with the jewelry business.

In Wood's original discussions with Ingersoll, the *Fortune* Survey was envisioned less as an instrument for measuring political opinion than as a device for discovering consumer preferences and thus unlocking market secrets withheld by most corporations. However, Eric Hodgins, who was the editor in charge of the Survey, and Cherington, Roper & Wood soon found that the answers on political and social questions were more interesting than the brand preferences of consumers. In introducing the Survey, *Fortune*'s editors cited Walter Lippmann's thesis, developed in a book entitled *Public Opinion* published in 1922, that a knowledge of public opinion was essential in a democracy. They pointed out that, having advanced that thesis, Lippmann himself confessed thirteen years later that he "knew of no better barometer of business opinion than the discredited barometer of stock-market averages." The editors advanced their claim to fill this obvious gap in public information: "It is the hope of the editors that by experiment and correction the *Fortune* Survey may come in time to enjoy a certain authority as a barometer of that public opinion the importance of which has been so well described—the nature of which has been so blankly ignored." The first contract with Cherington, Roper & Wood called for four surveys a year at an agreed price of $10,000, a figure which, Roper feared, would be unprofitable

223

In the first two installments of 1935 the Survey reflected the social revolution that was taking place in the country. Over three quarters of those polled believed that the government should see to it that every man who wanted to work had a job. The Survey provided statistical proof that public-relations efforts by a corporation *did* influence the public's opinion of it. It revealed the wide split between economic classes on the question of whether or not labor was fairly treated in the U.S. And while it recorded the widespread apathy among Americans toward foreign affairs, it discerned an uneasiness and fear about the intentions of Japan and Germany and showed a U.S. bias toward the British on the part of those expressing interest in the world. In 1936 the Survey broke ground with a daring poll that demonstrated not only that an overwhelming majority of people approved of birth control but indicated that people were willing to discuss a subject theretofore considered taboo.

The Survey won amazingly quick acceptance. Somewhat to their embarrassment, the editors found it being credited even with the gift of prophecy. The editors carefully explained that the poll was intended as a barometer, not as a precision instrument, and was subject to a mathematical margin of error as large as two percent.

The President became a regular follower of the department, and made arrangements to get advance reports as soon as Roper's figures were assembled. At one time the editors, not altogether sure that Roosevelt was really looking at the report, decided to withhold it. They promptly got a message ("Where is the Survey?") from the President's assistant, Judge Samuel Rosenman.

Its first big test came in the election of 1936; the Survey published in the October issue reported that 61.7 percent of the people with opinions were favorably inclined to F.D.R. He was re-elected by 60.5 percent.

For many years the *Fortune* Survey played an important part on the U.S. social and political scene, carefully watched by the White House and the leaders of both parties. It had the effect of extending *Fortune*'s name and influence far beyond its immediate circulation and contributed to the growing prestige of the magazine.

_____

Time Marches On the Screen

O N FEBRUARY 1, 1935, at the Capitol Theatre on Broadway, then the flagship house of the mighty Loew chain, and at other theaters across the country, there was shown the first release of a new series of short subjects, _The March of Time_. Time Inc. had entered the business of making motion pictures in an attempt to make the cinema an instrument of more effective journalism. In terms of the millions who would see this and subsequent releases, _The March of Time_ was the most ambitious publication Time Inc. had yet undertaken. As in the case of _The March of Time_ on the air, the company was venturing an experiment in mass communication which departed radically from the rationale of the magazines with their carefully selected audiences.

The first release of _The March of Time_ was the culmination of eight months' experimental work. By coincidence, just as Luce had decided to disband the Martin Experimental Department, Louis de Rochemont, director of short subjects for Fox Movietone News, was calling on Roy Larsen to propose translating the _March of Time_ radio program into motion pictures. This project became the major new

225

undertaking of Time Inc. in 1934 and 1935.

De Rochemont's was not an original idea. A few months after the first *March of Time* broadcast Larsen had learned that two Hollywood agents were trying to sell the idea to the studios, and he had written his friend Paul Hollister of B.B.D.&O.: "As this is an idea which Fred Smith and I have had ever since we started the radio re-enactments, no one can have any copyright . . . and if you know anyone who wants to make some money and have a damn interesting job, here it is." Shortly thereafter Luce's friend David O. Selznick [1] suggested that Time Inc. look into the newsreel business. Larsen replied: "Harry and I are agreed that before we even consider it, we must be sure that there is a lot of money to be made in it," adding that if they entered the field "we would of course try to change the technique." All this was in 1931. No more was done about the project until de Rochemont sought the meeting with Larsen.

De Rochemont was a man of imagination who from early boyhood had been deeply involved in newsreels; he had made his own crude camera from designs in *Popular Mechanics* and sold footage taken with it to his hometown movie theater in Chelsea, Massachusetts, where it was shown under the title "See Yourself as Others See You." As a free-lance newsreel cameraman he scored his first news beat when officers re-enacted for him the arrest of a suspect in the attempted bombing of the international railroad bridge at Vanceboro, Maine, in 1915. When the U.S. entered World War I, de Rochemont enlisted in the Navy and was commissioned; remaining in the service after the Armistice, he was attached to U.S. headquarters in Istanbul, where as officer-cameraman he shot newsreel-type footage for recruitment films. In 1923 he resigned from the Navy to enter the newsreel business, though he continued to make Navy films on contract. His work involved worldwide travel, in the course of which he scored a notable exclusive with his pictures of Indian rioting following the arrest of Gandhi, films which he had to smuggle past the British censor. On his own initiative he financed and produced a documentary, edited from newsreel archives, called *The Cry of the World,* which won critical acclaim but was not commercially successful. While

[1] Then vice-president of RKO-Pathé.

226

at Fox Movietone News he produced a series of travelogues, *The Magic Carpet of Movietone,* and another series, *The March of the Years,* foreshadowing in format *The March of Time.* These films, centered on great news stories of other years, were largely based on archival material combined with brief re-enacted scenes. De Rochemont felt the technique could successfully be adapted to *The March of Time,* and this is what he proposed to Larsen. Previous proposals for making *The March of Time* in motion pictures had been based on the assumption that the episodes would have to be wholly re-enacted, at prohibitive cost. De Rochemont proposed instead that current newsreel footage be linked with archival material, reducing re-enactment to a minimum.

Larsen was immediately enthusiastic and avid to get started. Luckily, de Rochemont had arrived at just the right moment. Luce, well disposed to some new venture, gave Larsen the go-ahead to experiment. With no other assurances whatever, de Rochemont quit his job with Movietone, setting up an arrangement with his former employer for the use of footage from its library and rental of a projection room and working quarters in the Movietone offices at 54th Street and Tenth Avenue. In June 1934, he and Larsen began work with a staff of six—film cutters, a negative matcher, a writer and an office boy. Luce did not meet de Rochemont until some time later.

De Rochemont and Larsen had no small ambition; their objective was to revolutionize the newsreel and give it a new journalistic purpose. The newsreel business was at a low ebb, one reason why de Rochemont wanted to leave Fox Movietone. But it had not always been in such sad shape. The motion-picture camera had entered journalism almost with its invention. Since before the turn of the century, it had been recording history—President McKinley's inauguration, Admiral Dewey at Manila Bay, Queen Victoria's funeral. There were cameramen following the Balkan wars and in the trenches on both sides during World War I; immediately afterward worldwide organizations for covering news had been developed. The silent cameramen risked their lives and fought one another for exclusives, and the cinema archives are richer for their initiative.

The film companies which controlled the newsreels were not run by men with journalistic aspirations; their interest was in profits to be made from the feature films, and the expenditure on newsreels seemed to them unnecessary and excessive. There was little or no profit in the newsreels because they were sold as part of a package, a sideline to the features which kept customers coming to the box office. Moreover, the editing of most newsreels was wretched. They were little more than moving snapshots of disasters or sporting events interspersed with such trivia as bathing-beauty contests and lunatic fashions. With the addition of sound in 1928, a new dimension was added to the camera's coverage but with it a new item of expense. The sound cameras were costly and heavy, and with them the cameraman lost his old-time mobility. There was more pressure to economize. Neither initiative nor creativity was encouraged, and any venture into controversial ground was positively discouraged. The producers and the exhibitors alike were spineless when confronted with any protest by politicians, local censors or patriotic groups. In 1934 Adolf Hitler was scarcely seen in any newsreel, and never in any context that might be considered unfavorable. Yet the public liked newsreels and expected exhibitors to provide one as part of every program. A phenomenon of the 1930s was the opening of theaters devoted solely to newsreels and other short subjects.

Larsen and de Rochemont aimed at producing each week a short film dealing with contemporary subjects that might be found in any issue of *Time* and *Fortune*. They did not, however, obligate themselves, as did the radio program, to draw the material directly from a current issue. What they wanted to do on the screen was what *Time* did in print—tell a story with a background and insight and in a coherent form. They first aimed at an over-all length of ten minutes —the average running time of the current newsreel—divided into five episodes of two minutes each, the whole a blend of news clips, re-enactment and dialogue, linked, as on the radio, by the vibrant voice of Westbrook Van Voorhis. One episode from the first of two short experimental reels illustrates the technique.

The subject chosen was the three-way naval-arms race among the U.S., Britain and Japan; it was introduced by pictures of Admiral Heihachiro Togo, just deceased, and as these flashed on the screen "The Voice of *Time*" reminded viewers that Admiral Togo was

228

honored and revered . . . for his victory at Tsushima—the kind of victory for which nations and navies build and spend and strive and dream for generations—the kind of victory for which Japan has built her present navy.

The film then cut to the British fleet steaming back from spring maneuvers, and the episode concluded with shots of Franklin D. Roosevelt at a recent grand review of the U.S. fleet. As the camera panned over the assembled ships the narration came to its climax:

. . . U.S. citizens have new assurance that in their navy they have a mighty fighting machine, trained, equipped, prepared to protect every foot of America's ten thousand miles of coastline.

TIME MARCHES ON!

The reactions of colleagues and friends to the first reels encouraged further experimentation. Over-all length of a third film was extended to twenty minutes, permitting fuller treatment of the episodes. The subject matter was certainly not to be found on current screens. The lead episode was devoted to the business of strike-breaking, based on an article in *Fortune*. For comedy relief, viewers were invited to consider the case of Moe Buchsbaum: an American arrested in France for speeding, he refused to pay his fine unless the magistrate agreed to remit it to the U.S. as a payment on France's war debt. The closing subject was the upcoming Saar plebiscite. The viewer saw the busy factories of that industrial basin, then shots of the statesmen of Versailles—Wilson, Clemenceau and others responsible for the impending crisis—and the film concluded with current pictures of French and German troops on the march. The narration stated the issue, explained how it had arisen, and suggested that the outcome might bring a new confrontation of ancient enemies.

The new reel was clearly an advance. Luce complimented Larsen and de Rochemont on its quality, but he also was disturbed by it, writing:

The best thing I can do is to go down into the storm cellar and try to collect my thoughts. . . . The shattering point is that Reel

229

No. 3 is not a newsreel. Then what the hell is it? Or (since it is something very swell) doesn't it matter?

With Luce no "shattering point" ever failed to matter. The retreat into the storm cellar produced another Time Inc. prospectus, largely the work of Larsen, who during the experimenting had prepared for Luce nineteen pages of handwritten notes criticizing the newsreel of the day, demonstrating how Time Inc. editing technique could be applied to the cinema, and glowingly stating the opportunity that was open in a new medium. Luce took these notes and paraphrased them into another document garnished with his own philosophizing about the importance of pictures in journalism. The document is an excellent example of how a couple of eager young men, excited about a new medium, argued themselves into venturing a fair-sized amount of their none too plentiful capital in the highly speculative business of making motion pictures.

The document—it was not formally labeled a prospectus—began by stating "The Opportunity," which was defined as "First . . . to make a better Newsreel. Second . . . to evoke articulate, nation-wide public appreciation of it." The second section described the dismal plight of newsreels. The third section, "The Moving Picture as Journalism," reflected much of Luce's thinking about pictures and journalism, some of it prophetic of a picture magazine still to be created; but principally the question was posed: Could the newsreel be regarded as a unique branch of journalism?

> *Time* believes it can [he answered]. And the purpose of the Editors of *Time* in creating *The March of Time* is to pioneer in the possibilities of moving-pictures as an instrument of significant journalism.
>
> (Parenthetically, let no one suppose that *Time* is toying with the Newsreel as a possible by-product proposition for any advertising or other subsidiary purpose. *The March of Time* is to be a major effort on the part of Time Inc., if anything.) . . .
>
> *Time* . . . believes the status of the Newsreel can be revolutionized as soon as the public realizes that the Newsreel has become a product of Journalism, produced and morally and

230

intellectually underwritten by one or more potent Journalistic reputations.

With no more ado Time Inc. was in the movie business, although the original ambitious goal of a reel on a once-a-week basis was reduced to the more practical program of producing one release a month. Approximately $40,000 had been spent on the experimental reels; another $150,000 was earmarked to see the enterprise off to a fair start, a ludicrously small sum in a field where magnates talked in millions. Luce made no bones to the directors about the fact that he was playing a long shot:

> I can give Directors little assurance as to its financial success. My guess, however, is that *The March of Time* pictures will be a big hit with a large part of the public and that out of that circumstance, despite the chicanery of the movie business, we can make some money. . . .
>
> Failure of *The March of Time* will not, I believe, positively damage *Time*'s reputation—it will simply mean that in this case *Time* will have used its reputation without profit.
>
> But there is one final point. The movie field is a colossal field. It is a field to break into which requires characteristically millions rather than thousands of dollars. Messrs. Larsen and Stillman and those who have worked with them present you with a product and with a plan by which *Time* can break into this field with some chance of success at a cost of, say, $200,000. Time Inc. can certainly afford the money and it can probably afford the "intangibles." On that basis, I think it is an opportunity that should be ventured.

The Board agreed, but only on "the express condition that such business shall be conducted separately . . . by a new corporation to be organized for that purpose." March of Time Inc. was set up as a subsidiary.

It was one thing to produce a film; it was another to book it into the theaters. Who was to undertake distribution? The reels were shown

231

to the major distributors. They evidenced little interest in taking on a new and probably unprofitable short subject that would be competitive with their own films. Stillman moved in with a suggestion to RKO, which controlled Pathé News, that Time Inc. refinance Pathé and take over its management in return for distribution by RKO of *The March of Time*. But this deal fell through. A struggling independent distributor, First Division Exchanges, Inc., was willing to handle *The March of Time,* but needed funds; for $100,000 Time Inc. acquired a 25-percent interest in First Division as an investment and thereby obtained a desperately needed distributor for its new product.

Luce could justify his gamble in grandiose arguments about journalism; *The March of Time*'s first distributors were baffled in trying to explain just why their customers should buy a brand-new short subject. Larsen recalled how one salesman sold it to the buyer of a West Coast theater chain: " 'Sam, I've got something new, something colossal—it's called pictorial journalism, but there's no point in you or me trying to understand it. To you and me it's just spaghetti on spools, but you buy it!' And Sam did."

Before its appearance *The March of Time* was heavily promoted in *Time* and *Fortune,* in advertisements in trade papers and on posters. The campaign evoked an enthusiastic response: one chain reported inquiries from more than 100 theaters; a theater owner in Washington received letters and telephone calls from more than 100 patrons asking when the picture would be shown. One manager for the Loew theater chain reported: "In all my years of experience . . . I have never seen such enthusiasm." A week before the release of the first film its editors, alarmed by the expectations aroused, reminded their loyal readers in a house advertisement that "after all, *The March of Time . . .* cannot vie with a *David Copperfield. . . .* Its only star is an idea. It will be only two reels long. . . . Nor is the idea of a single issue . . . so great as the idea of a series . . . coming, once a month, as a continuous cavalcade of our times."

The critics' reaction to the first release was encouraging; Abel Green in *Variety* called it "potent b.o." But the trade was less enthusiastic. In an account of *The March of Time,* published in 1936, the producers confessed, "*The March of Time,* it seems, had been overballyhooed." The public liked it, although Larsen watched in dismay as half the audience at the Capitol walked out after the main feature; many in the audience were unaware that a short subject had been added to the program.

Although Luce thought that *The March of Time* still needed a lot of work, *Time* gave its new sister enterprise friendly notice. The first release was reviewed not in the Cinema section, but under The Press:

. . . Just as regular newshawks make the events of yesterday live again in print, so *The March of Time* undertakes to recreate them on the screen by the simple process of going back to the scene of action and getting the characters to repeat themselves in word and deed. Examples from the first release of *The March of Time*:

—In Washington, NRA will go on trial before the U.S. Supreme Court because a small-time battery manufacturer in York, Pa. could not pay the 40¢ per hour minimum wage required by his code. No newsreel camera was on the spot when Fred Perkins was visited by the Federal marshal, told he was violating the law, but he and his wife and his workmen will never forget the scene. To York, Pa. and into Fred Perkins' home and battery shop went *The March of Time*'s photo-reporters (script-writer, director, cameramen). The story was reconstructed and rehearsed just as it originally happened. . . . Result: On the screen, *The March of Time* audiences see & hear Fred Perkins call his workmen together for counsel, hear him tell them he cannot pay more than 25¢ per hour, see him enter his kitchen after a hard day's work, hear him tell his wife that NRA has cracked down, that he must post $5,000 bail or go to jail. To jail he goes; after 18 days, out on bail he comes. [It would still be some years before *Time*'s up-ended sentences got on their feet.] Then to his aid go eminent volunteer counsel—David Aiken Reed and John William Davis—who personally re-enact their conferences with their client following his conviction in Federal Court (*Time*, Dec. 17). And *The March of Time* camera takes the Perkins case to the doorstep of the Supreme Court. . . .

233

—News to millions of cinemaddicts is the fact that the political balance of Japan, hence the peace of the Orient, centres on 85-year-old Prince Kimmochi Saionji, Last of the Genro. It is this Elder Statesman who most often makes up the imperial mind of the Son of Heaven. Yet this potent old Japanese has been completely missed by U.S. newsreels. Therefore to the tiny fishing village of Okitsu went the newscameras of *The March of Time,* with the result that shots of Prince Saionji, guarded night & day by 40 soldiers, sitting on his flower-bordered porch reading the newspapers, are the first to appear on any U.S. screen. . . .

Other subjects covered in the first release were "Speakeasy," wherein Jack & Charlie's "21" Club revealed the caches where it had hidden bootlegged liquor; "Belisha Beacons," the lights newly installed in London giving pedestrians continuous right of way; "Metropolitan Opera," the first sound pictures ever taken inside the Met (the cameramen were in white tie and tails); and "Motorist Moe" Buchsbaum's story, from the third test reel. The first release played in 417 theaters in 168 cities.

But the project was almost immediately in trouble; First Division Exchanges was a badly run, money-losing outfit. C. D. Jackson, after a trouble-shooting trip, reported, "There is no head, very little middle, and a lot of tail. We will never get anywhere with this crowd." Meanwhile Stillman was telling the Executive Committee that the company's investment had been "rendered practically worthless by the pending insolvency and possible bankruptcy of First Division." To salvage the situation, Stillman set up a new subsidiary to guarantee continued distribution of the picture. To increase revenues and entice exhibitors into showing the series, he had devised an ingenious sliding scale of rentals based on U.S. Department of Commerce reports on each city's retail sales. This produced higher returns, but involved a guarantee that if box-office receipts failed to meet expectations, half of the fees would be refunded. It was not a satisfactory arrangement. It was with relief, therefore, that management finally persuaded RKO to undertake distribution of *The March of Time* in July 1935.

234

The RKO deal led to a windfall. Before signing with the company, which was being reorganized after filing under the Bankruptcy Act, Stillman discovered that its 6-percent notes, which it had been forced to issue at one period in near-bankruptcy, were now selling at a heavy discount. Among those who held these notes and were not selling was John D. Rockefeller, Jr., who had been forced to take them in lieu of unpaid rentals for the Radio City Music Hall and the Center Theatre. On Stillman's recommendation Time Inc. purchased for $241,097 notes having a face value of a million dollars, an investment which, with the sale of some and the later conversion of others into RKO Common, repaid the company many times the loss on the investment in First Division.

The total start-up costs of *The March of Time* for 1934–35 were $900,000. But Luce felt the money was well spent; in the 1935 annual report he told shareholders they could be proud and pleased: proud because the film had "done a publishing job which can rank with either *Time* or *Fortune* in significance; pleased because profits are already in sight." There was no doubt about the public acceptance; the forecast of profit was premature.

The production of *The March of Time* was demanding, difficult and physically exhausting. That the film series was produced on schedule was due to a combination of the talents of Larsen and Louis de Rochemont. For two years Larsen devoted himself almost wholly to *The March of Time*. He went into the movie business with no knowledge of the techniques of editing film. "I started from absolute scratch, and Louis was my teacher," he said. But he brought to the new medium news judgment, writing and editing ability, and business and administrative skills. Louis de Rochemont was a man of enormous creative energy. He lived only to make pictures; the business side interested him relatively little. The staff they brought from their respective fields formed an interesting organization. Miss Celia Sugarman, Larsen's secretary, who moved over to *The March of Time* with him, recalled that "each group was fascinated by what it saw of the other and each was occasionally startled by the ignorance of the other. . . . The particular combination of top executives was in itself bound to create difficulties. They were brilliant and exceptionally

235

able, but as to temperament they had little in common."

The de Rochemont-Larsen partnership, for the first year at least, was also a silent contest of wills. Larsen was soon making and editing sequences, as well as supervising and managing. He would tell his film cutter, "Now hide this and don't let Louis see it until we are ready." De Rochemont, viewing the sequence, would re-edit it, a process inevitably leading to further changes before the final release. "One producer might have been counted on to have to stop for breath or sleep once in a while," said Miss Sugarman, "but two producers spelling each other could outlast the clock." On one occasion de Rochemont did not leave the premises for five days, snatching catnaps on the office couch and having his meals sent in. Larsen worked just as hard, often through the night in the final days before the release. One day he showed up at 9:30 a.m. and apologized for being late; he had left the office at 2:00 a.m. but on the way back to work had indulged in a couple of sets of tennis. Louis de Rochemont, according to one of his fellow workers, "could only work under pressure"; as to Larsen, "whatever the hour, he seemed to be right there, looking at you."

Something of the tension that was generated by *The March of Time* can be gathered from a memo Larsen wrote asking non-production staff to keep out of the projection room:

> . . . Please consider how apt you would be to bust in on the Editor of *Time* when he was trying to write captions . . . or change the lead of a story. . . . The Editors of *The March of Time* have to work out these problems in the projection room. . . .
>
> The closing days of a release, when the pictures are getting into final shape, and it might seem to the uninitiated to be the time that the Editors are relaxing and that your curiosity should be satisfied, are their worst days.
>
> This is sort of a defensive memorandum because the writer can understand its being taken as a sign of temperament. It isn't temperament—it's nerves. . . .

But while tension was high, so was morale. An old *March of Time* hand said, "We shared with the magazines, and with Time Inc. in

236

general, that feeling of elegance, of doing things tremendously well, and of taking pride in the least tiny thing."

The March of Time combined newsreel, documentary and a dramatic presentation in a new form of compelling journalism. In an age of electronics when television can intrude scenes of actual battle into the cocktail hour, the method of *The March of Time* is no longer accept-able as journalism. Yet TV, the modern film documentary, the new school of *cinéma vérité* owe much to its pioneering methods. The much-praised Italian movie *The Battle of Algiers* is a superior recent example of what *The March of Time* achieved in a more limited way —the re-enactment of an event so effectively that it simulates reality itself. A. William Bluem, a student of the documentary, wrote that *The March of Time* "stretched the limits of journalism by implicitly arguing that the picture as well as the word was, after all, only symbolic of reality. What mattered was not whether pictorial journal-ism displayed the facts, but whether, within the conscience of the reporter, it faithfully *reflected* the facts." [2] Luce put it somewhat more succinctly: *The March of Time,* he said, must be "fakery in allegiance to the truth." The producers did not in every case use actual films of an event or person even when available; they often used re-enactment by preference if this served better to clarify or dramatize the narra-tive. The viewer could not in most cases—nor did the producers intend him to—distinguish re-enactment from reality. But every se-quence was anchored in fact. However, as *The March of Time* matured and its resources expanded, the producers relied less and less on re-enactment and more and more on their own documentary films.

The achievement of *The March of Time* was not so much its technique as its introduction into cinema of subjects of current con-troversy and significance. In its first year it tackled such subjects as the re-arming of Germany, the Nazi persecutions and the emigration of the German Jews to Palestine, the struggle between Church and State in Mexico. On the domestic scene it focused on such current and worrisome phenomena as Huey Long's Share-the-Wealth, Father Coughlin's Social Justice movement and Dr. Townsend's Townsend-ites. It did a documentary on TVA, then big news, touched on the

[2] *The Documentary in American Television* (Hastings House, 1965).

237

Nye investigation of the munitions industry and the debate over the Neutrality Act. It also prided itself on some exclusives: the first motion pictures of Sir Basil Zaharoff, the legendary "merchant of death," and of Anatole ("Papa") Deibler, the official French executioner.

In maintaining "allegiance to the truth," the *March of Time* cameramen had remarkable success in persuading public figures and just ordinary people to become participants. Making the sequence in the first release in which Fred Perkins re-enacted his struggle with the NRA, the producers discovered that real people are often better at portraying themselves than any actor. The producers were soon stage-directing Cabinet members, Senators, politicians, labor leaders and hundreds of individuals to perform more effectively than any Hollywood extras. Colonel François de la Rocque mustered thousands of his fascistic Croix de Feu supporters to a torchlight rally in Chartres for *The March of Time*'s cameras; Father Coughlin posed for *The March of Time,* which re-enacted the extinguishing of a fiery cross that had once burned on his rectory lawn; Huey Long cooperated in a sequence which turned out to be a devastating satire; Wendell Willkie, counsel for Commonwealth & Southern Corporation, appeared as one of the principals in the TVA episode; General Douglas MacArthur assigned U.S. Army units to cooperate with a *March of Time* film unit and appeared in the same release. In the beginning, hired camera crews were used. Soon *The March of Time*'s own cameramen were on special assignment in the Far East, in Europe, in Latin America and on location across the U.S.

After seeing the test reels, Creighton Peet, a movie critic on the old New York *Post,* had warned the producers that they would be getting into trouble because "what people see in films is twenty times more powerful than what they read in print. This is the real basis of all censorship complaints. The movies have power . . . no other means of conveying ideas begins to touch the films. . . . In this reel you have dynamite. If it builds up a following, it can, in time, become a terrific force in the land. The only question is whether the timid movie people will stick with you; they are yellow-bellies from the word go."

His prophecy of trouble proved correct. *The March of Time* was in hot water from the beginning. Ordinarily, newsreels were exempted from censorship by the then omnipresent municipal and state censors; *The March of Time* was not always granted the same right. The Province of Ontario Censor Board turned down the second release, which contained episodes on Hitler and the Hauptmann trial. In Ohio and Illinois, censors rejected a sequence on the Nazi persecution of the Jews as "gruesome" and provocative. In Britain the censors snipped out pictures of Father Divine on grounds of blasphemy (he claimed to be God). Huey Long disappeared from an issue shown in New Orleans theaters. Pictures of the Dominican Republic dictator, President Trujillo, brought a diplomatic protest. (Secretary of State Cordell Hull reminded the Dominicans of the freedom of the press, but the Radio City Music Hall dropped the film. The New York *Times* commented: "You could probably count off the patrons of the Music Hall from the Dominican Republic on a book of matches, but that's the way they are over there.") The National Legion of Decency was outraged by scenes showing Lady Godiva's Ride, a feature of the Texas Centennial celebration at Dallas. The Hearst newspapers attacked *The March of Time* because of pictures taken in the Soviet Union, which they declared to be overt Communist propaganda.[3] But from Lord Beaverbrook in Britain came a note of commendation: "It is bound to become an influence exercising great power over the minds of men."

The March of Time, like *Time,* tried to indicate "which side it believes to have the stronger position." Implicit in a film on Gerald L. K. Smith, as in the one on Huey Long, was a vein of heavy satire. The pictures on the Jewish emigration to Palestine were sympathetic and therefore, by contrast with the scenes of persecution in Germany, a condemnation of the Nazis. But, like *Time* and *Fortune* at that period, the series did not consistently follow a specific editorial policy. This irritated some critics; George Dangerfield wrote in the *New Republic:* "I wish [the editors] would say—outright, beyond question

---

[3] The sequence on the Soviet Union was purchased from Julien Bryan, an independent cameraman who had Soviet cooperation. Extremely naïve, the film showed crammed food shelves in Soviet stores and described consumer goods as plentiful at a time when there were notorious shortages of everything in Russia.

—that somebody was right or wrong." Soon the criticism would change; *The March of Time* would be accused of following a definite and internationalist line.

A year after its founding *The March of Time* was playing in more than 5,000 theaters in the U.S. and 709 in Great Britain, and its international monthly audience was estimated at 15,000,000. An elaborate illustrated book was published by Time Inc. to celebrate *The March of Time*'s anniversary, referring to the film as the company's "third major publication":

> . . . not a product of ink-on-paper to be distributed to individuals through the mails . . . a product of acid-on-celluloid . . . distributed from the screens of cinemansions to big and little crowds. *The March of Time* had, therefore, to earn its right to existence under rules quite different from those which ordinarily govern the practice of journalism. That right . . . has now been earned—a franchise granted by the owners and managers of thousands of theatres to serve the demands of a large public.
> . . . *The March of Time* is now established in the world. . . .
> It is a chapter in the history of pictorial journalism. . . .

In support of these claims were impressive testimonials from the men who then were leaders in Hollywood—Darryl F. Zanuck, Walter Wanger, Irving Thalberg and David O. Selznick. Selznick was quoted: "I feel the inauguration of *The March of Time*—with its courage and its novelty—will prove to have been the most significant motion picture development since the invention of sound." A year later, on his nomination, *The March of Time* received a Special Award Oscar from the Academy of Motion Picture Arts and Sciences for "having revolutionized one of the most important branches of the industry, the newsreel."

CHAPTER
19

"A Little Big Business"

HARRY LUCE was so deeply immersed in his company that he seemed to have no personal life apart. And from the time of Hadden's death the company was so centered on him that the least diversion of his attention had repercussions. Luce was well aware of both the strength and weakness of the situation. From time to time he made some efforts to free his colleagues from a sense of dependence on him, yet at the same time he was reluctant to yield an iota of personal authority. In 1930, for instance, after he had devoted almost two years to the launching of *Fortune* to the neglect, he said, of *Time,* he wrote that he would attempt to work out a new organization to provide that "I am not essential to *any* operation at *any* time. The publisher [by which he meant himself] should have no duties whatever. But let this not be misconstrued. For, per contra, the publisher should (and, I trust, will) be in a position to watch and control every operation, no matter how trivial."

Again in 1933, after Howard Black was formally named advertising manager of *Time,* Luce returned to the subject in a letter to the salesmen. "There is a paradox about Time Incorporated," he wrote.

241

"On the one hand, the evidence is pretty convincing that it has first-class business management; on the other hand, it sometimes looks as if we just didn't have any business management at all; only recently our auditors were in despair because a diagrammatic chart of our organization would resemble the blueprint of a rabbit warren. . . ." His own concept of the organization, Luce went on to say, was that of a partnership, and "to the extent that we can retain this partnership idea, we will preserve the virtues of common enthusiasm and informality of relationships." He did not believe that Time Inc. could be successfully organized "along the lines of a 1929 bank with ranks and rows of officers, sub-officers and sub-subs. In a business which requires so many different *kinds* of talents, you can't judge everybody's worth by a preconceived notion of title. . . . Let us not have to fret about rank or authority."

However, in the same letter he once again made it plain he intended to surrender none of his own authority. There had come to his ears the stirrings of office "politics"; this he was determined sternly to suppress, for he bluntly closed his letter with this warning: "A certain amount of latrine gossip is harmless and good for the soul. But real internal politics, though it is the most widespread disease in American business, is not necessary in this business. And I will tell you why. Whenever you feel like talking organizational politics, you are cordially invited to come to me. I may be just as dumb a politician as John F. Curry [then boss of Tammany Hall] but as long as I am President of this company, I intend to be its political boss. I will share with my associates the handling of our civil service on a basis of merit only. But the patronage—I intend to dispense that."

Luce could effectively suppress the natural tendency to politicking so long as he was present and approachable, a man whom everybody in the shop knew and trusted. Continual expansion was steadily altering this situation. In 1935 a series of events tended to disturb the close-knit relationship among the executive group. From the middle of 1934 onward Larsen was almost wholly preoccupied by *The March of Time;* it was a major venture into which the company was now pouring not a few experimental dollars but hundreds of thousands of dollars, an enormous public success bringing the company favorable attention, but not profitable and requiring the closest supervision of the man junior only to Luce himself. Larsen's loss was compounded by that of Vice President Robert L. Johnson, who took leave of absence to become Relief Administrator of the State of Pennsylvania. Now independently wealthy by reason of his Time Inc. stock, Johnson was eager to leave advertising and find a second career in public service. As the senior advertising executive, he had played a useful role as moderator between the conflicting personalities and ambitions of Howard Black and F. Du Sossoit Duke. Following Johnson's departure Duke resigned and joined *Newsweek*.

All this occurred at a time when Luce, quite uncharacteristically, was diverted from company affairs to a personal problem. His marriage was breaking up.

The marriage was, in one sense, a casualty of the company's success. After a few years' residence in Manhattan following the move back from Cleveland, Luce established his family in New Jersey; the demands of the business, his presence at public dinners and other functions required of the head of a publication increasing in influence left him less and less time for family life. He also fell in love with a young woman who shared his interests in journalism and politics, Mrs. Clare Boothe Brokaw, the onetime *Vanity Fair* editor who had thought him "a dull fellow." Mrs. Brokaw had divorced her husband, George Tuttle Brokaw, some five years earlier and had already left *Vanity Fair* when she met Luce for the first time in 1934. The occasion was a dinner party; seated next to each other, they quite naturally talked shop. She told him that while working for Condé Nast she had prepared a dummy and written Nast a memorandum about a picture magazine, for which she believed there was a great opportunity. Luce asked a number of questions (John Martin and his Experimental Department were then working on the same idea), and the conversation continued after dinner until Luce suddenly terminated it by pulling out his watch and announcing, "Good night, time to go to bed." He promptly left the party.

They met a second time several months later at the apartment of the Countess Rose Waldeck. He said, as she remembered, "Come

243

over here and sit down. I want to talk to you more about this magazine—this idea you have for a picture magazine." He put to her a hypothetical situation—the death of the Emperor of Japan—saying, "All right, you have a picture magazine—published here in New York. The Emperor dies. What are you going to do about it?"

"Well, you know, Mr. Luce," she recalled answering, "I should think anyone like yourself would have complete access to the best photographers in Japan. Make a contract with them to buy the first magazine rights."

"That solves the problem if you can get it from Japan in time."

"I don't know why that worries you, because if *you* can't get it from Japan I don't think anyone can," she said.

This second conversation was as abruptly terminated as the first; once again out came the watch and he said, "Time to go. Good night." Her opinion was revised; she no longer thought him dull, but she did think he was "enormously rude."

They next met at a Turkish Ball given by Elsa Maxwell at the Waldorf on December 9, 1934. Mrs. Brokaw had been dancing, and her partner had stopped to speak to someone when the lights began to dim for the floor show. Coming toward her across the floor was Luce, with a glass of champagne in each hand. She thought, "Here comes that rude man," but "just as he reached me I said, 'Oh, Mr. Luce, you're no doubt bringing me that champagne.' At that moment the lights went out, and we sat down together and talked during the performance. When the lights went up he looked at me and said, 'Will you come downstairs in the lobby with me? I have something I must tell you, and I think I must tell you now.' So we went downstairs. He said, 'I've read about it happening. I've heard about it happening. But it has just happened to me. The French call it a *coup de foudre*. I think I must tell you—you are the one woman in my life.' "

She thought perhaps he had had too much champagne. He told her this was no place to talk, but he would call at her apartment at four o'clock the following Thursday. When he appeared, he told her, "What has happened to me is very important, and I know now that it's going to be the most important thing in my life—unless you kick me out of it."

244

Mrs. Brokaw was understandably disconcerted by this sudden and importunate suit. On his departure, she decided to visit her mother in Miami. Within twenty-four hours of her arrival there Luce wired that he was following. They spent two days sight-seeing and he returned to New York, saying that he would be back the following week. Nothing was resolved by the Miami visit; she found him troubled and unhappy —in love with her but distressed at the prospect of breaking with his wife. Mrs. Brokaw flew to Havana to visit friends, the Cuban representative of Pan American Airways and his wife, again thinking to escape him. Luce followed her there; she learned from him that, whether she accepted him or not, he had decided to ask his wife for a divorce. But before accepting him Mrs. Brokaw decided to put the Atlantic between them, and left on a long trip to Africa and Europe. Before she sailed, she remembered, he told her, "I don't think Time Inc. wants any new babies, but if you and I get married I will start the picture magazine and you can be co-editor."

The divorce was granted to Mrs. Luce in October 1935. *Time* reported in its December 2 issue under Milestones:

Married: Henry R. Luce, 37, editor and publisher of *Time, The March of Time, Fortune,* the *Architectural Forum, Letters;* and Clare Boothe Brokaw, 32, playwright (see p. 68), onetime managing editor of *Vanity Fair;* at Old Greenwich, Conn.

The page reference was to *Time*'s review of Clare Luce's *Abide with Me,* which had opened two days before the wedding to devastatingly critical reviews. The première presented Luce and *Time*'s drama critic with a dilemma. John Billings, the managing editor, noted in his diary:

What to do about reviewing *Abide with Me?* Can we say it is rotten? We wrote several drafts to get the proper degree of innocuousness. Luce, in his hotel, finally snapped out of it, called Ingersoll, told him what he wanted. . . . Drafts were written and rushed up to him, only to be sent back for changes. Luce wanted to eat his cake and have it, too; say the play was rotten, and yet good. The final version . . . didn't get back to me until 8:30 the night we went to press.

245

Luce showed the versions to Clare; she promptly sat down and wrote a review describing the play as "stinking." But he said, "No play is that bad," and they collaborated on a final version that combined mild censure with faint praise. As he left her that night with the amended copy, he hesitated, she remembered, and said with a smile, "No Marion Davies she." [1]

From early summer onward in 1935, Luce's preoccupation with his personal affairs distracted his attention from Time Inc. to an extent greater than ever before; at the same time Larsen, busy at *The March of Time,* had been relieved of his duties as general manager, although he shuttled back and forth as much as possible. The situation prompted a suggestion from Ralph Ingersoll to Luce which each man remembered differently in later years. As Ingersoll recalled it, what he suggested was the appointment of a publisher for *Fortune* in addition to himself as managing editor, plus a general manager of the company to whom the publisher could be responsible. Luce's recollection was that Ingersoll suggested the appointment of a general manager, with himself as the nominee. In any case, on August 12 Luce named Ingersoll general manager of Time Inc.; Eric Hodgins succeeded him as managing editor of *Fortune.* Luce wrote the Executive Committee that while the "office would be an experiment . . . Mr. Ingersoll would be an admirable choice."

It was not so received by the staff of *Time.* Billings, whom Luce consulted on the appointment before it was made, assented, but only on the assurance that Ingersoll would not interfere in editorial matters; he noted that "a great groan went up from the back benches." The reaction was understandable; the interposition of a new man, to many a relative stranger, between them and the man to whom they felt intense personal allegiance was upsetting. But Ingersoll was not one to be overly troubled by the opinions of others, and he launched himself aggressively in his new job, confident in the friendship and backing of Luce.

The announcement of the appointment, drafted by Luce and dis-

[1] The films of Miss Marion Davies, Hearst's friend and companion, were invariably reviewed with high praise in the Hearst newspapers.

Henry Robinson Luce
Tengchow, China

Leaves
From a Company
Album

Briton Hadden
Brooklyn Heights, N. Y.

Luce Age 16
On Vacation 1914

Hadden Age 16
On Vacation 1914

Yale 1920 News *Board. Hadden (center) Chairman;*
Luce (at his right) Managing Editor;
P. I. Prentice (left, rear) later Publisher of Time.

Hadden, front row center, Luce, seated far right,
on Editorial Board of Hotchkiss Record.

Hadden was unhappy at Harvard Military Camp, summer 1917.

Luce was eager Officer Candidate, Yale 1917.

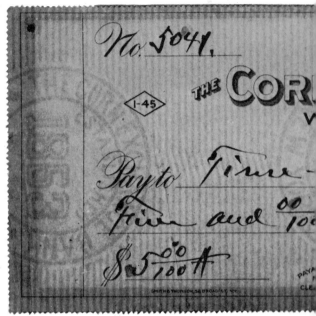

Judge Robert Luce
drew up the incorporation papers and insisted on
becoming the first subscriber.

Subscriptions were
solicited by this circular
with its Latin motto.

In the winter of 1922
a dummy was produced for
prospective advertisers.

A trial issue
was printed
before Vol. I, No. I

FIFTEEN CENTS

TIME

The Weekly News-Magazine

VOL. 1, NO. 1   MARCH 3, 1923

The first issue of Time
with cover designed
by Gordon Aymar
and drawing by
William Oberhardt.

Time's *editorial staff 1924. Hadden at top of steps;
left to right, John Martin, T.J.C. Martyn,
"William, the Clipper," Niven Busch.*

Time's *office at 236 East
39th Street formerly
housed Hupfel's brewery.*

*The Penton Press Building, Cleveland,
where* Time *made its headquarters 1925-1927.*

It was in an upstairs room in this building
on East 17th Street that Hadden and Luce
wrote prospectus. Left, the entrance hall.

Hadden, Luce and City Manager William R. Hopkins
with first copy printed in Cleveland.

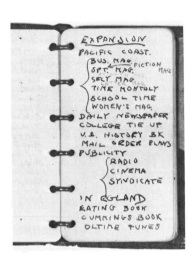

Hadden's notebook;
Ideas for New Magazines.

Roy E. Larsen, Harvard '21,
was Time's first
Circulation Manager.

Robert L. Johnson,
first advertising salesman;
later a Vice President.

John S. Martin, Hadden's cousin,
became Time's M.E. after his death.

Manfred Gottfried
Time's first writer.

This photograph of Hadden
was taken shortly before his death in 1929.
He liked to wear green eyeshade.

Howard J. Black came
rom New York Telegram.

Charles L. Stillman, hired as
Business Manager, became Treasurer in 1930.

Thomas M. Cleland sketched first cover of Fortune *upside down on a tablecloth. Left below: The cover.*

Parker Lloyd-Smith, right, was the first Managing Editor of Fortune.

Ralph McAllister Ingersoll,
who succeeded Lloyd-Smith,
came from The New Yorker.

Eric Hodgins followed
Ingersoll as M.E., later became
Fortune *Publisher.*

Miss Patricia Divver
was first woman to join
Fortune's *Board of Editors.*

Archibald MacLeish from
1930 to 1938 was a principal
contributor to Fortune.

The March of Time, *first broadcast March 6, 1931*
over 20 stations of the Columbia Broadcasting
System, was one of the most elaborate programs
of its time, employing a versatile cast and the
23-piece Columbia studio orchestra conducted by
Howard Barlow. In the picture above Mrs. Ora Nichols,
CBS sound-effects chief, and Harry Von Zell, star
announcer, are at microphones to left, Barlow
raises his baton, and producer Donald Stauffer
is seated at far right. The March of Time
was heard over CBS and later NBC until the
program finally left the air in 1945.

The March of Time *in cinema, the first release*
of which opened at the Capitol Theatre, New York,
on February 1, 1935, was awarded a special "Oscar"
by the Academy of Motion Picture Arts and Sciences
in 1937. Larsen, left, who accepted the award,
is shown with other winners (Bette Davis,
Victor McLaglen, Paul Muni and Jack Warner).

Distaff side of Time *editorial, circa 1933. l. to r.: Margaret Bassett, National Affairs; Lillian Lerner, Religion; Cecilia Schwind, Foreign Affairs; Alice Weigel, copy typist; Lilian Rixey, National Affairs; Elizabeth Sloane, asst. copy chief; Mary Fraser, rear, copy chief and head of research; Pat McKeefe, general; Elaine Slocovich, asst. Foreign Affairs.*

Laird Goldsborough discusses Time *Foreign News schedule with Managing Editor Gottfried at a story conference, the beginning of the editorial week.*

Russell Davenport, Managing Editor of Fortune, *head of table, presides over meeting of Board of Editors. He left magazine in 1940 to work for G.O.P. candidate Wendell Willkie.*

The Life *editorial team 1937. l. to r.: Wilson Hicks, Picture Editor; Daniel Longwell, Executive Editor; John S. Billings, Managing Editor; Hubert Kay, National Affairs Editor; Howard Richmond, Art Director; Margaret Bassett, researcher.*

Fortune's Charles J.V. Murphy, Life's *David Scherman taken prisoner on high seas by a Nazi raider, on their release provided* Life *with a notable scoop.*

*Mary Fraser became
Chief of Research of
Time Inc. in 1939.*

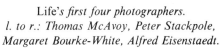

*Life's first four photographers.
l. to r.: Thomas McAvoy, Peter Stackpole,
Margaret Bourke-White, Alfred Eisenstaedt.*

As Time's *offices were pictured in the old* Life, *1932.*

*"If it ain't 'Life,' it's 'Time,'
and if it ain't 'Time,'
it's 'Fortune.' "*

John Mackey, the New Masses

*"Edward! What will the editors of
TIME have to say about this!"*

*"If their circulation
keeps going up, Joe, I swear
I can't go on."*

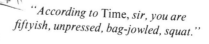

*"According to Time, sir, you are
fiftyish, unpressed, bag-jowled, squat."*

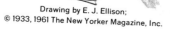

*Mr. and Mrs. Luce
returning from Europe 1938
aboard* Queen Mary.

*Luce and Chungking Correspondent
Teddy White in China, 1941.*

*Rear Admiral Richard E. Byrd and
Luce received Honorary Degrees,
Rollins College, Fla., 1938.*

Luce at bat during first "Time Out,"
a company picnic held at Westport, Conn., 1940.

David W. Brumbaugh, first accountant, became Executive Vice President.

Charles Douglas Jackson, first General Manager of Life.

Allen Grover joined Time as writer in Business, became a Vice President 1939.

Ralph Delahaye Paine, Jr.
became Fortune *M.E. 1941.*

Thomas Stanley Matthews
joined Time *1929. Became M.E. 1943.*

Howard Myers
Editor-Publisher, Architectural Forum.

Henry Robinson Luce
A Contemporary Photograph 1941

tributed without checking, contained two factual errors. When he learned of this Luce apologized to Ingersoll in an irate memorandum: "Let me state a principle which is perhaps not understood by all my associates and which should be understood p.d.q. . . . that I expect other people to keep me from making detailed mistakes. I will take responsibility for big mistakes. If the company is ruined, it's my fault. But I'll be goddamned if I will take responsibility for detailed mistakes, however attributable they may be to me. . . . Barnes [2] says trouble is some group around here thinks every word I say is inspired by God. I doubt that—but anyway the thing I want to get across . . . is that the Pope is likely hereafter to murder any Cardinal who permits the Pope to err. To cuss once more—what the hell are junior executives for?"

Early in 1936 Luce was as deeply immersed as ever in every phase of company operations. The two years just completed had set new records for profits—$1,733,094 in 1934 and $2,249,823 in 1935. The 1935 figure included $478,000 realized from investments, which amount partially offset the heavy costs incurred by *The March of Time*.

The annual report noted with pride that the company had offices from San Francisco to Paris (where European headquarters of *The March of Time* were located), that the company's salesmen were doing business with more than 1,000 industrial concerns and the payroll numbered 644, not including part-time correspondents. The company, Luce wrote, had now reached the point . . . "beyond which it will cease to be even a big Small Business and become a small Big Business.[3] Problems of consolidation and coordination march with problems of further expansion. The problem of public

[2] Bernard Barnes, promotion manager of *Fortune,* later a vice-president.

[3] Luce made frequent use of the capital letter. He once wrote a managing editor: "Will you kindly concede me a whim and issue a ukase to the effect that a capital letter at the beginning of an important word is not only not to be discouraged but . . . is to be in every way encouraged. I have tried for months to intimate my strong feeling in this matter. . . . I beg to ask as a favor that capital letters be encouraged . . . and, further, that whenever a writer has sense enough to feel like capitalizing any letter (even Z in Zither) he be allowed this aid to freer communication with his reader."

relations also arises. *Time,* The Weekly Newsmagazine, has been, and still is, its own quite adequate apologist. Ditto, *Fortune.* But with a motion picture journal, a nightly radio broadcast [4] and with four magazines, the public interpretation of your company's alleged viewpoint or viewpoints must be taken with great seriousness."

[4] In 1935–36 *The March of Time* on radio was a fifteen-minute nightly broadcast sponsored at various times by Remington Rand, *Time* and the William Wrigley, Jr. Co.

248

CHAPTER

20

A Year of Tumult

"THE EDITORS OF *Fortune* are graying over the sitch-ee-ay-shun at *Time,* owned by the same group," wrote Walter Winchell in his newspaper column in February 1936. "Some *Fortune* eds are liberals. They are said to be alarmed over *Time*'s 'Fascist attitude.'" The flippancy, candor or manners of *Time* and *Fortune* often roiled readers, but not until recently had either magazine been seriously accused of following a political line. The Winchell squib was an interesting straw in a rising wind, signaling an important change in the climate of public opinion. Time Inc.'s avowed posture (that of "unbiased, objective journalism," as Luce put it to one critic, "and as such we cannot defend or attack, play up or play down") was becoming increasingly hard to maintain. *Fortune*'s objectivity, too, was being challenged, but on different grounds.

It was inevitable that the passions and emotions that racked the American community should be reflected within the company. The year 1936 was tumultuous. Added to the political strife inherent in any Presidential election were strongly divisive currents. The short-lived unity that Roosevelt commanded at the beginning of his regime had long since been shattered. At the extreme Right the frightened inheritors of wealth and privilege coalesced around the reactionary and embittered Liberty League. The business establishment was alienated from the Administration by policies which it felt were hostile to the enterprise system. A surging and militant labor movement was girding for a final assault on the great unorganized industries—automobile and steel. At the extreme Left there was the small but active Communist Party maneuvering under the cover of the Popular Front to sell Communism as twentieth-century Americanism. And in the summer there broke out the agonizing prelude to World War II, the bloody Spanish Civil War, which further polarized U.S. opinion. Over all hung the pall of a sick industrial society unable to solve the desperate problem of unemployment.

In February, when the Winchell column appeared, the label "Fascist" was not bandied about so freely as it would be after the Spanish Civil War began; and therefore the extremity of the charge was all the more startling. But there was no doubt that Winchell's tip was accurate. Soon after it appeared MacLeish wrote Luce:

I don't think anyone up here has ever thought *Time* was fascist in intention. To that extent Walter the Winch is all wet. It is, however, true that quite a lot of us think that *Time* has a strong unconscious bias, particularly in labor stories and in foreign news relating to revolutionary developments and to all things Russian. What we think is, of course, only interesting in so far as our individual and personal judgments are valued. But since we are very much concerned with the continued success of the journalistic venture in which we are all jointly engaged, our opinions at least have the merit of being well-wishing instead of destructive.

By "our opinions" he said he meant those of managing editor Eric Hodgins, Wilder Hobson, Dwight Macdonald and himself.

We have no desire to be officious [MacLeish added]. We think *Time* is an indispensable adjunct to American living. We think it is beautifully edited. We know damn well we couldn't do the job

250

as well. But there is enough truth in the Winchell dope—however he came by it—to call for names and numbers. And also—if the editors of *Time* will permit the observation—*Time* is so nearly an impartial magazine in most things that it seems a pity it should present a seeming bias in the controversial matters where impartiality is hardest to maintain. . . .

Along with the memorandum, MacLeish submitted "exhibits" of *Time*'s "bias" prepared by Macdonald. Macdonald also wrote a memorandum:

> My personal sympathies happen to be liberal. This doesn't mean that I advocate *Time* going "left"—any more than I want *Fortune* to do so. In times like these, a truly objective and impartial magazine would perform a unique and extremely valuable service. This is what *Fortune,* it seems to me, is beginning to do.

He mentioned the "often heard charge of 'Fascism' levelled at *Time,*" and complained that the magazine had "developed a technique of implying things by shrewdly chosen adjectives and neatly turned phrases." He contrasted *Time*'s articles with some on the same subjects which had appeared in the *New Republic* and the *Nation,* adding:

> I've been reading the *Nation,* the *New Republic* and the *New Masses* in the last few months and I have frequently found their reporting of events far more revealing and complete than *Time*'s account. For years *Time* has had a contemptuous attitude toward these magazines as mere "journals of opinion" and as prejudiced and non-factual. Comparing *Time* with the *Nation,* I can see no ground for this point of view. I urge that *Time*'s editors read these "prejudiced" magazines for a few months, with open minds. There is a great deal that *Time* can learn from them. . . . At present, the chief difference between *Time* and the *Nation* seems to be that the *Nation* is consciously left-wing (and can therefore allow for its own bias and make an honest effort to dig down to the facts) whereas *Time* is ostensibly impartial but actually (perhaps unconsciously) right-wing (and therefore, its

251

bias being unadmitted and perhaps even unrecognized by its own editors, unable to allow for its prejudices). I should like to see *Time* become really impartial.

With a patience that was frequently surprising in such circumstances, Luce returned a noncommittal answer:

Thanks for your notes and exhibits. This is the kind of "steering" criticism which is most valuable to *Time* at this stage in its career. I shall study the question at the earliest opportunity, and meanwhile shall insert a caveat into the *Time* thinking machine without raising an issue.

Macdonald could scarcely be counted as a credible advocate of journalistic impartiality. He was at the time, according to his own later account, "a mild fellow traveler" who, after reading Marx, Lenin and Trotsky, "leaned toward the Communists because they alone on the American Left seemed to be 'doing something' " [1] What Macdonald defined as "really impartial" would almost certainly have been rejected by Billings and his associates as a radical bias. Under Billings, as under Martin, *Time* continued to be edited with no particular point of view; by and large, writers were given their heads to express their own opinions, and the result was that *Time* could be said to be consistently inconsistent—sometimes to the point of giving flagrant offense to some of its friends and supporters. One instance of what appeared to be journalistic irresponsibility occurred in the magazine's report of the execution of Bruno Hauptmann for the murder of the Lindbergh baby. *Time* commented, "Many a plain person in & out of New Jersey feels that Hauptmann was railroaded to jail and death by invisible wealth and power and points, right or wrong, to the Lindbergh-Morrow-House of Morgan connection. Conceivably Governor Hoffman's activities would, if successful, be rewarded with political dividends from such persons." An enraged Thomas Lamont, Morgan's senior partner, scribbled this note to *Time*'s first investor, Harry Davison: "My G--! Harry, has *Time* come to this? It far surpasses

[1] Dwight Macdonald: *Memoirs of a Revolutionist* (Farrar, Straus and Cudahy, 1957).

252

anything I have seen in the yellowest of yellow presses. *'Right* or *Wrong'?"*

Davison felt impelled to protest to Luce:

Dear Harry,

Don't you think this is pretty raw, particularly when you know it is bunk? I am quite reconciled to swallowing a lot of "yellow journal" stuff from time to time but this really makes me sick.

Undoubtedly Luce was much embarrassed; he was often put in a difficult position with his friends and acquaintances by what his magazines published. But as an editor he did not like to lay down guidelines and rules; he understood that creative editors and writers worked better if given wide latitude. He was often disappointed in their work, but he accepted the risk as part of the price of aggressive journalism.

Fortune was caught up in a squabble in which Macdonald was the central figure. He had been assigned to do a series on U.S. Steel, with Charles Stillman detailed to assist in the analysis of the corporation's finances. The research took months and was one of the magazine's most ambitious undertakings. Politically, Stillman and Macdonald could hardly have been farther apart; they were agreed, however, that the corporation had a poor record of return to stockholders and maintained high prices to customers by monopolistic practices. They were also agreed that U.S. Steel's technology was outmoded and its labor policy, to say the least, antediluvian. Macdonald wrote three of the articles. A fourth, on U.S. Steel's labor, was assigned to another writer, Robert Cantwell.

When the first of Macdonald's articles—" 'The Corporation' "—was sent to the company for correction of errors of fact, U.S. Steel's chairman, Myron Taylor, was predictably upset. *Fortune* and U.S. Steel were soon at loggerheads: some truculence on the magazine's part made it appear to Taylor that the editors were unwilling to make corrections; and some allegations by U.S. Steel of a radical bias on the part of the writer angered *Fortune*. The row soon involved Ingersoll, Grover and Hodgins as well as Stillman and Macdonald. The manuscript was finally wrenched into a form acceptable to everyone; most of *Fortune*'s criticisms survived, and U.S. Steel felt that the article was fair enough to warrant cooperating in the ensuing three articles. However, when Macdonald's final article was going through the editors' hands, he suddenly resigned because, he said later, the piece was being "bowdlerized."

The editors did not, in fact, "bowdlerize" the Macdonald article; they scrapped it altogether and substituted another. Ingersoll, who had a hand in editing the series because it had been originally assigned when he was still managing editor, told Luce it had been done because Macdonald had written "an interpretative analysis of the whole subject—an editorial" which had to be denied publication because it was "an opinion of a member of the staff." But Ingersoll felt that this was unfortunate because Macdonald's viewpoint was "an informed and intelligent one"; he suggested to Luce that the magazine formula should be altered to accommodate such articles, perhaps by using a byline.

Macdonald, a year after leaving Time Inc., opened fire on Luce and the magazines with a three-article series in the *Nation*. In these he charged Luce with being a "great mouthpiece" of the ruling business class, concluding: "The decay of American capitalism is pushing all these people in a certain direction. But it is premature to call Time Inc. fascist. Proto-fascist would be more accurate." The articles, as we shall see, had a certain internal impact on the Time Inc. organization. Macdonald himself, however, admitted later that his prognosis —that the magazines would become more, not less, Fascist—was wrong.

The U.S. Steel series carried quite a wallop. Some years later, in a memorandum to Luce, Eric Hodgins recalled "the truly enormous clattering in the streets that resulted from this highly critical series. Whereas hitherto we were 'the mouthpiece of the House of Morgan' we now became 'paid with Moscow's gold.' We certainly shook the pillars of the temple and shook them hard—and I privately think it was very good for the temple." A high-ranking official of the C.I.O. declared that the U.S. Steel series did more than any other one thing to pave the way for the precedent-making agreement between U.S. Steel Chairman Myron Taylor and John L. Lewis in March 1937. In any case, *Fortune* scored an exclusive in its May issue when it was the first publication to reconstruct in accurate detail the steps leading to that agreement.

The *Fortune* series on U.S. Steel, appearing at a time when the coming Presidential election was sharpening the hostility between the Administration and business, caused a number of the magazine's readers to charge that *Fortune*'s editors harbored a bias against business. This was maintained notwithstanding the fact that *Fortune* gave much space to Roosevelt's opponents in the pre-election months, printing articles by Ernest T. Weir, chairman of National Steel, who proudly proclaimed himself an "Economic Royalist," and Senator Arthur H. Vandenberg, who presented "The Republican Indictment." (Under Roosevelt, the Senator wrote, "Capital has constantly faced 'capital punishment.' ") *Fortune* salesmen were running ever more frequently into the complaint that the magazine was anti-business. Toward the end of the year Luce was somewhat startled when, at a meeting with W. B. ("Tap") Kegg, *Fortune*'s Cleveland representative, the salesman asked whether it was ethical to solicit advertising if the magazine had in fact a bias against business. This was an unusual thing for a salesman to do; the separation of advertising and editorial at *Fortune* was strictly maintained, and the salesmen took an almost Marine Corps pride in being able to accomplish their mission no matter what the editors said.

Luce arranged a meeting between Hodgins, Kegg and the advertising manager to discuss the complaints. In reporting back to Luce, Hodgins attributed the main cause of the trouble to the U.S. Steel series, but assured Luce:

No one in the Editorial Department thinks that *Fortune*'s charter is to "pan business." Its charter continues to be thought of as one to interpret, to praise *and* to criticize according to the Department's best and most unbiased abilities. It is beside the point that I happen to feel that *Fortune*'s writers (with two exceptions now happily liquidated) have discharged this duty unusually well this year. It is also beside the point that 1936 was, because of political feeling, a year of unusual contention in

255

which the U.S. Businessman all too often made a fool of himself by yelling "Communist" at all non-members of the Liberty League. . . .

But it is not beside the point that the criticisms are being made, or that it seems to me that our own Advertising Department is perhaps acquiring a slight feeling that maybe there is some justice in the criticisms. . . .

"It seems obvious," Hodgins concluded, "that many a person, both within and without Time Inc., needs re-education in the *Fortune* editorial philosophy. The considerable change in that philosophy which was caused by the Depression has never, to my knowledge, been expressed in print." To that end he suggested a new promotion campaign telling the business world just what *Fortune*'s editorial purpose was. Luce, agreeing to this suggestion, answered:

The only trouble with *Fortune* is that it often forgets it is a Journalist and imagines itself to be the Oxford Union—Junior. (Socialist, these days, of course.)

Every time we tell a *good* story we are right—or, every time we tell a *right* story we are good—that is a damn funny thing about Journalism. All the troubles are when the stories aren't very good or aren't very right. . . .

The Presidential election was not much of a contest. Luce, who had attended the convention which nominated Landon, voted for him though he early wrote the Republican candidate off as a serious contender. *Time* came in for the increasingly familiar charge that it was betraying bias. Otis Peabody Swift, a public-relations man who was riding the Landon train, complained to his friend C. D. Jackson that *Time* had failed to reflect the exuberance and feeling of victory which those who were with Landon felt so strongly. Jackson replied that Billings, *Time*'s managing editor, had shown him another letter from the Landon train that "boo for huzzah" gave "the 100 per cent other side of the picture." Jackson added: "Why should *Time* play up Marion Talley against the accomplished artistry of Lotte Lehmann? The fact that Lehmann's voice is six months ahead of cracking for good doesn't make Talley the prima donna that she may be two years from now. We are passing history in review, not attempting to make it." In its final article on the campaign *Time* made it clear it was not rallying around either candidate:

> . . . Alf Landon read the closing speech of his campaign, not a much better orator than he began it. But the crowd which his oratory could not sway continued to cheer, for they had come like most Alf Landon crowds because they liked the big sign that hung in the Auditorium. Its letters spelled out, "You Can Believe Landon," but it was no compliment to the Republican Nominee. It expressed the crowd's opinion of Franklin Roosevelt. For peace and good will to men, both parties were content to wait until after election.

On Roosevelt's election *Time* said he had "won the undoubted right to call himself the ablest master of U.S. politics in a century." The reaction of *Fortune* was astonishing—and must have seemed to many of its readers confirmation of a deep-set bias toward the radical Left. A *Fortune* article rejected the post-election thesis, widely held in some Republican circles, that the victory represented a shift of the electorate to the Left. Wrote *Fortune*: "There is unfortunately no reason whatever for supposing that the election of November, 1936, proves the country has completed a mass migration to the Left." Defining "liberalism" as "an attitude which sets human rights above property rights at every point of conflict," *Fortune* went on to say that Roosevelt had avoided the issue "with a skill and assiduity which would have done credit to an African dodger. The problem of the power of the Supreme Court to upset humanitarian legislation he never once debated. . . . Instead he offered as the principal and most persuasive reason for his re-election an argument which appealed primarily to the defenders of property . . . the argument of prosperity."

It was not the election but the Spanish Civil War that most sharply divided Time Inc. in 1936. Some twenty-seven years later Luce, in the McKinsey Lectures at Columbia University, recalled, "We of Time Inc. in the middle Thirties began to take our stand. Not without great troubles among us—in the family. There were among us men and women of the left, even as we would say today, of the far left; also of the right. The Spanish Civil War was fought in the *Time* & *Life* Building—with some bitter consequences. . . ."

The target of those who supported the Loyalists was *Time*'s Foreign News editor, Goldsborough. For eleven years he had written the Foreign News section almost single-handed, filling pages of copy week after week with a precise, legible script, leaving wide spaces between the lines for editing. But so readable were his articles that a succession of managing editors scarcely altered a line. Hadden, Luce, Martin and Billings regarded him as a mainstay; his department was one of the best read, most often quoted.

Goldsborough was a complicated character. Lame from childhood and therefore limited in exercise, he was stout, depended on a heavy cane to move about. He was also deaf. These handicaps tended to isolate him, as did his personality. He was a prima donna who preferred to work alone, impatient of assistance, prone to anger when contradicted. Luce thought of him as a man with the viewpoint of an "eighteenth century gentleman"; he was certainly a romantic. When he married Miss Florence McConaughy the couple journeyed to Goldsborough, Yorkshire, so the religious ceremony could take place in the church of his ancestors. He did not adjust easily to the new climate of the 1930s.

He had a solid background in European politics. Beginning in 1927, he went abroad once a year for *Time* to meet political leaders, pick up tidbits of personality, gossip and rumor that enlivened the magazine. At first he had few contacts abroad, and *Time,* virtually unknown then in Europe, had no overseas correspondents to smooth the way for him. But he was a man of style and he moved about in the manner of a roving ambassador, staying only at the best hotels, hiring Rolls Royces, entertaining lavishly.

His excursions, while approved by Luce, were nevertheless the occasion for numerous disputes between them over his expense accounts. Jackson, finally deputized to handle this problem, left a report of one encounter with Goldsborough on the matter of an advance: "Every year that Goldsborough has gone abroad there have been monster preliminary negotiations and bitter acrimony on Goldie's return due to the Scotch blood in both Harry and Goldie. Year after year Goldsborough has whittled, wheedled, chiseled and frowned his way through an expense account which has finally assumed almost laughable proportions. . . .

"Having armed myself with complete dollar information on hotel rates in England and on the Continent, car hire, breakfast, lunch, dinner, tips, ocean rates, etc., we squared away. Goldie said that he would like to have a lump sum allocated to him to spend as he wished with no questions asked. I mentioned a lump sum but when I explained how it was arrived at he no longer wanted a lump sum arrangement. At the end of the third session we arrived at a figure acceptable to Goldie. . . . It isn't worthwhile making Goldie feel that his imperial progress through Europe is being dimmed by his having to fish in his own pocket."

Goldsborough's virtuosity was best demonstrated, perhaps, in *Time*'s handling of the romance of Edward, Prince of Wales, and Mrs. Wallis Warfield Simpson of Baltimore. After Edward succeeded his father, George V, on the throne in January 1936, only to abdicate less than a year later, some U.S. newspapers credited *Time*'s coverage of the story with a critical role in the ouster of the King. Actually, the magazine's circulation in the British Isles was only 3,200 (1,400 subscribers and 1,800 newsstand sales). But *Time*'s reports, together with others appearing in the U.S. and foreign press, were used by Prime Minister Stanley Baldwin to pressure Edward into the decision to step down.

The British censorship of *Time,* at the time, was the most blatant of any imposed on foreign periodicals. It was not official (throughout the crisis *Time* subscribers receiving their copies through the mail read an unexpurgated magazine) but was imposed by W. H. Smith & Son Limited, which then and now enjoys a virtual monopoly on periodical sales; offending stories were cut out before *Time* was allowed on their newsstands. There had been other instances of Smith censorship: when *Time* reported the "seduction" of Ramsay MacDonald by Lady Londonderry (the "seduction" being the fact that Lady London-

259

derry had persuaded widower MacDonald to accept invitations in British society once more); and again when *Time* reported that the Duchess of Kent was ". . . the Empire's greatest expert in getting around . . . Queen Mary. The forbidding Queen-Empress, seldom overgenerous with other members of the Royal Family, constantly gives the Duchess of Kent this or that costly trinket because 'she is so sweet.' " The British press gave the latter item a big play under such headlines as "TIME MAGAZINE INSULTS QUEEN."

The first of *Time*'s stories about Edward and Mrs. Simpson, two years before the abdication crisis, had a blithely innocent ring:

> Such fun was Edward of Wales having at Cannes last week with beauteous Mrs. Wallace Wakefield [sic] Simpson that he sent back to Marseilles an airplane he had ordered over to take him up to Paris.
>
> "To the delight of hundreds of onlookers last night," cabled a British correspondent, "the Prince danced the rumba with an American woman identified as a Mrs. Simpson."
>
> She became THE Mrs. Simpson last month at Biarritz where His Royal Highness welcomed her as she arrived, carried her suitcase out of the railway coach.

The misspelling of her name produced a letter from her fellow Marylander Mrs. Mark Sullivan, wife of the historian and Washington columnist, correcting the error. It was published in the Letters column; the editors appended a paragraph noting, "Mrs. Simpson is now traveling on the Continent, closely attended by H.R.H." When British newspaper proprietors decided to black out all news of the Prince's romance, *Time*'s continued coverage again brought censorship down on the magazine. A cable from London informed the home office that the censorship was because of "insulting and inaccurate references to Prince. . . . Diplomatic protest expected for previously censored story [the Duchess of Kent item] but Court officials who saw Prince story do not yet contemplate action as references not political." There were no grounds for diplomatic protest and none was made. When King George died and the Prince became Edward VIII, *Time*'s editors voluntarily decided to report only the new King's public life if he kept his private life private, and so informed its British distributor.

What broke *Time*'s silence was Edward's own insistence on inserting Mrs. Simpson's name in the Court Circular. Thereupon *Time* resumed its coverage of the romance.

Edward appeared to be less distressed by *Time*'s reporting than some of his subjects. He granted Goldsborough an audience when Goldsborough showed up that spring on his annual trip to Europe. On that same sojourn Goldsborough presented himself to President Albert Lebrun of France (the first audience the President had given to a foreign journalist) and interviewed France's Premier Léon Blum and Premier Manuel Azaña of Spain.

However skillful at titillating readers, Goldsborough was not always a man of balanced judgment. He was ridden by prejudices which he made little effort to conceal and which his editors did not police. In reporting the Ethiopian war *Time*'s Foreign News section clearly reflected Goldsborough's pro-Mussolini sentiments. It pictured Haile Selassie as "squealing for protection," termed his country "squalling Abyssinia" and spoke of Africa's "dreary little war." He seemed to have no sense of the offense he gave when he wrote of Léon Blum as an "exquisitely cultivated Jew and famed rabble-rouser" or, in reporting his rise to the Premiership, as "a prosperous and infirm Old Socialist whose spidery limbs and thin beaked nose give him the air of a flamingo. Flapping gestures complete the illusion."

Goldsborough espoused Franco's cause in the Spanish Civil War from the beginning. The Madrid regime was characterized as one of "Socialists, Communists and rattlebrained Liberals" which "had emptied the jails of cutthroats to defend itself and swell what could be called 'forces of law and order.'" *Time* later described the leader of Spain's Rightist insurrection as "singularly humorous and carefree," a man of "caution, thoroughness, quick decision, forehandedness" whose "program was Back to Normalcy for Spain."

Fortune was about to draw an entirely different picture. In one article of a series, "Background of War," MacLeish would define the issue in Spain as lying between Fascism and liberalism:

Hitler and Mussolini had been swelling and blowing on the Rhine and in Ethiopia for some years [MacLeish wrote] but prior to the Spanish war their swelling and blowing had been

261

directed against Russia or against the Jews or against such remote figures as Haile Selassie. They had sneered at democratic institutions but they had not actually attacked a democratic government. Now suddenly they were supporting . . . an attack upon a government which was republican and liberal in form. . . .

Goldsborough and MacLeish carried on a duel-by-memorandum (copies to Luce), enriching company archives with a record of the emotional heat aroused. Here is MacLeish to Goldsborough, commenting on Goldsborough's stories in *Time:*

> . . . It is my feeling that entirely objective journalism would have presented the facts in such a way as to indicate that the fascists, backed by landowners and church, were the aggressors against a popular government lawfully elected.
>
> More specifically, I have continually objected to the use of the phrase "Red militia" in *Time.* . . . Briefly, I feel that *Time* has never presented the war in Spain for what it was—an inexcusable and unjustifiable act of aggression by reactionary forces against a popular government. . . .

Here is Goldsborough to MacLeish:

> On the side of Franco, and we have rubbed this in more than once, are men of property, men of God and men of the sword. In so describing them, I presume that I condemn them to particularly nether depths, but what position do you suppose these sort of men (irrespective of nationality) occupy in the minds of 700,000 readers of *Time? Time* is obliged to bear in mind the set of values with which we have every reason to believe that our readers are equipped. They do not, I am convinced, recoil at the sight of a United States Marine, a clergyman or a prosperous householder, and they are of a quite contrary opinion as to Communists, Anarchists, and even "Republicans," so-called, of a stamp who resort to political gangsterism and philosophically apostrophize the native Violence of the Spaniard. . . .
>
> Red is the one and only color which accurately covers the

262

various political shades of Red which comprise the followers of Largo Caballero.

Luce's viewpoint was different from both. A few weeks before the exchange between the editors, Luce had received an appeal from MacLeish to help finance a motion picture which MacLeish and John Dos Passos were interested in producing on behalf of the Loyalist cause. At that time Luce wrote MacLeish:

. . . Suppose that one is neither pro-Fascist nor pro-Communist, but stalwartly and closed-mindedly pro-Freedom and Democracy—does Spain provide the issue for such an one? I think not. Last year, Spain was perhaps Democratic rather than Communist. But there is certainly strong evidence that Spain has now only two significant camps—the Fascists and the Communists (or Left-dominated Popular Front).

Ultimately the world may be divided between these two camps but I do not think it is yet, and I think that anyone who thinks that Communism is to be trusted as an ally of Liberty is, quite simply, a mistaken theoretician and a hopeless politician! I know you will be glad to be called the latter but I trust you would be insulted by the former.

Luce's memorandum did not change MacLeish's opinion. This was made amply clear by Goldsborough's own report of a meeting between MacLeish and him, which was arranged by Luce in connection with the Background of War articles. In the memo Goldsborough refers to himself by name:

. . . consultation with Goldsborough has been begun by MacLeish and will now take its amicable course, although they managed to reach an interesting stage within the first 60 seconds.

According to MacLeish *"The* issue" in Europe and perhaps in the entire world "used to be between Communism and Fascism, but is now between Democracy and Fascism."

It is immaterial to Goldsborough, who tries to form his own judgments independently and assumes that MacLeish does the same, that this thesis matches word for word the official thesis of the Soviet Union's Ambassador, Mr. Troyanovsky, in Washington and that of the leader of the United States Communist Party, Mr. Browder. This is in fact the official thesis of the Komintern. To uphold it . . . makes the question of definition arise as fundamental.

Goldsborough told MacLeish that, in his opinion, the *Fortune* series—which must necessarily be much concerned with Communism, Socialism, Democracy, National Socialism, and Fascism—should contain at the outset a brief series of definitions of what *Fortune* means by these terms. . . .

To this MacLeish replied warmly that he is altogether opposed to defining any such terms. . . .

In Goldsborough's experience it is only in extreme pro or extreme con circles that the very mention of defining fairly and squarely the terms one intends to use touches off anger. . . .

Goldsborough assumed that he spoke for Time Inc. and had had the best of the argument. He assumed too much, but Luce was not ready to intervene and did not; for the time being, *Time* continued to reflect the views of its Foreign News editor, *Fortune* those of MacLeish.

In the fall of 1936 it was common knowledge that Time Inc. was about to publish a new magazine. Inevitably this drew a renewed scrutiny of Henry Luce, phenomenally successful at thirty-eight and married to a witty and beautiful woman, a celebrity in her own right. He was, of course, an obvious subject for a profile in *The New Yorker*.

The New Yorker's brilliant and erratic founder, Harold Ross, had never forgotten or forgiven *Time*'s review of his first issue. Hadden thought *The New Yorker* essentially snobbish; Ross thought Hadden's style "barbaric." Ross had been still further angered by an article on *The New Yorker* which *Fortune* published in 1934.[2] The late James

---

[2] Ross's opinions about *Time* did not prevent him from doing business with Time Inc. In 1934 he sold 2,190 of his shares in the F-R Publishing Corp., which owned *The New Yorker,* to Time Inc. for $104,000, a deal made over a luncheon at "21" with Stillman. The shares were purchased purely as an investment, sold two years later for a capital gain of $61,315.

Thurber, in *The Years with Ross*,³ said that the *Fortune* article in retrospect was more like "a bouquet of roses than anything else, with only here and there the buzzing of a bee among the blossoms." It was not so regarded on publication. The manuscript was shown to *The New Yorker*'s editors before publication. They fiercely resented it because it listed the salaries of principal staff members. They felt that in publishing these Ingersoll had taken advantage of his privileged position as a former managing editor of *The New Yorker*. Ross, who was pictured as an editorial genius though slightly mad, in retaliation posted a notice on *The New Yorker*'s bulletin board reading, "It is not true that I get $40,000 a year." His public riposte was a cryptic sentence in *The New Yorker*'s "Talk of the Town" column: "The Editor of *Fortune* gets $30 a week and carfare." Luce was only distantly aware of the feud; he was not a regular reader of *The New Yorker*.

Two years elapsed between the appearance of the *Fortune* article and the profile of Luce. The *New Yorker* staff in the interim had weighed and rejected various suggestions for retaliation. The forthcoming publication of a new Time Inc. magazine offered an appropriate occasion. Wolcott Gibbs, whom *Fortune* had described as a man who "hates everybody and everything [and] takes an adolescent pride in it," and who was *The New Yorker*'s most able satirist, was assigned to write the profile, with John Bainbridge as his researcher. It was to become one of the magazine's most often quoted articles.

Ingersoll scented danger and advised Luce not to cooperate. But Luce felt that as a journalist he must do so. When the manuscript was completed, Ross submitted it for correction of facts. Ingersoll, who read it first, flew into an immediate rage, accusing Ross of "Hearst tactics"; Luce agreed to a meeting with Ross to discuss the article. With difficulty this was arranged, Ross insisting they meet on his own ground for dinner at his apartment, where he was flanked by his managing editor, St. Clair McKelway. Ingersoll was Luce's second. It was a fruitless, acrimonious evening; at one point Ingersoll and

³ Atlantic-Little, Brown, 1959.

McKelway nearly came to blows and Luce and Ross had to separate them.

The article characterized Luce as an "ambitious, gimlet-eyed Baby Tycoon . . . efficient, humorless . . . brusque, contradictory, hostile." In a famous sentence parodying *Time* style Gibbs wrote, "Backward ran sentences until reeled the mind." At the end Gibbs made grudging acknowledgment of his subject's importance and achievement: "Certainly to be taken with seriousness is Luce at 38, his fellow man already informed up to his ears, the shadow of his enterprises long across the land, his future plans impossible to imagine, staggering to contemplate. Where it all will end, knows God!"

Ross, in his contradictory way, seems to have been troubled by what he was publishing; in a five-page single-spaced personal letter to Luce [4] he tried to justify the article. At their dinner meeting Luce had complained that there was not "a single favorable word" in the article. Ross wrote that, on the contrary, the article presented Luce as "practically heroic," and that he, Ross, was astonished that Luce was apparently "unconscious of the notorious reputation *Time* and *Fortune* have for crassness in description, for cruelty and scandal-mongering and insult. I say frankly but really in a not unfriendly spirit that you are in a hell of a position to ask anything. . . ."

Ross then quoted Gibbs as saying he had thrown out "a lot of stuff that would have made the boys' hair stand up." He gave it as Gibbs's opinion that *Time* "gratuitously invaded the privacy of a great many people" and regularly accused others of "harlotry, bastardy [and] physical deformity." Concluding, Ross wrote:

> After our talk the other night I asked at least ten people about *Time,* and, to my amazement, found them bitter, in varying degrees, in their attitude. You are generally regarded as being as mean as hell and frequently scurrilous. Two Jewish gentlemen were at dinner with me last night and, upon mention of *Time,* one of them charged that you are anti-Semitic, and asked the

[4] Thurber said that no copy of the Ross letter exists in *The New Yorker*'s files, but that a young woman once sent him a copy, commenting that it had been used in courses in journalism schools across the country. The original of the letter remains in the Time Inc. archives.

266

other if he didn't think so too. The other fellow said he'd read *Time* a lot and he didn't think you were anti-Semitic especially; you were just anti-everything, he said—anti-Semitic, anti-Italian, anti-Scandinavian, anti-black-widow-spider. "It is just their pose," he said. . . . I feel rather childish writing all this. It's all over now, anyhow.

Sincerely yours,

Harold Wallace Ross

Small man . . . furious . . . mad . . . no taste.

In his reply Luce did not pursue the argument:

Dear Ross:

. . . it was not "up to you" to make any explanations so far as I was concerned, but in any case I want to thank you for the personal trouble you took with the *Time*-Luce parody. . . . I only regret that Mr. Gibbs did not publish all he knew so that I might learn at once exactly how mean and poisonous a person I am.

Mr. Gibbs, like you, is undoubtedly sick of the whole subject. But, having located a poison more or less at large in society, he may perhaps like to help mitigate it. And this, I assure you, he can do if he will take any current copy of *Time* and red-pencil every example he finds of "cruelty, scandal-mongering and insult"—and send it to me. . . .

Two years later, on the anniversary of the Luce profile, in somewhat childish reprisal Ingersoll put the name of Eustace Tilley, a mythical character used in *The New Yorker*'s promotion, on the *Time* masthead. He intended to keep it there for a while, then drop it and announce that Tilley had been fired. But the name disappeared sooner than planned, under threat of suit from Corey Ford, the writer who had invented Tilley.

James Thurber years later passed this judgment: "As parody, the Luce profile was excellent, and often superb, but it seems to me that Luce and Ingersoll were justified in resenting the tone of the piece, here and there, and some of its statements." Gibbs himself had an afterthought; when the piece was reprinted in a collection of his writings he wrote Thurber that he had asked his publishers to change the description of it from "the fabulous profile on Luce" to " 'the ill-advised etc.,' and they are still trying to figure out what to make of that."

A few years after the profile appeared Luce, at Rollins College to make a speech, dropped in on a class in Contemporary Biography. "And who do you suppose the class was discussing?" Luce exploded to a colleague. *"Me!* And what do you suppose they were using as their text? That goddamn article in *The New Yorker!* So now my question is: *Is* this thing going to be engraved on my tombstone?"

"To See Life; to See the World"

Just as every floor of a skyscraper is said to cost
one life, so every important magazine costs nervous indigestion for at least ten people. . . . A year
ago we had, or fancied we had, some viscera to
spare. What did we choose to do? We chose to
create a magazine called *Life*.

HENRY R. LUCE
to the American Association
of Advertising Agencies, 1937

IN FEBRUARY 1936 Luce returned to New York from a two-month
honeymoon in Cuba and at once called a group of his executives into a special meeting; an important decision was pending.
John Billings noted the occasion in his diary: "Luce took me to lunch
at the Cloud Club with Ingersoll and Larsen in a private room. The
subject up for discussion: starting a picture magazine. Larsen was
doubtful, wanted more pictures in *Time*. I agreed to that, but argued
that a picture supplement would not prevent others from starting a

picture magazine. Luce was all for the picture magazine. He's got it in his blood bad."

Luce had been thinking about a picture magazine for a long time and had shelved the work of the Experimental Department in 1934 with reluctance. His enthusiasm for *The March of Time* increased his long-standing interest in pictorial journalism. From the first issue of *Time* onward Hadden and he had taken the greatest care in the selection of illustrations. In *Time*'s first issue one of the eleven meager illustrations was obviously chosen because it so well matched the accompanying article. Senator Smith W. Brookhart of Iowa, noted for his determined informality in dress, was pictured in farm clothes stroking the nose of a horse. The caption: "I have never owned evening clothes and never propose to." As money and space permitted, *Time* steadily increased the variety and range of its photographic illustrations. Edward Steichen, the distinguished photographer, called *Time*'s combination of pictures and captions one of the "really meritorious" uses of news photographs in the 1920s. In 1933, at Luce's express order, *Time* ran one of its first major picture features, an eight-page picture layout on the London Economic Conference.

Luce's experience with *Fortune* extended the range of his experimentation, for *Fortune* was almost as much a magazine of pictures as of words and provided a showcase for an exciting new generation of photographers—most notably the pioneer in the use of the miniature camera, Dr. Erich Salomon, whose "candid" photography came as something of a revelation. The miniature cameras created an almost contagious enthusiasm for pictorial journalism in the early 1930s. Everyone, Luce recalled, seemed to be interested in publishing a picture magazine. "You would go to '21' and places like that," he said, "and people would buttonhole you and tell you what a natural it was. When you asked what you would put in such a magazine or how it should be made up, they could not tell you."

In October 1934 *Time*'s involvement in picture journalism increased with the appointment of Daniel Longwell as special assistant to *Time*'s managing editor, John Billings. His job, Luce told the staff, was "to introduce more pictures . . . in a unique *Time*-like manner . . . under the firm control of an Editorial Purpose." One of Long-

270

well's credentials for the job was his enthusiasm for photography and picture journalism. He first met Luce in *Time*'s early days through mutual friends in Doubleday, Doran and Company, where Longwell was publishing manager of trade books. Longwell, Nebraska-born and a Columbia graduate, had edited a number of picture books for Doubleday. A man of great enthusiasms and bubbling with ideas, Longwell was one of those who tried to sell Luce on a picture magazine. In 1933 Luce offered him a job on *Fortune* which Longwell turned down; a year later Longwell was back asking to join Time Inc. His first assignments were in promotion for *Architectural Forum* and *The March of Time;* then came the appointment as assistant to Billings.

Longwell's work was soon evident in *Time*'s columns. In the issue of February 25, 1935, there appeared three pages of candid photographs of Franklin D. Roosevelt which offered a vivid contrast to the usual run of news pictures. They were the work of Thomas McAvoy, a young photographer on the Washington *News* who, experimenting with a newly purchased Leica, had brought off a scoop. Ushered into the President's office along with the other news photographers with their more conventional gear, McAvoy began shooting, using only available light. When the photographers were ushered out they joshed McAvoy: "In that light and with that box, boy, you could not get anything." McAvoy did not tell them that he had prepared for shooting in the weak light by immersing his film in ammonia to make it specially sensitive. Soon McAvoy was a regular photographer on Longwell's budding staff.

Another enterprising young photographer, Peter Stackpole, was trying out the new fast camera on the West Coast. On assignment from the Oakland (California) *Tribune,* he snapped a picture of Herbert Hoover dozing gently during a speech by Secretary of Labor Frances Perkins. The *Tribune*'s city editor sent it to *Time*. Longwell bought the picture, and soon other Stackpole pictures were appearing in *Time* and *Fortune*.

In September, with the Italian invasion of Ethiopia imminent, Longwell proposed that Time Inc. bring out a picture magazine on a crash basis, arguing that "a war, any sort of war, is going to be natural

271

promotion. . . . If the Italians march into Ethiopia and if eight days later we can have a magazine on the stands, it ought to sell 100,000." This was impractical, but Longwell's budget for pictures in *Time* was increased. Among the pictures of the Ethiopian war that *Time* published were those of Alfred Eisenstaedt, who was one of the great photographers of Europe. Born in Dirschau, West Prussia, Eisenstaedt had been drafted into the German army in World War I, been wounded and decorated with the Iron Cross. For the Associated Press and other agencies he had covered scores of major assignments before the Ethiopian war. In December 1935 he came to the U.S., and soon after joined Longwell's staff.

As the use of pictures in *Time* expanded, Longwell was given as his assistant Joseph J. Thorndike, Jr., Harvard '34, who, like himself, was interested in the new art of photo journalism. Longwell also had as his consultant one of the foremost European picture editors, Kurt Korff, the former editor of the *Berliner Illustrirte Zeitung,* who had recently been driven from Germany because he was a Jew. Longwell credited Korff with teaching him how to read pictures, how to look for "a little more of something" that sets the great photograph apart.

Little by little, as Longwell's department expanded, the idea of a picture magazine revived as a possible new venture for Time Inc. There were rumors that other publishers were interested: J. Stirling Getchell, an advertising man, was trying to raise money on a dummy which he had produced; there were rumors that *Collier's* was installing new presses. *Newsweek* was advertising itself as "the illustrated newsmagazine." *Time* could raise a challenge to that description and strengthen it by putting out a picture supplement of, say, six to twelve pages. Longwell and Korff were instructed to produce a dummy.

At about the same time, in December 1935, T. E. Donnelley, president of R. R. Donnelley & Sons Company, which printed *Time,* and his executive vice-president, H. P. Zimmermann, paid a courtesy call on Luce in New York. Merely to open the conversation Zimmermann asked Luce if he was planning any new publications and if they could be of service. Luce laughed. "For God's sake, Zim, I can't be your salesman. What have you got to sell?" Then, quite seriously, Luce asked his visitors to figure out the best make-up of pictures in magazine format that could be put on the newsstands for five or ten cents. Luce added some general requirements: the printing must do justice to the photographic illustrations and be of high definition. The Donnelley executives returned to Chicago, where in their pressroom, quite coincidentally, experiments were going forward that would make such a magazine possible. Prior to this time it was impracticable to print halftone illustrations on coated paper at high speeds. Ink dried by penetration and by oxidation and would smear on coated paper on high-speed rotary presses. The paper used on such presses had to be absorbent and of dull finish, which seldom did full justice to the illustrations. The alternative method, rotogravure, also left much to be desired in quality of reproduction.

On his return from Cuba, Luce called the Cloud Club meeting and, afterward, put in a call to Zimmermann in Chicago: "I am ready to talk." So were the men from Donnelley. Their experiments pointed the way to a dramatic advance in the art of high-speed printing. A new fast-drying ink had been developed which could be used on coated paper running through rotary presses. When the first samples were studied in New York, Luce said, "This is it. This will enable us to start an entirely new kind of magazine."

The printers returned to perfect the process; in New York the planning of a new magazine began.

John S. Martin, who had been assigned to *The March of Time* after the break-up of the earlier Experimental Department, was put in charge of the Longwell-Thorndike-Korff group, which became the nucleus of a new Experimental Department. But first Luce ventured an experiment on his own: with the help of Longwell and Mrs. Laura Z. Hobson, a writer in the *Time* promotion department, he undertook the production of a seventy-two-page clothbound book celebrating the achievements of *The March of Time*. It was intended to promote the movie, but it also must be regarded as an experiment in picture journalism. Entitled *Four Hours a Year,* it was a retrospective account of *Time*'s and *Fortune*'s pictorial journalism as well as that of *The March of Time*. In the introduction, the editors spoke of pictures as "a new language, difficult, as yet unmastered, but incredibly

273

powerful and strangely universal," and of opportunities as yet unful-
filled: "The gathering and writing of news-facts and the taking and
gathering of news-photographs are carried on as two separate and
unrelated functions of journalism. Word-journalism being senior in
point of time and custom, photo-journalism is still regarded as a sort
of mechanical sideline to the serious business of fact-narration—a
social inferior which, on certain regrettable and accidental occasions,
may steal the show. The webbing of the news-photo into the woof of
journalism is an evolutionary process barely begun."

The staff of Time Inc. was excited by rumors of the new project. In
March, C. D. Jackson tried to quiet these with this memo: "The
current activity on the 51st floor may give rise to the query, what's
up? Something is up, and until further notice it should be considered
an office secret. The Experimental Department is working on the idea
of a picture supplement for *Time*. The less said about it, the better."
His memorandum was very obviously a diversionary tactic. Some hint
of Time Inc.'s intentions had appeared in the newspaper columns
because of the company's increased activity in picture procurement,
an interest that obviously outstripped the immediate requirements of
Time and *Fortune*. In March, for instance, Time Inc. had signed a
reciprocal agreement for use of the full pictures services of the
Associated Press; and Time Inc., through a wholly owned subsidiary,
Pictures Inc., became the sales agent for non-newspaper rights to
Associated Press pictures. The real purpose of Pictures Inc. was to
acquire for the Time Inc. magazines the rights to pictures from all
foreign and domestic agencies. At the same time there was set up a
central picture-procurement bureau within the company. All of this
was to ensure that the editors would have unlimited access to the
output of news photographs from every available source.

In June 1936 Luce made a formal presentation to the directors.
The magazine would have a page size approximately that of the
Illustrated London News, be printed on "shiny" (coated) paper
"much better than *Time*'s, not quite as good as that of the most
expensive magazines," contain 40 to 48 pages of editorial matter to
be supported by 20 pages of advertisements. The contents were to be

a bigger and better collection of current news photographs than is available in all the current events magazines plus all the Sunday gravure supplements combined. Altogether about 200 photographs with full explanatory captions.

The tentative price: ten cents on newsstands, or $3 a year. The name: *Dime, The Show-Book of the World.* (Within the office the staff called it "Uncle Harry's Show-Book.")

The basic premise was that "people like to look at pictures . . . but nowhere are all the best . . . pictures brought together and printed clearly on good paper in logical, coherent sequence so that you can enjoy and study them in one comfortable sitting." *Dime,* said Luce, would not be a "mere selector" of pictures; it would edit as well as select, and would

> seek to advance the art and function of pictorial journalism. It will have its own staff of four or five outstandingly good camera men [and] be a ready purchaser of the best product of the best free-lance camera men. . . . *Dime* will be the complete and reliable *record* of all the significant events which are recorded in pictures [and] will seek to reveal more of the current events . . . and more of the contemporary life of the world . . . than has hitherto been revealed in pictures.

The financial outlook for the magazine was admittedly uncertain, inconclusive on the prospect for profit:

> It is easy to imagine how millions can be made out of *Dime.* Since it is by far the biggest and best package of pictures for the money, and since "everybody" likes to look at pictures, it will achieve millions of circulation and, having achieved five or ten million circulation, it will be the most potent advertising medium in the United States. Result: profits sufficient to pay off the national debt.
>
> But alas, short of this dream bonanza, it is difficult to find a logical profit formula. Truth is that *Dime* is not an investment —or even a speculation—which is likely to appeal to an unimag-

275

inative Scotsman. For example, here is a budget for 500,000 circulation with an advertising rate of $2,000 a page:

Income

1,000 pages of advertising @ $1,700 net	$1,700,000
500,000 circulation @ 5 cents per copy	$1,300,000 [1]
	$3,000,000

Expenses

Paper and Printing (plus some allowance for replacement of circulation)	$2,200,000
Editorial	250,000
Selling Ads	250,000
Circulation Promotion	200,000
General	100,000
	$3,000,000

A magazine which cannot make money on 500,000 circulation and a $3,000,000 turnover is not one which is calculated to separate a Scotsman from his whiskey.

Dime was set up on a financial pattern radically different from that of *Time* and *Fortune*. Those magazines had relatively low break-even points; by reason of their high subscription prices, nearly all the cost of printing and publishing could, theoretically, be paid for by a small number of subscribers. To apply the same principle to the new magazine would require a price of 25 cents a copy, "which would put it out of the reach of the middle-class American [and] thereby deny one of the chief characteristics of pictures, which is that 'everybody' likes them." *Dime*'s circulation would pay only for the cost of printing and paper for its 40 to 48 editorial pages and the cost of maintaining circulation. The advertising revenues had to cover: the cost of printing the advertising pages, and of selling them; the cost of putting together the editorial content; any increased costs of circulation; and all overhead. The margin of profit rested entirely on the sale of

[1] Figure represents not gross but net returns from newsstand sales.

advertising, which meant that "the gamble is largely on the question of whether or not *Dime* will prove to be a popular advertising medium."

The publishing plan envisaged publication in early autumn 1936 in order to take advantage of the Christmas gift subscription season, which it was hoped would enable the magazine to establish a circulation base of 200,000 (not the 500,000 in the imaginary budget) for 1937; the basic page rate for advertising was to be $1,200, or $6 per thousand. The goal was to sell 1,000 pages in 1937. On this basis, the presentation concluded:

> Investment in 1936 will be between $250,000 and $400,000. If all goes well, *Dime* will theoretically break even in 1937. But if all goes well, *Dime* must drive on to bigger circulation, which will require an additional $300,000. If things do not go well, the $300,000 will be needed for repair and for retreat purposes. That comes to a total of $700,000 indicated outlay. Add to that another $300,000 for bad (or good) luck and it can safely be assumed that $1,000,000 will see *Dime* safely through to a break-even 500,000 circulation or to an honorable grave.

The directors voted to proceed.

Luce's associates had mixed feelings. Stillman, an enthusiastic supporter of *Fortune,* was lukewarm—possibly, he admitted, "because the subject matter of *Fortune* was of more intense interest to me." Allen Grover wrote: "The sums involved, the long odds against success, the small return to the company from anything except an enormous circulation, make it a gamble which puts Wall Street and Broadway to shame." But he was for the venture because he felt the company should invest in publishing.

The staff was virtually unanimous that the name *Dime* would not do. Gottfried wrote: *"Dime* is a swell name but it will soon rival syphilis as a cause of insanity—among telephone operators, office boys, newsstand boys, newsstand buyers, advertisers and everyone who has to use Dee-ime and Tee-ime in a business way. . . . You might even call it 'Tent'; it covers everything." Another argued, "I don't like *Dime;* after all, you might want to change the price some day." Nick Wallace wrote from Chicago: "When I visualize the countless errors in handling which are sure to result from a name that sounds and looks so much like *Time,* I start picking me out a nice, comfortable sanitarium. One of our worst bug-bears is the illegible writing of most people. We can now pick out the word *Time* without much difficulty, but when that is complicated by deciding whether it is *Time* or *Dime,* we will all be dizzy. . . . Call the new magazine (1) Scene—or Seen (2) Pictures (3) anything but *Dime!* Please!" Larsen was for the name: "It strikes me as crazy enough to make sense."

Between June 8 and 29, Luce produced a prospectus for the new magazine that has seldom been surpassed as a piece of promotion:

> To see life; to see the world; to eyewitness great events; to watch the faces of the poor and the gestures of the proud; to see strange things—machines, armies, multitudes, shadows in the jungle and on the moon; to see man's work—his paintings, towers and discoveries; to see things thousands of miles away, things hidden behind walls and within rooms, things dangerous to come to; the women that men love and many children; to see and to take pleasure in seeing; to see and be amazed; to see and be instructed.
>
> Thus to see, and to be shown, is now the will and new expectancy of half mankind.
>
> To see, and to show, is the mission now undertaken by a new kind of publication, *The Show-Book of the World,*[2] hereinafter described.

The need and opportunity for *Show-Book* existed because while there were many pictures in a week's harvest of news, nowhere could be seen at one comfortable sitting "the cream of all the world's pictures," and almost no attempt had been made to

> edit pictures into a coherent story—to make an effective mosaic out of the fragmentary documents which pictures, past and present, are. . . . And, more than that . . . reveal to us far more

[2] A footnote said, "Actual name will appear on Vol. I, No. 1."

278

explicitly the nature of the dynamic social world in which we live.

The magazine promised to scour the world for the best pictures, to edit them with feeling for form, history, and drama, and to publish them on fine paper in a "complete and reliable record." The magazine's content would be built, the prospectus promised, on two cornerstones: the Big Newspicture Story of the Week—"the biggest news that is best recorded by the camera"—and the Big Special Feature, "some subject of major current interest and significance." As distinguished from the News, the function of the Feature

> will be Revelation—taking you intimately into the life of a famed personage, be it Shirley Temple or the Pope; or intimately into the inner workings of a celebrated institution, such as The Jockey Club, The Japanese Army, Alcatraz, Vassar or Father Divine's Heaven. . . .

The rest of the contents would vary as pictures vary, but at least two or three "great photographs" were promised, and pictures recording "the shifting mores and fashions," Broadway openings and Hollywood movies; and *Show-Book* undertook to "crash the Party-of-the-Week." Finally, the prospectus promised to produce the unpredictable,

> so that while *Show-Book*'s readers will usually know what to expect they will never be quite sure that they will not get a whacking surprise. . . .

All in all, *Show-Book* promised to be quite a package. The editor of *Advertising and Selling,* on reading the prospectus, commented: "The fine promissory glow, conviction of success and siren seductiveness which Luce wraps up in a prospectus is lost on a publication, but would make millions for an enterprising pre-SEC underwriting house. . . . Seems sort of a shame that they have to get out a new magazine and can't just sell the prospectus."

Life: Vol. I, No. 1

T
HE CREATION of a new magazine, Luce wrote in describing the
launching of *Life,* is "a compound of hundreds upon hundreds of decisions, varying in importance from agreement on
an editorial point of view, frequency of issue, schedule of prices, etc.,
to style rules on the use of commas. These decisions are based upon
innumerable individual experiments, mock-ups, make-ups and make-
believes—trial copy, trial photographs."

It was a far from orderly process, extending over eight months in
1936, and before the first issue appeared the nerves and physical
resources of the company were stretched to the breaking point. The
decision to publish was taken before any number of essentials had
been determined. The first sales staff was hired before a dummy had
been prepared; the men were handed a copy of *Four Hours a Year*
and told to study it. They made their first calls on the trade before the
date of publication had been set, a circulation guarantee established
or the page size chosen—and the magazine had no name. (In the
office, *Parade* was a working title.) Yet such was Time Inc.'s reputation in advertising circles that some agencies were willing to take a
chance. And, of course, the Luce prospectus, circulated to the trade,

became a powerful persuader. Ben Duffy of Batten, Barton, Durstine & Osborn immediately signed a space contract. Dr. George Gallup, of Young & Rubicam, predicted the magazine would be successful because Time Inc. "had the intelligence and initiative to grasp an idea which has been a natural ever since pictures were born. . . ." On the basis of a series of test mailings in late spring the circulation guarantee was set at 250,000 and the advertising rates at $1,500 for a full page, inside color at $2,250 and the fourth cover in color at $3,000. Advertisers who signed contracts prior to publication were guaranteed these rates for the first twelve months—as it turned out, one of the greatest bargains in the history of periodical advertising, and a near-disaster for Time Inc.

The circulation guarantee proved to be conservative, because prior to the first issue the new magazine had 235,000 charter subscriptions. The first major mail solicitation, a letter over Luce's signature, went to 755,000 subscribers to *Time* and *Fortune*. It consisted of a description of the magazine and concluded with a direct personal appeal:

. . . before we take our final plunge, before we risk upwards of $1,000,000, we need some friendly assurance that you and people like you—the alert, newsminded audience for whom we are planning our new venture—are willing to risk with us the price of a year's subscription.

We must reach our final decision this month—to publish or not to publish.

So if you think we are right—

If you have faith that we can create with pictures a new magazine you would value as you now value *Time* or *Fortune* . . . if you are willing to join us in the venture as an Original Subscriber—

Then may I ask you—please—to help us to our decision by signing the enclosed card today and rushing it back to me airmail.

It was one of the most successful mailings in Time Inc.'s experience; 26,151 cards were returned in a single day, 72,955 in the first week (almost 10-percent return).

Financial and production planning was enormously complicated.

281

Pierrie Prentice, who had succeeded as over-all circulation manager after Larsen moved to *The March of Time,* prepared a series of budgets based on a variety of plans—"for a 25¢ fortnightly at 100,000 circulation," for a weekly of the same circulation and "one last shot at a 10¢ quality magazine" at 100,000, 200,000 and 500,000 circulation. By mid-May fourteen production and distribution budgets had been produced for magazines with a circulation of 200,000 and a 280,000 print order. They included page sizes ranging from 9⅜″ x 13⅜″ (*Parade*) to 10½″ x 14″ (*Illustrated London News*), and a variety of qualities of paper. In the absence of firm decision there was an air of unreality about much of this budgeting.

In the preliminary stages the production planning was handled by a committee, which apparently added to the confusion at the Chicago end. There Nick Wallace was rapidly running out of patience. He remarked that things were being done the way Baptists prepare for a picnic, with "no allowance for rain, and it always rains." On his own initiative Wallace came to New York to confront Stillman with the situation and to demand that Stillman take charge of production. Stillman did so with the help of the company's assistant treasurer, David W. Brumbaugh.

Brumbaugh, a man of rising importance, had been hired by Stillman in 1933 through a want ad in the New York *Times* which brought hundreds of responses. Among these was a letter from a Dr. Seay, who said he knew just the right person and hoped Time Inc. would make no final choice until his nominee could be interviewed. Stillman did not know Dr. Seay, or that his candidate was his prospective son-in-law. Purely on a hunch, he took Seay's advice and interviewed Brumbaugh. In advising the directors of his choice, Stillman wrote that the new man was "a native of Virginia, where he worked his way through Roanoke College, emerged with an A.B. and a scholastic average of 90. He then borrowed the money to go to Harvard Business School, specialized there in Accounting, was graduated with Honors in 1931." His starting salary was $3,000 a year.

It was Brumbaugh's memorandum, entitled "Recording of a Decision of Major Importance," that justified the adoption of the large page size. The choice had narrowed to a *Vogue*-size page (9¾″ x

282

12¾"), which offered the prospect for greater profit, or the larger *Illustrated London News*-size page, which the editors preferred. The decision was to settle on the 10½" x 14" page size; this was slightly larger than that of the *Saturday Evening Post,* offered excellent display for photographs but at the same time would accommodate advertising plates made for either *Vogue* or the *Saturday Evening Post.* An appendix to the memorandum reflected the philosophy that still guides Time Inc. management:

> Never in our history have we come out of any tight spot by a choice of conservatism or economy *in the usual sense of those words,* but always by expenditure of more money and more effort to gain greater income at greater expense. This will always be the right choice as long as the ideas and the vitality are flowing freely to keep pace with the increased outlays. This has produced profits which must be considered the result of the most effective and hence the most economical use of an enviable concentration of manpower, an element in success far scarcer than gold, no matter what price per ounce.

It was relatively easy to decide on a page size; it was far more difficult to fulfill Luce's prime specification—the quality reproduction of photographs on coated paper. The technology required in both printing and paper-making was far from perfected when Donnelley delivered to New York their first experimental samples. Prior to 1936, for instance, coated paper in rolls was not readily procurable because there was little demand for it. Magazines which used coated paper were printed on sheet-fed presses and therefore the paper was delivered in the form of sheets rather than rolls. The Mead Corporation, which supplied paper for *Time,* would supply coated paper in rolls on demand, but it was produced by a costly and cumbersome method, each side of the paper being coated separately. While patented processes did exist for coating paper on both sides of the sheet in one continuous operation, they had not been developed. One of Stillman's first problems was to determine whether an adequate supply of coated paper could be guaranteed. The Mead engineers went to work on the problem, came up with a paper which they called Enameline, offered at a tentative price of $98 a ton, well within the budget projections for the new magazine. While the Mead production was limited, Stillman felt that sufficient progress had been made so that he could gamble that additional supplies would be made available if a market developed.

There was a problem in printing; the experimental pages Donnelley had shown in New York were produced on makeshift equipment specially converted to accommodate the new quick-drying ink. The ideal procedure would have been to design and engineer new presses, the construction of which would have taken a year or more. The men at Time Inc. were determined not to wait. The men at the Donnelley plant therefore took two presses which had previously been used to print mail-order catalogues, equipped them with gas-fired heaters needed to speed the drying of the ink. They had many misgivings about this equipment. A few weeks before the first issue went to press, T. E. Donnelley recalled, he told Zimmermann, "We may have overestimated our ability to deliver. The foreman just told me he has yet to get a satisfactorily printed sheet out of those converted presses." The two presses alone were not adequate to handle the job; pending the delivery of new machinery, the magazine had to use, as standby and auxiliary equipment, a rotogravure press and outmoded sheet-fed presses.

The Luce prospectus seemed to provide a coherent and clear editorial blueprint; it proved more difficult to translate into a printed magazine than was at first anticipated. The earliest surviving dummy was produced—so the editors said—"from the 5,000-odd pictures that came into existence or were for the first time available to U.S. magazines during the week of May 18–23 . . . selected and arranged experimentally to demonstrate our conviction that, while the camera has achieved high efficiency as a reporter and recorder of our time, a journalistic job remains to be done in articulating a language of pictures." It was, by common agreement of all who worked on it, a failure. It lacked taste and distinction and was too sensational. Among the pictures were those of a lynching, brutally captioned "Nigger Hunt," a murderer strapped in the death chair and a nudist colony at the San Diego fair. "One nude is nude," MacLeish hooted on seeing this spread, "twenty nudes are just bare."

A printed effort, entitled *Dummy,* was produced in midsummer; it went to press in twelve days under conditions intended to simulate actual publication. A good deal of confusion prevailed; Thomas Cleland, the designer of *Fortune,* had been hired as a consultant, but complained to Luce that he had been ignored: ". . . I was never even consulted . . . or given any opportunity . . . to correct or revise any of my own part of it. It appears to have been immediately subjected to the criticism and suggestions of all the Toms, Dicks and Harrys except the particular Tom engaged for that purpose by the particular Harry who engaged him." The editors, well aware of *Dummy*'s shortcomings, asked its readers to "please pretend . . . a magazine like this has been coming to the house every Thursday. This is no special issue—indeed it is below par and suggests that the regular editorial staff had gone on vacation leaving this issue to be put to press by inexperienced juniors."

The selected audience to which *Dummy* was shown was not impressed. "It was a complete flop, as far as we were concerned," said Longwell. While Director Robert Chambers objected that the pictures were "lurid—reminiscent of the graphics [the tabloids]," former director Harry Davison told Luce he doubted that the magazine would interest "the average straphanger."

Luce agreed with both of them. To Chambers he wrote: "Most of the criticisms were on the other side of the fence. . . . The point is, of course, that we do not intend to appeal to the mob, but we do hope that the magazine will appeal to a million or more people who are not all of them high-brow." And to Davison: "The dummy was a disappointment. . . . I hope it proves we can't do any worse. . . . We are now setting out to get the job done right."

Another critic was Paul Hollister, a friend of Luce and Larsen and one of the most creative advertising men of his generation. When *Dummy* appeared he was executive vice-president of R. H. Macy & Co. in charge of advertising. He wrote Luce: "It is inconceivable that even an avowed dress rehearsal just for 'fun' should have turned out so far short even of where you intended. . . . Great God, that a

LOOKS paper should make even a tentative *peek* looking like this.
. . . The dangerous thing is you have good raw material; it must not
be 'bootchered.' " He added that he was taking off for a vacation at
Manchester-by-the-Sea in Massachusetts, but that for $1,000 he
would rework *Dummy* and show how it should be done. He did not
expect this offer to be taken up, but Monday morning in Manchester
his telephone rang. As he remembered the conversation:

> Luce: "I got your note. It is very intriguing."
> Hollister: "Oh."
> Luce: "What do we do now?"
> Hollister: "What do you mean, what do we do now?"
> Luce: "I mean what do you do next? I want your comments."

Hollister asked to have twenty copies shipped to him; he then drove
to nearby Gloucester, bought a drawing board, a can of rubber
cement, scissors, art gum and a T-square. For ten days he holed up,
forgoing beach, tennis and golf, re-making *Dummy*. Longwell went up
to see the result—a new dummy, pasted up accordion-style so it could
be spread out on the floor. Longwell said it was "fine."

That was all Hollister heard for several weeks. Finally he wrote
Luce: "Was it that bad?"

Next day he was invited to lunch in New York with Luce, Longwell
and Ingersoll. Luce described to Hollister the work-in-progress, then
turned to him and said:

"Now we have an editorial prospectus. Now we have a basic
format. . . . Now what do we do?"

"What you do," replied Hollister, "is to get an art director and put
him at a drawing board. Put tape over his mouth, because whatever
he has to state should drain off through his fingers onto paper. Never
let an art director talk. On a table at his left put your basic format
dummy for reference. Onto a table at his right, feed him batches of
photographs with a note saying you want 1, 2, 3, 8—any number of
pages you need, for each batch, and any suggestions you have for
playing up any particular angles of the picture story.

"So he makes layouts from the pictures. If they are right, you pat
him on the head. If they have strayed from the mood of the basic

286

format, you take a small hammer, rap him smartly on the skull, point severely to the dummy and cry 'No, no, no! Naughty!' He then repents and makes the layout right or you get yourself a new art director."

"Fine," said Luce. "Will you get us an art director?"

In September, Hollister recommended his own art director at Macy's, Howard Richmond, for the job.

Luce designated himself as managing editor "for an unstated term of months or years." His alternate, he said, would be John Martin, who, when the magazine was successfully under way, would take over, enabling Luce to "retire to his sinecure as General Editor of Time Inc. publications"; Longwell became picture editor, "supremely responsible for the flow of pictures. . . . Every nickel spent for pictures and all work of photographers must be regulated by him. . . ." There were three associate editors (writers): Joseph Kastner, drafted from *Fortune*;[1] Thorndike, who had been with the Experimental Department from the beginning; and David Cort, transferred from *Time*. The first staff photographers listed were Eisenstaedt and Stackpole; the names of McAvoy and Bourke-White were added within a few weeks.

Miss Mary Fraser, designated by Luce as copy chief, would, he said, "be in the unhappy position of having two bosses, but as between the two she is more responsible to the Picture Editor than to the Managing Editor."[2] "Fra" (Wellesley '23) was outstanding among many dedicated and resilient women who played an important role in Time Inc.'s development. On graduation she had joined the company as a circulation-department typist, then become secretary to Hadden. She resigned in the summer of 1924 to get some newspaper

---

[1] Kastner, who had had to resign as copy boy when *Time* moved to Cleveland, had been hired back in 1930 after his graduation from Yale. According to Eric Hodgins, Luce demanded one day at lunch: "Is there anyone on your staff who can be concise?" Hodgins replied that Kastner had been writing the "Off the Record" department for *Fortune* and managed to keep it within four columns. " 'Joe Kastner,' said Luce, 'that's the boy I want.' That afternoon I had to tell Joe that I had apparently and inadvertently sold him down the river."

[2] This turned out to be true in her personal life. She married Dan Longwell in December 1938.

experience on the New Brunswick (New Jersey) *Home News,* then returned to *Time* in November 1927, where she became head of research and copy chief until drafted temporarily for this new job.

This staff was largely responsible for the second printed dummy, *Rehearsal,* which was printed in September. The content, the editors said, was "suggestive" of the magazine to be; it carried some sample advertising pages, although advertisers were warned that the make-up was "not to be considered as an ultimate guide to advertising positions available" in the actual magazine. In format and content, *Rehearsal* closely approximated the magazine that appeared on the newsstands six weeks later. It had good spot-news photographs—the fall of Irun in the Spanish war; the Nazi rally at Nürnberg; a "biography," in Soviet paintings, of Stalin "as Communists *must* see him." But the photograph that caught all eyes was Paul Outerbridge's full-page color study of a seated nude, entitled (presumably because her face was averted) "Modesty."

This was long before the day of *Playboy,* in whose columns "Modesty" today would scarcely raise an eyebrow. In 1936 the editors knew all too well that so explicit a nude would not be acceptable in a magazine of general circulation. In a dummy printed for limited circulation, directed to the trade, they obviously enjoyed being a little naughty. The alarm bells sounded. The head of the American News Company warned that "while the picture will undoubtedly create sales, it would be better not to print a picture of this type in a magazine published by a house that has the wonderfully fine standing of your company." From Chicago, Nick Wallace wrote that he did not want his subscription agents to see *Rehearsal* because "it would rub them the wrong way." A *March of Time* crew, dispatched to Hyde Park to film a sequence on the Roosevelt family, took along a copy; when the President's mother's eye fell on "Modesty," she announced firmly that it was not the kind of magazine her family would wish to have in their home. T. E. Donnelley wrote Luce, "You will lose no subscribers by leaving such pictures out, and you will keep a great many more if you do." Luce replied, "As to the nudes, I'll agree. . . . Of course, I had in mind the fact that actually this dummy was not for general publication—I thought the Outerbridge color (with or without nudes) would be of special interest to advertising men."

The over-all reception of *Rehearsal* was somewhat mixed. Dorothy Thompson, the columnist, wrote Luce that she and her husband, Sinclair Lewis, thought it "curiously unmodern, a combination of Bernarr Macfadden and the *Illustrated London News*. In fact, Henry, the magazine does not look like you. I should expect from you something handsome, dramatic, speedy. . . ." Prentice was also disappointed, commenting, "If the magazine we turn out is going to be anything like that, I do not believe we will hold more than 50% of our prepublication subscribers. . . ." But Longwell was enthusiastic and told Luce: "Encouraging is the attitude of . . . people like Larsen, Billings, Hodgins. . . . They criticize [details], yet with publishing-editorial imagination enough to see what we are aiming at and how we are approaching what we shall be. Frankly, they think we could go right on the stands." Luce decided that the period of experimentation was over. "We won't experiment any more," he said to Longwell. "We'll learn how to do this in actual publication."

Some months before the first issue of *Life* went to press, there occurred an incident that had a lasting influence on the relations of Mrs. Luce to the Time Inc. magazines. Apparently neither she nor her husband had taken too seriously his promise, when he was courting her, to make her co-editor of the new picture magazine. But throughout the pre-publication period he had constantly discussed the project with her and she had been most enthusiastic. One afternoon Luce called her and, as she remembered it, said that Ingersoll and Dan Longwell had invited them to dinner, adding with a chuckle, "I think I know what's coming." " 'I said, 'What?' He said, 'I think they want to offer you a place on the magazine.' I said, 'Oh, that's wonderful!' "

At dinner at Voisin it soon became evident, at least to Mrs. Luce, that her hosts had no intention of making her an offer. Toward the end, Ingersoll asked if they could go back to the Luce apartment at River House. There, he began talking about how well Luce had handled *Time*. Then, according to Mrs. Luce, Ingersoll turned and said, "Harry, you have got to make up your mind whether you are going to go on being a great editor or whether you are going to be on a perpetual honeymoon. When you edited *Time* you stayed in the office until ten and eleven o'clock every night. Now you catch the 5:10 back to the country.[3] You clear out of that office at five o'clock every afternoon. Clare, if she really loves you, won't get in the way of the success of this magazine. And what I have to say to her is that you cannot publish a great magazine with one hand tied behind your back."

Her husband, Mrs. Luce recalled, was thunderstruck. She said to Ingersoll, "Mac, I have something to tell you, and I hope you'll remember it and Harry will remember it. Harry Luce can publish a better magazine with one hand tied behind his back than you can publish with both of yours free." And with that she went upstairs "to have a little cry."

When Ingersoll and Longwell had left, Mrs. Luce said to her husband: " 'I've been hoping and thinking of how I could be of most help to you and it's perfectly clear the way I can help you most is to set about my own business. And for some time I have been thinking what I'd like to do is to write another play.' And I did, and it made a million dollars." The play, *The Women,* produced in December 1936, ran for 657 performances on Broadway, was twice made into a movie, and has been many times revived in summer theaters.

The prospectus said that the name of the new magazine would not be announced before publication. Charter subscribers and the staff were invited to submit suggestions; the list covered several pages: *Affairs, Candid Camera, Graphic, News-Views, Pageant, Scene, Show, Witness, Sight, Eyewitness, Picture.* Paul Hollister called Luce in great excitement one morning, saying he was coming over with the ideal name. He appeared with a drawing of an eye with the word *See* superimposed. *Look* was actually used in some cover mock-ups. Larsen argued that because of the broadcast and movie, *The March of Time* should be considered.

The name finally chosen was the one Mrs. Luce had mentioned in her memorandum to Condé Nast several years before; it was also

---

[3] The Luces had a house in Connecticut as well as the apartment at River House.

suggested by James A. Linen, Jr., the father of the present president of the company and an old family friend of Luce. On reading the prospectus, he wrote, "The name *Life,* if it were to be preempted, would appear to me to best typify the proposed publication." A month later, when Luce had finally decided to buy the old *Life,* he wrote Linen, "We have been trying to get the use of the name *Life* and I had hoped [to] write you before this that we had been successful. . . . As you can see, I agree with you fully that it is the perfect name. . . ." As the prospectus said, "To see life; to see the world; to eyewitness great events . . ."

The old *Life* was in its fifty-fourth year. Founded by three young Harvard men, it had reached the peak of its circulation (a quarter million) and influence in World War I years. After the war its long-time contributor, the famous illustrator Charles Dana Gibson, acquired a controlling interest. *Life*'s pages were graced by the writing of Franklin P. Adams, Robert Benchley, Dorothy Parker and Frank Sullivan, and the drawings of Gibson himself, Gluyas Williams and the great political cartoonist Rollin Kirby. One of its editors was Robert E. Sherwood, later to become a distinguished playwright and a personal assistant and ghostwriter for Franklin D. Roosevelt. But *Life* failed to keep up with changing modes and manners; it lost ground to *The New Yorker,* was changed from a weekly to a monthly. In 1932 its ownership passed to a trio of advertising men, Clair Maxwell, Henry Richter and Frederick G. Francis. By 1936 circulation had declined to 70,000.

Was it for sale? When Luce decided on a Friday afternoon in August that *Life* was the name he wanted, he called in *Time*'s advertising manager Howard Black, a friend of Maxwell: "I practically whispered the name to him, and then asked him if he thought we could buy it. I never spent such a long, nervous weekend. It was Monday before Black reported back. 'The answer is yes,' he said, 'if you'll give jobs to the small staff.' " The matter was settled immediately; the price was $92,000.

The intention was to keep the sale secret until Time Inc. was ready to launch the new magazine, but Walter Winchell broke the story on the day of sale. However, the last issue of the old *Life* was not withdrawn from the newsstands until the day before the new *Life* appeared. The sale of *Life* touched off many sentimental tributes, among them H. I. Phillips' verse in the New York *Sun:*

> Life takes time, I always knew
> In this drab world of strife,
> But truer is the headline still
> That tells me *Time* takes *Life.*

Prior to the publication of *Life* the management of Time Inc. was aware that another picture magazine was about to be published. In fact, as a hedge against the possible failure of *Life,* it invested in the venture. John Cowles and his brother Gardner, publishers of the Des Moines *Register* and *Tribune,* were friends and stockholders of Time Inc. With full knowledge of Time Inc. plans, they showed Luce, Larsen and company a dummy of *Look.* It was planned as a monthly, printed in rotogravure on cheaper paper, aimed at a mass audience, with production costs budgeted so low that newsstand sales could produce a small profit in the first year. No advertising was to be solicited in the first year, pending the establishment of a circulation base.

The Cowleses felt there would be no competition between the two publications; they therefore offered Time Inc. a 20-percent interest in their magazine—50,000 shares for $100,000. John Cowles wrote Larsen: "Although it is an extreme gamble, we think it is a chance worth taking. . . . Circulation might conceivably go to 600,000 or 800,000 the first year. . . ." Larsen and Stillman recommended the investment, arguing that "if our plans for *Life* prove to be top-heavy with overhead and bigness, as they might, the modest scale of operations proposed by the Cowles brothers is so much the opposite extreme that they might well succeed where we might fail."

The Executive Committee agreed to the investment, taking note of a reservation by Luce, who was "afraid their journalism would prove to be too 'yellow' for us to be in entire sympathy with it." However, Larsen noted that the Cowleses "feel that they will be able to become less 'yellow' as they go along, as did the *Daily News.*" The Time Inc.

investment, at the Cowleses' request, was reduced to 45,000 shares before publication started. In July 1937, with both *Life* and *Look* in operation, the Cowleses requested that Time Inc. resell them its interest, which the company did for $157,500, a profit of $67,500.

Six months before *Life* went to press Luce took Billings aside and said, "There is going to be a lot of talk about this picture magazine. Everyone is going to want in on it. I want you to be the one person who doesn't bother his head about it. Just keep *Time* going." Luce knew his associates only too well; before the magazine appeared the company executives, with the exception of Billings, were almost wholly involved in one way or another. There was a good deal of confusion as to who was doing what, as is evidenced by a small aberration on the part of Longwell a few weeks before publication. He wrote to Ingersoll, the general manager: "May I shift off onto you lettering for the *Time* cover and stationery? Will you see that no stationery is printed until you have the final lettering for the cover?" To which Ingersoll replied acidly, "The lettering of *Life*'s (not *Time*'s) cover is your problem, not mine. When Harry and you have chosen the lettering, I shall be happy to take on matters of masthead wording, etc. . . . Stationery will not be printed until it is necessary. But in view of the tardiness of the editors, it may be necessary—in the interest of collecting money—to print stationery without benefit of cover type."

The cover design is attributed to artist Edward Wilson; his idea, said Longwell, was "to get the best damn picture we can find every week and slap *Life* on it wherever it fits on top and agrees with the design of the picture." The lettering and distinctive red background of the logotype and the red border band below were contributed by Art Director Howard Richmond. It was first proposed that the color should vary from issue to issue, but Luce and Larsen, on the basis of their experience with *Time,* decided to stay with red.

Then, only weeks from the publication date, *Life*'s editorial management underwent a shake-up. John Martin's erratic personality had begun to have a corrosive effect on everyone. He handled Longwell roughly, criticizing him before an embarrassed staff, and arbitrarily rejected pictures and layouts. He was at odds with Luce; at one luncheon he shouted down all of Luce's suggestions as "buckeye." On October 23, Billings recorded in his diary:

> At 5 o'clock Luce called me to his office, shut the door, and proceeded to tell me that a great crisis had arisen on *Life*—a crisis due to Martin's behavior. Luce and Martin just don't pull together as a team. As a result *Life* is still badly disorganized and nowhere near ready to go into publication. . . . Now Luce wants to put Martin back on *Time* and make me Managing Editor of *Life*. He thinks he and I could work well together, and so on. I was surprised and startled at this proposal. I know nothing of the philosophy of *Life* and am devoted to *Time,* which is clicking along well. . . . Yet *Life* is a new job with fresh excitement—and much harder work, I suppose. My answer to Luce was: I am ready to do whatever he thought best for the organization.

Luce wrote Martin:

> . . . You and I have not been enough of a success to date as collaborators. . . . Perhaps, without alibi, I should take most of the blame, since it was my job to organize *Life* including the "collaboration." But I must also express candidly the opinion, which is shared by others, that you are a most able editor and an equally difficult collaborator. Roy and I . . . are agreed . . . that there is one obvious good solution—namely, that you should forthwith take post again as Managing Editor of *Time* and that Billings should come to *Life* as my collaborator-in-chief. . . .

Billings took over his new assignment just seventeen days before the first issue was scheduled to go to press. "I had so much to learn in so little time," he recalled. "The staff was green and Longwell was out with the flu. . . . Everything had to go to Luce for a final yes or no. When he wasn't squinting critically at layouts or editing captions, he was filling me full of *Life*'s principles and purposes. *Life* would inform, but it would also entertain. There was to be a lot of show business about it. It would have unity in flow, pace and change of pace, charm and shock—phrases that persisted for years."

Typical of the confusion, not to say near-chaos, attending the birth of *Life* was a curious episode involving Ingersoll, who withdrew from current operations, retired by himself to a hotel room and produced a seventy-four-page memorandum re-examining the whole project. He handed this massive document to Luce on November 2, just two weeks before the first deadline. Luce dropped it into his desk drawer unread. Ingersoll felt that he was being slighted. Luce then had to take time out to mollify him, writing:

> Your work is neither lost nor wasted nor unappreciated. . . . If I am petulant, I am sorry and will try to reform. Meanwhile, what is most on my mind is *getting things done*—and for the next few weeks the emphasis should be on volume rather than quality of work. By quality, I mean whether I cause the right or the wrong thing to be done. If my instincts are wrong, it's too late to change them or me now. . . . Right now I'm afraid, alas, it's got to be the spirit of the Light Brigade—disastrous as that proved to be. Here's hoping we survive!

The cover for Vol. I, No. 1, was Margaret Bourke-White's picture of the massive Fort Peck Dam being built by the WPA in Montana. The frontispiece, captioned "Life Begins," showed an obstetrician holding a newborn baby by its heels. The news section began with further pictures of Fort Peck, showing the workers at a Saturday-night jamboree and the frontier shanty towns where they lived. There were pace and variety in its pages—the first aerial photograph of Fort Knox; Fort Belvedere, Edward VIII's country residence; a spectacular shot of the newly opened Bay Bridge linking San Francisco and Oakland. There were scenes from the Broadway hit *Victoria Regina,* with a family album of the star, Helen Hayes, and from *Camille,* about to open with Greta Garbo and "today's Great Lover of the Screen," Robert Taylor. The magazine offered a three-page color portfolio of the paintings of John Steuart Curry, the first of many which would acquaint *Life* readers with America's contemporary artists. The magazine closed with a party—a hunt given in honor of the British Ambassador to France. The last picture in the magazine was the enormous bag: row on row of dead hares.

Editorially the first issue made a pleasing impression, giving no indication of the infinitely complicated process of putting it to press. With the exception of one advance form, *Time* had a single deadline. *Life* had to be put to press in sections, which meant that the editors had to meet a succession of deadlines. The *Life* editors had to assemble a layout with the original photographs and captions and ship these to Chicago nightly by the Twentieth Century Limited. In an emergency, substitute pictures could be sent by wirephoto and corrections teletyped, but this added a further complication best avoided. Thus the struggle to keep pace with the production schedule and current with the news imposed a constant strain on the editors, writers and artists. The pictures for the lead in the first issue did not arrive until twenty-four hours before the final deadline; Luce and Billings were so swamped with detail at that moment that they had to turn them over to Ingersoll for layout. He drafted MacLeish from *Fortune* to write the captions.

The deadline was Saturday night, but Stillman, who had gone to Chicago to oversee the first printing, reported that on Monday morning when he arrived,

> Wallace had just sent through some changes on two pages that had come by teletype. At around 10:30 a.m. Chicago time (11:30 a.m. New York) Ingersoll telephoned four more changes.
>
> There were four rotary presses supposedly all made ready and set to go, but it wasn't until 4:30 p.m. that the first press started turning out acceptable work. The rest followed along, but it didn't make much difference how fast they turned over, as the bottleneck of the operation proved to be the collating of the twelve sections.

The sections printed in advance had to be assembled with the later pages and fed into machines—stitchers—to bind the magazine together. Crews of girls did the collating:

There were four gangs working. But the paper being slippery and the sheets larger and heavier and the line longer than they were used to, they made very heavy going. Furthermore many of the girls were green. . . . Desperate efforts were made to speed up, including taking two crews off the *Farm Journal* and putting them on *Life.* . . . They averaged about 7,000 an hour and with all available girl power on the job, they were just barely keeping their heads above water, running about 50,000 copies behind schedule.

When Luce saw the first proofs from Chicago "he thought the whole issue had gone sour on the press," Billings recalled. With the actual delivery of finished copies the mood changed. "As the congratulations and cheers began to roll in, we all felt better," wrote Billings. "Of course there were always the jokers who were quick to write, 'You stink!' [But] we seemed to have a success on our hands. But one issue does not make a magazine, and we had to push on and on."

On Thursday morning, November 19, 1936, some 200,000 copies of the first issue of *Life* were placed on sale, 475 of them in Worcester, Massachusetts. These 475 copies were sold out in a few hours, as were copies in other cities; scores of telegrams from news-dealers poured into the headquarters of the American News Company asking for additional magazines. The orders could not be filled because the press run of 466,000 had already been exhausted. Gratifying as was the demand, management partially discounted it, attributing the initial sellout to curiosity. The following week the magazine sold out again, and again in the third and fourth weeks. The press run could not keep up with the demand. Management was totally unprepared for a situation unparalleled in the history of periodical publishing. Until 1936 the largest circulation ever attained by any magazine in its first year of publication was 500,000, a figure *Life* had apparently surpassed in weeks. A Time Inc. executive, asked how the new magazine was doing, replied, "Having *Life* isn't like having a baby. It's like having quintuplets."

In an attempt to gauge the market, management decided to flood the newsstands of Worcester. The test began with the December 4 issue and a shipment of 2,000 copies; they disappeared as quickly as the original 475 copies. In successive weeks the shipments were raised to 3,000, then 4,000. After 9,000 copies of the March 8 issue were sold, the Worcester distributor telegraphed: "Send 12,000 next week." Another sellout. This figure—12,000—projected on a national scale, indicated that the potential demand for *Life* was between five and six million copies, an all but incredible figure in view of the fact that the biggest newsstand sale for any national magazine was one million—at a per-copy price of five cents v. ten cents for *Life*. Tests in other cities confirmed the figure.

In publishing the story of the Worcester experiment as a two-page house advertisement, *Life* said: "There are many reasons why the Publishers . . . cannot feed endless freight trains of smooth stock paper into the maws of innumerable presses. The demand for 5 or 6 million copies a week is the kind of demand we can *not* follow. So we can only settle down to producing our 1,000,000 a week now and gradually raise production to 1,500,000 by the end of the year. Meanwhile our principal efforts will be devoted to making *Life* a magazine of continuing pleasure and profit to the millions of people who will read each issue this year."

CHAPTER

23

"We Are Poor Again"

IN MARCH 1937, to the surprise of some associates—Ingersoll
said it was "a bolt from the blue"—Luce announced a decen-
tralization of management by the appointment of a publisher for
each of the magazines. Larsen was named publisher of *Life* (a job
that he had been filling *de facto* since pre-publication days), Ingersoll
of *Time,* and Hodgins of *Fortune.* The purpose of having a publisher,
Luce wrote, was to have "one executive . . . continuously and exclusively engaged in promoting the welfare of one publication from every
point of view. (I found it possible to be the continuously responsible
editor-publisher of two magazines but it is long since apparent that I
cannot be the continuously responsible editor-publisher of each and
every one of our present publications)." [1] The table of organization
for the magazines, in the future, would comprise a publisher, a
managing editor and an advertising director. Thus, after long fretting
over the ideal form of organization, Luce in one stroke created the
Time Inc. division system that still obtains.

[1] Louis de Rochemont, responsible to Larsen, produced *The March of Time;*
Howard Myers was editor-publisher of the *Architectural Forum.*

299

"This form of decentralized organization will mean that less will be done by what is known as 'General Management,' " Luce added, explaining that general management consisted of the president (himself), a general manager, a treasurer (Stillman) and a comptroller (Brumbaugh). His memorandum did not mention the circulation department, which, under Pierrie Prentice, continued to serve all the magazines. Ingersoll retained the title of general manager of Time Inc. as well as publisher of *Time*,[2] an anomaly which Luce admitted "violates the theory of this scheme. However, while we must achieve a clearer definition and delegation of responsibility, we need not become slaves to an organization theory." The title of general manager was dropped a year later.

Luce's decision to decentralize was a direct consequence of the staggering problems arising from the soaring circulation of *Life,* which caused feelings of triumph coupled with consternation at the tremendous losses following in its wake. Luce remained deeply involved in the perplexing questions of *Life* for the better part of 1937. He hoped, of course, that the appointment of publishers would free him from too much involvement with the other magazines. In one sense it did, but the new publisher of *Fortune* and his successor as managing editor, Russell Davenport, soon were themselves engaged in making important changes in that magazine's editorial direction— changes that Luce himself instigated. On *Time,* to which Luce was devoting the least of his attention, Ingersoll on his own initiative undertook an internal reorganization. The inauguration of the new system therefore set in motion a period of the most intense activity in every division at a critical and exciting moment.

On *Life,* the result of the Worcester experiment precipitated a debate on the magazine's long-term objective. The immediate decision—to limit circulation for the time being to a million copies, then to increase to 1,500,000—was of necessity. It was impossible to produce any more copies. In fact, it was only by prodigies of effort on the part of the Donnelley company that *Life* was able to deliver a million copies each week. The pre-publication plans called for weekly production of

[2] He had also been made a vice-president the year before.

300

400,000 increasing slowly to a million over a three-year period to permit the orderly introduction of new equipment. The delivery of a million copies weekly was achieved by running the presses around the clock, shutting down only to change plates for the next issue. During the first months there was literally no print order; Publisher Larsen took all the magazines that could be printed. The circulation department was never certain how many copies would be available. The equipment was not geared to such a demand and the weekly runs were subject to many hazards. The early heaters used to dry the ink were gas-fired and as the web was exposed to the heat a thin sheet of flame could be seen spreading across the paper as the volatile solvents were released. If for any reason the web slowed or the press stopped, the paper was liable to catch fire. One visitor to the Lakeside Press was told that fires were so frequent that there was no time for fire drills. But, by some miracle, there were only two damaging press fires in the first year of production.

Production was also endangered by shortage of coated paper. Prior to publication, Stillman had contracted for 10,000 tons from the Mead Corporation; he estimated that *Life* in its first year, with 350,000 circulation, would consume 11,000 tons and that consumption would increase gradually to 35,000 tons in 1940. Within six months *Life* was consuming more than three times the pre-publication estimate. There were no facilities in existence for producing such quantities. Stillman and his associates bought the best paper they could at whatever price in the open market, much of it of inferior grade. The day-to-day supply was so precarious that in Chicago members of the *Life* production staff could be seen leaning from their office windows counting the incoming freight cars being shunted onto the Donnelley siding, hoping the day's delivery would be sufficient to keep the presses going.

As the circulation increased, losses skyrocketed and very soon were running at the rate of $50,000 a week; the original estimate of $1,000,000 to see *Life* break even or to "an honorable grave" proved a major miscalculation. As early as December 1936 *Life* announced that in February 1937 advertising rates would be doubled; even the new rates did not fully reflect the actual delivered circulation. More-

301

over, the holders of pre-publication contracts had the privilege of ordering additional space at the original rates, and many were quick to make the best of a bargain. The more circulation and the more advertising, the greater the losses.

The losses could not be avoided ad interim. But the urgent long-range question concerned *Life*'s future. Should facilities be expanded to meet the demand indicated by the Worcester experiment—expansion which would require the company and/or its suppliers to make capital commitments running into millions of dollars? Pushing *Life*'s circulation into the millions also meant that *Life* would be entering direct competition with long-established mass-media magazines like the *Saturday Evening Post* and *Collier's*. As Ingersoll put it, a race with them was one in which "there is a big cash purse for the winner and only a silver-plated cup with your name engraved on it for the runner-up." Stillman, who had long since overcome initial reservations as to the wisdom of the new enterprise, was now for going all out. On the back of a place mat from the Hollywood Palace Hotel in Los Angeles he wrote Larsen: "I believe we have got the chance of a lifetime. . . . We should have a set statement which we all make about the money we are losing and why we are losing it. Then we should proceed to lose it without hysterics in an atmosphere of *complete and serene confidence* that we know what we are doing and that we are building a great property for the advertiser and ourselves. Any limitation policy smacks of hysterics—an admission that we are taken by surprise by our own creation instead of exuding confidence, which is what will sell the big-time advertisers a year from now."

Larsen was in agreement; he argued for a policy based on

(1) Recognition of *Life* as a *Satevepost* with circulation of 2,500,000–3,500,000.
(2) Recognition of possible short-lived business boom to 1939–41.
(3) Recognition of necessity for leadership in weekly mag field once we pass 1,500,000.
   (a) Leadership can ask and get highest price; runners-up take lower than leader's price.

302

(4) 1938 profits must pay '36–37 losses.

(5) 1938 must be another stepping-stone year.

Luce was not wholly persuaded; he still wanted to move more slowly, not get the company too much involved with capital expenditures, paper plants, etc., and avoid a direct confrontation with other magazines. His answer to Larsen:

> *Yes,* as to the unabashed recognition that a well-edited *Life* may be destined to have and to hold 2,500,000 or more circulation. But *No,* as to direct comparison with *Satevepost* as advertising medium. . . . Let us recognize that *Life* may develop into as *"different" a thing advertisingly as it is editorially.* As a matter of fact, *Life* has to be defined editorially before it can be defined advertisingly. . . . It will take at least one year to see what our editorial definition will lead to for better or for worse. . . . In 1938 we have to determine whether *Life* is a sound and profitable advertising medium. If *Life* is a good advertising medium, it will be good at 1,500,000—without any reference to whether it will go to 3,000,000.

He did not agree with Larsen on the necessity of "leadership" (i.e., being top dog in circulation):

> The more we concern ourselves with the leadership angle, the more we have to fight the price battle—until we have achieved sound leadership. We need a higher price. But I don't think we need leadership to get it. I am for having a pretty low price in 1938—to make unmistakably sure the advertiser gets his money's worth. . . .

However Luce tried to skirt the idea, his decision meant that *Life* was going to head for a mass circulation and rigorous competition. Years later Howard Black recalled that in 1937 a million dollars was bandied about rather freely. He remembered being at a meeting in the Cloud Club with Luce, Larsen and Stillman. Luce asked those assembled, "Shall we lose another million dollars on *Life* this year?" All agreed they should.

303

Luce's comment that *Life* still needed editorial definition reflected his belief that its editors had not yet mastered the art of editing pictures. It was a technique to be learned by trial and error. The readers, intrigued by the novelty of pictures, were unaware that for the first year of publication the editors were still experimenting. The pattern of the magazine changed weekly. For instance, an early rule adopted by *Life* editors was that no photograph would be retouched. But they often forced photographs into strange shapes—ovals, circles—and even tried cropping them diagonally. John Billings called such layouts "cookie cutouts"; the contorted shapes were eventually abandoned. A means of telling a complete and coherent story in pictures also had to be worked out. In the European picture magazines and the Sunday rotogravure sections little effort was made to relate one picture to another; *Life*'s editors worked as hard as *Time* writers to lay out picture stories that would have a beginning, a middle and an end.

The marriage of words and pictures required the evolution of a *Life* writing style quite different from that of *Time*. "Most of the first editors and writers on *Life* had worked on *Time,* and they instinctively brought over their favorite words and rhythm of *Time* writing," said Billings. "As managing editor I sought to eliminate all traces of the so-called '*Time* style' and to develop a fresh literary form, clear, simple and factual, which would blend smoothly with the predominating pictures." Writing for *Life* had its special problems. The format demanded that all captions should square off; this meant that writers were required to conform to a predetermined character count, a difficult literary exercise.

The prospectus referred to the magazine as "the Show-Book of the World"; soon the staff was referring to sets of pictures as "acts," a theatrical term that was peculiarly apt. The managing editor, in assembling his raw material, was in some ways more a producer than an editor; he had to be concerned that his sequence of acts had variety and change of pace. Every editor seeks to avoid repetition of subject matter, but the editor of a picture magazine has to be on his guard twice over because quite dissimilar subjects often turn out to be visually repetitive.

Life's editors thought originally that their raw material would be

304

provided mainly by the photographic news services. They soon discovered that a week's run of news photos produced only a few outstanding pictures; one automobile accident looks very much like another. The services seldom provided a sequence of pictures telling a coherent story. *Life* needed photographers who not only understood the art and technique of photography but could be journalists as well. To recruit and direct the corps of staff photographers and free-lancers filling *Life* assignments became a job almost as important as that of the managing editor. To fill this post, in March 1937 *Life* hired Wilson Hicks, the picture editor of the Associated Press; on *Life* he played a role second only to Billings and Longwell in developing a successful format. To the original quartet of staff photographers—Eisenstaedt, McAvoy, Stackpole, Bourke-White—were added other gifted professionals: William Vandivert, Carl Mydans, Hansel Mieth, John Phillips, to mention a few of the names that soon appeared on *Life*'s masthead. Robert Capa, Fritz Goro, Walter Sanders and Wallace Kirkland were among those who undertook *Life* assignments within the first year. Hicks's presence made a difference in the quality of photographs, and six months after the first issue Larsen told Luce that *Life*'s own photographers were now dominating its pages.

The critic Bernard De Voto was one who noted and commented on the significant change in *Life*'s editorial approach in its first year of publication: *"Life,* whose original formula called for equal parts of the decapitated Chinaman, the flogged Negro, the surgically explored peritoneum, and the rapidly slipping chemise, has decided to appeal to more normal and more intelligent minds. It now spends much more energy on the news and on a kind of visual journalistic investigation which becomes increasingly interesting as it becomes more expert." One of *Life*'s most famous acts in its early period was a domestic strip-tease entitled "How to Undress in Front of Your Husband." Luce voted to print this in spite of misgivings on the part of some editors. "Crude and vulgar as it was," said Billings, "this act did a promotional job. It got the magazine talked about, and by March we had attracted enough attention to be denounced, burlesqued and reviled." And, in consequence, to become more circumspect.

The public continued to buy every copy available. The early *Life* was lively and unpredictable, amusing and entertaining. One memorable stunt was the printing of two photographs of a hippopotamus, back to back; the captions read "Lotus Fore" and "Lotus Aft." "Aft" was placed opposite the Campbell Soup advertisement; the advertiser canceled his contract.

As a mirror of its times *Life* was also a serious magazine. The news made it so—the Japanese invasion of China, the Spanish Civil War, the growing menace of Hitler and the Nazis provided dramatic photographs. "Though we did not plan *Life* as a war magazine," said Luce, "it turned out that way." In its first year *Life* had some notable journalistic coups: the first photographic study of cancer, for which it won commendation from the American Cancer Society, and Edgar Snow's exclusive pictures of the Chinese Communist leaders Mao Tse-tung and Chou En-lai in their Yenan redoubt.

Life's major emphasis was on the news, but Luce felt that in the new magazine he had made an important journalistic discovery. "While journalism accents the abnormal," he wrote, "the hopeful fact is that the photograph can make normal, decent, useful and pleasant behavior far more interesting than word journalism usually does." He felt this was best exemplified by what he defined as "the photographic essay." In 1965 the New York Museum of Modern Art had a major exhibition entitled "The Photo Essay"; before the publication of *Life* the term was unknown, and Luce can be credited with originating it. He used it first in connection with photographs Eisenstaedt took at Vassar which greatly pleased *Life*'s founder. The picture sequence, Luce wrote, left "mountains to be written about Education in general and Vassar in particular. It is not an account of Vassar. It is a delightful essay on Vassar. But it is vital. It does communicate. Both to those who know about girls' colleges and to those who do not, it tells something about Vassar and Education and America and Life in 1937. And it tells the kind of thing that only the most skillful (and now obsolete) literary essayists have hitherto managed to tell in words."

Luce devoted much time to the *Life* editorial department and kept closely in touch with the planning of every issue, but the company's

306

demands on his time soon forced him to surrender day-to-day operations to John Billings as managing editor.

Managing editors at Time Inc. have always exercised considerable power. They are the men on the firing line who make the decisions in the critical minutes when the magazine is going to press. They must draw the best performances from the staff. Their decisiveness and sense of direction, or lack thereof, affect both the quality of the magazine and the whole production process. Billings proved to be a brilliant managing editor of *Life*. He had an instinctive liking and feel for pictures and made up his mind quickly. He saw most pictures, approved all layouts. To his staff he was a formidable figure. Only Luce, Larsen and a few of the older hands addressed him by his first name. To others he was always "Mr. Billings," and his summons on the inter-office communicator brought them running. His deadlines were met promptly. Under him morale was high and the staff enjoyed a sense of freedom and adventure. Carl Mydans, in *More Than Meets the Eye*,[3] recalls the atmosphere:

> No idea was too absurd to be tried as a story. Sometimes two people found themselves on the same assignment, each representing a different department. And sometimes when the story came in the department assigning it had moved along to new interests or had died along the way and the pictures, finding no takers, finally came to rest on heaps of others, now repositories for discolored coffee cups and ash trays.
>
> But it was a magazine for expression and creation and for youth, and never mind the fatalities. The death of one creative urge simply cleared the way for another. We had an insatiable drive to search out every facet of American life, photograph it and hold it up proudly, like a mirror, to a pleased and astonished readership. In a sense our product was inbred: America had an impact upon us and each week we made an impact on America.

The impact of *Life* produced almost a sense of wonder in the staff, the management and even outsiders that is reflected in a memo from Larsen to the advertising department. Summing up progress in sales

[3] Harper & Brothers, 1959.

307

and promotion, he wrote: "Arthur Kudner [the head of an important advertising agency] suggested the other day that we should strive to keep for *Life* the wonderment about *Life* that we have displayed so far. In other words, he is suggesting unconsciously a return to our old 'amateur spirit' slogan of the early *Time* days, and I think that all of us will admit that in guiding the destinies of this new big lion we have by the tail, we are a bunch of amateurs." But the advertisers were not altogether convinced that the demand for *Life* would continue when the novelty wore off. In April 1937 Luce was invited to address the American Association of Advertising Agencies; his subject was the mutual responsibility of editors and advertisers in maintaining a free press. He used *Life* as an example of this unique interrelationship, and the heart of his talk was a bold sales pitch for his new magazine:

. . . A year ago . . . we chose to create a magazine called *Life*. This magazine, as you know, has published pictures of corpses, of nudes, of snakes, of the rear of a hippopotamus and a lecture on How a Wife Should Undress. It has been an enormous success. Evidently it is what the public wants more than it has ever wanted any product of ink and paper. Nevertheless, I confront you with a question. . . . Should we publish *Life?* And this is not a question only for my partners to decide. We have decided. We like *Life*. We believe it to be immensely important. We intend to be proud of it. We propose to put into it all the wisdom and understanding of which we are capable. . . . But it is also for you to decide. It is a question for each and every one of you to decide in your heart and in your mind because each of you is deciding it in the pocketbook of your client. . . . I stand before you as before a court. Your court is also the Appropriations Committee of the American Press: you are the Commissars, you exist as an alternative to the People's Commissariat of Public Enlightenment. Here today I make application not for a few incidental pennies; I ask that you shall appropriate over the next ten critical years no less than one hundred million dollars for the publication of a magazine called *Life*. You cannot escape a reply to this question. We will not let you. We will keep hammering persistently on your doors, asking for the money week after week. You will either give it to us, or you will not. If you do, there will be *Life*. If you do not, there will be no *Life*.

In retrospect, in the light of *Life*'s subsequent record as an advertising medium, the appropriation seems modest enough. It did not seem so in 1937. To many of his listeners, Luce must have sounded downright presumptuous.

In June, Time Inc. removed any doubt as to the direction in which *Life* was heading; it was definitely committed to becoming a mass-circulation magazine. A new circulation guarantee of 1,600,000 was announced for the year 1938; the advertising rates were raised to $5,700 a page, or $3.56 per thousand circulation. However, following Luce's line of reasoning that *Life* should charge a higher price, the new rates did not reflect the competitive situation; they were distinctly higher than the rate per thousand of the *Saturday Evening Post* ($2.96) or *Collier's* ($2.61). This was to prove a mistake.

Notwithstanding Luce's hope that Time Inc. might be able to avoid getting too involved in printing presses and paper-making plants, *Life*'s rising circulation required increased press capacity and new sources of paper supply. The company was fortunate in being able to persuade its suppliers to make the capital expenditures required. Time Inc. was thus able to concentrate its energies on publishing rather than manufacturing. This was largely made possible as a result of an enlightened policy, originating with Stillman, in which Time Inc. took the position that even though it was losing millions in publishing *Life,* it would guarantee its suppliers a fair margin of profit. Stillman also worked out with the suppliers a cost-plus formula by which Time Inc. shared in savings that resulted from efficiency, new techniques or volume. This policy, at first applicable only to the paper suppliers, was extended to printers as well. By the end of 1937 Time Inc. had invested $5,000,000 in establishing *Life;* its paper manufacturers had invested $3,500,000 in new machines and the printers $2,000,000 in new equipment—in all $10,500,000 in the middle of a depression.

The major problem continued to be a suitable paper supply. The specification that *Life* must be printed on coated paper was costly. Unless a way could be found to produce such paper by less expensive means, *Life* would continue to run in the red. Strangely enough, at no time was it suggested that the specification be altered and *Life* use less expensive stock. "Maybe coating paper is all a mistake," Stillman wrote in 1937, "but as long as it is associated with fine printing, it is what *Life* will buy. We may use floor wax for coating, but coated it must be. . . . This is of the essence of *Life* paper buying policy. The thing that differentiates *Life* as conceived from *Life* that is is that ten times as many guinea pigs want it as we thought would want it."

In exploring new sources of supply, Stillman discovered that the Consolidated Water Power & Paper Company of Wisconsin Rapids, Wisconsin, had acquired in 1933 a patent for making coated paper on a groundwood base. The prejudice in the printing trade against using paper with a groundwood base in quality printing was very strong. But the Consolidated process gave the paper a finish comparable to that of paper of much higher quality. Stillman decided that Time Inc. would experiment with the Consolidated product; many difficulties had to be overcome before the paper proved to be satisfactory. At first it blistered as the ink was dried because of its high moisture content. With experience the paper was improved; as Stillman said, *"Life* was the midwife [for] long overdue children of other people's inventive genius." The decision to use the groundwood paper was very important in reducing *Life*'s physical costs; in 1940 *Life* was paying $88 a ton for coated paper that in 1937 had cost $100 to $200 or more. The contract Time Inc. signed with Consolidated in May 1937, calling for delivery of 40,000 tons a year, represented a long-term commitment for $17,000,000, the largest contract Time Inc. had made up to that moment.

Fortune's course, during this period, was relatively unaffected by *Life*, although it could not be described as serene. The principal effect of *Life* on *Fortune* was to divert Luce's attention temporarily from Hodgins and his staff. As managing editor, Hodgins had shown himself to be an administrator of grace and wit, an accomplished writer and an able technician. Under his editorship *Fortune* had produced some extraordinarily good editorial matter. Its single-subject issue on Japan (September 1936), suggested by Luce and written largely by MacLeish and Wilder Hobson, both of whom spent three months in Japan, remains a journalistic landmark. The issue was focused on a single question: "How long can Japan continue her phenomenal commercial, industrial, and military expansion?" It was an examination of Japan that necessitated looking into the astonishing contrasts presented by Japanese life. To a colleague MacLeish summed up his own impressions with another question: "How long can one century exist inside another?"

Hodgins had his troubles with a small and pampered staff accustomed to a high degree of independence and autonomy. On the whole, he handled the writers with great humor and patience, although their eccentricities were a trial. One of them turned up in the office of a corporation president wearing a sweater, a shirt with collar open and no tie, baggy slacks and blue sneakers. When there was a complaint from the president's office, Hodgins wrote the following memo:

TO—Staff
FROM—Mr. Hodgins
SUBJECT—A SWEET DISORDER IN THE DRESS

By no stretch of the imagination could the Managing Editor be thought of as a Snappy Dresser. In fact, his tendency toward old pepper-and-salts has been a matter of frequent remark by one of his more elegant confrères.

But he must, in all seriousness, ask the staff to preserve, in the matter of dress, something more closely approaching what the late Mayor Gaynor of New York was fond of referring to as "outward order and decency." In the office, *Fortune* writers may garb themselves like the Aga Khan or Isadora Duncan's brother, depending on the whim that seizes them. But when they are calling on business men, executives, bankers, educators and others with whom *Fortune* deals, it is up to everyone to remember that he is just as much an Ambassador for *Fortune* as is the Publisher, the General Manager or any of the Managing Editors, and to guide and garb himself accordingly.

311

The uniform: one suit (pants to match coat and vest can be obtained at many establishments), one shirt, one tie, two socks of similar color, two shoes complete with heels, ditto. Underwear to taste. At many outdoor functions a hat may be worn without transgressing good usage.

The management rearrangement that placed Hodgins in the new office of *Fortune* publisher brought a quite different and distinctive personality to the managing-editorship. Russell Davenport, in the words of one of his colleagues and a devoted friend, was "in important ways the best managing editor *Fortune* ever had; in unimportant, the worst. As an executive, he was a fountain of anarchy, indecision, and disorder." Davenport was thirty-seven, a tall man whose strongly boned face and cleft chin gave him a crag-like appearance. He was enormously self-possessed and abounding in energy. During frequent leaves of absence from his *Fortune* job he had been composing a long autobiographical work, part prose, part poetry, the manuscript of which he carried about with him. In fact, he was preparing to ask for another leave to complete it when Hodgins asked him to dinner to offer him the managing-editorship. Reluctantly Davenport promised to think about it over the week-end. On Sunday morning he accepted. The decision had been made easier, he explained, because he had lost his manuscript in a taxi. It was never found, because Davenport did not try to recover it; when his wife commiserated with him, he said, "Hell, it's a relief."

He created an atmosphere of urgency and excitement. Full of ideas which he was often unable to communicate, he was habitually late, and the magazine's closings were chaotic, running through the night and often extending well into the next morning. It was not unusual for him to rush from the opera to the Jersey City printing plant, arriving in full evening dress and an opera cape. Once, finding that someone had miscounted the back of the book and there was a blank column to be filled in the middle of a page, he sat down and dictated directly to the linotype operator. In a preface to a book by Davenport, published posthumously,[4] John Knox Jessup recalled that

[4] *The Dignity of Man* (Harper & Brothers, 1955).

. . . Davenport brought certain qualities to *Fortune* which made it the most exciting periodical of that time. One was a readiness to back his own intuitions and gradually forming beliefs about the American political economy. He would attack any subject, however well guarded by experts or other obstacles, with the naked sword of his own layman's curiosity. . . . Corporate secrecy never stopped him from getting a story he wanted; he took a special pleasure in wire-pulling and porch-climbing, as in the case of stories on Allied Chemical and Diamond Match. He felt that *Fortune*'s journalistic ambitions, like his own curiosity, should know no bounds. Accordingly he turned the *Fortune* searchlight on such opaque subjects as the birth-control industry, the servant problem, air safety, the economics of a debut, the organization of the Vatican and of the State Department. . . . Davenport's notions of what was wrong with America were frequently in advance of his colleagues'; but the main difference was that he always thought he could do something about it. . . .

On Hodgins' accession to the publisher's job, Luce made a controversial suggestion which indicates that, although he was not presently involved in every issue, he was concerned about *Fortune*'s editorial direction. To Hodgins, Davenport and senior staff members he proposed the writing of a "Respectus." He did not dictate a change in policy; he solicited their ideas on "What *is Fortune?* What should *Fortune* be? What can *Fortune* be? How can it best get to be what it should be?"

By implication he reminded the writers of *Fortune*'s purpose by saying that the most important article *"for me"* in the May 1937 issue had been one on the Hitz hotels because

. . . Seeing the people as a hotel manager sees them, meeting bellhops not as Labor Problems but as bellhops; meeting Economics not as Economics but as putting the Hotel Adolphus out of the red—for all this and a lot more I am indebted to *Fortune*. I am indebted to *Fortune* for something which I cannot get at the most distinguished intellectual gathering—or from reading the *New Republic*.

313

He then suggested that

> *Fortune* shall have a platform with two planks. One plank it already has—the free and fearless journalism of inquiry. I suggest that it also acknowledge a bias in favor of private enterprise. . . .
>
> *Fortune*'s special field of inquiry is the industrial scene. The big question in that field is to what extent it should be controlled if not ruled by the State. . . .
>
> With all his controls, Mr. Roosevelt expects Private Capitalism to carry on. The country expects Private Capitalism to carry on. . . . Private Capitalism expects Private Capitalism to carry on—no matter how hobbled. We of *Fortune* expect Private Capitalism to carry on.
>
> Well then, if for no other reason than to enable us to be its effective critic, would it not clear the air, not only for the benefit of our curious friends of the extreme right and left, but also for the less obstreperous people in the middle [to acknowledge] that, pending a new Messiah and a fresh conversion, we are *for* Private Capitalism.

In a second memorandum some days later Luce further defined his proposition. He believed, he said, that *Fortune* not only had a field and a bias but also a philosophy which was best summed up by a quotation from the German writer Thomas Mann:

> "Materialism can be much more spiritual, much more idealistic and much more religious than any attitude of pride toward the material." If the spirit of man is to survive, it will do so only by conquering and absorbing the new, the very new material world which now suddenly exists.
>
> A magazine based on this philosophy and intending to deal directly with the new materialism can have one of two biases. . . . It can be either a great Communist magazine or a great Capitalist magazine. . . .

Luce concluded by saying that *Fortune* not only needed an abler staff but had to attract men with a more intense emotional interest in their subject.

314

From this point of view we could much more easily publish *Fortune* in Russia. Nevertheless, *Fortune*'s technique is journalistic rather than dialectical. . . . *Fortune*'s saddest failure is the publication of an article which bored the writer and also bored the American businessman. That is the new high of stupidity. That is the true indictment of *Fortune*. That is the indictment [Dwight] Macdonald was too stupid to understand. That is the indictment which will put *Fortune* out of business—with my hearty, if shameful, assent.

Once we get our bias clearly stated, we can let it rest happily in our subconscious, and devote our conscious efforts to making a vitally interesting magazine. And, for God's sake, have some fun.

Hodgins, with considerable inward resistance, had promised to try his hand at writing the "respectus" incorporating Luce's views for *Fortune*. He worked at it for some two months and produced a sixteen-page document which he considered a failure because "Whichever way I tried to tackle the question of *bias* (and I tried it in everything except iambic pentameter) I got stuck. A negative presentation is impossible, but every positive presentation I tried turned around and bit me by sounding either arrogant and blustery or mealy-mouthed and holier-than-thou. . . ." But, he assured Luce, there were no "sectarian" disputes between them "such as now and again put you and A. MacLeish on opposite sides of the fence." He found himself in a difficult spot—in the middle between Luce and the writers, who were, for the time at least, very much opposed to acknowledging a bias. Jack Jessup, Yale '28, who had come to Time Inc. in 1935 after spending five years as a copywriter with the J. Walter Thompson Company, was one of the most influential members of the staff. He told Hodgins that if the magazine got "the maximum literary validity out of its subject matter . . . [it] need not stoop to a profession of faith in the profit system. An artistic conscience (*Fortune*'s should be that) does not have to 'believe' in the profit system any more than it 'believes' in the Chrysler Building. . . . The profit system is a fact, not a cause." Davenport, too, was against the idea,

315

and so, for the time being, the idea of stating or acknowledging *Fortune*'s bias was dropped.

But not by Luce. In the fall he set up a committee of himself, Hodgins, Davenport, Stillman and Prentice to carry on the "re-think." Having made his opinions clear to his colleagues, he carried them to a presumably more sympathetic audience. In November, Luce made a speech before the Ohio Bankers Association. He did not believe that the reforms so far introduced by Mr. Roosevelt were necessarily inimical to a liberal society. Social legislation, he felt, was largely necessary and overdue. But it was time for a reassessment of the relationship between the Roosevelt Administration and capitalism. He told the bankers:

. . . The policies of a powerful President of the United States are based on the assumption that private capitalism will work whereas in fact private capitalism is not working. . . .

Whatever way you look at it, the smallness of our national production today is a national disgrace, a wicked disobedience of the ancient injunction to increase and multiply, a miserable failure to function as the intelligent creative animals we pride ourselves on being. . . .

If private capitalism is not working—why is it not working? . . . We know that private capitalism functions only under conditions of confidence and that today there is little confidence. . . .

Over the years Franklin Roosevelt has made most businessmen feel that he does not like Business—that he does not like Industrial Enterprise. The dangerous fact is this: while basing all his policies on the assumption that private enterprise will work, he has based his political popularity on the implication that Business is anti-social, unpatriotic, vulgar and corruptive.

The basic ideological change in American thinking, he said, was the new doctrine of potential abundance, the expectation and belief that there were means at hand for a better life for all. Out of this grew the idea of a planned economy; but planned economy, he felt, was completely inconsistent with political freedom and liberty.

316

What then? Must we reconcile ourselves to Planned Economy and bury our sweet dream of Freedom?

The answer, of course, is that in the real world of fact and logic no such choice exists. . . . The more abundant life may be problematical in a free society; it is utterly impossible in anything except a free society . . . for a very simple reason. The abundance which can be produced by an industrial society can be produced only by a very advanced degree of division of labor and by the most intricate and speedy exchange of the products of extreme division of labor. The economy of abundance is therefore so complicated . . . that it is incapable of being planned or directed by any conceivable human government. . . .

The hope of [Roosevelt's] ill-fed, ill-clad, and ill-housed depends upon the vastly greater productivity of free capitalistic enterprise under law. He knows that. We know that. . . .

The cause of freedom . . . is your business and my business. As a journalist, I am in command of a small sector in the very front trenches of this battle of freedom. . . . Let me assure you that I and my colleagues—we are enlisted in this war: for life. . . .

Make money, be proud of it; make more money, be prouder of it. School yourself for the long battle of freedom in this century. Look forward to victory—and to the achievement of a more abundant life which can be achieved only by free capitalistic enterprise in a free society.

A week after Luce's speech to the bankers, Davenport circulated a long memorandum, "Preface to a Revaluation of *Fortune*." Whether or not the memo was influenced by the speech, it marked a reorientation of the magazine.

I think that we must develop an editorial definition. Last summer when Harry broached this necessity, I did not recognize it and was very much opposed to some of the things that he had to say. I now feel, however, that he was on just the right track. It seems to me absolutely urgent that *Fortune* define or redefine itself in such terms as to reassure the American businessman . . . that our world is his world and not the world of either Stalin, or

317

Mussolini, or Trotsky, or even John L. Lewis or Mr. Roosevelt; that our basic principles are in a rough way his basic principles, the liberal principles upon which he has been reared; and that when we undertake to criticize him we do so as a member of his party.

The first major result of the redefinition took the form of a series of articles beginning in February 1938 on "Business-and-Government," dealing with such subjects as the utilities, the National Labor Relations Board, the SEC, monopoly. As an introduction to the series Davenport wrote an editorial which was so well received that the "Business-and-Government" series continued to be supplemented by editorials—the first editorials in any Time Inc. publication. Their theme was reconciliation, an end to the sterile and unnecessary warfare between American business and the New Deal. Davenport had friends in the New Deal (e.g., Thomas Corcoran and Harry Hopkins); he was on good terms with labor leaders. He also knew and liked businessmen. He felt that the American political economy was a bigger concern than that of any single interest group:

> It is now apparent that there exists a profound misunderstanding [he wrote] between Government (as represented by the New Deal) and Business. . . . To the New Dealer, the hurried Businessman has seemed stupid and stubborn; and to almost all Businessmen, the New Dealer has seemed erratic and untrustworthy. *But neither of these impressions is basically correct.* Each arises from a lack of knowledge and information concerning the other side. . . .
>
> Both sides go on the assumption that either one or the other must be right. . . . As a matter of practice . . . the logical development of either side to its conclusion would be cataclysmic. The liberal—the salutary—path lies somewhere between the two. And that path is the one that *Fortune* intends to explore.

The editorials were widely reprinted and commented on. President Roosevelt, calling *Fortune* "a discerning magazine of business,"

318

quoted approvingly from one of them in a major speech. Alfred P. Sloan, Jr., chairman of General Motors, found much to commend in them. The National Industrial Conference Board sent out 75,000 reprints of one on "Unmerging for Profits," and Davenport entered into a lively personal correspondence with such figures as Under Secretary of State Sumner Welles and Thomas W. Lamont. Larsen told Luce, "More and more I hear responsible and substantial businessmen praising *Fortune*'s current job and either consciously or unconsciously quoting it."

But some members of the staff were definitely upset by the new line. The researchers rebelled. An anonymous verse appeared in the bulletin of the leftward-inclining Time Inc. unit of the Newspaper Guild, sardonically entitled, "The *Fortune* Researcher's Dilemma, or How Can a Girl Help Not Going Wrong?"

> I've a passion to be palpably impartial
> With reporter's objectivity I burn
> You will find me neither militant nor martial
> But for *Fortune* I don't know which way to turn.
>
> For the middle of the road has been denied me
> And I cannot stay on either side for long
> If I'm left or if I'm right, they're there to chide me
> How can a poor girl keep from going wrong?
>
> Chorus
>
> The writers are left and the editors right
> And no matter which way I may lean
> The stuff that I check
> Gives me pains in the neck
> And I always get caught in between.
> I try to be fair, but I'm tearing my hair
> And I'm weeping by buckets and gallons
> For the writers all say
> I'm in Morgan's pay
> And the editors say I'm in Stalin's.

319

Soon after the poem appeared, seventeen researchers (all but the three junior members of the staff, who were not invited) held an indignation meeting in the apartment of Miss Emeline Nollen. It ended prematurely when someone dropped a lighted match on the hostess' brand-new rug and the Fire Department had to be called.

When the meeting reconvened, the girls drafted a formal protest, which they delivered to Hodgins and Davenport with all the formality of a diplomatic démarche. Their complaints:

1) A series of editorials accompanying the Government and Business stories which either confuse the stories or, still worse, constitute a tacit denial of their essential facts.

2) An increasing tendency toward a pre-established bias which the investigator is expected to prove and which the facts gathered often conspicuously fail to prove. This situation has not been mitigated by the fact that the bias has on occasions not been made clear to us or to the writer until very late in the story's life, at which point the story has often been taken out of the writer's hands completely. Nor have memoranda to the effect that the writer is sole master of his story helped to create a happy frame of mind.

Davenport brought all his charm into play. He sent off a short memorandum as "an earnest of a new and better order," promptly followed this up with a twenty-one-page document in which he tried to reconcile bias and objectivity. The editorial policy of the magazine was merely, he said,

. . . the *explicit* statement of what has been *implicit* in *Fortune* all along. . . . Suppose a *Nation* writer and a *Fortune* writer were each to do an article about a business. Suppose the articles were to be the same length; that the same facts were available; and that the same doubts were outstanding after the facts were gathered. . . . Let us suppose that the *Fortune* writer and the *Nation* writer believed *equally* in objectivity and sought, within the limits of fairness, to be objective. Nevertheless, the *Nation* article might appear to *Fortune* as hopelessly biased, and the *Fortune* article might appear to the *Nation* as hopelessly biased.

320

. . . The infinitesimal resolutions of the doubt will have made
the whole difference. A quick way to qualify for the nut house is
to follow this train of thought any further.

The girls were at least mollified. Eric Hodgins further reassured them
by telling them their protest was "an excellent example of Back
Talk. It is not only the right, it is the obligation, of every researcher
to Talk Back. She must talk back to every writer, every editor, every
publisher, every founding father, with whom she comes into professional contact in the course of a story."

Ralph McAllister Ingersoll was valued by Luce for his talent at
stirring things up. When Luce recognized that he and Larsen would
be preoccupied by *Life,* he picked Ingersoll to be publisher of *Time*
because he knew that Ingersoll would tackle the job energetically.
While Ingersoll might have preferred to be in on the *Life* adventure,
he knew that *Time* was the source of all profits and its publisher
would be in a position of power, and he relished power. Moreover
Time was in some trouble; the *New Yorker* profile, the Macdonald
series in the *Nation* and other unfavorable publicity had made the
young men at Time Inc. fully aware that their public relations needed
improvement. Ingersoll had some very positive ideas about what must
be done and no hesitation about making them known to Luce.

Ingersoll's journalistic ideas differed widely from those of Luce. He
was a fervid New Dealer; he shared MacLeish's and Macdonald's
general attitude toward the Spanish Civil War; he didn't think much
of the way *Time* was being run and he was determined to make
changes. He had hardly moved into the publisher's office when he
fired off a first barrage of memoranda on Time Inc. in general and
Time Magazine in particular. (He was one of the most prolific memo
writers in Time Inc. history, not outdone by Luce himself.) The story
of the company's success—"My, my, how those two young Yale boys
are getting on!"—was no longer an unmitigated blessing, he wrote,
because now that the company was successful it was recognized as an
active competitor for the dollar. There was also "a peculiar arrogance" about the company, "a survival from the days when the
struggle for existence really was so intense . . . that nothing seemed

321

of importance to us comparable to ourselves." The company needed to mind its manners and cultivate the public by discarding the theme of "Success Success Success" for "Service Service Service." Luce returned the memo with a penciled "Noted by H.R.L."

As to *Time,* Ingersoll told Luce, in another memorandum: "Many sincere and intelligent people have satisfied themselves that *Time,* consciously or unconsciously, prejudices the news scene against things they believe in—and thus is a positive force for evil—and therefore feel that they must in conscience attack it." He cited as an example *Time*'s coverage of the labor movement, adding, "I can entirely understand those people who saw in it evidence that *Time*'s editors were well-fed, newly-rich Yale boys in whose world labor movements were things to be laughed at, baited, ignored." He blamed some of this on *Time*'s dependence on the U.S. press: "The U.S. press was stupid and reactionary. *Time*'s news is based on the U.S. press. Hence *Time* was stupid and reactionary. Q.E.D. That, at least, is the oversimplification."

He also attacked Goldsborough, who, he said, "confuses and confounds *Time*'s critics. They do not know where he stands. He can come into their court any day with overwhelming evidence that he stands for or against anything they like." The Foreign News editor's mind was "a mare's nest" of "prejudices and preconceptions and emotional biases." To this blast Luce entered only a mild demurrer:

The case you make against *Time* is a little unfair in that it does not take into account a pre-Depression perspective. *Time* began in the days of Mr. Harding. It came out every week during the long reign of Calvin Coolidge and on through Hoover. In those days *Time* was favorably regarded by liberals . . . and was never regarded as a conventional or pro-existing-order sheet.

Today it may seem otherwise. But perhaps there's a reason and a good one. Perhaps *Time* stays in the middle of the road while the country has swung further to the left than it is in its nature to remain. In one sense, at any rate, it is right that *Time* should be of the *minority* opinion——in exactly the same sense as it can be said that the majority is always wrong.

322

The big question in the reformulation of *Time*'s purpose, said Luce, was whether it should take its interpretative function more seriously in the future than in the past:

> I think it must. The problem is how to take ourselves more seriously as interpreters and yet retain a dispassionate attitude. . . . I am not sure that we should present ourselves as an essentially political paper. . . . One word as to Goldsborough. His is a *unique* mind . . . whose uniqueness amounts almost to genius, and which respects Truth.

Luce concluded with the injunction, "Continue on your line of thought and write me again when you feel like it."

Ingersoll needed no encouragement. In May Luce left for a vacation in Hawaii; while he was away *Time*'s publisher rewrote the original prospectus and constructed a new series of memoranda as a basis for carrying it out. He argued that the concept of "group journalism as opposed to impresario journalism" had been implicit if not clearly articulated in *Time*'s original prospectus and that the time had come to emphasize it and improve its practice. It should be dedicated to "a thing called The Scientific Principle." To that end he argued for an expanded budget to provide better research and an improved writing staff. Ideally this should consist of "at least ten or twelve brilliant young men—zealots to the religion of keeping people well informed, with boundless curiosity and energy and ingenuity; thoughtful, broad, experienced, specialists." The present *Time* staff did not practice "group journalism by even a remote conception of the word. It is run by two eccentric autocrats, each autonomous: John Martin and Laird Goldsborough."

Ingersoll circulated his prospectus to his colleagues in Luce's absence. The staff was well aware of Luce's attempts to persuade *Fortune* to acknowledge a bias, and Allen Grover pointed out that it might be very difficult to reconcile a *Time* prospectus that dedicated the magazine to the "scientific principle" with a *Fortune* "respectus" proclaiming its dedication to private capitalism. But C. D. Jackson liked the prospectus and applauded "group journalism" as "something pretty juicy for the public to get its teeth into." Jackson also

323

thought that if *Time* could have better research it would be "no exaggeration to say that 80% of *Time*'s external problems will disappear." He went on to say that Time Inc. had gone through two phases and was now entering on its third. Phase one, Jackson wrote, was that of *"Enfant Terrible":*

> In the *enfant terrible* days we could be guilty of practically anything and get away with it, because when we committed the uncommittable there always were sufficient apologists to jump up and utter their particular version of, "Okay, he killed his sister, but ain't he cute, he's only six,"—and no more rational explanation was necessary.

He thought that phase ended when the combination of the *March of Time* radio program and the *Time-Fortune* Building at the World's Fair in Chicago introduced *Time* to "the millions." [5] Then began, Jackson argued, the "U.S. Phenomenon" phase:

> We evolved at whirlwind speed. . . . We became a storm center in the public eye—Congressmen and Senators discussed what we wrote—President Roosevelt requested that we no longer imitate his voice on the air—Communists called us Fascists and Fascists called us Communists. . . . We changed from being a vague interest in the public's mind to an absorbing object of curiosity, and from an absorbing object of curiosity we became an irritating object . . . and some of the toes on which we had trod got back their power to kick, and kick they did. And all this time our manners did not improve because in the early days we had been too busy to develop manners, and in lieu of manners we developed brusqueness. . . . So people began to take an unholy glee in calling us names and whispering and sneering at our journalistic and business mannerisms. I think this second stage reached its peak and its end the day Wolcott Gibbs's story was published in *The New Yorker.*

Now, said Jackson, *Time* was entering a "Golden Age." Unlike Ingersoll, he thought he detected "a lull in the animosity":

[5] The pavilion—"the longest magazine rack in the world"—was visited by more than 2,000,000 people in the 1933 season.

We have recaptured our pristine charm via the launching of *Life*. "Those *Time* boys have done it again" seems to have stilled even our most ill-wishers. (Note well "Those *Time* boys." Nobody says *"Life* boys" or *"Fortune* boys" or "Luce boys" or "Chrysler Building boys"). And because of the present lull this is the psychological moment to do something about consolidating the feeling of respect and friendship which has started up again. . . . We can't go on forever feeling that we are a people apart and to hell with the rest of the human race. And I absolutely disagree with anyone who says, "To have an acute awareness of responsibility and to act in conformity therewith means a loss of those juices and spices which have made *Time* and Time Inc." Harry has said, and quite rightly, that *Time,* by its very nature, creates the necessity of an occasional apologist. But let that apologist at least be apologizing for something worth the apology—not because we think it is smart to eat peas with a knife.

Jackson concluded: *"Fortune* and *Life* are going to get by on their own. It is to *Time* that Time Inc. must look. . . . And on the way *Time* comports itself, personally and editorially, will depend what the world thinks of Time Inc."

Luce's reaction to all this when he returned from Hawaii is not recorded. His recollection was that he thought "the scientific principle" was nonsense when applied to journalism.[6] The Ingersoll prospectus was printed, but received only limited promotional distribution. However, Luce did give Ingersoll authority to spend more money on the editorial department.

There was very little that Ingersoll could do about *Time*'s editorial department so long as John Martin was managing editor; he was not

[6] Though Luce found himself subsequently using the phrase "group journalism," he finally rebelled against it, and in 1947 wrote a memo to John Billings, then editorial director of the company, asking that it be expunged from the Time Inc. vocabulary: "It goes without saying that we are both devoted and addicted to what is mis-named group journalism. We believe in teamwork, in cooperation, in division of labor; i.e., we believe that two or more heads are often better than one. We believe in intellectual partnership and in what might be called 'basic agreement,' etc. But we do not believe in any such subordination of individual responsibility, or in any such subordination of individual imagination or whim or fancy, or in any such subordination of individual intellectual sweat as is suggested by 'group journalism.' "

interested in attuning to Ingersoll. But matters played into the new publisher's hands. Martin was unhappy about his shift from *Life*—an unhappiness which manifested itself in long and intermittent absences. One week he did not appear at all, and the magazine was put to press by a young assistant, Frank Norris. Like Martin a Princeton graduate, son of the president of the Southern Railway System, he had been hired eight years before. He had written Education and The Theatre and had been Billings' assistant in National Affairs. When Billings was made managing editor Norris had become National Affairs editor until Luce, not altogether satisfied with the arrangement, put Gottfried in that post. So Norris became an assistant to Billings, and after Billings moved to *Life,* he remained as assistant to Martin.

It was finally decided that Martin must go on a year's sabbatical. Luce and Ingersoll then turned to Gottfried, offering him Martin's job with the proviso that he share the title with Norris. It would be, Ingersoll explained, like a law partnership: Gottfried the senior partner, Norris the junior. Gottfried agreed, although not liking the arrangement. Who would take over his job as editor of National Affairs? Luce said it would have to be *Time*'s movie reviewer, Noel Busch. "The suggestion had a comic side which even Harry appreciated," said Gottfried. "Busch was probably the most talented writer on the staff but he had not a political thought in his head. Busch protested against the new assignment; but there was no one else."

"Harry reassuringly told me not to worry," Gottfried recalled. "*Time,* he said, had passed through a difficult period but it was now running fine; I would have no problem but to keep it running on an even keel. This judgment was such a surprise to me that I didn't even protest. Perhaps because Harry was so engrossed in *Life,* he was not aware of *Time*'s weaknesses in its editorial set-up. Or perhaps, from the early days, he was so accustomed to *Time* skating on thin talent ice that it seemed perfectly normal to him to have to draft the film reviewer to write National Affairs."

The sometimes eccentric way in which *Time* editorial posts were filled was never better demonstrated than at this moment. Gottfried had not yet seen the end of the development, for Thomas Stanley Matthews now appeared on the scene with a claim which he felt

326

ought to be honored. Martin had hired him away from the *New Republic* in 1929; he had written in Religion, Press and Books for a time and then, by a special arrangement, confined himself to book reviews for seven years. He had an impressive background. His father was the Episcopal Bishop of New Jersey, his grandfather a U.S. Senator and Justice of the Supreme Court. His mother was a Procter, of the Procter & Gamble dynasty. He had been educated at St. Paul's School, Princeton (graduating a year before Martin), and taken honors in literature at New College, Oxford. He had had two novels published and his avocation was writing poetry. He later complained in his autobiography [7] that he was unhappy in his years with *Time,* but this was not the impression he conveyed to colleagues including Gottfried, who said that "During the five or six years that I worked closely with him he was having a love affair with *Time* journalism." In the summer of 1937, at a time when Matthews confessed he was tired of writing book reviews and not producing much writing on his own despite long leaves of absence, Martin had proposed that he take over the editing of the "Back-of-the-Book"— the critical departments. Martin had not told anyone else of this proposal, and by the time Matthews was ready to accept, Martin had disappeared.

So it was that on an August morning Matthews, "grim and erect" (as Gottfried recalled), arrived at the office to demand that Gottfried and Norris make good on Martin's offer. "His righteous wrath mounted as he talked to us," said Gottfried. "It was good comedy, because we were not trying to welch on anything. We had just never heard of what he was talking about." Gottfried and Norris suggested that he see Ingersoll, who decided that it would, in fact, be a good idea to have Matthews in this editorial capacity. He proposed that they not only install him in the role, but, after a brief breaking-in period, make him another managing editor.[8] (Ingersoll, to Matthews' amazement, almost doubled his salary—to $10,000.) "This suited me

[7] *Name and Address* (Simon and Schuster, 1960).
[8] On *Time*'s masthead all three were bracketed as "Managing Editors." But Gottfried internally was "senior managing editor," Norris "associate managing editor" and Matthews "assistant managing editor."

fine," said Gottfried. "Sharing titular authority with two people was a little better than sharing it with one." Matthews was to fill out a career of twenty-four years on *Time* and became a formidable promontory in its landscape.

The new team of managing editors was severely handicapped from the first by a shortage of able writers. "During the past five years, one competent man after another had been transferred to *Fortune*," said Gottfried, "and during the previous year *Time*'s staff had been raided for *Life*." While Gottfried addressed himself primarily to getting out the magazine, Ingersoll scouted for new talent and did replenish the staff. In a major departure from previous policy, an effort was made to hire writers of journalistic experience. Ingersoll brought in Leon Svirsky from the New York *World Telegram* to write Education, Robert Neville from the New York *Herald Tribune* to assist in Foreign News, Dana Tasker from *Newsweek* to take charge of pictures, and Bice Clemow from *Editor & Publisher* to write the Press section. Gottfried hired Winthrop Sargeant, a member of the New York Philharmonic Orchestra under Toscanini and former music critic on the New York *American,* to become the Music editor. Robert Cantwell, who had spelled Matthews as *Time*'s book reviewer before being transferred to *Fortune,* returned to strengthen the book-review staff, and Louis Kronenberger also came from *Fortune* to do theater reviews. Among the juniors hired (by Gottfried) was John Hersey, who, like Luce, was born in China. Graduating from Yale in 1936 he spent a postgraduate year in Britain, at Clare College, Cambridge. Before joining *Time* he had been for a few months secretary to the novelist Sinclair Lewis.

Ingersoll had reason to look back on the beginning of his tenure as publisher with some satisfaction. He had a Hydra-headed set-up, but his relations with Gottfried, first among equals, were harmonious and effective and he had largely rebuilt the editorial department.

The decision to increase the *Life* guarantee and Ingersoll's expansion of the *Time* editorial budget had been taken against a relatively good business background which prompted hope that economic recovery was under way. It was therefore anticipated that the money *Life* was losing could be recouped in 1938 and that the process would begin in the fourth quarter of 1937. Meanwhile *Time*'s earnings were building to the highest operating profit in its history, $3,069,000. But in September 1937 business started to slide, and by November the country was in the so-called "Roosevelt recession," a depression-within-a-depression. This hit *Life* particularly hard; the anniversary issue, November 22, carried 72 pages of advertising, but next week the number fell to 35 pages and there were blank spaces in the order books for 1938.

Time too was in trouble. Late in 1936 it had announced a circulation guarantee of 700,000 commencing in September 1937. But in the last quarter of 1937 newsstand, subscription, and advertising sales fell off. Ingersoll blamed the decline on the recession and on competition from *Life,* which, he wrote Luce, "competes with *Time* in the public's interest [and also] for the advertiser's dollar." He said that he was willing to meet this competition and believed he could expand *Time*'s earnings, "Provided only: that [*Time*'s] policies . . . are neither circumscribed nor compromised by policies originated not in *its* interests but in the interest of a natural competitor [i.e., *Life*]."

It is difficult to believe that Ingersoll expected to get what in effect he demanded—to publish *Time* as if it were independent of *Life* and *Fortune*. Ingersoll's sense of intramural competition (not unique at Time Inc.) would persist to the point where it would lead to new and more intemperate attacks on management and put him finally on a collision course with both Luce and Larsen.

Life did have an impact on *Time;* it was a competitor for the circulation dollar, and for advertising. But for the moment Luce was less concerned about internal competition than about the over-all prospects for the company; in December he broke the news to shareholders that Time Inc., which had so far that year paid $6 in dividends, would pay no year-end dividend and that it had incurred a loss of more than $3,000,000 on *Life*. The company was left with a net profit of only $168,430 after taxes. On December 21 Luce addressed a confidential memorandum to his senior colleagues (shareholders would have read it with very mixed emotions). "I write this in an attempt to take our bearings," he began, "to state where we have got to, how we stand, and perhaps where we ought to go from here," then continued:

> We have been coming awfully fast. We have been expanding like hell. . . . All this comes down to the proposition that expansion must cease, that we have created all the means of communication which any group of men can attend to. . . . We must devote ourselves to the proper and faithful uses of the instruments we have created.

Luce said that he had had "plenty of fun (and profit) as an entrepreneur," but from this point forward he wanted to be a journalist, and hoped that in the next five years "I can prove I was right about myself." A journal, he pointed out, was not a tool like a printing press, but a thing that grew and died—

> Sometimes it can be born again. But certainly it must die. I don't suppose we can establish the date for the euthanasia of our publications. But one way to look at them, at this date, might be to say that they have twenty years more of life. Which is to say that most of us have a work-life expectancy of some twenty years more. Now maybe during this period we can hand them over to new men who will successively carry them on for much longer than that. But our responsibility, I think, is not to have these publications going strong twenty years from now; our responsibility . . . is to make the fullest use of them during twenty years. If by so doing, they, or what evolves from them, are going strong twenty years from now, so much the better. But I suggest that what we want to do is not to leave to posterity a great institution but to leave behind us a great tradition of journalism ably practiced in our time.

Luce then turned to the financial history of the company, reviewing the successive investments in *Fortune, Architectural Forum* and *The March of Time,* all of which had come out of earnings which had been ploughed back into the company:

330

And then at last came *Life*—more than $800,000 we dumped into that in 1936 before we knew we had started. And then, at last, we no longer had more money than we knew what to do with . . . and by Gosh we found out how quickly money could go when you feel rich and encounter a really expensive idea. And, of course, it being in the best tradition of drama that Providence never takes care of spendthrifts, it was to be expected that a Recession should come along, destroy a million or two of profits that we thought were hanging ripe on the vine. So this year—for the first time in the history of Time Inc.—we don't plough back anything into the company. Instead of that, we dip into surplus to pay dividends.

Now all of this indicates to me that we are poor again. We are no longer a rich company. . . .

So, what's to be done about it? What's to be done about it is, obviously, to go get rich again. We did it once before. Let's see if we can do it again.

CHAPTER
24
_____

"Making a Nickel—
Interpreting the World"

ARRY LUCE wrote to a colleague early in 1938: "The business
of Time Inc. is not easy business. It involves everything
from the hard business of making a nickel to the equally
hard business of interpreting the world. (To observe the number of
people at lunch and dinner who quite easily interpret all cosmological
phenomena—perhaps the only really hard thing to do is to make a
nickel!)" This was a complaint that could have been made by any
responsible publisher in the critical year 1938. It was characteristic of
Luce that he took both "businesses" with equal seriousness; it is the
measure of his ability that he was able to manage both. The Roosevelt
recession made the earning of a nickel difficult; as the Civil War
racked Spain, as civilization retreated before Nazism in Central Europe, as Japan tore savagely into China—and as Americans sought
escape in cynicism or indifference—Luce discovered both the inade-
quacies of his publications and a mission: he and they could not be
indifferent. He turned more earnestly to the task of interpreting the
world, and his publications turned with him.

He announced his intention, as the year began, to devote more time to editorial matters; in January, in a memo to his associates, he nominated himself "for a new job, namely Editorial Director of *Time, Fortune* and *Life"* because "I must, ex officio, acknowledge more responsibility than any other individual for at least the general editorial direction of our papers. In recent years, you have all at various times carried the actual burden of this responsibility without help from me. This has been due to major emergencies such as *Life.* In 1938 I'd like to pretend that no emergency exists."

When Luce decentralized the operations of the company by the creation of the divisional system, he had overestimated the extent to which this would lessen the demands on him; his executives continued to be too dependent on his personal calendar for decisions. Toward the end of 1937, while he was still general manager, Ingersoll had made the somewhat astonishing proposal that Luce appoint "a Second in Command, whose sole responsibility is to head this company and who has full authority to speak for you—a man in whom you must be determined to have such confidence that you can trust him when to take action and when to refrain. . . . His title: Executive Vice President." Luce refused that bait, but he did elevate Allen Grover, who had left *Fortune* the previous year to become his personal assistant, to Assistant to the President; his job was to be "the President's manager . . . if the President is stalling on something to your dissatisfaction you can insist to Grover that he get the President to quit stalling." Grover's authority was further increased when, a short while later, he was made a vice-president of the company. Luce also added to his staff another Assistant, Ralph Delahaye Paine, Jr. After a two-year stint on Wall Street, Paine, Yale '29, joined *Time* as a cub writer, then worked four years as Business writer and spent a short time writing in the National Affairs department. Paine's job was "to act as continuous 'liaison' between the several editorial departments and between them and the President of Time Inc."

Life, in addition to imposing new pressures on management, had produced some other lasting effects. For one thing, it had caused a population explosion. To the total payroll—in 1936—of 650, there had been added in that year alone 228 new employees in New York and 344 in Chicago. The New York staff had long since outgrown the original two floors of the Chrysler Building, and new quarters were needed. The company therefore signed a lease for the top seven floors of the eleventh and newest of the Rockefeller Center buildings which had been rising since 1931 in defiance of the Depression. The rent was $220,000 a year. Over the weekend of April 29, 1938, the last of 641 employees moved to the newly named Time & Life Building at 9 Rockefeller Plaza, overlooking the skating rink (and westward, giving restless writers a view of ships leaving for Europe). With the staff went 544 desks, 103 tables, 975 chairs, 391 filing cabinets, 380 typewriters, 20 water coolers, 174 coat trees, 10,000 pounds of stationery, a library of 13,000 reference books, a morgue of 100,000 folders and a picture collection that had grown to 300,000 photographs.

If all the problems in 1938 could have been solved as easily as that of housing, Luce would indeed have been able to pretend that no crisis existed. But he and all his associates were still troubled by the paradox of *Life:* here was a new magazine which was a dazzling success with the public but which continued to lose money at such an alarming rate that late in 1937 and through the first few months of 1938 there circulated rumors that *Life* would be forced to discontinue publication. Later Luce could look back on this anxious time and joke about it. "I once lost a trifling $5,000,000 on a wild-steer ride with a hot baby called *Life,*" he said, "and believe me that was an awful lot more excitement than I ever got out of *making* money. Of course, I didn't really *intend* to lose all that money, but then on the other hand I had to sort of *pretend* I had intended to, otherwise all my friends would have thought I was a dope. It got so that every night when I came home, my wife would tell me how another one of her dear friends had consoled her about my forthcoming bankruptcy. President Roosevelt even asked me about it once. He said was it true that I was making such a hell of a success I was going bust. And in my innocent eagerness to reassure him I said, 'Well, Mr. President, I've got my next year's budget balanced.' And then did I blush! But he just

334

laughed a good-hearted laugh and I immediately began thinking up schemes to unbalance my balance and get in step again."

He did not have to think very hard. As 1938 began, *Life* was a long way from balancing its budget. The company was in no danger of going broke; the thought of discontinuing publication was never entertained. At the same time it was evident to everyone in the trade that the losses on *Life* were running in the millions. *Life*'s competitors, aided by a little wishful thinking, encouraged the rumors. In a letter to the advertising agencies Larsen sought to counter these reports: "We fully expect *Life* to turn in a profit to the company this year." Pointing out that the magazine had established itself within a year as a property comparable to the *Saturday Evening Post,* he declared that Time Inc. was prepared

> to guard it with every dollar within our reach. . . . We have put some five million dollars into *Life* to date, and we think we have something pretty big to show for our money. . . . When a new magazine produces editorial content so interesting that the reading public will voluntarily spend $10,000,000 in a year to read that magazine, it does upset many of the publishing theories of the past. . . . When a publisher has such a property [there] can be no question of the success of that magazine—and if the reading public wants it, the advertiser cannot help but profit. . . .

Larsen's case was amply supported by the circulation figures. In the first issue of the new year *Life* carried an inside-cover house advertisement in which the magazine extended New Year's greetings to "800,000 subscribers, 1,000,000 newsstand buyers and 14,400,000 other readers." In its first year of publication *Life*'s circulation revenues had been higher than those of any other weekly publication in history. This had been achieved with little promotion; and some 60 percent of sales were on the newsstands, where *Life* sold at ten cents —twice the per-copy price of the *Saturday Evening Post* and *Collier's. Life* was also meeting the competition of *Look* and a dozen other picture magazines that had been launched in the wake of its first issue.

335

But the advertiser was not buying *Life*. The basic reason was price. It was recognized that to be successful *Life* had to be accepted as a vehicle for mass-consumer advertising. Somewhat naïvely, perhaps, Luce had also assumed that the advertiser would pay a premium for what Luce considered to be *Life*'s self-evident values: superior printing on quality paper, speed of distribution, and news coverage. The experience with advertising sales in the first year had also been misleading. In this period *Life*'s rate, as measured by the cost per thousand, was less than the competition, and media buyers seized a bargain. In 1937, when *Life*'s rates were raised to reflect the increase in circulation, many advertising contracts were not renewed. The *Life* salesmen argued *Life*'s values; the space buyers quoted rates: the *Saturday Evening Post,* $2.96 per thousand; *Life,* $3.56 per thousand. Larsen himself began to canvass agency heads; he was told bluntly that *Life* must meet the competition. "We thought they had been buying *Life* because of quality and glamour," he recalled sadly, "but instead they were buying by the slide rule." At the $3.56 rate (based on a circulation guarantee of 1,600,000) *Life* had to sell 1,000 pages of advertising to break even. To meet the *Saturday Evening Post*'s rate or undercut it meant accepting further losses unless substantial reduction could be made in physical costs.

Luce was for maintaining the rate; Larsen, fresh from his canvass of the agencies, argued that this could not be done. He proposed instead raising the circulation guarantee to 2,000,000 with no increase in the page rate, thus reducing *Life*'s rate per thousand to $2.85. At this point Stillman provided figures that clinched Larsen's argument. Substantial savings in production made possible the reduction of the break-even point to 924 pages on a $2.85 rate. The makeshift presses on which *Life* had originally been printed delivered copies at 5,000 an hour; new ones now installed and scheduled at 6,000 an hour were producing at the rate of 6,700. The bindery was being mechanized, reducing the dependence on hand labor. And improvements in the technology of producing paper made with a groundwood base indicated that further substantial savings were possible. Because *Life* had sold 2,224 pages in 1937, when its advertising rates were competitive, Larsen argued that, with increased

336

circulation and a rate lower than the *Saturday Evening Post,* the magazine might reasonably expect to sell at least 1,000 pages in 1938. Luce's objections were overcome; the new rate was announced to the trade on February 1.

Larsen decided then that he could afford to take some time out for a cruise in the Bahamas. Before he left, newsstand sales had been a little soft, but *Life* was still selling out on most newsstands. Soon after he left, Jackson and Stillman, alarmed by reports from the American News Company that *Life* for the first time was taking newsstand returns, decided they must call Larsen by radio telephone. They did not know that Gerard Lambert, head of the firm that manufactured Listerine, a big advertiser, was also cruising near Larsen's boat and was at that moment using his radio telephone to assure friends in New Jersey that, in spite of an accident which had injured one man on his yacht, his passengers and the rest of the crew were safe. "The air was full of advertising ears listening in," said Larsen, "when this message came over the air waves about *Life* taking returns. I stood there listening and trying to tell our guys to shut up. They didn't realize they were talking to the wide, wide world. I finally got them to understand I didn't want to hear any more. They thought I was just cold—casual about the whole thing."

He was far from casual. "Returns"—unsold copies—are normal in newsstand sales; as circulation manager of *Time,* Larsen had learned to predict and live with them. But with *Life,* which had a smaller proportion of subscriptions, newsstand sales were the critical area; any falling off jeopardized the new circulation guarantee. In its first year of publication *Life* had taken almost no returns. Did returns mean that the novelty of *Life* was wearing off? Larsen put in to the nearest port and hurried home.

There occurred at this moment an incident that gave *Life* a tremendous lift. A film documentary on the birth of a baby, produced by the American Committee on Maternal Welfare (with the support of such prestigious bodies as the American College of Surgeons, the Association of Obstetricians, Gynecologists and Abdominal Surgeons, and the U.S. Children's Bureau), had been refused an exhibition permit

337

by the New York State censors. There was an immediate outcry from both the medical profession and the press. Joe Thorndike, *Life*'s movie editor, suggested that the magazine show up the stupidity of the censor by publishing stills from the picture. Larsen recognized that it was a promotion opportunity not to be missed. Publication was planned with the greatest care to blunt any charge of sensationalism while exploiting the controversy to the hilt. Said Larsen: "Our build-up is going to way over-sell the story to sensation-seekers, and I think it would be grand to disappoint them all"; he deliberately did not increase the print order.

In those days the constitutional guarantees of a free press were frequently and unconstitutionally abridged by various censors, national and local. The Post Office, for instance, often held the idiosyncratic view that displaying the bare breasts of African women was not offensive in the *National Geographic,* but showing those of white women was reason to bar any magazine from the mails; newsstands were rigorously policed by local prosecutors. In this case the Post Office said there would be no objection to the "Birth of a Baby" pictures. Trouble at the local level was anticipated; newsdealers were assured in advance that *Life* would defend and indemnify them if they were prosecuted.

There was some apprehension about reader reaction. The pictures were deliberately kept small, none more than a column in width. The sequence of the actual birth showed only the head and shoulders of the infant emerging from voluminous sheets that draped the mother during delivery. In advance of publication, $13,000 was spent on a letter to subscribers alerting them and pointing out that the four-page form in which the pictures appeared would be placed in the middle of the magazine for easy removal if parents did not want their children to see them.[1] Another mailing went to clergymen, civic leaders, etc., soliciting approval.

The issue came out April 8. Immediately, Governor George H. Earle of Pennsylvania ordered the magazine off the newsstands; the Canadian Customs impounded all shipments; *Life* was banned in thirty-three American cities, seventeen of them in New England,

---

[1] Money largely wasted—most of the letters arrived after delivery of the magazine.

including Boston, Hartford and Providence; in Boston and New Haven criminal prosecutions were instituted. The real test case was in the Bronx; there Assistant District Attorney Samuel J. Foley took action against newsdealers, and Roy Larsen presented himself in Foley's office, sold a copy to a detective and was formally charged with selling an obscene publication.

Before the case could be brought to trial—within hours of publication, in fact—many arbiters of U.S. morals rushed to the magazine's defense. "The motion picture cannot be harmful, because it is honest," said Mrs. Franklin D. Roosevelt. Miss Dorothy Thompson declared: "If the pictures are obscene then the birth of a baby is obscene . . . and we had better face the fact that that's the way life (small 'l') is." The Surgeon General of the United States, Dr. Thomas Parran, congratulated *Life*.

Larsen was acquitted; the case in New Haven was dismissed peremptorily by the bench without a trial, much to the disappointment of Jackson, who had gone there hoping to be arrested. Only in Boston did the prosecution win, in spite of a brilliant defense of *Life*'s newsdealer by Joseph N. Welch (who would attain national prominence in 1954 as special counsel for the Army against Senator Joseph McCarthy). Following Larsen's acquittal, the ban was rescinded in many cities, and all but 10,000 of the seized copies eventually were sold.

Ten days after the pictures were published, Gallup's Institute of Public Opinion, taking an independent poll, estimated that 17,000,000 adults had seen them, a minimum of eight readers for each copy; of these, 76 percent said the pictures were not obscene and 61 percent approved their publication; approval was slightly higher among women than among men.

"The Birth of a Baby" was useful and timely promotion when it was much needed; it demonstrated editorial influence, and was a reminder to advertisers of *Life*'s enormous readership. Moreover, an unassailable cause had been upheld: better and safer motherhood.

Time, since the last quarter of 1937, had also been having some trouble on the circulation front due to the recession and competition from *Life*. In 1937, as in 1936, *Life* had siphoned off some of the

Christmas gift subscriptions that ordinarily would have gone to *Time*. As circulation manager Prentice explained it to Luce, *"Time* is probably a better magazine than *Life* but *Life* is definitely a better Christmas present than *Time*."* In May 1938 *Time*'s circulation problem was eased by the purchase for $25,000 of the name, good will and unfilled subscriptions of the *Literary Digest*. There was some irony in Time Inc. taking over a magazine that sixteen years before (so Hadden and Luce had been told so often) had preempted the market that *Time* was about to enter. In 1920 the *Literary Digest,* with gross advertising revenues of over $12,500,000, was second only to the *Saturday Evening Post* in dollar volume of national advertising. It once had a circulation of more than 1,500,000, but it fell into a decline which its publishers were unable to reverse. Its demise was hastened by the disastrous error of the long-established *Digest* straw poll, which in 1936 predicted that Alf Landon would win the Presidency. In February 1938 the *Digest* suspended publication and Time Inc. undertook to fulfill 250,000 unexpired subscriptions; 150,000 subscribers chose *Time* and 45,000 selected other Time Inc. publications, mainly *Life*. Ingersoll wrote, with obvious relief, "It seems odd not to have any more circulation concerns."

The *Digest* subscriptions transferred to *Life* provided an essential cushion, though a small one, for Larsen's new circulation guarantee. The main difficulty on *Life,* in spite of the readjustment of the rates, continued to be advertising sales. Howard Black, who on the permanent retirement of Robert Johnson in 1937 became the senior advertising executive of the company, was now devoting himself solely to *Life.* He had as his assistant a young Williams graduate who joined *Time* in 1934: James A. Linen III, the grandson of Luce's father's great friend and sponsor. After trying his hand briefly at writing, Linen had switched to sales and been transferred to Detroit. There his work won a direct commendation from Luce: "I have before me the list of ten accounts which you recently got because, as Howard said, you didn't know any better than to go after them!" With *Life* under way, Linen was transferred to that magazine, then recalled to New York to be "assistant to the advertising director." His first job, Black told him, was to work the words "to the" out of his title.

340

Black's sales force had high morale and a tremendous conviction about the magazine. One of the first salesmen recalled that he and his associates were so sure that the advertising in *Life* would create sales that they went out and bought stock in one company that had just signed up for a campaign. Joseph C. Goulden, an independent witness,[2] has testified to their fervor; *Life* salesmen, he wrote, fought for advertising with "the ferocity of Dead-End Kids." But in spite of competitive rates and a responsive readership, freshly demonstrated by "The Birth of a Baby," they were having difficulty in signing up the major advertisers. In Detroit, where the *Saturday Evening Post* and the automobile industry had grown up together, *Life* in its first two years had the greatest difficulty in even being considered for the top schedules.

The sales problem had several facets, but it was essentially a simple one. Luce had said in the beginning that *Life* might develop as an advertising medium into something quite as unique as it was editorially and therefore had ruled out presenting it as a competitor to the *Saturday Evening Post*. This proved to be true; in fact, *Life* differed so much from the norms accepted by major magazine advertisers that they had difficulty in fitting it into their media picture. It was not so obviously oriented to a predominantly male readership as were the *Saturday Evening Post, Collier's* and *Liberty*. Its readership among women was nearly equal to that among men, but it had no service function as did the women's magazines *Good Housekeeping, Ladies' Home Journal* and *Woman's Home Companion*. It had an enthusiastic following among young people. It also differed in format; other magazines concentrated their editorial display in one bank of pages and continued text through the advertising pages. *Life* provided a number of editorial sections, which dispersed its pictures and text through and opposite the advertising pages. This gave the advertisers many more positions opposite editorial matter, which not every advertiser knew how to exploit; some argued that *Life*'s editorial pictures directly competed with the advertisements.

Larsen and Black addressed themselves to a sales strategy to overcome *Life*'s problems. Larsen had perceived that *Life* would be a more attractive magazine if it could win over the soft-goods and

[2] *The Curtis Caper* (G. P. Putnam's Sons, 1965).

341

fashion trade, whose colorful advertisements would brighten its pages. As a group, these advertisers were not easily persuaded, so *Life* undertook to sell them indirectly by a demonstration of merchandising. Its merchandising expert H. Ford Perine organized a group that worked with department stores from coast to coast on a series of spectacular fashion promotions that created tremendous consumer excitement and increased store traffic. Soon the merchandising effort spread to the food and drug chains.

However, *Life*'s real trump card lay in its tremendous pass-along readership. This was a distinctive feature of *Life* from the first issue onward; in fact, the readership seemed almost too great to be believed. One questionnaire inserted in every 100th copy of the magazine returned a figure indicating that each copy had 14 readers; the publisher arbitrarily reduced the figure to 10.76 readers. A series of surveys continued to give impressive evidence that the readership outran the actual circulation by millions. The media buyers, however, based their judgment on the Audit Bureau of Circulations report; in circulation *Life* trailed the *Saturday Evening Post, Liberty* and *Collier's.* Larsen was the first to suggest that *Life*'s readership was more characteristic of a radio audience than that of the conventional magazine, and Black realized that if they could validate this tremendous pass-along readership in a convincing manner *Life* would have a unique and powerful sales argument.

The problem was how to establish a measurement of readership that would be accepted. Cornelius DuBois, *Life*'s market-research director, turned to the opinion-sampling techniques of Dr. George Gallup and Elmo Roper, which had been triumphantly vindicated by their forecast of the vote in the 1936 Presidential election.

In July 1938 *Life* called in a group of marketing and research specialists, headed by Paul T. Cherington and assisted by both Gallup and Roper.[3] This group of experienced professionals became the controlling committee of *Life*'s Continuing Study of Magazine Audi-

[3] Others in the group: Mr. Archibald M. Crossley, President of Crossley Inc., and Mr. Samuel Gill, Crossley's director of research; Dr. Darrell B. Lucas, Associate Professor of Marketing at New York University. Dr. S. S. Wilks, Professor of Statistics at Princeton University, helped with methods and analysis.

ences (CSMA), turning itself, said an observer, into "a veritable laboratory of market research, breaking new ground with new methods." Though financed by *Life,* the committee's work was fully independent; later the group became an agency known as the Magazine Audience Group, handling research projects for publishers other than Time Inc.

Its goal was to determine just how many people were reached by a single issue of the four leading weeklies. The phrase "Magazine Audiences" had the merit of suggesting a comparison with the total "listening audiences" claimed by the radio networks. The first survey was conducted in 115 cities and hamlets on the basis of more than 8,000 interviews; later the study widened.

The findings showed that while *Life* was smaller in circulation, its total audience was 17,300,000, compared to 15,900,000 for *Collier's* and 14,000,000 for *Liberty;* the *Saturday Evening Post,* the leader in circulation and advertising, showed 12,900,000 readers.

The committee's figures were at first indignantly challenged by *Life*'s competitors. The Crowell Publishing Company took a full-page advertisement in the New York *Herald Tribune* to denounce the findings and the theory, asserting that for its part it would make no claim beyond its circulation figures in the Audit Bureau of Circulations report. But the thoroughness of the study, the caliber and independence of the supervising committee, were difficult to dispute, and the new concept was finally and generally accepted. The committee's findings were a tremendous factor in finally establishing *Life* with advertisers.

In August 1938 Larsen made a significant report. The year's losses on *Life,* to be sure, he said, would be greater than anticipated because of new editorial and promotion expenditures. But this money was being spent "not with the feeling that it must be done to maintain a position, but rather to enhance *Life*'s general value as a magazine property—spent with the feeling that *Life* has definitely turned the corner and that now is the time to snowball its success trend." Newsstand sales were improving against a general fall-off; but, most important, there began to develop a new advertising acceptance, with fashion advertising "over the top" and even an indication of a break-

343

through in Detroit. Through a series of big editorial features the editors had (Larsen noted) "established in people's minds the fact that *Life* is 'important.' Before that, *Life* was a sensation, yes, a novelty and interesting—but not important." Now he looked ahead confidently to a whole new phase in Time Inc. operations. Luce's "wild-steer ride" was beginning to turn a corner. "In *Life* we have our first big-volume, small-profit-margin operation," Larsen wrote. "A large profit for *Life* must come with a tremendous volume of advertising, which means that *Life* must be a *Saturday Evening Post* or a *Good Housekeeping.*"

If only the rider didn't lose his seat. Luce distributed the Larsen report to the other publishers and managing editors with the comment:

> I would like to make the point that by all odds the No. 1 immediate task and indeed obligation of Time Inc. as a whole this Fall is to put *Life* over.

While Luce was deeply engaged in the foregoing "hard business of making a nickel," he was increasingly concerned about his magazines' responsibility for "the equally hard business of interpreting the world." Personally Luce had always been willing to and did take responsibility for what the magazines printed, but, until he had urged *Fortune* to adopt a bias in favor of private enterprise, he had not imposed his views on any of them. In 1937 and early 1938 he made a number of speeches, which were intended, so he wrote to a friend, "in some degree to put Time Inc. on record." He thus began in his own mind to formulate an editorial policy for all the magazines, a process that carried forward through the whole of 1938. The first of these speeches, made at Williamstown, Massachusetts, before the Institute of Human Relations, dealt with the public responsibility of a free press. "The give-the-public-what-it-wants-theory" was, he said, the prevailing theory of publishing. In it lay

> the danger of sensationalism and the danger of mediocrity. . . . But there is another and a greater danger: the danger that such a press will not give the people what they must have—what they will perish without.

344

The present crisis in world affairs may be described as a crisis in journalism. Fundamentally and at bottom the reason why the modern dictatorships are unspeakable is not merely because of their murders and their concentration camps and their treason trials. Men can fight that kind of tyranny. They have fought it before and overcome it. . . . Modern dictatorships are unspeakable [because] they corrupt the mind from within. They suppress the truth. They lead men by lies and fraud to desire and acquiesce in their own enslavement. And how is this corruption brought about? *By the destruction of journalism.* . . . What then can the Press do to ensure its survival? There are, I believe, two answers. The first is that the Press must assist the people to govern themselves. . . . The Press today may be roughly divided between entertainment and information—perhaps 70% entertainment and 30% information. . . .

Luce said that the Press in entertainment could not hold its own with the movies, radio and "perhaps . . . television." On the other hand,

Nothing . . . can compete with the Press in information [and] publishers will find an expanding market for information and all journalists an increase in the dignity of their strange profession.

The second thing the Press could do to ensure survival was to perfect its craftsmanship:

There is today great need for great argument. And to the great debate, the journalist must and will respond in his emotions and in his conscience. It is not peculiarly the mission of the Press to exorcise the Doubt which is conquering the Western World or to discover and rediscover standards of faith and excellence by which men may live. But if there is such a mission in the world . . . that mission can succeed only if it succeeds in and through and with the Press. . . .

There is a mission which is peculiar to the Press—the mission to inform. Through all the alarms of the future, the true journalist will continue to believe in the paramount importance of the purely informative function of journalism. . . . His proudest boast will be . . . that he has, fearlessly, eagerly, and effectively

345

transmitted significant information from the boisterous news-fronts of the world into the minds of living and literate and free people.

In a second speech, the one to the Ohio Bankers, he had reaffirmed his belief in free enterprise. In February 1938 he made a third address, at Rollins College in Florida, in which he exhorted students

> to discover in this present confusion the standards of excellence by which free men may live together in broad and general agreement—standards of conduct, criteria of Truth. . . .
>
> For Democracy, I suppose, makes one great assumption. It assumes the persistence among men of a vigorous sense of right and wrong. It assumes that in any given society of free men and women there will exist strong moral sanctions broader and more compelling than the statute books. Democracy assumes that the people will construct a government in their own image of right and wrong and that it is therefore not necessary that the government should construct the people in its image of right and wrong. Democracy assumes that there can be and must be a law higher than the state. To that law many names have been given. And one of the names is Truth, and another among the philosophers is Virtue, and another, in the common affairs of man, is Morality.

His approach to his editors on such matters was roundabout—not because he was in any sense intimidated by them but because he respected their positions. On one occasion when he sent Gottfried a number of suggestions for stories which *Time* largely ignored, Gottfried wrote and apologized for his neglect. Luce replied: "Don't ever worry about ignoring my story suggestions. I try to make them with, of course, a feeling for *Time*. But well I realize that they are made without benefit of a systematic knowledge of all the story possibilities for the issue. And certainly they always (or almost always!) are offered to aid rather than to harass!"

He was not, however, very happy about *Time*. Early in 1938 he wrote to Ingersoll:

346

In the '20s it seemed that a number of things had to be debunked. *Time* was no great campaigner. It was not so sure of itself in those days as it is supposed to be today. But it *was* regarded by a small group of truth-seekers as being on the side of truth versus the bunk.

Now it seems to me that recently, with all its research and with all its self-assurance, *Time* has been notably lax in its debunking job . . . has done almost no debunking of anything which is anti-capitalistic or leftist—except in the case of the lunatic fungus-like Townsend and of F.D.R. who, of course, is inescapable. And the reason for this is, I think, clear—namely, that over a period of years the mood of any non-Tory mind has been to try to understand the new social & economic forces or ideas. That was and is a good reason. I applaud, for example, your insistence on catching up on Labor. But now I think the time has come for a slight change of attitude—to take a deep breath, smile, and once again look at the cockeyed world—cockeyed to the left of us as well as to the right of us.

When *Time* eliminated the heading "Radicals" and fell into the current fashion of reclassifying radicals as liberals, Luce again wrote Ingersoll:

I understand that a recent internal triumph in *Time* is the elimination of the head *Radicals*. Maybe so. But several times lately I have seen *Time* use the word liberals when it meant radicals—or at least it meant to include people a good deal left of center, if not radicals. And what the hell, are there no honest radicals left? Are there no more guts left in American leftism?

I consider myself a liberal. Perhaps my kind of liberalism is considered far on the right. But certainly I don't want to be lumped with leftists—and especially not with gutless leftists. The same must be true of perhaps three-quarters of *Time* readers who consider themselves neither Tories nor Pinks. . . .

Ingersoll, who was running *Time* with the bit in his teeth, seems to have paid little heed to these or to other Luce comments. Larsen, for instance, told Ingersoll that Luce did not like the idea of promoting *Time* on the premise that the "departments are written for experts in the various fields they cover," adding, "If Harry doesn't feel that *Time* should be written that way, then unquestionably we shouldn't sell it that way." Ingersoll ignored Larsen. To mark its fifteenth birthday, *Time* included in the mailing to subscribers a facsimile copy of Vol. I, No. 1, and a seven-column article in the Press section of the February 28, 1938, issue pointed out: "The difference between the editorial mechanisms which produced the first and the 782nd issues of *Time* is the difference between a minipiano and a grand piano. It has many more keys but it is still the same kind of machine." There was no question that it had more keys, and some of them, Ingersoll promised, would play with more resonance and precision than the old "minipiano." In an anniversary letter to all subscribers he said that *Time* would henceforward strive

> *to make each department so sound that it can stand the test of the expert's microscope. . . .*
>
> Until today, *Time* has never dared to suggest that college presidents, for example, would find *Time*'s Education Department a real help in following the progress of education; that labor leaders would find *Time*'s Labor Column a real help in balancing their understanding . . . or that the German ambassador might find *Time*'s uncensored reports from Germany an important check on his own information from home. . . .

The new program, he added, was forcing *Time*

> to build up, independently, one of the world's great news-gathering and *news-verifying* systems and to make radical changes in all our editorial methods.

And he pointed with pride to editorial branch offices in five cities in the U.S. and abroad; and to 399 part-time "stringer" correspondents supplying and verifying reports from 357 U.S. cities.

Though Ingersoll and Gottfried had made progress in rebuilding the writing staff, the system of three managing editors was not functioning

348

to anyone's satisfaction. Ingersoll at one point wrote to Gottfried that "One of you must be responsible for having read every single item that's going in the magazine to be sure that duplications are caught, cross-references put in, tones of different stories jibe, etc., etc. . . ." While Gottfried agreed, he pointed out that it was impossible for the senior M.E. to do more than he was doing. He and Ingersoll then decided on a new arrangement that was the beginning of *Time*'s present system of senior editors. The work of editing was further subdivided and decentralized, with a limited number of departments assigned to each man, and Gottfried was assigned to be "a non-playing quarterback." This meant that he edited only the National Affairs section himself, but he read the final edited copy of all the other departments.

Harry Luce had the advantage of a continuing education freely handed out to him by his senior employees on the editorial side. It was MacLeish who came forward now with a long lecture. In 1938 MacLeish resigned to become curator of the Nieman Fellowship program at Harvard. Luce wrote him a note of appreciation for his work on *Fortune,* and MacLeish, instead of filing it in his personal archives and going quietly away, sat down and wrote an admonitory letter that warned of what the corporation might, in MacLeish's earnest estimate, become. It also bore on the important current question of Time Inc.'s interpretation of the world.

> I think I can say something to you which will truly be to your advantage. I refer to your courteous and kindly remark that you do not need to tell me of your appreciation of my work on *Fortune.* Well, my lad, you do. And I'll tell you why—and it applies to many other than myself. The last story of mine about which you had anything encouraging to say . . . was a long time ago. I will admit (with resentment) that *Fortune* is not the association of mutually assisting journalists it was for five or six very exciting years. I will admit (without enthusiasm) that it is now a part of a publishing enterprise in which not more than a dozen or so people know each other's names and not more than half that many wish each other well enough to stand by each

349

other in the only work that finally counts—the writing of the journal. But I will still reply that you do need to tell your associates when their work is good. Because if you don't the last element of personal humanity will drain out of that organization and you will be left with nothing on your hands but a business which earns money. I can speak of this freely first because I am no longer a part of that organization and secondly because your silence has never seriously hurt me—the reason being that I have always counted on a solid and substantial friendship between us and have always known that when the work *was* good you recognized its value. But there are a lot of others who haven't that solid basis and that mutual faith. And you owe them more than they get in the way of appreciation. They work for you—or for your magazines—harder than any comparable group in the country. And they value your praise more than you could believe possible. . . .

Then there's *Fortune* itself. . . . I think perhaps too enthusiastically that it has a future commensurate with its past. But then I'm not sure you would agree with me about its past. . . . I think when they take the final inventory of Time Inc. *Fortune* will stand out as by far the most important single item because *Fortune* will stand out as the one great journalistic innovation of our time. I don't know whether you are aware of the extent to which the jury of intelligent and disciplined minds has already come to that conclusion. I hear it everywhere. . . . It is a very great magazine. It's a very great magazine because it is a true and honest and efficient journalistic technique. And God help the editor who ever meddles with that technique—who ever puts the editorial wish above the research girl's yes-say or nay-say. Because there is no better way to kill an egg than to murder its mother the goose. . . .

I wish you hadn't been so successful. Because it's very hard to be as successful as you have been and still keep your belief in the desperate necessity for fundamental change. I think what you have done is amazing and I give you all credit and all honor for it. . . . But I don't know—you were meant to be a progressive—a pusher-over—a pryer-up. You were meant to make

350

common cause with the people—all the people. You would have
been very happy, I think, if you could have felt that the New
Deal was your affair. Because it was your affair. You would have
been very happy inside yourself as one of the leaders in a
democratic revolution in this country. . . .

I think you have been an honorable journalist. You would
have been happier in a fight though. . . .

A few weeks later MacLeish wrote that he was sorry if he had said
anything that might offend.

I had come to the end of a piece of my life which meant (or did
for years) a great deal to me—much of it in association with a
gent who—I wish perhaps too earnestly—was on the same side I
find myself on. . . .

Luce would never share MacLeish's enthusiasm for the New Deal, but
he was not offended by the exhortation, or by MacLeish's personal
criticisms. In fact, he entertained the hope that he might someday get
MacLeish back. He replied:

Last fall (before things began to get so bad so fast) I had hopes
we might undertake some big step in the evolution of *Fortune*.
One of my ideas was an editorial page (but different both in form
and purpose from the one which Russ [Davenport] is doing) and
another of my ideas was that you might be persuaded to be The
Editor of *Fortune*—editor in the sense of Editor of the New
York *Times,* specifically responsible for a responsible editorial
page, generally responsible for a certain amount of ideological
coherence in the mag., i.e. keynoter—but distinct from the terrific journalistic grind of Managing Editor. In a big gossip with
Mac [Ingersoll] the other day, he thought I should tell you
this—partly because he thought it had been a good idea, and
partly because it might happen some day. Anyway, we like to
think it might.

MacLeish did not come back to Time Inc. After a year at Harvard,
Roosevelt offered him the post of Librarian of Congress. MacLeish
remained on cordial terms with Luce in spite of continuing political

351

differences. After Luce's death he wrote, "My admiration (and affection) for HRL remains and increases. He was a better and bigger man than most of his colleagues ever guessed—or guess today. Wrong and opinionated, sure—but a memorable human being."

Luce devoted most of his attention in the first six months of 1938 to the editorial problems of *Life*. The dozen imitators that had come along in *Life*'s wake were, with a few exceptions, edited with the viewpoint of a circus sideshow—heavy on cheesecake and the freakish. *Life* too was printing its share of trivia: Alexander King (author of *Mine Enemy Grows Older* [4]), who worked briefly for *Life,* counted it among his achievements that he managed to find a midget whose life-size photograph exactly filled a double-page spread. And although Luce was not against such acts (*Life* had been conceived as a showbook), he was not satisfied with such limited horizons. Inspired by his discovery that the camera could make "normal, decent, useful and pleasant behavior far more interesting than word journalism usually does," he pressed his editors to get the photographers into the byways of America. They did indeed produce Americana that were beautiful and sometimes new. On one occasion *Life* recorded a local sauerkraut festival. Luce was delighted, although Longwell objected that this was carrying the search for beauty in the commonplace rather far.

Perhaps the most important editorial question of 1938 was whether or not *Life* should carry full-length articles. Some editors objected that the introduction of articles would negate the basic concept of a magazine dedicated to pictures. But against this was the argument, advanced by a number of advertising agencies, that *Life* was a magazine that could be "flipped through" and therefore did not hold its readers long enough to give proper exposure to the advertisements. This argument took little account of the fact that in both captions and text blocks *Life* carried thousands of words of reading matter. Luce himself thought the advertisers' point was "a bum argument, but let's grant it." It was therefore decided that each issue would carry at least one important article. The first was a biographical sketch of the Democratic National Chairman, James A. Farley, by Joseph Alsop

[4] Simon and Schuster, 1958.

352

and Robert Kintner. In the long run the decision was wise and important to *Life*'s future and status; as circulation expanded, it offered important writers an enormous audience, a forum for ideas, and finally, because of the decision, the magazine in later years would be able to publish the memoirs of world figures—among them, Sir Winston Churchill, Harry S Truman, the Duke of Windsor.

It was a trip to Europe in May and June that brought home to Luce, if they needed bringing home, the responsibilities and obligations that rested on a free press. The problems of journalistic inquiry and interpretation would preoccupy him for the rest of his career. The May–June trip was the first of three European trips he and his wife made before the U.S. entered the war. He had several meetings with U.S. Ambassador Joseph Kennedy in London, had tea at the House of Commons with Harold Nicolson and dinner with Brendan Bracken, chairman of the *Financial News* and later wartime Minister of Information. Luce also talked with Lord Southwood of Odhams Press; he had an interview with the chief Diplomatic Advisor to the Government, Sir Robert Vansittart, an implacable foe of the Nazis. Everywhere people talked fearfully of war. "The smell of Munich was already in the air," said Luce.

In Hitler's Berlin the Luces were entertained by the German representative of a great American corporation. A fellow guest, the corporation's vice-president for foreign operations, told Luce that Germany was the place to study "the ways and destiny of man in the Twentieth Century" because "whether or not you like it, Germany is the place where you are likely to learn the most about what you are going to get in the U.S. and elsewhere in the world." The impression Luce got was that these people believed in National Socialism as "a socialism which works mightily for the masses however distasteful it may be to them personally in many ways." Reporting this to his editors in New York, he was skeptical: "The great apologetic slogan in Germany is 'Everyone has enough—no one has too much.' Of course, to my old Liberal-capitalistic mind, it is extremely doubtful if everyone can have enough unless some lucky (or unlucky) bastards have too much. . . . But the extraordinary thing about Hitler, at least for the moment, is

353

that he has suspended the class war; not, at the moment, by making the poor like the rich but by making the rich like, or damn well pretend to like, the poor." He observed that, despite a façade of luxury (e.g., waiters in tailcoats at the Hotel Adlon), the menus were poor, the bathwater was muddy and the toilet paper "the worst I have encountered in years."

Luce, for the first time, saw a copy of Julius Streicher's notorious anti-Semitic newspaper *Der Stürmer*. "A traveler is always prepared to learn that a sensational circumstance within a country has been greatly exaggerated," he wrote, "but there has been no exaggeration as to the important role which anti-Semitism has played in the Third Reich or as to the intensity of this brand of hatred. . . . There was no evidence that they [the Nazis] were letting up on anti-Semitism. . . ."

In Prague he had an hour's audience with Dr. Eduard Beneš, Czechoslovakia's President. "He believed," Luce reported, "that war can be avoided and that if a general war is avoided during the next five or ten years, the totalitarian systems will collapse and democratic systems will again triumph in Germany, Italy, etc. I challenged him on the collapse of the totalitarian regimes and he said they would go broke. The little man's faith in democracy was very convincing— especially as he backed it up with the assurance that the average man in the street far down below his gleaming palace was ready and willing that very moment to fight for country and for liberty." (A year later Luce admitted to his editors he had overestimated Czech determination to fight.)

As they were leaving Europe, Luce cabled to make sure the *Time* cover story on Beneš scheduled for June 27 did full justice to an "able idealist, great leader of a brave people."

Luce had evidence that Time Inc. magazines were being read with attention in foreign chancelleries, even though their circulation abroad was minimal. He had been received everywhere as an important, influential editor. Back home, however, he was reminded of the magazines' prominence by all too frequent complaints about them. As publisher of *Time,* Ingersoll had been lectured by such disparate

354

critics as Mrs. Helen Reid, of the New York *Herald Tribune,* and officials of the Sinclair Oil Company on the need to assume a more responsible attitude. From Washington *Time*'s correspondent reported numerous pleas from the State Department that the publications treat foreign leaders more respectfully. The President of Peru did not like a portrait which *Fortune* published and made an official protest to Washington. Under Secretary of State Sumner Welles complained in a confidential letter to C. D. Jackson that a picture spread in *Life* was detrimental to U.S.-Turkish relations. A Catholic publication, the *Sign,* objected because a group of Time Incers were publicly listed as sponsors for a party to raise funds for Loyalist Spain. This invalidated any claim the magazine made to impartiality, the *Sign* felt. Luce wrote the editor of the *Sign* that he had not approved of the group's action: "We do not object to individuals in Time Inc. associating themselves with various 'outside' causes, as individuals, but we do object to groups of Time Inc. editors or writers sponsoring various causes."

An insight into the attitude prevalent among members of the editorial staff during this period has been provided by Alfred Kazin:

> . . . There was a curiously pretentious show of intellectual "guilt" around the *Time-Fortune* offices, an unnecessary need to show oneself pure and uncorrupted. Professional liberals—not the poet-reporters like James Agee and other gifted writers who were fascinated by the social material of the Thirties opened to them—liked to think that their gifts were misused and exploited; grumbling about the boss made them feel that their wine had not yet turned into Luce's corporate vinegar. . . . Although they were glad of the generous salaries, the constant stir around the place and the travel, they found it necessary to insist that not Henry Luce himself, and above all not Mrs. Henry Luce, could ever control their opinions.[5]

Luce recognized that certain inter-office relations were coming to a head. He saw a need to define fairly explicitly an over-all editorial policy, but was reluctant to make any show of imposing his opinions.

[5] *Starting Out in the Thirties* (Atlantic–Little, Brown, 1965).

He himself was never cynical or neutral on matters that he felt required moral judgments; it therefore never occurred to him that men who merited his respect would bow to his judgment merely because they happened to work for him. So instead of laying down a policy, he hoped to persuade his colleagues to accept one.

In the fall of 1938 he invited thirteen of his senior associates to dinner at the Union Club. It was evident to them that he had been thinking about the confusion that existed over such questions as "objectivity." He sought, said Gottfried, "consensus and the collective support of his colleagues." No record exists of the night's discussion, but some weeks later he sent the people who had been at the dinner a seventeen-page memorandum on "The Principles, Policies and Attitudes Which Guide, Inspire and Motivate Time Inc." It began with "objectivity":

> People say they do not "understand" Time Inc. . . . Even within our company there is occasionally some confusion on this score. For example, there is a persistent urge to say that *Time* is "unbiased," and to claim for it complete "objectivity." That, of course, is nonsense. The original owners-editors-promoters of *Time* made no such fantastic claim. . . . You will find an acknowledgement of bias in the first circular. . . .

While Time Inc. "does not have and does not propose ever to have any formal creed," Luce pointed out that he had made within the last year three personal statements reflecting his attitude toward journalism, contemporary political economy, and truth and morality. Luce asked his colleagues to reread these speeches and ask themselves if there was anything in them to which they would seriously object. No one was being asked to applaud the style, he said. But if there was "general concurrence" in the attitudes and biases revealed in them, "then we may nail down one plank—namely, that the attitudes of Time Inc. on these subjects are approximately, and as far as they go, the attitudes as indicated in my statements."

By "general concurrence," Luce said, he did not mean unanimity but some agreement by "two-thirds or perhaps 75%" of "all our more responsible members." If there was such concurrence, he suggested, "it becomes the first and major policy of the company to see to it that these policies and attitudes are exemplified to the best of our abilities in our work." But he added,

> It is not only conceivable, it may even be highly desirable and salutary to have in responsible positions in this company men and women who are fundamentally not in sympathy. . . . We like dissenters [but] the dissenter must be the exception rather than the rule. We must seek characteristic agreement, leaving room for uncharacteristic dissent.

His memorandum then addressed itself to the question: Why is Time Inc. in business?

> First, but not in order of importance . . . to make money . . . Second . . . to earn, to maintain and to leave behind it a great and good reputation as a Journalist . . . Third . . . to make some contribution to the general welfare.
>
> As to these last two purposes, we regard the profession of journalism as in itself of such overwhelming importance at this time that we believe that the effective and honorable practice of our profession is by all odds the greatest contribution we can make. . . .

As to making money,

> We believe that Providence may look after the sparrows and the lilies, but there is no Providence which we can see lying around which is likely to subsidize our publications. None, that is, except Advertisers. We do not want to be subsidized by anybody. . . . But if we have to be subsidized by anybody, we think the Advertiser presents extremely interesting possibilities. We believe we can be subsidized by the Advertiser by giving him value for value received and without compromising more than a small fraction of our journalistic soul. That small fraction we are frankly willing to sell for a price. Thus, for example, we agreed

357

never to name the middle name of Walter Percy Chrysler. . . .
But the important thing about this compact, this compromise
with the advertiser, is that it should be clearly understood by us
and by him. . . . Once having decided to solicit and to take
advertising, we must keep the bargain . . . not only to deliver
full statistical advertising value, but also the implied bargain of
being appreciative of and grateful for our customers. The journalistic independence of Time Inc. has been made abundantly
clear to the advertisers of America. It has been a long, and to us,
at times, an intensely dramatic struggle. We won. There is not an
advertiser in America who does not realize that Time Inc. is
cussedly independent. . . . The fact is that there is not and there
never was a magazine publishing house which took advertising
that is so damned independent as we are. . . .

Luce pointed out that no "biggish magazine house" in America had
ever relied so little on the advertiser, because Time Inc. had insisted
upon a greater circulation revenue proportionate to advertising than
any other publisher. But the corollary of this, he said, was that the
editors were doing business directly with the readers:

Our position is definitely that we must publish a great deal of
material which either in substance or manner or both is not
calculated to increase circulation. But the problem cuts both
ways—the problem of conscience. Any writer who is not enthusiastic about the job of increasing our circulations *by his own
writing* is here on a misunderstanding. There is no proper place
for him. . . .

He set forth his view of the separate purposes of *Time, Fortune* and
Life:

Time . . . to keep the more literate people of America well-informed . . . *Time* is a liberal magazine. Does anyone boggle at
that? I do not think it can be denied. If *Time* is not liberal, it is
certainly mugwump, and I take it that a mugwump is a species of
liberal. The mugwump is a liberal who is not willing to accept
the responsibilities and duties and hazards of consistent partisan-

ship. . . . But the mugwump is not simply an indifferent, careless cynic. Quite on the contrary, a mugwump is someone who cares a great deal about human society. . . .

Time is or will be again the most powerful journal in America. But the paradox is that *Time* will maintain its power only on condition that it never uses it for partisan, personal, or ulterior purposes.

Fortune . . . to give a view of and insight into contemporary industrial society . . . The main fundamental problem seems to be whether it can be a liberal magazine and still enjoy the advertising patronage of industrial and luxurious America. In my view the advertising problem is no problem at all—except for the advertising department and high-powered publisher-promoting. The problem lies entirely in the circulation. . . . [We] did successfully publish a liberal *Fortune*. . . . There is one thing which makes me goddamn sore and that is the suggestion that *Fortune* had no social consciousness in its planning and beginning in 1929–1930. The fact of the matter is that *Fortune,* not as a matter of ivory-tower theory but as a matter of desperate practical fact, launched itself into Coolidge-Hoover society on the basis that all business was invested with a public interest. And there never has been since that time any proposition seriously laid down in this country by anybody in any position of public responsibility which is more important or more radical than that. . . . I think it will take us pretty near the rest of our lifetime to run out the implications of the proposition. . . .

The cause of "effectively informative journalism" . . . is again proven in *Life*. . . . It probably publishes more solid information to more people than all the other mass magazines in America put together. . . . *Life* does not give nearly as much information as *Time* (except in the very limited sense that one picture equals 1,000 words) . . . but "effectively informative journalism" is now just as definitely *Life*'s cause as it is *Time*'s.

There was no reason, he concluded, if each periodical were what it ought to be, why one of the three should get in the way of the others, and all should "profit by the good name and the good will of the others."

If thirty men of the company in responsible positions could concur in what he had written,

> then Time Inc. officially has got a coherent system of policy and principle. . . . Then the next step is with confidence and without bashfulness to make clear to every member of Time Inc. what the principles and policies of Time Inc. are. . . .

Most people who received the memorandum, according to Larsen, "took it that Harry was laying down the word and you either accepted it or you didn't, and if you didn't, you could get out. But Mac Ingersoll didn't like it—and he didn't get out." He did write Luce a caustic note: "For me to rebel against it would be the kind of insanity which rebels against the necessity of eating every day."

But having decided that the magazines should have policy direction, Luce, characteristically, did not then personally proceed to dictate it. Instead he cast around for some mechanism by which specific policies would have the collective sanction of his colleagues. A Policy Committee was formed and met on Friday mornings in Luce's office. The minutes of the first meeting, November 11, were kept by Allen Grover and read as follows:

> Present were: Luce, Ingersoll, Larsen, Hodgins, Gottfried, Grover, Paine, and toward the end, Longwell. Meeting lasted about an hour.

It was decided that:

1) *Re Munich*

Time Inc. policy: we don't now know whether it was a good thing or not.

2) Time Inc. magazines will be against government regulation of business or government in business just for the sake of government being in business.

3) Time Inc. will be against the persecution of Jews or anyone else.

360

The Policy Committee continued for some time. It was not a legislative body which required the editors to conform exactly to its resolutions; it was rather one of many devices by which Luce was to keep both editors and writers alert to what he considered to be their responsibilities.

Paid Back Measure for Measure

LUCE HAD optimistically theorized that if each of the magazines were what it ought to be, all should "profit by the good name and the good will of the others." It was valid enough as a theory, but practically it could not be accepted by some of his associates. The first to challenge it was the harassed circulation manager, Pierrie Prentice, who throughout 1938 had borne the burden of seeing that both *Life* and *Time* made their guarantees. He was therefore infuriated when Ingersoll passed on a casual remark by Luce that "there is nothing the matter with *Time* that cannot be fixed up by a good circulation letter." In Prentice's judgment there was much wrong with *Time,* and he said so in a sixty-two-page memo (Time Inc.'s executives were never as succinct in internal communications as in their magazines). The memo, addressed to Ingersoll, raised two highly sensitive points—how the competition of *Life* had affected *Time*'s circulation, and what Prentice considered to be the indifferent editorial performance of *Time.* The nub of what he had to say was summed up in a few indignant paragraphs:

362

The nearest thing to an analogy that I can think of is the case of a captain of a liner who has been on the bridge in a storm continuously for two years and then gets a note from the President of the company and the Chief Passenger Agent down below telling him that there isn't any storm at all and the only trouble is that he doesn't know how to steer a boat. There is a storm and *Time* has sailed square into the middle of it with all sails set. . . .

The storm, of course, was *Life,* which this year is taking $10,000,000 out of the pool *Time* took its $3,300,000 from in 1936. It is all very well for Harry to say that *Life* has one function and *Time* has another function. It is also true that an automobile has one function and a house has another function, but the Brookings Institution in its last report states quite flatly that one reason people are spending less money on housing is that they are spending more money for automobiles.

One of Prentice's recommendations was that he be allowed to reduce *Time*'s rate for renewing subscriptions from $5 to $4. (It was not accepted.) As for the editors of *Time,* wrote Prentice:

We have sent out millions of letters urging people to read *Time* because the news was so exciting and so important this year and *Time* was the place to get it. But when they did turn to *Time,* I think we let them down. The very definite reaction I get from reading *Time* is that the editors don't think the news is very hot. When I asked the man in this company whom I consider just about the shrewdest critic on our payroll why he thought *Time* wasn't getting anywhere, he got epigrammatic and said, "The trouble with *Time* is that it is edited by too many young men who smoke pipes." More specifically, he said, "The trouble with *Time* is that it is not edited by men who are excited about the news."

Ten years ago I think the attitude of Brit and Harry and Gottfried and Goldsborough and John Martin and Lloyd-Smith toward the news used to be, "Here's another hot one you certainly don't want to miss—let me tell you about it"; now I think the attitude is a bit pedagogical. . . .

It is not clear whether Luce read the Prentice memorandum. But a month later, on October 28, he received a blast from Ingersoll, thirty-eight pages portentously headed "Subject: The Earning Capacity of *Time,* The Weekly Newsmagazine, Its Commercial Policy and Recommendations for a Budget for 1939." It was triggered obviously by forecasts of *Time*'s profit for 1938, which showed there would be "an all-time record decline in earnings from one year to the next"— amounting to a drop in operating profits of roughly $2,000,000. One may fairly surmise that Ingersoll was both embarrassed and frustrated by having to submit such a figure; in any case, the thirty-eight pages constituted a defense of his record as publisher and an attack on *Life* and the over-all management policies of the company.

From the viewpoint of *Time,* wrote Ingersoll, corporate management had made "at least two large, identifiable mistakes":

The first: failing to realize the uniqueness of its achievement, the Management had hardly got its first million dollars under its belt when it immediately began to dilute the essence of its earning capacity—its wits—by creating one new property after another. . . . The energies of *Time*'s management went, in succession, into:

1. Creating *Fortune* Magazine
2. Creating *The March of Time* in moving pictures
3. Buying and remodelling the *Architectural Forum*
4. Experimenting with and finally founding a newspicture magazine. . . .

It might have been sounder *business* for *Time*'s proprietors to have minded their knitting and used their wits to move *Time* forward to an unquestioned Number One position in the magazine world. . . .

Once you accept, upon demonstration, the fact that *Time* earns its living by its wits, then it becomes clear that the distraction of these wits into other enterprises constituted a serious and continuous threat to *Time*'s earnings. . . .

364

The strange unevenness with which the management of *Time* has regarded its money is also largely attributable to the management's failure to understand the true relationship of its new ventures to the whole enterprise. What do I mean? The phenomenon of the same group of people pinching pennies with one hand and scattering hundreds of thousands of dollars with the other (continuing the enormous expense of *The March of Time* on the radio . . . the precipitous entrance into the moving picture field in a spot in which only a year's research could have proved that it was impossible to make substantial returns on the invested capital). A businessman from Mars would certainly be confused by the fifteen-year record of how Time Inc. spent the money it earned—the management now tight-fisted, now open-handed, now tough, now sentimental. Since the same people were in charge throughout, this erratic behavior seems to me only explainable by a confusion in their minds as to what they were in business to do: to make money or to have fun spending it. . . .

The second mistake, Ingersoll said, lay in the fact that the company's year-to-year operations had come to be conducted on the assumption

of continued and uninterrupted and always-profitable expansion. . . . The key decision in *Time*'s commercial operation, in any given year, is the arbitrary determination of what circulation to guarantee—on which decision the advertising rate is based. Throughout *Time*'s adulthood, the practice has been to make this guarantee in advance, upon a projection—an optimistic estimate. . . .

So one way of looking at *Time*'s 1938 debacle is simply that the world at last caught up with it. . . . In 1938 we were simply caught between two poles—forced for the first time in *Time*'s career to spend large sums to make good our guarantee, forced in this depression time to sell advertising in *Time* at the highest rate in its history.

So the setback in *Time*'s business was due (1) to the Depression and (2) to *Life* Magazine, whose "success was carved out of a very real

365

piece of *Time*'s hide. I estimate it," said Ingersoll, "as a $750,000 to a $1,000,000 piece."

For 1939 he proposed that *Time* maintain the 700,000 guarantee but not increase it, concentrating instead on improving the product. To that end he asked $1,000,000 for the editorial budget, to be spent largely in increasing the salary scale and hiring new writers. In October *Time* had advanced its production schedule to deliver copies east of the Rockies on Thursday instead of Friday to reduce *Life*'s competition. Ingersoll said that extending this to the Pacific Coast was being investigated. He also envisioned improvements in *Time*'s printing, to make it more attractive to the advertiser.

There was another section to his document. In it Ingersoll returned once more to a savage attack on *Time*'s Foreign News editor, Goldsborough, and *Time*'s foreign-news coverage: "If ever the returns were in on the failure of a major department," he wrote, "the returns are in on *Time*'s Foreign News. . . . Throughout this year *Time*'s circulation has sagged. I hold the Foreign News department responsible. . . . People do not buy hundreds of thousands of copies of the writings of a tired, tired Jesuit—'Jesuit' in the philosophical sense. And a tired, tired Jesuit is Laird Goldsborough." He recommended that Goldsborough be sent off immediately on a leave of absence.

Ingersoll said he intended to anger Luce, and he succeeded. Luce waited twelve days before he answered, in fifteen pages which constituted his own view of the company's history:

> It is necessary for me to challenge certain of your statements and implications and to reply to them as if to an indictment. You did indeed say to me verbally that your memo was a "rough draft" and therefore more "blunt" than you might have intended. However, the bluntness is okay with me. . . .
>
> You repeatedly accuse the "management" of "confusion," of "absurd optimism," of "dangerous malpractice" . . . of "short-sighted presumptions," of harboring "illusions.". . . The kindest impression you give of Time's "management" is summed up in your phrase "another of the management's idiosyncrasies.". . . You can at every point substitute for the word "management," the name Henry R. Luce.

366

The best way to meet an attack is usually by counterattack. But that method is not open to me. . . . I have no strong attack to make on you. . . . I have therefore no choice but to accept the difficult gambit of defense.

In setting up my defense, what I must do is to draw a big line, the hugest possible line, through the year 1936; that is to say up to the beginning of *Life*. I am prepared to defend all the charges you make in so far as they relate to prior years. But I will agree with you and I will grant that *Life may* have been one big mistake for Time Inc. I realize that all my previous record—and it was a good record—will go for very little if *Life* is a failure and if its failure causes *Time*'s failure. I am too much in midstream now to defend *Life* now. What I can say, however, is that just about as soon as it was apparent to anyone except nonexisting prophets that *Life* was going to be such a disturber of the peace, and as soon as it was apparent that I was not going to be able to give adequate attention to *Time*, I picked the best man I could find to give it his full attention, and, from the moment he took charge, he was permitted in accordance with his wishes to spend vastly more money on *Time*, editorially and otherwise, than had ever been spent before. But I'll agree, it is yet to be proved that *Life* was not a mistake—for *Time*.

Luce defended the various company ventures: *Fortune* had paid the company at least 200 percent on its money investment; the *Architectural Forum* had proved to be "a trouble" but no great loss; *The March of Time*, "the most daring venture we ever made," represented an actual investment of $700,000, and "if *The March of Time* has not been worth $700,000 in advertising—then a lot of people are spoofing us who think that if it cost us $700,000 a year, we'd still have a bargain."

But all this is of little importance compared with the impression which your analysis leaves as to the motivation for these adventures. There is not one which has not appealed to some large or important group of thoughtful people as being of really great significance. . . . Some people may exaggerate the importance of Housing, but certainly Housing is important and certainly there is no publication whose impact on this problem compares with the importance of the *Architectural Forum.* . . .

As for *Fortune* . . . surely MacLeish's instincts were not entirely screwy when he said, as he has often said, that *Fortune* is the greatest journalistic invention of the century, that it is the most important magazine in America.

And finally, there is *The March of Time* [which] may lay claim to being the most important thing we ever did. If there is one phenomenon of our times which people concerned for the mind and future of our race bewail more than anything else, it is the failure of the motion picture to achieve integrity and significance. *The March of Time* is not merely one lucky flicker of integrity—it is, apart from possibly Disney, the one and only continuous achievement of significance in the motion pictures of our land. . . .

So what does all this add up to? . . . Ours is a series of radical pioneering ventures, none of them failures, all of them in some way great successes, all of them dealing with the immediate stuff of our common life in a period of great human crisis, and above all, all of them regarded by various groups of discriminating people as outstandingly important contributions to the journalism of these great days. There must be something more, Horatio, than is mentioned in your philosophy.

To the charge that management assumed "continued and uninterrupted and always profitable expansion," Luce answered:

I ceased having that assumption when not later than 1928 I assured Donnelley's that *Time*'s circulation would never exceed 300,000—not at any rate for years. Years later, in 1935, I spent two solid days arguing against the 600,000 guarantee. . . . There was only one guarantee in all *Time*'s history which ever slipped by me easily. That unfortunately was the last one. . . . And when we made the 700,000 guarantee, you were, if I recall, Vice President and General Manager of Time Inc. . . .

All through 1936 I was worried about only one thing—

368

whether *Time* was strong enough to carry itself through the joy-ride we might have with *Life*. There was one question which I asked . . . "How's *Time*? How is *Time editorially*? Do people really read it as they used to?" I could get not one single corroboratory reply to my suspicion that *Time* was losing a little of its old "it.". . . My conclusion, therefore, was that if I, myself, found *Time* a little dull or not quite the equal of events, that must just be a reverse English on my own vanity—that I only found it a little dull because I wasn't so actively engaged in making it. That is one mistake I shall never make again. Hereafter I shall trust my own judgment.

You are right—there was a flaw in *Time*. It was weakening editorially—due mainly to management neglect & Time Inc. distractions. At last, you are right, we were about to take on one distraction too many.

The Ingersoll memorandum had two important consequences. First, Luce agreed that Goldsborough should be given a year's leave of absence. Ingersoll was not alone in feeling that, as Foreign News editor, Goldsborough had outlived his usefulness. Gottfried also thought so, as did many others. As Billings said, "The times changed but he didn't." Luce himself had to admit that *Time*'s attitude toward events in Europe fell short of his own standards and expectations. In reporting Hitler's mobilization of 1,000,000 men in August, a major power play that was to bring Britain's Prime Minister Chamberlain to Munich, *Time* had said blithely: "Last week Europe was in a mood to let Adolf Hitler exercise his boys and put on a show." It is difficult to say how much Goldsborough bore the responsibility for *Time*'s attitude; he was now being edited by the associate managing editor, Frank Norris, and he had two assistant writers. But there was a common estimate that he had become an obstacle to any change. Luce left to Ingersoll the conditions on which Goldsborough was granted leave. It was agreed that he would be retained on the payroll, and travel in Europe as *Time*'s Foreign News editor. But Ingersoll refused to give him a guarantee that on his return he would continue in that post.

369

Luce announced the decision, paying Goldsborough an earnest tribute for his past services:

> It would be impossible for me to state adequately how much *Time* owes to Goldsborough's brilliant and tireless work during the thirteen long years since first he joined the Newsmagazine. The Western European era of Locarno, War Debts, League of Nations and Peace Pacts; the rise of the Dictators, all of them; the entrenchment of the Soviet regime and the first Five-Year plan; the epoch of the War Lords in China and the rise of the Nationalist Government; Gandhi, a score of British Parliaments —of all these things in addition to the more recent and world-shaking events from the rape of Manchuria to the partitioning of Czechoslovakia—of all these things he has written to hundreds of thousands of devoted *Time* readers. No writer has contributed more to *Time* than Laird Goldsborough.

Those who celebrated his departure most enthusiastically were the editors of something called *High Time,* a strange little egg that had been laid in Time Inc.'s nest. It was a shop newspaper published blatantly by "the Communist Party Members at Time Inc." Under the heading "Goldie—The End of *Time*'s Minister of Propaganda," *High Time* gloated over his downfall and made no secret of the fact that the Communists had made common cause with Goldsborough's enemies on the staff.

Almost immediately on taking leave Goldsborough fell critically ill. His recuperation took a long time. When war broke out in September 1939 he returned to write in the Foreign News section but was never again an important influence. In April 1941 he resigned from *Time* to be a Special Assistant to Luce, and in December of that year he was retired with a lifetime pension. In 1943 he was made coordinating officer for the New York Counter-Intelligence Division of the Office of Strategic Services. On February 15, 1950, his colleagues and friends were shocked to read of his death the previous evening; he fell or jumped from his private office in Rockefeller Center, clutching his heavy gold-headed cane.

* * *

370

The Ingersoll memorandum had a second consequence. It sent Luce down to *Time* to preside as managing editor over two issues—the first in November, the second in December—something he had not done for a long time. He took to *Time,* said Eric Hodgins, "a shirt-sleeves-and-green-eyeshade attitude. He got down on the floor and wrestled with every problem as it came up. He never niggled over small points—would usually pass without comment two-thirds of the stories in their first draft form for the sake of concentrating with all his might on the one-third which claimed his real attention and which he considered truly important. Vigor, not minuteness, was the key to every editorial thing he did." He concluded at the end of the two sessions that whatever was wrong with *Time* was rooted less in the managing editor than in the publisher.

Ingersoll was presumptuous; he was also elusive. There occurred at about this time an incident over the choice of illustration for the Man of the Year cover. The Man for 1938 had to be Hitler. The only good available color photograph showed him, according to Gottfried, "looking as innocuous as a file clerk dressed in khaki uniform and cap. Nobody liked it but we accepted it *faute de mieux.*" The more Ingersoll brooded over the picture, the more he felt that *Time* could not put it on the cover without conveying a kind of innocent endorsement. He decided, therefore, to substitute a lithograph by an Austrian refugee, Rudolph Charles von Ripper. It depicted a little man easily identified as Hitler playing a monstrous organ surmounted by a Catherine wheel from which hung his naked victims. Ingersoll captioned it "From the unholy organist, a hymn of hate." It was undeniably effective anti-Nazi propaganda. The decision was made while Gottfried was on his weekend. "I was bloody angry when I found out about it," he said. "I could see it was questionable public relations to run a deadpan cover of a man people were beginning to hate. But we had never before used the cover as a deliberate instrument of propaganda." Neither had Luce been consulted. The change had been made and the presses were running when Ingersoll told him what he had done. Ingersoll recalled that Luce was angry, but only said, "Spilt milk—let's not discuss it." Ingersoll said that after the cover incident he never again talked to Luce frankly about an editorial matter. Luce's recollection in later years was that he did, at the time, think the cover was too polemical but it was not the decisive moment in his relations with Ingersoll. His dissatisfaction with *Time*'s publisher had been building up for some time, and after his brief sortie at editing *Time* he sat down to collect his thoughts. He had Ingersoll in his sights, but it was not any one man who bothered him; the magazine that he and Hadden had launched with such conviction sixteen years earlier had got strangely off the track. "Okay—here goes for a memo about *Time* without any predictable terminal facilities," he wrote. "Anyway I haven't written a long memo about *Time* in gosh knows how many years." There ensued a kind of dialogue with himself which reveals in detail what he thought about the magazine. Perhaps it said too much; in the end he consigned it to his desk drawer.

Obviously I must think there is "something wrong" with *Time*. . . . Well, I do. . . .

There have, of course, been earnest attempts to make *Time* "new" in various particulars—new cover, new typography, not to mention greater facts such as new direction for some departments and, above all, an almost entirely new cast of editors. Now there is nothing unnatural or weird about a publication striving to improve itself. . . . But it is not always necessary that such efforts should involve disparagement of the publication's past. . . . Leaving aside all the invidious comparisons on editorial performance and personnel, even such an aspect as Advertising Promotion has been subject to, I think, unfruitful comparisons. As one rather intimately concerned with bringing *Time* to a No. 1 position among all publications in the world in advertising pages, I have listened with mingled feelings to suggestions that *Time*'s advertising promotion was characteristically pretty inept. . . .[1]

I am an Old Bolshevik who hopes to be a good Progressive for

[1] Ingersoll had criticized *Time*'s past promotion thus: *"Time*'s advertising promotion policy was once summed up by President Luce quoting the late Briton Hadden: 'To stay in this business you have got to stick your head out of the window and yell every once in a while. It doesn't matter what you say—just stick your head out the window and yell.' *Time*'s policy has been to grind out an enormous volume of dull statistics and every once in a while stick its head out the window and yell. Not saying anything in particular, just yelling."

at least another decade. Specifically, I think that it is incontrovertible that there were virtues in the old *Time* (many of which are still in the new, of course) which are essential to any *Time* any time anywhere in a journalist's world. Rare virtues, easily lost and difficult to regain. . . .

The editors and writers are not sufficiently eager to please *Time*'s 700,000 customers. *Time* did not invent its most famous slogan: "cover-to-cover." That was given to us by hundreds and thousands of readers who unselfconsciously used the phrase. . . . What delighted people was to find that they could read something about this and something about that and something about something else—none of which bored them. *Time* either attracted people intensely or repelled them. But it bored nobody. . . .

Different people are bored by different things. Most women, like many literary journalists, are bored by Business. But women, being the greater realists, are far more interested in money than most men are. Therefore if you want to interest a woman (or an artist) in Business, get down to brass tacks and talk *dough*. . . . So there are no rules about what will bore whom and what won't. But there is one rule we have to accept for practical purposes—namely that different things bore different people. And that puts *Time* smack up against the issue of whether or not it is going to be a cover-to-cover magazine. And that means that if you are going to ask one man to read *Time* from cover-to-cover, you have got to work like hell to edit *Time* *for one man*. [This was a reversal of Ingersoll's theory that *Time*'s departments should be written expertly for experts.]

The conception of *Time*'s reader is hard, very hard, to put into words, but terribly simple for anyone to grasp if he wills to grasp it. *Time* is edited for the Gentleman of Indiana. At this point I cannot say what I want to say without indulging in a little Americanism. America, for example, is not New York. New York is in the bloodstream of America and America flows hot through New York. But New York is not America. Perhaps we should seriously consider moving *Time* (not *Life* or *Fortune*) to

373

Chicago. For Wall Street is not America. Broadway is not America. Café Society is not America. Park Avenue is not America. The Intelligentsia are not America. Columbia University is not America. New York is the fascination of America—where vices easily become virtues and virtues vices.

Time is edited for the Gentleman of Indiana and for Madame the Lady of Indiana. I will not launch into a description of him and her because I don't want to jar your imagination with my own inept drawing. But—you know what I mean? Yes. Sure.

Time is going to write for the Gentleman of Indiana, writing to him as man to man, in straightforward decent language, no punches pulled, but no dirty below-the-belt cracks either at God, the Constitution or his fellow gentlemen of Indiana. If we have anything unpleasant to report to him about himself or his country or his God we will tell it to him straight. . . . What we can't say straight out—let's don't say it. . . .

If I had to say what is wrong with *Time* in one word, I would say it lacks *Unity*. . . .

The Managing Editor is the key to Unity because he is and must be the ultimate broker between the reader and all the possibilities of news and writing. . . . It is his job to get out the paper. It is the job of the Publisher to coordinate all the phases of publishing a magazine and see that they all work together for good, including a good profit. . . . At about this point, I better introduce myself into the picture. The system we have assumes also a sufficient sympathy between all three of us as to the purpose and policies of *Time*. Now, while I am plenty interested in "successful publishing" financially speaking, it is my hope in the years to come that I can spend relatively more time on the Editorial side and relatively less on the Publishing or Business side. . . .

This seems to put the Publisher pretty much on the vulgar money-making side of things. And in view of the fact that Ingersoll is considerable of a journalist, maybe this is psychologically wrong. But I should like to think not. Just as I should hope that the President of Time Inc. would always be a man of strong

374

journalistic leanings, so I would like the Publishers to be journalists. If I give to Ingersoll a job I would prefer to have less of, it is partly because I have had so damned much of it and not because I think it lacks imaginative values. . . .

What is *Time*'s editorial target, goal or purpose? Once again I am baffled by the difficulties of putting into words what is best defined in action. Who has ever defined the word News? Who, then, can adequately define Newsmagazine?

The purpose of *Time* obviously is to inform. To inform about what? Obviously to inform about the news. What is "the news"? Well, at least the very phrase "the news" suggests something a little more definable than "news.". . . Among us in recent years, there has been more and more a tendency to distrust *Time*'s original boldness. "It is not enough," the cry has been, "just to tell yesterday's or last week's story." I deny it. Any time any magazine editor wants to compete with me on that proposition for at least 500,000 high class circulation, I will gladly accept the challenge. . . .

I have heard much muttering and some loud talk about the new conditions facing *Time* competitively—the radio, the commentators, the more serious attitudes of readers—and *Life*. . . . All that talk bothers me not one bit. If I had to make my fortune over again, and there were no *Time,* you wouldn't catch me wandering off looking for gold mines—you'd find me peddling stock right now in a real genuwine Newsmagazine. Good grief, in 1923 the basic premise of *Time* was that the newspapers were excellent and the magazines were excellent B U T. The more means of communication there are, the bigger that B U T. . . .

In devoting ourselves to putting together "the news," we stoop to a task no weekly journalist has ever before stooped to and we render to hundreds of thousands of influential Americans a service greater than that rendered by any contemporary journalist—and the hell with the Pulitzer Prize. . . .

Time is even a *better* magazine than it used to be. But somehow it does not give the feel of being desperately, whimsically, absurdly, cockeyedly, whole-souledly *determined* to in-

375

form, to inform, to inform. *Time* is heavy with Information but it does not *burst* with Information. Please don't hit me over the head if I say that at times *Time* gives the impression of being fat but not pregnant. . . .

A lot of the effort and discussion about *Time* has had to do with what may be crudely called its "intellectual" level or its "interpretative" profundity.

Well, let me deal with this question in a peculiar and personal way. I am worrying about *Time*'s journalistic appeal to its readers or potential readers. Someone else around here, call him Mr. "X," is worrying about *Time*'s intellectual or interpretative level. Well, now, what I would like to do is to change places with Mr. "X." Dear Mr. "X," if you will guarantee that *Time*'s newsstand circulation will move steadily forward, I will gladly be responsible for *Time*'s intellectual level. . . . I fancy I could be a pretty hot intellectual myself if I ever had the chance to be. I, too, could probe the European situation to its very gizzard. . . . I realize it's a little late in my old age to take on a new career. . . . But, I'd like to have the chance. So, Mr. "X," if you'll take on the job of guaranteeing *Time*'s circulation, I'll take on the job of being its intellectual mentor and elevator. . . . As Ivory Tower editor, I'd like to be in a position of saying, sure, your circulation is fine but I want more intellectuality. I'd like to bawl you out for printing too much triviality, for bad taste, for shocking puns, for childish enthusiasms. I really don't like being the low-brow around here! . . .

I do not conceive of myself as having to be the continual Moral Schoolmaster of this place. But I think I cannot escape being the custodian or depository of *"Time*'s conscience." Possibly therefore an informal, unwritten custom should be established—namely that any senior editor or senior executive of any Time Inc. publication who is troubled about any tendency involving editorial conscience should understand that he can and should come to me about it at any time. Practically, and recognizing that we are all frail mortals, it is a question of mutual confidence and respect. If fundamentally any senior does not

376

have sufficient confidence and respect for my ethical attitudes, he should, I think, put me on notice to that effect. . . .

Luce's reflections on *Time* were written just before a dramatic change in *Life*'s outlook invalidated Ingersoll's criticism of that venture. In February 1939, while Luce was on a brief vacation at his South Carolina plantation, he received a telegram from C. D. Jackson, general manager of *Life:* "LIFE IN BLACK FOR JANUARY." To which Luce replied: "HOORAY FOR THE FIRST OF ONE HUNDRED CONSECU- TIVE MONTHS. HEARTIEST CONGRATULATIONS." Not only had the pic- ture magazine made a breakthrough into profit but its future earnings would establish it as one of the great publishing successes in magazine history. Moreover, *Life* was developing as Luce had predicted in his policy memorandum: it was no longer a direct competitor of *Time* in either circulation or advertising. So far as 1938 was concerned, the company took a loss of $749,000 on *Life;* but the year was a sub- stantial improvement over the preceding one, with profit after taxes of $1,129,422 (v. $168,430 in 1937). But the most reassuring news, stockholders were told, lay in the important item of surplus, which

. . . was up $339,000 at the end of 1938, after payment of $949,000 in dividends. . . . Turning back again to January 4, 1936, surplus was at that date $2,895,000. On December 31, 1938 it is recorded at $2,278,000. Accordingly, in the three years there has been a reduction of $617,000 but this was due to the use of surplus to maintain the continuity of dividends in 1937. . . .

If we total up the dividends paid to stockholders during these last three years, we can summarize the record of accomplishment during that time, as follows:

Life has been created and become established, and $4,639,000 has been paid to stockholders in dividends, with Surplus reduced only $617,000.

Luce, free of anxiety about *Life,* continued to give much thought to his as yet unspoken dissatisfaction with *Time.* But he did not act until April 1939, when the staff was startled and surprised to learn that

Ingersoll was taking leave of absence "to develop plans for a new kind of daily newspaper." Ingersoll had been working privately on this project for many months although few in the company other than Luce knew about it; to him Ingersoll had talked about the problem—"endlessly," said Luce. One morning Ingersoll brought the subject up again. Luce abruptly and, he thought, to Ingersoll's surprise, suggested that Ingersoll should henceforward devote his whole time to the newspaper. The Board of Directors took note of the leave and stipulated that it involved Ingersoll's retirement from the offices of vice-president of Time Inc. and publisher of *Time*. The Board also recorded that there was no commitment as to job or salary should he return to the company. In recognition of past services, Ingersoll was paid until the end of 1939.

Thus was a difficult situation resolved. Luce and Ingersoll had reached a point where their differences could not have been reconciled. Ingersoll was no longer content with a subordinate role and longed for individual recognition. T. S. Matthews observed that he loved power so much that "his own allegiance became intolerable to him." [2] Ingersoll's relations with his senior associates had also reached a point where he was isolated from them; Gottfried observed that when he left "I think I was the only one who was not stone-cold hostile to him."

Ingersoll's influence with Luce was short-lived, but for that time he carried considerable weight. He won Luce's confidence and admiration for the way in which he took over and handled *Fortune* after Lloyd-Smith's death. Luce, in after years, felt that making Ingersoll general manager had been a serious mistake; in that role Ingersoll, by his politicking, had alienated his associates. It was only after he became publisher of *Time,* however, that Luce began losing confidence in Ingersoll; their differences were not personal but journalistic. Luce could not, and obviously would not, surrender or delegate the editorship of the magazine which he had helped to found and which remained the foundation on which the whole Time Inc. publishing business rested.

* * *

[2] *Name and Address* (Simon and Schuster, 1960).

378

Luce left no doubt of this on Ingersoll's departure; he announced that he would take over the duties of publisher and in addition would regard himself as editor-in-chief of *Time* with principal responsibility for "general character, tone, direction, ambition and ideals." Gottfried, as managing editor, was to see that "creative, aggressive, knowledgeable journalism shall be represented in every issue . . . in short, that each issue shall pack a punch—meaning at least three punches." Norris, with a new title, executive editor, was told to see to it "that all the news of all the world that can be put into two hours' reading is put there"; he was also to "cause stupidities to vanish, realities to abound." Matthews received the title of associate executive editor, because "in the job of executive editor there is too much for one man to do well." To handle the magazine's business, Luce drafted Charles Stillman to be general manager, a job which was added to his corporate duties; he was also elected a vice-president. F. D. Duke, returned from *Newsweek,* was made advertising director.

One of Luce's problems in resuming direct control of *Time* was getting to know the staff: most of the writers felt themselves to be virtual strangers to the editor-in-chief. Most of the old-timers had either departed or had been moved to one of the other magazines. To the group of new and talented men, most of them of a liberal turn of mind, who had been taken on in the past year, Luce was an unknown quantity. It was Matthews who suggested to Luce that he have dinner with a half-dozen of them and try to explain himself. Glad of the chance, Luce invited them to his apartment at the Waldorf Towers.

One of the guests, Charles Wertenbaker, who had written for *Fortune* as well as *Time,* years later told Luce that the occasion had given him the idea for his novel *The Death of Kings,*[3] a story revolving around a group of journalists who work for a newsmagazine like *Time.* While its principal character, Louis Baron, is a composite differing from Luce in his career and personality, he gives a dinner where he presents to his associates the idea that they should all support the American revolution—"the one with the most vitality in it." Wertenbaker described the climactic moment of the dinner:

[3] Random House, 1954.

As he [Baron] kept on developing his thesis, Berkeley [the narrator] began to believe in Louis Baron as he had never quite believed in him before. He did not believe his argument truer than any other simplification, or better able to solve the problems troubling what was called the liberal mind. But, better than most such pronouncements of faith, it admitted the insolubility of problems, the uselessness of conventional slogans, the unattainability of final, utter victory. Most of all, it exhibited Louis Baron without the spurious protection of his money, his position, his success, his power, his loneliness, his reserve; it revealed him clad only in the purity of his belief. . . . He had won them; Berkeley saw it; and Louis, lifting [his] heavy brows to stare each one in the face, could not fail to see it, too. . . .

There were two other such dinners. Matthews later described one held at The Players:

By this time we felt that we knew him a lot better, and we had only a few more things to ask. But some of them were awkward questions—things like "How much is your financial interest in *Time?*" and "Under what circumstances would you consider using *Time* as a political instrument?" When Luce arrived . . . he handed us each a copy of a memo he had written. As we read it, we saw that he had anticipated all these final questions and had written his answers. Furthermore he had lifted the argument to a general discussion of journalism, its purposes and possibilities and ended with a statement of his own journalistic faith. He had cut the ground out from under us. We looked at each other and shook our heads. There was nothing left to say.[4]

The memo Matthews referred to was a four-page summary of the long memorandum on principles and policies that Luce had written the year before (Chapter 24). To that general statement he had added several points:

Time now has an implicit obligation to make money . . . but this obligation can be liquidated in an orderly manner at any

[4] *Name and Address.*

380

time that Management feels that what it wants to do is in fundamental ethical conflict with profit-making probabilities. . . . It is the intention of *Time* to be fearless in the performance of its task, self-appointed and publicly announced . . . the peculiar *Time* purpose is to get information—a whole special bundle of information—*into* people's heads.

Luce observed that *Time* had been reasonably successful in achieving that purpose; he noted that a survey had shown that *Time* readers were better informed than any of several different groups and that this was "pretty important to me. It tended to prove I hadn't been a patent-medicine liar all these years."

Years later Luce recalled these three encounters: "I felt I convinced them that *Time* indeed had a serious purpose." Larsen reported to Luce some months after the change-over that *"Time* has maintained its grand new—or renewed—editorial pace which you inspired it to. . . ." Stillman, somewhat closer to the situation, felt, nonetheless, that *Time* still had an old problem—i.e., in the area of its public relations.

Time cannot escape the fact that it is the bellwether of the most successful journalistic group in the world. When it jumps on somebody's toes *Time* is not only a smart aleck—it is a big bully as well. People rush to defend people and things thought to be attacked by *Time* because *Time* is so influential and so powerful and so rich. Too many people do not consider *Time* as well-intentioned. They think of it as coldly objective, every now and again dropping its objectivity to take a crack at some poor son of a so-and-so.

Luce took note of the criticism. "We are eager that our journalism should be enterprising, fearless, forthright, and all this is what makes *Time* interesting to us as well as to others. But before we can be any of these things, it is first of all necessary that we strive with all our power to be Fair." The first job of the Letters column was "to do justice" by correcting errors which may have harmed people and "if in any week dull correction letters would fill up the whole Letters section

381

. . . then that is just too bad."

Luce differentiated, however, between kinds of "squawks." There were those "which are not essentially matters of fairness but rather of point of view. . . . It is not the duty of the editorial department to win friends and influence people . . . [only] to be fair."

The problem of a certain alienated readership was partly resolved by the news itself. As war approached, the American public was avid for information, which *Time* supplied. Its circulation prospered.

By the middle of 1939 Time Inc. had become perhaps (the point is debatable) the most effective publishing force in the country. Luce enjoyed the prominence, which he commented on in a speech to *Life*'s advertising salesmen at their convention that year. They were remarks of the kind he would never have made in public but relished making to his employees; whatever was pompous in them was saved by the grace of humor.

Every hour of every day streams of people come to our offices pleading causes. . . . Every cause to which any of us are indifferent suffers thereby. Every cause which arouses our interest gains thereby. Of all the pleaders I see only a small fraction. But here are the causes I can hear on one day. The Belgian Ambassador comes to see me. He is a charming gentleman. He wishes to point out that there is an idea brewing to appease Germany by giving her the Belgian Congo. Why, he asks, should Belgium be the goat—although of course he didn't use just that language. And Belgium, he says, has done a very fine job in the Congo. Won't I please send an expert reporter to the Congo to make plain the good news about Belgian rule. When the Ambassador has departed with all felicitations, I get a telephone call about the Museum of Modern Art. Won't I please put Nelson Rockefeller on *Time*'s cover. In my mail are two special personal invitations for *Life* to Come to a Party—each a worthy cause. After the necessary personal acknowledgment I route them down to join the 36 other invitations to a party which *Life* has received that same day—most of them "causes" of one sort or another. The next letter is from a high-ranking Republican

382

leader asking me to please play down the Taft-Bricker rivalry in Ohio because this will do the Republican Party no good. Before I have figured out how to reply tactfully to that letter, two very chic ladies come in to talk about birth control. They recall that *Time* was one of the earliest, perhaps the very first forthright reporter of the cause of birth control, and that *Fortune*'s article on contraceptives was a milestone in their cause. They want me to blast hell out of the World's Fair because some "sinister" influences have sabotaged their show. Comes then a telegram from a very kindly old gentleman, one of my father's dearest friends, a Bishop now turned Buchmanite. Here is the telegram:

YOU HAVE GONE TOO FAR YOU ARE ALIENATING THE BETTER ELEMENT AMONG YOUR SUBSCRIBERS AND HINDERING IN- STEAD OF SUPPORTING THE CONSTRUCTIVE FORCES OF THE NATION AT A TIME WHEN OUR CIVILIZATION IS THREATENED WITH COLLAPSE STOP IF NO REVERSAL OF POLICY OUR CON- NECTIONS MUST BE SEVERED PLEASE PASS ON THIS MES- SAGE TO YOUR FATHER

Buchmanites have spent hours trying to convert *Time* editors. Alas, if Buchmanism is the voice of God, the Editors of *Time* will, I fear, have a hard time getting past the pearly gates. Comes then a brilliant Italian journalist to tell me that the American Press has completely misrepresented the facts of Europe. But he doesn't want me to do anything. It is too late, he says. There will be war—and he expects to die.

In his talk to the salesmen Luce could touch on only a few facets of his personal involvement with an expanding and adventurous organi- zation. *The March of Time,* for instance, was continuing to stir up the motion-picture business because it insisted on presenting films on controversial subjects. This drew criticism from certain in- fluential leaders in the industry—men like Spyros Skouras and Martin Quigley, publisher of the *Motion Picture Herald*—who felt that the cinema should stick to entertainment. One of the most controversial of all *March of Time* releases had been "Inside Nazi Germany," its first single-subject issue. It depicted scenes of prosperity within Germany and dwelt on the extent of Nazi propaganda abroad as evidenced by the activities of the German-American Bund in the U.S. But while the pictures tended to emphasize the strength of the Nazi movement, the commentary was an indictment of Nazi rule. *The March of Time* said: "Of the Fascist nations in Europe today, Germany emerges as the supreme example. Democracy is destroyed. The dictator is a demi-god who can do no wrong. . . . Nazi Germany faces her destiny with one of the great war machines in history. And the inevitable destiny of the great war machines of the past has been to destroy the peace of the world, its people and the governments of their time." Within three weeks of its release "Inside Nazi Germany" prompted more than a million words of newspaper comment.

The reactions were strangely contradictory. The German Consul General in New York demanded changes in the film, which he said was detrimental to his country; he was refused. Harry Warner, on the other hand, refused to exhibit it in his theaters because he believed it was German propaganda. Warner's view was challenged by two other prominent Jews: David O. Selznick called it "one of the . . . most important reels in the history of pictures," and Rabbi Stephen S. Wise said that no one could object unless "he is an enemy of the Democratic order. . . ."

On the heels of "Inside Nazi Germany," de Rochemont put out a more explicit indictment of Nazi policies, "The Refugee—Today and Tomorrow." It concentrated on the story of "a new kind of refugee —the victim, not of warfare, but of an intolerance and persecution unparalleled since the Dark Ages." This release was banned in Cleveland, much to the disgust of the Cleveland *Plain Dealer*'s critic W. Ward Marsh, who wrote, "With *The March of Time* [the spectator] accepts fact as fact which either helps him form opinions about a world tragedy or cinches the opinion he has already formed. Political censorship . . . has long since outlived any usefulness it may ever have had."

A side effect of "The Refugee" was to put an end to the efforts of a free-lance cameraman, Paul Dorsey, who was trying to get into Germany and do still another picture for de Rochemont. He had been ardently cultivating Hitler's actress friend, Leni Riefenstahl, then visiting the U.S., but Dorsey sadly reported: "We had arrived at the hand holding stage, were calling each other pet names, and were on the verge, I suspect, of spending the night in the same bed. . . . ["The Refugee"] fixed my business, and it's no trip to Germany for me. Before that she had promised to speak a good word for me to Goebbels and Hitler. Now we call each other Mr. Dorsey and Miss Riefenstahl."

In the spring of 1939 the Board gave de Rochemont the go-ahead on his most ambitious project to date—a feature-length film based on Major George Fielding Eliot's best-selling book *The Ramparts We Watch,*[5] a plea for American preparedness.

Under the creative, if somewhat tumultuous Russell Davenport, *Fortune* added a good deal of luster to the corporation. Although its profits were not large and its paid circulation was relatively small, it claimed a readership of over a million, and was one of the most widely quoted magazines in the U.S. The *Fortune* Survey had become, along with the Gallup Poll, a carefully watched barometer of current opinion. In March 1939 *Fortune* introduced another feature that would have a significant influence on American opinion—the *Fortune* Round Table. It was the idea of Raymond Leslie Buell, the president of the Foreign Policy Association, that if he could bring certain leaders of opinion together around a table they would be able to reach a consensus on important and controversial public questions. Luce, Hodgins and Davenport bought the idea, and Buell resigned from his Foreign Policy job and joined the *Fortune* editorial staff. In introducing this journalistic innovation the magazine described the Round Table as "neither a discussion nor a report. It is, with the exceptions noted in the text, *the unanimous expression of men who, in their private and public utterances, are known to disagree concerning the subject selected.* It is based upon the theory that Americans, no matter how embroiled in controversy . . . can speak as one man upon certain fundamental principles. . . ."

Fortune was able to attract to these symposia men of national prominence. The first Round Table included Chester I. Barnard, presi-

[5] Reynal & Hitchcock, 1938.

dent of the New Jersey Bell Telephone Company, best known for his seminal work, *The Functions of the Executive;* Clinton Golden, Regional Director of the Steel Workers Organizing Committee; Beardsley Ruml, Treasurer of R. H. Macy; Sumner Slichter, the Harvard economist; and Allan B. Kline, later head of the American Farm Bureau Federation. Another early participant was a man whose career was to become closely involved with *Fortune*—Wendell L. Willkie.

Fortune leavened its more important and serious features with a lively issue in July 1939 wholly devoted to New York City. In 248 pages weighing 3.466 pounds, containing twenty-one articles (v. the usual nine or ten titles) and specially commissioned paintings, the editors explored the life of the great city.[6] It was the first issue of *Fortune* offered for sale on the newsstands; it sold 169,000 copies over subscription circulation. Larsen reported jubilantly to Luce that the issue had been "a complete and howling success [and] brought back a readership to *Fortune* which I believe was sadly lacking . . . among advertising and New York business friends."

By the middle of 1939 *Life,* a publishing success in every way, was growing from strength to strength, in circulation, in advertising and in readership. At the same advertising convention in which Luce had described for the salesmen the pressures on him as head of the company he told the men:

> The fact that *Life* is now a success makes Time Inc. once again a success. As long as the success of *Life* was in doubt, as long as *Life* was unsure of itself, unformed, immature, its uncertainties cast confusion over the whole of Time Inc. Overnight, *Life* made us big but added nothing to our strength. Indeed, it sapped our strength. As all of you I think know, Time Inc. put nearly $5,000,000 into *Life* before it turned the corner. . . . Now

---

[6] It presented a multitude of fascinating facts about the city. Polly Adler, New York's most famous madam, was thrilled to have been mentioned. "I entered the Valhalla of the American executive," she wrote later in her book *A House Is Not a Home* (Rinehart and Company, 1953). "I could feel that my name would go down in history inscribed on the rolls with Morgans and Mellons and Du Ponts, with Henry Ford and John D. Rockefeller."

386

[*Life*] is paying us back measure for measure. I am glad *Life* is paying us back the $5,000,000. But it is doing much more than that. Indeed it has done already far more than that. For *Life* has restored to Time Inc. in unbounded measure its good will, its good name. . . . It is a far greater Time Inc. today than ever before—and of course I do not mean merely greater in obvious bulk, but greater in spirit, more adventuresome, more humane, greater in its grasp and what is more, greater in its reach. And thinking of the irrepressible enthusiasm of Robert Browning we may well add, saying to each other:

> "Grow old along with me!
> The best is yet to be,
> The last of life, for which the first was made."

In Personnel Matters— "A Considerable Lack of Definition"

IN FEBRUARY 1939 Pearl Kroll, one of the few women ever to become a *Time* writer [Sport], wrote Luce expressing her concern at evidence of dissension in the ranks. She was moved to do so by the appearance of the Communist gossip sheet *High Time*. Luce replied, "You are quite right in putting the bee on the 'heads of the organization' to work out the problems of organization so that men and women can work together harmoniously and effectively. I can only promise you that I am sticking leech-like to this job until I succeed or have sense enough to call myself a flat failure! The year 1938 was primarily concerned with 'putting *Life* over.' The year 1939 is dedicated to making Time Inc. a happy family. Of course I do not mean happiness in any bluebird sense. But if by Christmas 1939 Time Inc. is not the best damned organization in the country, a lot of people, besides myself, are going to feel terribly, terribly hurt."

The problem of staff morale had been neglected. Not deliberately, but because Luce had long felt such a personal responsibility for everything and everybody at Time Inc. that he had difficulty in adjusting to changes brought about by growth. Three years earlier, in

1936, Mary Fraser had written him that while she "would not call a halt on this zooming expansion, I am still alarmed and uneasy at a growth which seems, little by little, to take away the intimacy and loyalty of the group of two years ago. New faces appear with dizzying rapidity, and in self-defense floor after floor becomes isolated and ingrown. It is also obvious that the time has passed when the energy and will of every single person employed here was directed toward only one thing—a swell magazine, personified to them, as a small group, by a man they all knew." Luce did not disregard the warning; when he announced the publisher system soon after, he urged the new publishers to get to know their people.

But while recognizing a problem, he did not fully comprehend it, particularly the attitude of the new employees. He worked closely with associates whom he knew and trusted and had little contact with the new employees who were strangers to him and he to them. They were often hired on a hit-or-miss basis and sometimes fired in the same way without his knowledge. Those who swarmed into the dozens of new jobs resulting from *Life* often found themselves working for others who were perhaps only weeks or months their seniors. The talented found unlimited opportunities for initiative, but others were confused, did not know to whom they were responsible or what was expected of them. It had always been a hard-working shop with a lot of self-generated overtime, but overtime was also imposed on some who did not see the reason or necessity for it and were not paid for it. The pay was higher than in most New York offices during the Depression, but there were many disparities; people doing the same work in different divisions were often paid at different rates.

The conditions made it easy for the *Time* Unit of the American Newspaper Guild to recruit the new employees, for it offered an outlet and focus for their discontent. A management consultant who conducted an independent study of staff relations fairly summarized the situation in 1938: "Many thousands of people over the country would give their eye teeth to work for the *Time* enterprises. . . . The new individual's morale at the time of his joining the staff . . . reaches higher on the psychological thermometer than for perhaps any other organization in the country. But does the sentiment last? For some, 'yes.' For

389

many, 'no.' The failure of the management to give the attention to morale that it deserves has squeezed out loyalty, has killed initial buoyancy, has indeed dumped the Guild on your doorstep. . . . Your employees have not been abused but at strategic points they *have* been seriously neglected."

Until a small number of Communists infiltrated Time Inc. and the Newspaper Guild, there had been no note of active dissension and disloyalty. The Communist infiltration of Time Inc. was less important and less influential than the Party's inroads into the Guild, where for several years they were in control of the New York chapter. In the middle and late 1930's there was no New York publication of any size that did not have some Communists or fellow travelers on the editorial staff. A shop newspaper similar to *High Time* was published at the New York *Times.* In the case of Time Inc. the tactic of publishing *High Time* with its burden of slander and gossip did the Party more harm than good. It was fiercely resented by most members of the staff. There were those, Miss Kroll among them, who wanted Luce to root the Communists out.

Luce firmly rejected any idea of a company Red hunt in a memo which he circulated in reply to the first issue of *High Time* (the paper ceased publication after three issues). In it he said the Communists had damaged the reputation of the company by using its name in partisan propaganda. ("A publication by 'The Communist Party at Time Inc.' is just as offensive as one would be by a 'Nazi Bund' . . . and far more offensive than a publication by 'New Dealers of Time Inc. Staff' or by a 'Time Inc. G.O.P.' ") Luce felt that the greatest injury inflicted by *High Time* was that it jeopardized the freedom that had hitherto prevailed within the staff; this, he said, he was determined to uphold at all costs.

It has been a cardinal principle with us that editors, writers and researchers have a right to spout to one another their views— well considered, half considered, or ill considered—so that editorial give and take shall be honest and free. We have had people of all shades of political thought on our staff and I maintain the right of every one of them to speak to every other member of the staff with as much intellectual freedom—and carefreeness—as

390

he would in his own family. I also maintain the right of members of the staff to gossip, kick, criticize and laugh about what others of the staff have said, done or written. *Free speech in confidence* is essential to group journalism. It would be intolerable if our editors had to feel that they could not open their mouths without having some half-uttered thought plucked out and used to stab them publicly in the back. It would be just as intolerable if any writer had to feel that if he repeated in the office what some other member of the staff had said, it might be twisted and publicly used against Time Inc.

It was against this background that Luce promised Miss Kroll to make Time Inc. once more "a happy family."

Luce's choice of words, "a happy family," had a paternal ring; it was very difficult for him to feel otherwise about a company in which he was designated—according to the rather quaint usage of the Securities and Exchange Commission Registration Statement—a "parent" of the company. Luce found it difficult to think of or discuss Time Inc. in the cold abstract terms usually applied to corporations. He also was reluctant to proclaim himself "the proprietor," a term which his associates often used in affection behind his back. In the years prior to 1939 he often talked of the company in terms of a partnership in which he was the senior partner. He believed in equality of opportunity, with rewards based on individual merit.

This thinking had led him to create the first stock-ownership plan in 1929. At the time the company purchased stock from the Hadden estate to set up the plan, Luce explained that this would give the key employee "a two-edged interest in *Time*. Keen for the enhancement of the value of his stock, he will work for the future. . . . He will do all he can to keep down waste and inefficiency. Just one example— Mary Fraser. She is the copy chief. She runs all the editorial girls. . . . Next to the Managing Editor, it depends more upon her than anyone else whether *Time* gets to press on time and avoids $200 overtime or late deliveries. . . . She gets a good but modest salary— probably saves very little of it. If she should lose her health or leave for other reasons, she would have nothing to show for her services to

Time except the appreciative sentiments that would go with her. But 10 shares of stock which some day might be worth $500 each—that would make all the difference."

Seventeen employees shared in that first stock-purchase plan; thirty-three participated in a second one in 1933.

Apart from the early stock plans the company's personnel policies prior to 1938 could be summed up as simply a good day's pay for a hard day's (and often night's) work. The staff worked without benefit of contracts, guarantees of security, or pensions; infirmity and old age seemed remote perils to that youthful band. There was one exception. Robert Johnson had a contract which guaranteed him not only a modest salary but 10 percent of the profits. He was older than Hadden, Luce or Larsen, he had given up an established position to join them and he stayed with them after the quarrel with Crowe. It was quite usual for advertising salesmen to work on a commission basis. So long as profits were low the contract was not really important in determining his compensation, but when the tide turned Johnson stood to make a good deal more than his associates. In 1929 Luce decided to renegotiate the contract, which did not terminate until 1941. It was becoming increasingly probable that the small company had ahead of it the payment of unreasonably high compensation to Johnson, entirely out of line with the compensation of others, especially of Larsen, who was regarded as more valuable. The existence of the contract was straining relations among the small group.

Luce proposed a cash settlement. The matter was negotiated by Johnson's father-in-law, Albert Rathbone, a distinguished attorney. Rathbone suggested that the accounting firm of Price Waterhouse & Co. be asked to value the contract; they estimated its worth at from $150,000 to $200,000—a sum far beyond the means of Time Inc. in 1929. However, the company had just received payment of $100,000 from an insurance policy it had carried on Hadden's life. Luce asked the directors to approve the payment of this amount in settlement of Johnson's contract; in addition Johnson was given a new three-year contract raising his salary to $30,000 and guaranteeing him annual increases to a maximum of $40,000. On concluding this arrangement Luce asked the Board to raise Larsen to $30,000 and in a formal

minute noted that he expected Larsen's salary would exceed Johnson's in future. It was not a formal agreement, he said, for "Larsen is
quite willing to be fired when no longer worth his hire."

As the company grew and prospered, salaries increased and staff
morale continued high. Luce did worry from time to time that the
company might not be able to maintain the old spirit. He observed on
one occasion, "From now on, we will have to employ a lot of people
who know exactly when they have done a day's or a week's work and
who propose to do no more. We will also have a few who do not
count the strain on their backs. Let us distinguish between them when
it comes to pay or other privileges." This remained the basic policy.

In the deepening Depression in January 1932, Luce, Larsen and
Johnson voluntarily cut their own salaries, but not those of the staff. In
the spring of 1933, however, an over-all reduction of 10 percent was
ordered, though exempted from it were members of the editorial staff,
the circulation girls in the Chicago office and all employees earning
under $30 a week. This was the only and very small reduction at a
moment when larger pay cuts were the order of the day. Moreover,
during 1934, salaries were increased on an individual basis, and most
employees found that their wages had been restored to the previous
level or better. Throughout the Depression, Time Inc. remained a
very good place to work.

The original appearance of a union at Time Inc. was not due to any
employee dissatisfaction; it began as a well-meaning gesture of solidarity with the labor movement that was sweeping the country in the
mid-thirties. The few staff members who first formed a unit of the
Book and Magazine Guild did not approach management or seek a
contract. Some time later some senior writers on *Fortune*—Russell
Davenport, Archibald MacLeish and Wilder Hobson—invited Luce to
lunch and told him they proposed to organize a unit of the American
Newspaper Guild. Luce's first reaction was "Can I join? Why not?"
He also told them that he did not think much of organizing a union
merely to show solidarity with other journalists; a union's purpose was
to fight for better wages and working conditions and he plainly indicated that he did not think his luncheon companions had any complaint on either score. Nor did they.

393

The next Luce heard of the Guild was in the fall of 1936; Heywood Broun, the national president and a columnist on the New York *World-Telegram,* was coming to address a meeting of Time Inc. employees. Luce asked Grover to "round up some people so that we will be sure that Broun has an audience." The Broun meeting created little excitement and aroused some apprehension. Gottfried, who stumbled into the meeting by accident, fired off a note of objection to Luce, telling him "the union does not represent anything like all your employees. . . . If in trying to be good hearted you should give the union any privileges which would tend to make our position outside the union untenable, you would be doing us no good turn. There are at least a few of us who damn well intend to do a better job than the next fellow and damn well intend to be paid better than he for doing it. . . ." Gottfried feared that Luce "in his rather moralistic reasoning" might decide that his employees ought to join a union. If Gottfried's sentiment was not wholly representative of the staff, it was characteristic of the deep-seated individualism of the older hands.

The Guild continued to organize without hindrance or help from management and with little real awareness of the consequences on either side. The original organizers were soon outvoted by the newcomers, who took over the union's campaign. In June 1937 when a dispute arose at *The March of Time* over (according to an indignant Larsen) "whether a couple of the idealistic union joiners were Management or Labor," Larsen was told that no member of the *Time* Unit was permitted to discuss the matter with management so long as the union had no contract [1] with Time Inc. Larsen reported to Luce, "So the little gesture of our idealistically liberal writers ends up in a hard-boiled, non-old-*Timer*-manned Guild which intends to pursue a completely hard-boiled union-and-constitution-guided course with

---

[1] Larsen to Luce: "The word 'contract' was a considerable shock to me and I had to change the subject the three times the word was mentioned in order not to commit myself one way or the other . . . in fact, to avoid registering on the awful word."

A Guild brochure: "[Mr. Larsen] was told there was no machinery inside Time to adjust differences because there was no contract between Time and the guild. Mr. Larsen . . . pondered and asked: 'Then why don't we have a contract?' "

Time Inc.'s Management." Management-employee relations had indeed changed.

The company agreed to the Guild's proposal for contract negotiations, and at a small informal meeting in September 1937 the Guild submitted a list of suggestions. Luce, in an opening statement of the management's policy, said, "Many men and women, of differing abilities, of differing opinions and of differing temperaments, have been happy in their work in Time Inc. We are open minded toward any suggestion [but] we believe we have as little right to coerce any man or woman into joining an organization as we have to coerce them not to join. We ask only that there should at all times be a common agreement on a common purpose—namely the improvement of Labor Relations of the groups within Time Inc."

The principal negotiator for management was Ingersoll; the prevailing naïveté about labor relations is evidenced by the fact that in one discussion about the Guild, Ingersoll startled his associates by announcing that he was for the closed shop. "You would have thought I had blasphemed the Virgin Mary at a Eucharistic Congress," he said. It turned out that he thought a closed shop meant a company union. Later he admitted to the union representatives that management had given little thought to the possibility of collective bargaining. "This may seem strange to you gentlemen who are professional labor negotiators," he said, "but it is a fact which it is vitally important for you to know in order to understand Time Incorporated. You have to grasp its peculiar and untypical executive management —by working editors. And you have to understand the implications of its literally breath-taking growth."

The first negotiations dragged on for ten months. "Both sides were naïve and often silly," Ingersoll said. "The weekly meetings were often hilarious." There was little serious disagreement except on the Guild demand for a Guild shop,[2] on which the company was adamant, and the demand for a 35-hour week (they settled for 40 hours).

[2] This would have permitted Time Inc. to hire non-Guild members, but after thirty days they would have been required to become members. It would also have required all current editorial employees to join the Guild after the signing of the contract.

The negotiations with the Guild did lead management to re-examine personnel policies and to establish definitions and classifications for certain jobs, and minimum rates of pay were included in the contract. These things Luce conceded were necessary, but he resisted pressures to carry such measures to bureaucratic extremes. He remained a confirmed individualist in the matter of handling men and women. For a 1939 confrontation with the Guild he defined his views in this statement:

> Management is often tempted . . . to take a "fish or cut bait" attitude—i.e., settle a man's worth (to us) once and for all by giving a man a big raise with the idea of firing him if he doesn't prove worth it. It sounds like a good clean, clear-cut method. My experience tells me that it sounds a great deal better than it is. At any rate, it will not be the characteristic method of personnel management as long as I am chiefly responsible for running this company. For while it is undoubtedly true that we have wasted too much time fussing with people who are just never destined to be of any great use here, it is also true that a great many of our most useful people would not be here, if we had adopted a more decisive attitude toward them at various times in their careers here. . . .
>
> All kinds of considerations enter into a true estimate of a man's or woman's value to this company.
>
> Some men are uninspired but reliable. Some men are unreliable but have their brilliant moments. Some men work well in a team. Some men are good individual performers but are just too much of a nuisance in a team. Some men aren't very good today but did good work a year ago; others who are not pulling their weight nevertheless "show promise." . . . Endless are the varieties of considerations which enter into our estimates of the usefulness of various people.
>
> The kinds of management problems that I am suggesting here should be recognized by the Guild leaders—or if not, it should be clear that there is a basic difference in point of view between the Management and the Guild. . . .

396

This Management expects that its "personnel" relations will continue to be characterized by a considerable lack of definition.

Even before the Guild and personnel problems arose Luce had given a good deal of thought to employee benefit plans supplementing wages and salaries. In 1936, in her memo calling his attention to the problems created by expansion, Mary Fraser had observed, "I think Time Inc. pays extremely good wages, and that there is no kick coming there. But Time Inc. also expects, and gets, so much more than most other big businesses ask of their employees that some sort of special consideration is necessary." She recommended either a new stock-purchase plan or a company-wide bonus based on profits.

Stillman was working on another idea. After examining the idea of a pension plan, he rejected it as having little appeal to a group whose average age was as young as Time Inc.'s employees'. A rugged individualist himself, he believed "anyone with sufficient intelligence to work for Time Inc. should do his own thinking about his old age and make his own provisions for [it] on his own initiative." His suggestion was that a savings plan, to which the company would contribute, be established for those earning under $10,000, with a stock-purchase plan for those whose salaries were above that level; no action was taken on either the Fraser or the Stillman proposal. In 1937 a savings-cum-profit-sharing plan was again suggested. It too was rejected, but effective in January 1938 the company instituted for the Chicago staff, whose wage level was below that of New York, a savings plan to which the company contributed. With the losses then draining the company treasury, Luce felt that "with all the will in the world, this is simply not a propitious time to work out long-range schemes for profit sharing. . . . Perhaps no time ever is, but certainly now there are just too damned many unknowns."

But, despite the losses, he wanted to do something for key men. The publishers and managing editors, all new at their jobs, he thought should be taken care of by cash bonuses. "The first thing our friends require," he wrote, "is to earn a kind of proprietary right in their jobs

397

which they are presumably doing. . . . So, if they can make good on their jobs this year *and* get a good cash return . . . that would seem to answer both the financial and psychological needs *this year*." There was another group for whom he wanted to do something by way of a stock-purchase plan. They were men and women in the group below the top executives, "people we are pretty *sure* of mentally, morally, physically—who are mainly interested in their salaries and their work but for whom we would like to work out, without financial strain, a small conservative-speculative bet on Time Inc."

Stillman was disappointed by Luce's decision. He felt the emphasis on immediate rewards for top executives was psychologically wrong: he thought instead that Luce should set up an incentive plan for his top people based on profits, which he estimated at $75,000,000 in the next ten years. Incentives, he argued, would give the executives a substantial stake in the success of the company. So he entered a rebuttal to Luce, challenging his approach. The memorandum began with a study Stillman had made of twenty executive salaries:

No one who makes as much as $15,000 or $20,000 can have a case against his employer unless the employer has promised him actually or inferentially something, as for instance, a partnership which he subsequently fails to deliver. When a person arrives at this station in life [he] must make his own evaluation on his chances with the employer, including a decision whether the employer is a Henry Ford or a Du Pont, i.e. whether he is fated to remain an employee forever or whether he can if he wants and is good enough attain and enjoy the status of a privileged partner as Raskob, Sloan, F. B. Davis et al have been able to do as Du Pont partners. . . .

If the important people (employees or partners?) of *Time* have any case against their employer it is in the lack of policy on this important matter. The employer seems to go in one direction for a while, then in the other, or worse, to have no policy at all.

Knowing you as I do and recalling various conversations of the past, I wonder if you are not now more inclined to do business like Ford rather than like the Du Ponts. I think you would like to buy everyone out as Ford bought out Couzens, own 100% of the stock like Ford or Hearst, and solve everything through salaries and profit bonuses, payable in cash. . . .

One of the strongest arguments I know against the Ford or Hearst technique for us is that the entire 14 year history of Time Inc., one of the most successful companies anywhere, is the direct opposite. [Until Hadden's death] one of the company's principal characteristics was that for one magazine alone, there were five management stockholders who held 82 percent of the stock.[3] Now with three big and two little properties instead of one, there are only two large stockholders still in the business.[4]

It would appear to be preferable in the short and long run that the past history of *Time* as a self-perpetuating management of associated individuals owning stock . . . should be followed as the best solution practically and ideologically. . . .

A choice between a new deal to make the new Time Inc. more like the old and a Ford-Hearst method is a choice any one of your top executives is entitled to ask you to make sometime soon.

Stillman added that he knew Luce was fully aware that "the least possible one-man show is one-man show enough" and that the answer was to see that an adequately compensated first-class businessman was in charge of each of the operating divisions of the company. Stillman drew a basic distinction between a "business man" and a "hired man":

A successful Publisher in real life is first of all a business man with the profit motive or habit. . . .

Any man who is the man you are looking for as publisher of any of these three magazines ought to be good enough to make $1,000,000 during his lifetime and live well meantime, if his property is successful. . . .

Fortunately, you have as Publisher of *Life* [Larsen] a man

---

[3] Luce, Hadden, Larsen, John S. Martin and Robert L. Johnson.
[4] Luce and Larsen.

who has enough inducement through the preservation of his several millions—actual and potential—to present no compensation problem and who is a good enough Publisher . . . to be an eminently satisfactory choice.

The other two who are editor-publishers [Ingersoll and Hodgins] are on trial. . . . Are they business men? When you become satisfied that they are . . . they should be candidates for participation in the business . . . on such a scale reasonably calculated to make them each a millionaire at fifty or fifty-five. That's the importance of age. You want young men, so you don't have to make a millionaire every three or four years. . . .

In a modest bit of special pleading, Stillman included himself and Pierrie Prentice among those who might be considered "business men," and suggested they might not be "overly ambitious" in looking forward to making half to three quarters of a million dollars in the next ten years.

Those on the staff who were not "business men," whether editors, writers, researchers or advertising men, ". . . should be paid the market price for their services, *which may be very high in some cases* and more than business men may get in hard times. [They] should be spared as much as possible from the risks of the business which they are unable to appraise and whose policies they cannot influence much." His own committee on profit-sharing, Stillman felt, had approached the matter too much from the standpoint of rewards rather than incentives, and this was wrong: "Rewards promote loyalty and morale. . . . As to rewards, there need not be so much hurry. Because rewards come out of profits made by people with incentives. Incentives promote profits. Profits is what we haven't got enough of at the moment, to give out any rewards." Stillman then repeated his recommendation for some sort of incentive plan.

Luce did not accept the Stillman argument, stood his ground on his decision for cash bonuses and a small stock-purchase plan. He would not accept the premise that "business men" should be distinguished from editors, and in later years when the company did initiate incentive plans based on stock options which were to make millionaires of a score of Time Inc. executives, the editors and businessmen shared alike in the company's bounty.

Luce could accept and weigh an argument such as Stillman advanced without resentment. But what stirred him to fury was any charge that Time Inc. had been niggardly with its employees. In the fall of 1938, in his memorandum on the policy of Time Inc., Ingersoll had made such an accusation. Luce answered that the charge was resented

. . . because it is as untrue as it is unpleasant. Let us consider all the men—all of them—who up until 1935–36 were responsible for the editorial production of *Time*. There was first of all Briton Hadden. He died a millionaire at 31. There is then Henry R. Luce. He has edited and even written a good deal of *Time* in his day. He is a millionaire. The next senior writer is John S. Martin who never spent any time in the business office. He made a million. These were the lucky ones. And there was one who missed luck by a hair!—Gottfried. He would today be worth, on paper at least, $1,250,000 had he not felt the urge to be a novelist and given up his stock. Very gallantly, not letting this "would have been" bother him, he returned—at $10,000 a year, more, I suppose, than he could have got anywhere else and today is making what in my world is still called a big salary.[5]

Luce cited others who had been well rewarded—Goldsborough, Billings, the late Parker Lloyd-Smith—and he brought up *Time*'s treatment of the senior writers: "The record of the rewards given to the people who produced the successful *Time*," he said, "makes any charge of niggardliness or frugality nonsense."

. . . It must be said that the process of pie-carving did, of course, stop abruptly in 1936 with Time Inc.'s venture into *Life* —a process which had just previously been hit by the 1932–33 debacle. . . . If *Life* ever starts handing out pies, or if only *Time* recovers its pie-baking ability, they will start sharing again. . . .

If we can work out as effective a relation between reward and

[5] $22,500.

401

function as that which characterized the first ten years of *Time,* that in itself will be almost enough to guarantee the success of *Time.* The challenge is not to the past. The challenge is to the present and the future.

Luce's promise to carve up the pie again was kept in 1939, when *Life* began to make its substantial contribution to profits. In that year the company's revenues rose to a new record $29,311,057, and the after-tax profit was $3,206,751—an increase in profits over 1938 of $2,077,329. As soon as it was clear that the company had returned to affluence, a generous profit-sharing savings plan was instituted that covered all employees. Thirty-one key associates were excepted; for these men and women Luce inaugurated a still more generous plan. This "Senior Group" had, as Luce put it, "the main call on the jackpot"; a percentage of Time Inc.'s after-tax profits was set aside for them—half to be payable as a bonus and half to be retained by the company for later distribution. In the first of its seven years of operation the Senior Group shared a total of $304,661, a sum equal to 51 percent of their combined salaries.

In this new plan for the executives, editors and writers, Luce was trying to preserve in a new era and under different conditions the basic spirit that had characterized the early days of the company, that of a responsible group of friends working harmoniously to a common end. At a company dinner, Luce once described how he and Larsen conceived the idea: "We intended to have dinners . . . fairly often, with the sound of the cash register bells ringing in the background. It was to be an opportunity to look around, to look in each other's faces and to recognize ourselves as responsible men, responsible each to our own job and responsible to each other and perhaps responsible to some greater causes."

Rewards at Time Inc. continued to increase, not only for the key employees but for the rank and file, maintaining a scale of benefits unsurpassed in the publishing business.

A Full Share of
Responsibility

HESITANTLY, plagued by doubts and dissensions, the American people in 1939 began to shed the illusion that they could isolate themselves from events in Europe and Asia. The attitudes of Time Inc.'s editors also changed. In the sixteen years since the company's founding, the magazines' staffs had been more preoccupied with innovations in journalism and with the business of growth than engaged in public questions on the opinion-making level. As the world crisis deepened, the Time Inc. publications underwent a change, a change which Luce himself some years later—in the middle of World War II—described in a memorandum to his editors.

> Not that we had not always taken our work seriously [he wrote] for indeed we had, but in a sense, we had tried to limit our responsibility to the strictly journalistic and to avoid the responsibility (and with it the aura of self-importance) for what happened in the country or the world. . . . If, in the presence of crisis, we had adopted a policy of supreme indifferentism, that in itself would have been a factor in the scales. Indeed before Pearl

Harbor the principal factor that we attempted to combat was indifferentism. (Incidentally, this almost fatal indifferentism to war and the great issues of human destiny had been, to say the least, encouraged by the intellectual climate of the '30s; its scoffing at idealism; its parade of economic determinism; its suspicion of all human motives; its repudiation of the American past and of all the sterner virtues.) In any case we accepted our full share . . . of direct responsibility in crisis.

As far back as 1937 Luce had become convinced that the U.S. would inevitably be involved in the world crisis and probably in war. In a speech to the Montclair (New Jersey) Yale Club (where he was feted as the man who had won his "Y" in life) he startled his fellow alumni by telling them they were only "two jumps ahead of the Sheriff of Destruction," and predicted that the Yale campus would become, as in his undergraduate days, a military training camp. He also lamented the current attitude toward the old-fashioned virtues of patriotism and courage. Now he was impatient with the sluggish pace of the American economy, the blame for which he placed wholly on the New Deal. On the other hand, he found himself in agreement with the steps that Roosevelt had taken to rearm the United States and to aid France and Britain. While Luce was not numbered among the critics of Neville Chamberlain, he was not deluded into thinking that Munich did anything but buy time for Britain to prepare for war.

At the beginning of 1939 he initiated a debate among his editors on U.S. foreign policy. It was plain that while he was by no means committed to all-out support of the European democracies, he was several steps ahead of a number of his colleagues. "The younger men who graduated after I did in the '20s," he recalled later, "were, roughly, isolationist. But the men of my class and generation—Larsen, Billings and Longwell—*they* were interventionists." To get the discussion under way he circulated to the senior staff a paper written by John Chamberlain of *Fortune,* together with his own statement of what Time Inc.'s attitude toward foreign policy should be. Chamberlain argued that the U.S. should confine its over-all policy to the defense of its interests in this hemisphere, pointing out that "overseas

404

policy" in British history had always been a euphemism for "imperialism." Luce wholly agreed that the Monroe Doctrine must be upheld, but disagreed with any suggestion that U.S. power or policy be limited to the hemisphere or any other geographical area; he wanted his country to exert its influence everywhere. "No ideological war, not yet at any rate," he wrote, but he wanted American diplomatic action backed up by great military strength "and the evident will to use it in the maintenance of our clearly announced purposes." He also wanted the U.S. to use its economic power in defense of its interest. This policy might give considerable aid and comfort to such countries as France, Holland and Britain. "We have no obligation to help protect the British Empire," he wrote, but "we should be pleased rather than embittered if the policy which best fits the interests of the U.S. is also of use to Great Britain. We will not cut off our Irish nose to spite our Anglo-Saxon face."

The exchange seems to have been more for the education of the staff than the resolution of different viewpoints. However, as a result of the discussions, there was a large measure of agreement on the need for hemisphere defense. The Policy Committee recorded a decision that the Time Inc. publications would support the Monroe Doctrine and that they would undertake to inform their readers about Latin America. Whatever differences remained as to foreign policy, there were none about U.S. rearmament, to which *Time* and *Life* gave much space. They were also reporting the European scene with its rising tension. The Nazi seizure of what was left of Czechoslovakia, Mussolini's invasion of Albania ominously foreshadowed the coming hostilities, and *Time* began a series of articles explicitly entitled "Background for War." Luce himself moved closer to a position of active involvement. To the Foreign News and National Affairs writers on *Time* he wrote:

> Our involvement in Europe and Asia is overwhelmingly a moral (rather than a physical or "economic") involvement at this moment. Morally . . . we stand with the so-called "democracies." . . . Practically, there is a most difficult question as to what we should do. . . . It is clear that this country will not long

405

hold to any policy which is inconsistent with its moral sentiments. . . . We will not tolerate the defeat of Great Britain and
France. . . .

Luce introduced another topic: the state of U.S. morale. In preparation for a speech which he was to give before the Detroit Economic
Club, he had had a series of lunches and interviews with Wall Street
acquaintances. The meetings filled him with alarm over the prevailing
pessimism. His Detroit speech, therefore, was an exhortation to
American businessmen "to take part in the creation of the Great
Society." [1] He reminded them that they held the key to peace and
prosperity. And in a later speech to the New York Fashion Group, he
declared: "What is still not characteristic of America as it always used
to be is that feeling for the future, the confidence in the bigger and the
better, the spirit of you-ain't-seen-nothin'-yet. . . ."

He turned to *Life* as the most effective carrier of the message. With
Billings and Longwell, he plotted a special issue. It came out in a June
of strange contradictions: when nine million people were out of work
in the U.S.; when a World's Fair in New York was presenting "The
World of Tomorrow," a dream of wealth, luxury and peace. The *Life*
issue was intended "to take stock of some of the abiding things which
are magnificently *right* about America . . . to suggest, by examination
of our heroic past and hopeful present, the richer and happier America which will be ours when we have nerved ourselves to accept our
bounty and our destiny." On the cover the Statue of Liberty was
silhouetted against a blue background, and the theme of the issue was
summed up in an article by Walter Lippmann, who summoned Americans to "feel once more the exhilaration and the confidence that have
made them what they are"—and to abandon "the mentality of a little
nation on the frontiers of the civilized world."

Fortune made a characteristically philosophic bow to the problems
of the world beyond the U.S. borders by citing for special attention a

---

[1] A phrase anticipating President Lyndon Johnson but by no means original
with Luce. It was the title of a book by the British political scientist Graham
Wallas, published in 1914, and dedicated to Walter Lippmann, who had studied
under him at Harvard.

book that had just been published—*Union Now,*[2] by Clarence Streit, a New York *Times* correspondent who had watched and mourned the failure of the League of Nations. Editor Davenport wrote that Streit's vision of a federal union of fifteen democratic nations was probably not practical but that the book was nevertheless of "utmost importance to all those who believe in what *Fortune* has been calling the libertarian system. . . . In order only to keep what he has already won, man must always progress. . . . In order to progress he must always have a vision of something that he has not yet won. The union of the democracies is such a vision. . . . Out of Mr. Streit's dream may come some preliminary step such as a customs union, the pooling of resources, the coordination of national economic policies. These would all help to develop the free libertarian economy from which—imperfect as it is—mankind has already derived so much. And who knows? Visions sometimes come true."

In June the Luces went to Europe on a vacation; they left at a moment when there was a lull in the crisis and it seemed possible that war might be averted. But the trip confirmed Luce's own conviction that armed conflict was inevitable. While the Luces were at Aix-les-Bains, U.S. Ambassador to Poland Anthony Biddle invited them to visit Warsaw. The visit was made memorable for Luce by a ball given by the Ambassador. As he recalled: "Sometime late in the evening, I suddenly realized that these people, the Poles in their splendid uniforms, the women in their gowns, were eager to go to war. They talked about mounting their white chargers and riding to Berlin." In Paris, on the eve of sailing for home in August, Luce wrote to his editors: "Before leaving [for Poland] I had tentatively adopted the point of view that the Second Great War of the Twentieth Century was already being fought. On my return I am convinced that this is the only point of view from which to regard contemporary events in Europe and throughout the world."

While Luce was abroad the Time Inc. publications were making their preparations for coverage of hostilities. In the United States the news-gathering facilities had grown from a single out-of-town edito-

[2] Harper & Brothers, 1939.

rial office to six. Abroad, there were offices in Paris and London, established for *The March of Time* by Richard de Rochemont, brother of Louis de Rochemont and former head of French operations for Fox Movietone. Although the offices worked primarily for the movie at first, de Rochemont, an ex-reporter trained on the New York *Sun,* also supervised editorial coverage for the magazines.

Just before Luce returned to New York, he met his assistant Ralph Paine in Paris and suggested that Paine, who was on vacation, remain in Europe to coordinate editorial operations. With the crisis the Paris staff was augmented by the appointment of a *Life* correspondent, Sherry Mangan; in London, Paine and Walter Graebner of *Time* took on several full-time reporters. Working together, Wilson Hicks of *Life* and de Rochemont had discussed detailed plans for the assignment of photographic teams in Poland.

On his arrival in New York on August 14, Luce went directly from shipboard to *Time*'s offices to read the Foreign News copy, and virtually dictated to writer Robert Cantwell the lead article entitled "Weird War." It made the point that Europe was already at war—"a war of words and nerves, a war fought with weapons so strange and novel that they make machine guns look like good old crossbows— rolling barrages of slander timed to the minute; ceaseless bombard- ments of rumors, blankets of lies and alarms as blinding as poison gas . . . whispering campaigns, mystification, currency raids, posters, mass meetings, blackouts—weapons against which military men can only point their guns in vain. . . ."

The following Monday, August 21, the wire services carried the shattering news of the Nazi-Soviet pact. From Warsaw, where he was arranging for *March of Time* coverage, Richard de Rochemont cabled that the situation was grave but the Poles were calm; from London Paine cabled there was "resignation, even expectation of war." For the issue of *Time* that was to go to press the next week there had already been printed a million covers in color of Jack Benny. "Oh, God," wrote Luce, "how I hate the idea of Jack Benny this week." He ordered the covers scrapped and new ones printed with a color photo- graph of Winston Churchill, a far-sighted choice; Churchill was still outside the Government, a member of the House of Commons, shortly

408

to be called into the War Cabinet to his World War I post of First Lord of the Admiralty.

Until the Germans invaded Poland on September 1 (a Friday) there was much speculation about the possibility of a last-minute capitulation or another Munich. Even then some were not convinced that Britain and France might not still seek a diplomatic accommodation. The British and French declaration of war came two days later.

Luce, in the managing editor's chair at *Time,* scheduled a black-and-white picture of the Polish commander-in-chief, Smigly-Rydz, for *Time*'s cover. He now created a new department entitled World War. In the first article, under the No. 1 head "Polish Theatre" and the No. 2 head, "Grey Friday," *Time* reported: "World War II began last week at 5:20 a.m. (Polish time) Friday, September 1, when a German bombing plane dropped a projectile on Puck, fishing village and air base in the armpit of the Hel Peninsula."

Credit around the *Time* office for naming the conflict "World War II" was given to Frank Norris. As early as June he had been using this designation. "No one before," said Gottfried, "had thought of numbering wars like kings." In designating the conflict a *world* war *Time* was ahead of much of the American press. The New York *Times,* for many months, made no suggestion that it was other than a European war; *Newsweek,* in an editorial comment, pointedly reminded its readers that it had avoided "terming the conflict a 'second World War,' for it is still a European fight." *Time*'s phrase did not sit well with a lot of readers, particularly the isolationists. To readers who asked, "Why do you call it a world war when it isn't quite a European war?" the editors replied, "Because every nation is involved economically, most nations are already involved sympathetically and, with the British Empire at war, the sun cannot set on any continent or any sea on which there are no belligerents." One reader wrote indignantly: "You should be soundly condemned." The editors answered: "Nobody ever kept out of a riot by calling it an altercation."

The war did not go as anticipated. The French and the British were powerless to give direct military support to Poland. The French General Staff, mindful of the terrible blood-letting in World War I,

409

determined not to launch an offensive on the Western Front. The French and British air forces were held in leash and not permitted to attack the German cities for fear of retaliation on London and Paris, which were without adequate air defenses. All was quiet on the Western Front while Poland was crushed with a rapidity that stunned the world. Time Inc.'s advance plans for coverage went awry; two *Life* photographers assigned to Poland were not heard from for more than a week; the best coverage came from an agency man who was on the spot and managed to escape with pictures that were printed several weeks after the war in Poland was all but over. De Rochemont had been recalled from Warsaw to Paris as the fighting came nearer what was thought to be the center of operations. But there was nothing to photograph. Moreover, the French and British clamped down a heavy and frustrating censorship.

Under the issue date of September 25, before the final Polish collapse, *Life*'s editors rushed into print a special war issue which contained its first photographs—other than a few poor ones sent by radio—of the fighting. At press time there was only a forlorn hope that the Polish army could maintain any kind of resistance. The most significant item in the issue was an advance report of a *Fortune* poll reflecting the impact of the war on American opinion. Elmo Roper reported that 83 percent of all Americans wanted the Allies to win the war; one percent wanted Nazi Germany to win it; 16 percent had no opinion. There was considerable confusion, meanwhile, as to what the United States should do: 3 percent wanted to fight with the Allies at once; 13.5 percent wanted the U.S. to intervene militarily if the Allies should seem to be losing; 20 percent were for sending supplies to the Allies but not to Germany; a full 25 percent were against sending aid to either side.

A few days after the editors of *Life* had put their war issue to press, Luce met the Senior Group for dinner at the River Club. "There are occasions," he told them, "when to be in any sense responsible for the behavior of Time Inc. is not an entirely agreeable occupation [but] there has never been any month or week or day when I have been prouder of [our] work . . . than this month, this week and this day. This week's *Life* is a superlative answer to the journalistic challenge of war. . . . *Time,* entirely different from *Life* as it should be, establishes . . . its competency to deal with staggering events."

Then he turned abruptly to speak "not in any executive capacity but simply for myself . . . about this war." The American people were at a point of decision, he said, and if they decided to leave Europe alone "and devote all their will and energy to building here and building now the most successful society in the history of freedom, then they will have done their job in this generation. And if as an editor I can record *that,* I shall be prepared, if necessary, to record the downfall of the British Empire with polite regrets." He himself was far from reconciled to such a decision; he believed "this war is very different from the last war. . . . The chances of a happy outcome are none too great and . . . the nature of the peace to follow . . . will be actually decisive for something we call civilization."

Having come to this conclusion, Luce said he found himself embarrassed to be in agreement "with people with whom I had made it a point of pride never to agree on any conceivable topic," among whom was the New York *World Telegram* columnist Heywood Broun, whose radical views were anathema to him. He quoted the conclusion of a recent column in which Broun had written:

> This is the World War. And unless there is some feasible way for the United States to secede from the planet, we cannot declare ourselves wholly out. I am absolutely against our sending an expeditionary force abroad. I am completely for our lifting the arms embargo. And when the issue is drawn between democracy and the totalitarian state, I am not neutral. I am for my country and for my religion and civilization as I have known it. This is not a backroom brawl. This is Armageddon.

"That," Luce concluded, "is roughly what I believe."

They listened mostly in silence. Like most Americans, these members of Time Inc. were uncertain and unsure whether the U.S. had a role or mission in Europe or if this was indeed Armageddon. A year later Luce told his editors: "I thought the war about Danzig was awfully important—awfully important to the U.S. Many of [you] didn't think so. Very few of [you] thought it was what Heywood

411

Broun and I thought. You all agree with me now. . . ." And he blamed himself for not having pressed his point harder: "If we made any mistake last fall and winter, it was that we did not fight hard enough against isolationism, cynicism and lack of defense. We did make that mistake. It is my fault for not having insisted harder."

Actually, what followed in those months of 1939 and into 1940 was not Armageddon but anti-climax. With the collapse of the Polish resistance there ensued the "sitzkrieg," the phony war, the sullen silence on the Western Front. It strengthened isolationist sentiment in the U.S., heightened suspicions of the Allies' motives and expectations of a new accommodation with Hitler. Luce wrote to Paine in London:

> As to the war here—of course the great fact is the neurosis about Propaganda. This, of course, is all part of a piece with the progress of disbelief in this country for two decades—the distrust of all motives, etc. All this we have seen, and part of it, we must sadly admit, we have been. In these last few weeks, many of us have been trying to fight against the Propaganda of Disbelief internally as well as externally. With results good or bad, God knows.

A "stultifying ambiguity" (Luce's phrase) enshrouded the debate on America's role, even though the Soviet attack on Finland, on the last day of November, provoked a rash of anger in the U.S. But what constituted a "full share of direct responsibility" continued to be a matter for soul-searching among Time Inc. editors. T. S. Matthews, whom Luce had recently appointed *Time's* National Affairs editor, sent Luce a piece from the *New Republic*. It was, Matthews said, "a really respectable" warning against U.S. involvement. The evil abroad in the world, the *New Republic* argued, cannot "be crushed by exterminating those who seem for the moment to embody it." Luce responded in a staff memo that he thought there was no easy answer to what the U.S. should do about the war, but he felt that the American people "had best acknowledge that we are doomed to fight in one way or another, and then concentrate on choosing the best battlefield for the least bad kind of a fight for the best kind of a victory we can

412

imagine." The memo, Matthews answered, "somewhat perturbed" some of the writers who read it "as meaning that you are all for going to war. . . . Misunderstanding is always bad, but misunderstanding between you and *Time* writers is crucial."

"If I had my way," Luce replied, "the U.S. would most certainly not declare war on anybody tomorrow or under any circumstances which seem likely to me to arise in the near future." But, he added, he would have the American people decide what influence the U.S. was prepared to exercise and "proceed, enthusiastic, united, unambiguous and unafraid, to exert that influence. The people would make this decision with as little delay as possible and without 'waiting for more to happen.' " He felt his countrymen were still far too indifferent to events in Europe and Asia, distracted and lacking a sense of purpose and unaware of the need for action. Roosevelt had set the formula, "methods short of war"; what the methods could be was as yet untested.

Events in Europe had one immediate effect on the Time Inc. organization. In September 1939 Luce resigned as president and chief executive officer of the company, retaining the title of board chairman and editor-in-chief, thus confirming his determination henceforth to devote the greater part of his time to the editorial direction of the magazines. He recommended the election of Roy Larsen to the offices he had vacated, commenting to the directors that "by reason of the war abroad and the many problems in connection therewith . . . it would be advisable to have some rearrangement of responsibilities." Whenever absent on vacation or abroad, Luce had always designated Larsen as his deputy and second-in-command. Now, for the first time, he was delegating direct executive authority on the business side. It was overdue recognition of Larsen's position and contributions, which, over the years, had been second only to those of Luce himself.

413

The Loyal Opposition

AMERICANS DID NOT mourn the passing of the 1930s—"the worst decade of their whole lives," wrote Manfred Gottfried on New Year's Day 1940 in suggesting to *Time* writer Robert Cantwell a theme he might use in the lead article of that week's issue:

The '20s were a fool's paradise—the '30s were a fool's purgatory. In the '20s economics were unsteady, the social system was rotten and men lived carefree and gay and thoroughly enjoyed their lousy world. In the '30s we scuttled economics and re-formed the social system. We got rid of Warren Harding and Calvin Coolidge. We got figures and great liberals—men like George Norris finally got their due, and honest Harold Ickes instead of dishonest Albert Fall. We had La Guardia instead of Hylan. They put Whitney and Capone in jail. We spent millions on social service. We did all this and we starved and pinched and pitied ourselves. We had a thoroughly lousy time trusting neither ourselves nor the world. It was the decade of the great despair. An era of idiocy where we trusted neither our political nor our

414

economic future. There is not a man of 40, 50 or 60 alive today who would not admit that the '30s were the worst decade of their whole lives.

The point is, Bob, that I think this makes a very good background for a piece on Franklin D. Roosevelt, the great U.S. figure of the '30s. All that I try to give is a faint idea of what we might have in that first column.

It was an interesting thesis, coming from Gottfried, who generally took a cheerful, if sometimes anarchical, view of things. It was certainly not contrary to the views held by Luce in his bleakest moments. It was also an interesting sample of what *Time*'s editors expected of their writers; the points were all to be covered in an article of not more than 500 words, preferably less. The ensuing article closely followed Gottfried's outline and described Roosevelt as "the man of the decade." As Man of the Year 1939, *Time* named Hitler's temporary collaborator, Stalin.

In quite another mood and more characteristic of Luce was the Tenth Anniversary issue of *Fortune* (February 1940), dedicated to "The United States of America." On its white cover was a gold eagle by the artist Antonio Petruccelli, inspired by the Great Seal of the Republic.[1] The theme of the issue was affirmative; its thesis was that America's present problems arose not from the country's failures but from its magnificent achievements. The U.S., argued the editors, was "the greatest nation on earth" and

One can only *imagine* what will happen to the American when he wakes up to find that he has been moved to the very center of the world. A thousand years ago the city of Rome was the center of the Mediterranean world, and around Rome the *Pax Romana* radiated into the barbaric darkness of Africa and Eastern Asia. To prevent the modern forces of destruction from running a successful course, accomplishing the threatened extinction of

[1] In a subsequent issue the editors admitted to an aberration: ". . . The Department of State does all it can to discourage people from copying the Great Seal with too much fidelity. . . . But in our zeal not to transgress we did too good a job of infidelity: we faced the eagle's head to the right, toward the arrows of war, instead of to the left, toward the olive branch."

everything the human race has struggled for since prehistory, the citizen of the U.S., when he finds himself in the middle of the Atlantic World, may accept the thrust of destiny and turn to developing a *Pax Americana.*

Many American editors have played a direct role in politics: Greeley, Dana, Hearst and Pulitzer, to name four who sought to use the influence of their journals in partisan causes. Luce never conceived of his magazines as being political in the sense that their allegiance was engaged on behalf of any party; he had proclaimed them "mugwump." But in the Presidential year 1940 Luce and the Time Inc. magazines were for the first time directly engaged in the political arena.

The news on all fronts was kaleidoscopic, shifting every day from new alarms abroad to the interventionist argument at home, and suddenly revolving around the phenomenon of Wendell Willkie. His nomination as the Republican candidate for President was due in part to the prompting of Luce and *Fortune*'s managing editor, Russell Davenport.

Neither could be credited with "discovering" Willkie. He first emerged as a national figure when, as president of Commonwealth & Southern, a utilities holding company with properties in the area served by the TVA, he fought for the right of private utilities to survive against government-subsidized competition. Indiana-born, a Hoosier who had gone on to success in New York, he was the subject in 1937 of a two-part *Fortune* profile of himself and his company written by Jack Jessup. The article described Willkie as "quick-witted and resourceful" and "the Mississippi Yankee, the clever bumpkin, the homespun, rail-splitting, soil-eared, cracker-barrel simplifier of national issues in the style of Abe Martin and Will Rogers." But when a fellow editor suggested that Jessup might well hint that he was of Presidential timber, Jessup rejected the idea as too improbable. Early in 1939, however, Willkie was spotted as a Republican dark horse by Arthur Krock in the New York *Times* and, a few months later, by David Lawrence in his syndicated column. Willkie played it cool; his usual reply to such suggestions was "Wouldn't I be a sucker to say 'yes'?" The editors of *Time,* in a cover story on Willkie in July, had an answer of sorts; their cover caption: "Wouldn't he be a sucker to say 'yes'?"

Shortly after the *Time* story Russell Davenport met Willkie at one of *Fortune*'s Round Tables, and told his associates, "I have just met the man who ought to be the President of the United States." He invited Willkie and his wife to spend a weekend at his summer home, and, Jessup wrote, ". . . The two men talked continuously, locked in each other's ideas, the tennis court and the other guests ignored. Willkie was exactly the hero Davenport had been looking for: the American businessman at his candid, articulate best, large-minded, earthy, brave, wholly committed to a bigger and better America and to a bolder and more confident foreign policy." [2] Davenport introduced Willkie to Luce, who was impressed and wrote: "I think of Willkie as a force of Nature. I think of Davenport as a force of Spirit. When the two met . . . the chemical reaction produced an event of political history."

In the April 1940 issue of *Fortune* there appeared a Willkie-Davenport collaboration (signed by Willkie) called "We, the People." The article was deliberately intended to attract support for Willkie as a candidate, even though the idea still did not seem very realistic. In an accompanying editorial endorsing him, *Fortune* stressed his drawbacks: he would not play conventional politics; he was relatively little known to the great mass of Americans; he was identified with Wall Street and Utilities; and he had been a registered Democrat. But, said *Fortune:* "The principles he stands for are American principles. They are progressive, liberal, and expansive. One cannot dare to doubt that they will eventually prevail. But whether they will prevail in terms of political candidacy is a question that depends upon the political *sophistication* of the American people."

"We, the People" abounded in generalities and not a few clichés. It said little about foreign policy, mainly because Willkie and Davenport largely agreed with F.D.R. and, in any case, they believed the election would be fought and won on domestic issues. The article, while repudiating the embittered hard-shell Republican line and accepting

[2] Introduction to *The Dignity of Man,* by Russell Davenport (Harper & Brothers, 1955).

417

liberal reform, attacked the New Deal as doctrinaire and was a ringing manifesto on the theme of freedom for the individual against government encroachment. The *Reader's Digest* reprinted it.

The timing could scarcely have been better; the article dramatized and articulated a progressive point of view sadly lacking in the Republican Party at the time. It came when the race for the nomination appeared to have narrowed to two men, neither of whom had yet fully gained national stature. Thomas E. Dewey, the New York City racket-buster, was ahead in the opinion polls, but he was considered young for the Presidency and his attitudes on foreign policy were elusive and ambiguous; the runner-up was Robert A. Taft, a freshman Senator from Ohio, whose views on domestic issues made him a favorite among the Old Guard but who was an out-and-out isolationist. One Republican who was galvanized into action by *Fortune's* article was twenty-eight-year-old Oren Root, Jr., who, on his own initiative, mailed out declarations for Willkie under the heading "We, the People" to a selected list of Yale, Princeton and Harvard alumni. The response was so great that Root took leave from his law firm to campaign full-time for Willkie by organizing the Associated Willkie Clubs of America. In May, Davenport resigned as managing editor of *Fortune* to become the unacknowledged pre-convention campaign manager. Willkie earnestly asked Davenport not to make this financial sacrifice, but Davenport told Willkie (the New York *Sun* reported) that he was free and twenty-one and the best judge of what he should do.

Luce had taken little part in any of this. He would emerge later. By the end of April he was in Europe, more concerned about the war than about the next Republican candidate. Mrs. Luce had been in Europe since early March; from Paris she had signaled her husband by cable, "CURTAIN GOING UP."

The curtain had in fact just gone up with the Nazi attack on Norway and the occupation of Denmark on April 9, which had caught the press by surprise. *Time* was going to press when the news came and many of the staff had gone home. By daybreak Tuesday, Gottfried had written two and a half columns covering the events of the night in order to catch the beginning of the press run; later, the presses were stopped in order to add more details. Within one week of the invasion *Life* produced a sixteen-page illustrated report on the new hostilities, using artists' drawings and illustrated maps.

By the time *Life* appeared Luce was on his way. He had intended to fly on the newly established Pan American Clipper service to Lisbon, but when the flight was postponed he was the last passenger up the gangplank of the Italian liner *Rex*. With unsought leisure on shipboard, he found time to write "a letter of reflection" to his long-time friend and partner, Roy Larsen:

> . . . and the *one* reflection I have I want to make *before* becoming environmentally involved in Armageddon or whatever it is. The reflection is about your job and mine. . . . Our great job from now on is not to create power but to use it. . . . To see Time Inc. in perspective is to realize its tremendous potential power. As you know I get plenty bogged down in the *Time* & *Life* Bldg. by "responsibility"—but I have very little sense of the power at whose switchboard we stand. It's only when I get away that this picture really takes shape. I don't particularly like it. I don't think you do much—but there it is. . . .

The letter ended on a personal note:

> I have spoken of how Time Inc. looks in perspective. To no one else could I say with the same assurance of understanding: by God, what a job we've done. Only you & I know all the *unspectacular* headaches—& mistakes. . . .
>
> Selah! God knows what may happen before we meet. . . .

Luce landed in Italy, went on to Paris, where he joined Mrs. Luce and spent a week talking to French leaders. They convinced him of their need for airplanes and that the U.S. should ease restrictions on their shipment. He cabled home:

> What seems incredibly stupid to me here is that the United States should take most of airplane production for its own use instead of releasing to the Allies every single airplane which they are willing to pay cash for.

Grover replied: "On airplanes we think you have greatly over-simplified problem. But *Time* is getting facts. . . ."

Luce had crossed to Britain, which had at last awakened to its great danger; he and Mrs. Luce spent a weekend with Lady Astor at Cliveden and even in that Tory citadel, the center of support for Chamberlain and his policies, he found his hostess and her friends determined that the time had come to change leaders. "Chamberlain must go," Lady Astor told him. His talks in Britain more than ever convinced Luce that the U.S. should ship more planes, and he again cabled New York:

> In France I saw more than half of all people in most responsible positions and the three most impressively intelligent conversations focussed quite simply on airplanes. This view partially confirmed by important private conversation here last night. But, of course, I trust your judgment at world's greatest listening post.

On May 7 the Luces flew to Holland, a country in a state of crisis. German troop movements suggested an imminent invasion, and from The Hague, Luce cabled Larsen:

> A few great simplicities stand out. First, Allies probably will win a long war. Sheer weight of material and morale should triumph over German efficiency. Second, the kind of war Hitler may win and Allies may lose is an imminent blitzkrieg. All strategical, diplomatic, and, incidentally, editorial positions must be considered in light of Allied chances of withstanding blitzkrieg and changing it into long war. Answer to this question can be summed up in one word—airplanes.

The Luces had planned to stay in the Netherlands until May 10, but on the afternoon of the 9th U.S. Ambassador John Cudahy in Brussels telephoned that he had arranged an interview with the King of the Belgians and they must come to Brussels that night to be on time for it. By then everyone thought the war alert was over and that a détente with the Germans was possible. The Luces, arriving late that night in Brussels, found Cudahy waiting up for them. He told them he had been on the telephone day and night for three days but that the crisis was over, "Thank God." Exhausted, the Luces went to bed about midnight, and then, as Luce told the story, "At 5:30 in the morning the maid came in and shook me out of this deep sleep. I remember her saying, 'Les Allemands reviennent.' So I got up, wiping the sleep out of my eyes, and had to go and shake Clare and tell her, 'The show's begun.' We just had time to go to the window, which overlooked a lovely square, and in that beautiful early summer dawn I didn't quite have time to settle my chin in my hand, my elbow resting on the window, before 'boom,' the first bomb landed. This whole beautiful square was suddenly filled with dust from the bombs which had fallen on houses across the street. . . ." They learned later that Cudahy had been warned of the attack while they slept and had been the first to signal Washington in a telephone call to the President.

Luce immediately cabled Larsen:

> Your special correspondent, Clare Boothe, is sending Billings a brief eye-witness account of the first day of the Germans' grand attack on the western world. . . . If you were here today, remembering 1914, you would be sad but also you would be plenty mad. The word Boche is the only word used on the streets today to describe the enemy, and no other word would sound right. I deeply wish all priggish, pious pacifists could be here today. In the beautiful calm sunlight, rarely broken by siren's scream, there are only two realities—to suffer or to fight. I am sorry I failed to give you the steer sooner on the Lowlands, but even the highest quarters thought the imminent threat might pass.

The Luces insisted on staying in Brussels for a dinner planned for them that evening, in spite of Cudahy's warning to leave immediately. The next day they hired a car, picked up three members of the R.A.F. who had been interned during the period of Belgian neutrality, and headed for Paris. Luce recalled his first impression of the French now confronted with a real war: "The Ritz looked the same as ever, but the rich and prominent Frenchmen were terrified. I mean disgracefully scared and wanted to settle the war. They wanted to do any-

421

thing. This was my personal encounter with the fall of France."
He cabled his editors:

The remarks of Roosevelt and the Pope sound wonderful here.[3] I
am practically prepared to become both a Catholic and a third
termer unless the opposition offers some small degree of competition. Unless the others move awfully fast it looks like Davenport's man is the only Republican who can get this homecoming
vote. . . . The United States is indulging in complete and criminal folly unless it proceeds at once to build every single military
airplane it can possibly make in the next six months. Never mind
who uses them, never mind who pays, but for God's sake make
them. Similarly, all possible military equipment of every sort
should be ordered at once regardless of cost.

If *Life* and *Time* fail to sell this idea now, it probably won't
matter much what these estimable publications say in years to
come. The Germans have one weapon greater than all their army
and that is the blindness and stultification of those in every
country who are too fat to fight.

In a second cable to Gottfried he said:

You will never regret giving readers strong medicine whether
they like it or not.

Mrs. Luce's account of the air attack on Brussels appeared in the next
issue of *Life,* but neither *Time* nor *Life* made any direct reference to
the urgent need for planes. Nevertheless *Time* did hand out some
"strong medicine." In describing the attitude of the country, it said:
"Still clinging to its original determinations to stay out of World War
II, the U.S. was acquiring another—to prevent by other means a Nazi
victory." It reported the proposal of Argentina's Foreign Minister that
"The Americas should adopt an attitude of 'non-belligerency,' like
Italy's: wholly sympathetic with one belligerent. Toward this position,

---

[3] The Pope assured the invaded countries of his "paternal affection" and said
he was praying that "this stern trial may end with the restoration of full liberty
and independence. . . ." Roosevelt said that "I am glad that we Americans of
the free Americas are shocked, that we are angered by the tragic news. . . ."

unneutral but not yet belligerent, it appeared that the U.S. was moving, if not in theory, in fact."

Time's managing editor, without minimizing the seriousness of the news, did not have Luce's sense of disaster and urgency. As Hitler's army swept into France, Gottfried advised his editors: "We ought to offer as good a factual account of the Allies' defeat in France as we are able—bearing in mind that even when we go to press its real nature may well not be fully known. So let's not go out on a limb either way. The wave of fright and hysteria now sweeping this country may well look silly by next Thursday. Let's make a particular effort not to let any note of it creep into *Time*."

On leaving Paris, Luce said, half in earnest, half in jest, that he would come back soon and bring the American army with him. On arriving in the United States he broadcast two addresses, under the auspices of the Committee to Defend America by Aiding the Allies (organized by the Emporia *Gazette*'s William Allen White). The first of them was reprinted in the June 3 issue of *Life,* a special issue entitled "America and the World." Luce said:

> We may never fight side by side, comrades in arms of France and Britain. But we know now that, fundamentally, their struggle is our struggle. . . .
>
> If I know anything I know that . . . America, the America we love, has small chance of surviving the tyranny and chaos which everywhere advances unless those who love America make it plain that they are willing and ready to fight.

In an introductory box—the cover of this issue was the same picture of the Statue of Liberty which *Life* had used in the June special issue of the preceding year—the editors declared:

> Hour by hour, in these dark days, the events in Europe shape the course of America's destiny. In this issue *Life* looks first at the marvelous German Army in its swift, relentless invasion of the West. Then it proceeds to examine the beautiful, proud lands that lie in the conqueror's path—France and England, as they were and as they may never be again. How Americans live and

423

think for years to come will depend on whether the Nazi war machine wins its terrible goal or not.

The editors had to resort to rhetoric; they had little else to go on. All the *Time-Life* plans for war coverage, which, according to *Variety,* had been among the most elaborate of any journalistic enterprise, had been wrecked by the stupefying swiftness of the German victory on the Continent. Even during the phony war the Paris headquarters had found it almost impossible to function under strict French censorship. The New York office, for example, had received one cable: "Have complete, colorful Ministry of Information description of which the Ministry of Information will pass not one single word." In May *Life* sent twenty-four-year-old Andrew Heiskell to Paris to see what he could do about breaking through the censorship. Educated in Germany, Switzerland and France, he had a command of languages, particularly French, which it was thought would be useful. He had brief experience with the New York *Herald Tribune* before joining *Life* in 1937 as its Science and Medicine editor and later had been transferred to the business office as assistant to *Life*'s general manager, C. D. Jackson. Three weeks after Heiskell arrived the French government fled to Tours and the Time Inc. staff, numbering twenty-five with wives and children, set out after it. Leaving behind one reporter, Sherry Mangan, to cover the German entry (nothing he filed got by the German censor), the group divided into two cavalcades, one headed by Del Paine, the other by Richard de Rochemont.

During the stay at Tours, Heiskell and Carl Mydans decided to return to Paris to photograph the deserted city before the Germans arrived. It took them seven hours to cover a hundred miles because the roads were clogged with refugees. At dusk, rather than drive on in the blackout, they parked in a field to sleep the night. They were awakened by the local militia and seized as spies who had parachuted behind the lines. Their captors ignored their protests and at first dismissed their identification, saying, "All spies have perfect papers." Finally succeeding in establishing their true identity, they were released and tried again to reach Paris against the tide of refugees. Ten miles south of the city they learned that the Germans were already

424

within the gates, and they headed back to Tours. By the time they arrived the government had left for Bordeaux, and the Time Inc. cavalcade followed. With the French formal military resistance and the government collapsing, the Time Inc. group found they could do little in Bordeaux. They set out for Lisbon, where, free of censorship at last, they poured out their frustration: "We've seen," Heiskell wrote, "and at all times were aware that we were in, the greatest story of the century. . . . We did not tell the story because even before we knew it the government was falling apart. Though communications were still open, cables were super-censored. Mydans was sent on a mission to the front but of course it was the front where the battle was not taking place." An article by Paine on the fall of France appeared in the July 8 issue of *Life;* the essence of it was contained in three sentences: "France was not conquered in 43 days. France collapsed in 43 days. The French defeated themselves and they know it."

Luce returned from Europe convinced that "Davenport's man," Willkie, was the only possible candidate. *Time* reflected his views when in an early June report it said, "While Tom Dewey, with bravado, was fumbling with the topic of foreign affairs, while Taft appeared to be running toward the wrong goal posts, Willkie seized the ball, flatly declared: '. . . England and France constitute our first line of defense against Hitler. . . . It must therefore be to our advantage to help them in every way we can, short of declaring war.' It was what many a U.S. citizen believed." There remained however a large and influential segment of the party still to be won over if Willkie was to be nominated. Luce personally did all that he could on Willkie's behalf. Typical of his deep feeling on the crisis was this comment in a letter to a business friend in Dayton, Ohio: "I hope 90 percent of Republican business men will come to see that they had better play along with the principles of freedom with all its faults."

Some readers were confused by a *Time* cover story on Roosevelt in the June 10 issue which suggested to them that *Time* was "tossing in the sponge for the elections." The editors answered that "Far from suggesting that the U.S. in effect call off the 1940 election, *Time* is totally unimpressed with the cliché, 'Don't swap horses in midstream.' Citizens should ponder well who will make them the best President for 1941–45. For four years after election, the U.S.—unlike England, which got rid of Chamberlain—won't be able to swap horses no matter how bad the going gets." This again reflected Luce's opinion.

In the issue on sale as the GOP delegates converged on Philadelphia, *Time* quoted Raymond Clapper: " '. . . Republicans have just one issue in this campaign. It is whether Mr. Roosevelt or a Republican could do a faster, better job of obtaining the industrial production for defense. . . . On that point Mr. Willkie is the only man the Republicans have who stands a chance of making an effective case.' " Time Inc. fired another, psychological, gun as the Convention assembled. *Life,* which had been playing up Willkie strongly since May, stressed in its lead story the tremendous gains that the Willkie boom had made in the final weeks. Was a band wagon under way?

It was still a strange, emotional kind of boom. Willkie arrived in Philadelphia with the most makeshift kind of apparatus, centered in a small suite on the sixteenth floor of the Benjamin Franklin Hotel. The Benjamin Franklin's elevators were taxed beyond capacity; the Willkie rooms were jammed night and day with photographers, newspapermen and delegates curious about this amateur political upstart. They might get a brief audience with a hulking, rumpled-haired man who himself did not appear to be exactly sure of what was going on. They might catch a glimpse of poetic-looking Davenport, or of Luce. The candidate had to retreat into the bathroom in order to hold private conversations with his aides.

Time and *Life* covered the convention in force: the journalistic brigade included the whole National Affairs writing staff, researchers, the Washington bureau and men from bureaus around the country— augmented by fascinated onlookers from the New York office. In a tart memo after the convention, Gottfried complained of the influx: "*Time*'s working press did a more professional job than ever before but the home office turned our delegation into an amateurish spectacle."

Many years later Luce wrote an account of the nomination of Willkie in which he recalled his emotions and reactions to the nomination of the Republican candidate:

426

Except for one thing, Dewey would probably have been nominated—or perhaps Taft. That one thing was Adolf Hitler. [The convention met at] one of the most stupefying moments in the long history of Western Civilization. It was the horror of this moment which (in his eyes, not mine) justified Franklin Delano Roosevelt in seeking a third term—thereby shattering an honorable precedent established by George Washington. In this situation the delegates and guests in Philadelphia, and all the letter-sending station-wagoners,[4] came to feel, as if by a sort of prairie fire osmosis, that the man to nominate was Willkie. Why? Essentially because Willkie looked like the biggest and strongest man around. He had not come there with any clear position on foreign policy; he had made his way to Philadelphia with a powerful brief against the New Deal domestic policy. But, partly because he was an insatiable reader and so articulate about what he read, Willkie seemed to have a better grasp of the stupefying current events. Dewey, the racket buster, looked much too young for the job, and Taft, besides being so little known, was in any case not associated with a mastery of world affairs. . . .

Willkie was third on the first ballot—only 105 votes to 360 for Dewey and 189 for Taft. He was nominated on the sixth ballot. *Time* and *Life* recorded the event jubilantly. "For the first time since Teddy Roosevelt, the Republicans had a man they could yell for and mean it," wrote *Time*. *Life* hailed the victory as one of "progressive leadership over the stand-pattism of the Old Guard." Some readers took exception to the tone of this reporting. *Life* printed without comment a letter which said: "You certainly have dropped even the pretense of being a factual magazine. . . ." One *Time* reader suggested that the magazine "may have a lot more to do with this astronomical phenomenon than appears on the surface." To this the editors replied: "[The Willkie nomination] came about mainly through the normal operation of a free and alert press. . . . In particular it must be credited to that serious section of the press which over many months

---

[4] The Willkie supporters were afterward referred to as "the station-wagon set."

saw in Willkie a man with qualifications for making himself felt in a decisive period of U.S. history. With that press, *Time* gladly identifies itself."

When W. H. Kittrell, Jr., a Texas politico, wrote Luce to congratulate him on being "the man I believe to be most responsible" for the nomination, Luce was both flattered and pleased, but he argued that the magazines had done no more than present the case and that "If this coincides with a popular avalanche, such as swept Willkie in over the heads of a Maginot Line of politicians, certainly we can accept very little blame or credit." Years later he was more candid; in writing of the Willkie nomination he said: "I think I was influential, in a small degree, in the nomination of Wendell Willkie and of Dwight Eisenhower. . . . After Willkie got nominated, there were scores of columnists and others who thought they had played a notable part in his rise to power. It did Willkie no harm to have all sorts of articulate people thinking of him as their personal discovery. But whatever part other people played in the Willkie story, the man who made Willkie, next only to Willkie himself, was Davenport."

Luce believed that Willkie's nomination would help the nation prepare for war. He found himself impatient with the political equivocations—by both Willkie and the President—that placed emphasis on the U.S. keeping out of war rather than girding for conflict. When his friend Joseph Kennedy, the U.S. Ambassador to Great Britain, asked Luce to write an introduction to a book [5] which his son John had written as a Harvard senior, Luce used the occasion to needle Roosevelt and Willkie:

If John Kennedy is characteristic of the younger generation— and I believe he is—many of us would be happy to have the destinies of this Republic handed over to his generation at once. . . .

America will never be ready for any war . . . until she makes up her mind that there is going to be a war. And equally, as soon

[5] John F. Kennedy: *Why England Slept* (Wilfred Funk, 1940).

as she makes up her mind there is going to be a war, then there is no war she will have to fight which she cannot win. . . .

Mr. Roosevelt . . . really can't believe we are ever going to fight. Otherwise how can he so glibly guarantee that we will not need to sacrifice one tiniest bit of our "social gains." Or is he just playing politics? Surely Mr. Roosevelt wouldn't be just playing politics if he really thought we might be in for a war.

Nor is the spectacle of Mr. Wendell Willkie entirely encouraging. . . . All his genius of personality and industrial management will be bitter ashes in our mouths if Mr. Willkie goes forth to prepare for a war which he leads us to believe isn't really ever going to happen. . . .

Shortly after writing this, in mid-July, Luce sent a confidential memo to his senior executives stating "the position of Time Inc. with regard to the world crisis and America's part in it." He summed up their "journalistic duty" under five headings:

1. To continue to sound the Danger signal in all its aspects— Danger to the Sovereign U.S.A., Danger to our Constitutional Democracy.
2. To cultivate the Martial Spirit—without which we shall by no possible shadow of chance overcome the Danger.
3. To show that America is worth fighting for—since, incredible though it may seem, there appear to be those who doubt it.
4. To be hawk-eyed in our observation of Preparedness and to be savage and ferocious in our criticism of all delay and bungling.
5. Among as many readers as possible, to develop a sense of Foreign Policy.

Luce said that in foreign policy the U.S. should (1) try to avoid a full state of war with Germany but take all reasonable risks to keep Germany from subduing Great Britain, (2) redefine the Monroe Doctrine—i.e., insist that Mexico, the whole of Central America and all countries bordering on the Caribbean be friendly to the U.S. —and (3) give maximum support to China as long as China kept on

429

fighting, and be willing to negotiate a settlement in the Pacific whenever it was to the mutual advantage of the U.S. and China.

Billings of *Life* said he was for the memo 100 percent and that *"Life* is a natural for raising the Danger Signal, cultivating the Martial Spirit, for showing that America and its way of life are worth fighting for. We're all for that and are already on the way." To the distress of some readers, *Life* had already been sounding "the danger signal" all too loudly; in a sequence of drawings the magazine had demonstrated how the U.S. might be invaded. The sketches, the editors said, reflected *"Life's* long-held concern that the U.S. defenses were not all that they should be." Readers were shown the destruction of the U.S. fleet off Brazil, a Fascist army marching up Market Street in Wilmington, Delaware, and other disasters culminating in the spectacle of U.S. envoys suing for peace in Philadelphia's Independence Hall before a Fascist tribunal.

This somewhat far-fetched presentation of an extremely hypothetical situation drew an unfavorable reaction from readers who wrote in to accuse *Life,* among other things, of warmongering and sensationalism. Within the shop Pierrie Prentice protested to Luce that "praiseworthy concern over rearmament seems to have dimmed our perspective."

Life had also been devoting more and more space to military and patriotic subjects. Its special issues on America were intended to raise U.S. pride. In a June issue it had carried eight pages of pictures on the National Guard ("If You Want to Help U.S. Defense, This Is One Way"). The lead article in the issue on sale over the Fourth of July was entitled: "American Independence: Revolutionary Battlefields Mark Our Fight for Freedom." ("More than a century and a half ago America had to fight and bleed and nearly die to win its heritage of freedom and now in a darkening world it may soon have it all to do over again.") "There was a considerable deficiency of—to use an old-fashioned word—patriotism in this country," Luce later observed. "Never were the founding fathers in such low repute. What I tried to do—and *Life* was the place to do it—was to build up more feeling for the country—patriotism—to get Americans to have a stronger feeling about what their country stood for."

430

Gottfried on *Time* had reservations about Luce's dictum: "With the idea involved I agree 100 percent but in places I am put off a bit by the approach. 'Sounding the danger signal' does not appeal to me. It seems too much like ringing a bell. But I'm all for watching for danger like a hawk and describing it in cold blood. Similarly, 'the martial spirit' gives me a jolt—it sounds bellicose. I'm all for the U.S. being tougher than hell, knowing what it wants and being willing to fight for it anywhere, any time. But the toughest guys aren't bellicose. . . . While I want to look foreign policy in the eye, I don't want to commit myself to any one foreign policy. It's too much like loading the editorial dice." The attitude of *Time* was set forth in an editorial comment on a reader's letter in July 1940:

. . . *Time* does not favor U.S. entrance into the war. The only ax it has to grind is that U.S. citizens shall have the facts, welcome or unwelcome, to form intelligent opinions on what the U.S. must do to look after its own interests. Also to be plain, there are some circumstances in which the defense of the primary interests of the U.S. may require going to war. *Time* believes it as dangerous to refuse to consider that fact as to engage in warmongering.

Considerably less restraint was evidenced in *Time*'s promotion. Early in 1940 the company had launched its largest national advertising campaign, a series of advertisements highlighting incidents in the history of U.S. journalism and reminding readers that the Weekly Newsmagazine was also part of the Fourth Estate. Luce took a keen interest in these advertisements and they reflected the attitudes of his policy memorandum. Under the heading "Who Rides After Paul Revere?" a July advertisement began:

Wake up! Wake up! The Germans are marching!—Wake up! Wake up! The brownshirts are coming! . . .
Since the tenth of May, every flying bundle of newspapers that thumps against a way-station platform has been the thunderous knock of the rider sent out by the lantern signal in the Old North

431

Church. With editorial and news dispatch, cartoon, column, and special article, the far-sighted among America's newspapers have roused the town and the countryside. . . .

Where and how the present-day menace to freedom will strike, no man knows, or whether it will strike by direct invasion at all. We know that attack is possible—and that is enough. . . .

Fortune's publisher, Eric Hodgins, went along with Luce's call to a "Martial Spirit"; he also felt that more effort should be made to combat America's current air of defeatism. Luce concurred; he thought that *Fortune*'s "No. 1 task was to straighten out U.S. businessmen (and 'Liberals') on the great matter of Appeasement." Actually, *Fortune*'s greatest contribution during this period was to deal with problems of industrial mobilization and national defense.

The mood of the country was changing; although the overwhelming majority of Americans were against the country becoming directly involved in the war, a majority, according to the polls, were now for rearmament and for aiding the Allies short of war. Nevertheless there were still strong and vociferous isolationists, including Charles A. Lindbergh, who continued to muster significant support in opposing the Administration's course. They were heard from very loudly when *The March of Time*'s first full-length feature, *The Ramparts We Watch,* was presented.

It had been more than a year in preparation, Larsen joining Louis de Rochemont in its production; the original estimated cost of $150,000 had been more than twice exceeded and the picture was finally brought in at $400,000. A potpourri of patriotism and nostalgia, it attempted to re-enact the experiences of the average small-town American in 1914–18 and relate this response to the needs of the present crisis. The historical scenes, photographed in New London, Connecticut, where a volunteer cast of some 1,400 dressed up in clothes and uniforms of the period to stage Liberty Bond drives, patriotic rallies and parades, were perhaps the best. It was when it tried to project the lessons of World War I forward that the picture ran into trouble.

432

The film had its première in Washington, D.C., on July 23, 1940; it was shown later at the White House to President Roosevelt, who made no public comment. General John J. Pershing, World War I commander, praised it as "very moving. . . . We are faced with the same problems of preparedness today and this picture will help us make up our mind." Isolationists denounced it; George Sokolsky, the columnist, wrote after a preview, "I feel that [it] should not only be banned but that a Congressional committee ought to investigate the motives for its production." [6]

Dr. Gallup, commissioned to survey audience reaction, reported that viewers were "confused in their understanding of what the picture is about. . . . People who recognize it as the title of a recent best-seller assume that [it] is an inventory of national defense. . . . [Others] get a variety of vague ideas from association with the Star-Spangled Banner. . . . Some persons thought the message was that we should go into the war, others . . . that we should stay out." He recommended that, even at the cost of being accused of propagandizing, the picture should be revised to make its point of view more obvious. Larsen and de Rochemont had come to this conclusion, and were already at work on a new ending provided by the Nazis themselves.

For propaganda purposes the Nazis had made *Baptism of Fire,* a picture of the Polish blitzkrieg. Designed to intimidate neutrals, it demonstrated vividly and ominously the power of the German war machine. De Rochemont first tried to buy the film from the German distributor, U.F.A., but the Germans refused to sell unless they were allowed a veto over its usage.

Learning that the British had intercepted a copy which the Germans had shipped for use in South America, de Rochemont asked John Grierson, Canada's Film Commissioner, to get him a print, which he did. The Germans protested its use to "present propaganda . . . that we Germans are a threat to the United States." But this, of course, was exactly the point which de Rochemont was trying to make. He tacked *Baptism* onto the end of *Ramparts.* It made very

[6] De Rochemont was later summoned to testify before a predominantly isolationist Senate committee investigating the motion-picture industry.

explicitly the point that the Nazis were a threat to the civilized world and it suggested by inference that the U.S. had better do something about it. The ending added enormously to the dramatic impact, but it failed to make *Ramparts* a successful motion picture.

In the summer there was grave U.S. concern about the fate of Britain, and the disposition of the British fleet if Britain were forced to capitulate. The rate of British losses at sea, particularly of destroyers which were essential for defense against the U-boats, jeopardized British command of even the English Channel. There was one source of quick replacement—the fleet of over-age destroyers of World War I model which the U.S. Navy had returned to service. The British had been asking for these destroyers since May, but formidable obstacles, legal, emotional and political, stood in the way of their transfer. Roosevelt feared that the United States public was not yet ready to go so far in aid to Britain.

The William Allen White Committee to Defend America by Aiding the Allies had branches all over the country and it began to mount a campaign for the transfer of the destroyers. Working along parallel lines was a small body of influential citizens who joined forces because they wanted to go further and faster in helping Britain than did the White committee. It is a measure of Luce's rising influence and position in the community that these men asked him to join them in what became known as the Century Group.[7] Out of the Group came the proposal to trade destroyers for certain British-owned bases in the Western Hemisphere.

The Time Inc. publications used what influence they had to sway public opinion on behalf of the destroyer transfer by widely publicizing the debate. At the request of the Century Group, Luce was among those who tried to intercede with the Administration. With his former pastor and friend Dr. Henry Sloane Coffin he called on

---

[7] They were known as the Century Group because they met in the clubhouse of the Century Association in New York. The organizer was Francis P. Miller of the Council on Foreign Relations. Besides Luce and Miller, the others present at the first meeting were Herbert Agar, William L. Clayton, Henry Sloane Coffin, Lewis W. Douglas, Henry W. Hobson, Ernest M. Hopkins, Whitney Shepardson, William H. Standley, Henry P. Van Dusen.

434

Secretary of State Hull, but the meeting was not successful; Luce wrote his fellow Group member Lewis W. Douglas: "The noble old soldier has been working so long in an atmosphere of frustration and defeat that he has perhaps lost the necessary faith in the possible victory of his cause."

On the occasion of the White House showing of *The Ramparts We Watch,* the Luces, Larsens and de Rochemonts were invited to dinner at the White House as guests of the President. Afterward Luce made a note to himself: "After dinner Prex and I have a private talk in the Oval room. My big question is, has he or has he not made up his mind about sending destroyers to Great Britain. I understand him to say definitely that 'it's out,' but then later he says he is taking Chairman Walsh [David Walsh, isolationist head of the Senate Naval Affairs Committee] and Vinson [Carl Vinson, Chairman of the House Naval Affairs Committee] on the yacht this weekend and maybe he can bring them around to the idea. He makes much of the analogy of England and France after Dunkirk—Churchill having to decide on the basis of 'probabilities' whether or not to send the R.A.F. in full force to help the French Army and deciding 'No.' I do not think the analogy is good but do not argue with him."

To keep the destroyer trade out of politics, Willkie was sounded out and gave his word that he would not make it an issue. He apparently assumed, as did Luce, that it would be submitted to Congress for approval. When Roosevelt instead announced in September that the deal [8] had been made by executive agreement, Willkie felt impelled to denounce the President's method as "dictatorial" and "arbitrary." It rankled as well with Luce, who wrote Willkie, "For what little it's worth, I can give you my personal opinion, as a citizen, in a nutshell. I want nothing more done for Britain on the personal and exclusive authority of Franklin D. Roosevelt." [9] *Life* was more

[8] While the destroyer debate was on and the deal hung in the balance, a *Fortune* poll found that 70.2 percent of the people favored aiding Britain to the extent of selling her naval vessels. The figures were given to Roosevelt; he wrote to Elmo Roper, thanking him for his help. The President added that, of course, he had not made his decision on the basis of the figures.

[9] Luce resigned from the Century Group in November. The special circumstances which had led to his participation, he wrote, no longer existed; the

tolerant: ". . . Political shock at the method . . . was overwhelmed by popular approval."

By the time the Democratic Convention met, it was a foregone conclusion that Roosevelt would be renominated for an unprecedented third term. *Time* reported the event with a certain detachment, observing that "Few who heard his acceptance speech did not believe that before doing so he had convinced himself that his decision was for the best interests of the nation." *Life* was palpably outraged. It began its picture story of the convention with a photograph of Thomas D. Garry, Chicago's Superintendent of Sewers, who had stampeded the convention by commandeering the public-address system and bawling out, "We want Roosevelt!"—"The Voice of the Sewers," as the press described it. In an accompanying text block *Life* said, ". . . No amount of rationalizing could disguise or demolish the solid fact that at Chicago last week, in a time of world democratic crisis, the greatest democracy treated the world to one of the shoddiest and most hypocritical spectacles in its history."

As for Willkie, he returned to his native Indiana and set up his campaign headquarters in Rushville (pop. 6,000)—a maneuver intended to remind the electors that at heart and in origin he was just a simple small-town boy. Rocking on his front porch, the candidate joshed newspapermen, but said little about the issues. With London being bombed and the Battle of Britain reaching a high pitch of fury, the corny, informal spectacle of Wendell Willkie revolted Luce and he made this clear in a couple of memoranda to his friend Russell Davenport. Hoping that Willkie would quit "this cracker-barrel dawdling," Luce observed that "running for President may be fun for Mr. Willkie but it's a God damn serious thing for 130,000,000 Americans and maybe for the world. . . . Willkie's campaign is to be a Crusade. But a crusade for what? The campaign must be a Crusade for Free Men in a Free Land. . . ."

---

country was now fully alert to the danger overseas and aid to Britain was assured, and "while of course it is eminently proper for a group of citizens like yours to confer and collaborate, I think that as an editor I should not be an active member of a policy-promoting group outside of my own organization."

But as Willkie's campaign developed, it had few aspects of a crusade. In its September 9 issue *Time* let Willkie have it:

GOPoliticians last week were sure that the thing they had dreaded all along had come to pass: the holy-rolling crusade of Wendell Willkie had gone sour.

The first rumor to get around was that Wendell Willkie was just a super-hawker who had sold the Republican Convention a bill of goods. Last week, spreading rapidly through professional ranks was the belief that maybe Willkie was only a fatter, louder Alf Landon. . . .

He still drew curious crowds. . . . As one sad Old Guardsman pontificated to another: dead whales on flat cars also attract crowds. . . .

Yet Willkie was obviously the hardest-hitting extemporaneous, day-by-day debater of public issues whom Republicans have had for a candidate since Roosevelt I. . . .

The story created a minor sensation. The New York *Post* and the Philadelphia *Record* headlined it. The *Post* captioned its story: "Says *Time,* Ex-Backer: Willkie Just a Fat Alf." The Washington staff of *Time* was jubilant; they had fretted under taunts from their fellow newsmen that *Time* was becoming a mere house organ for Willkie. Felix Belair, who had left the New York *Times* to become bureau chief for *Time*'s staff, wrote New York: "It did more to clinch Time Inc.'s reputation as an objective publishing house than any other recent development. . . . The Republicans freely conceded that the story was entirely true."

Luce was deeply embarrassed, fearful that the magazine had dealt a severe blow to the candidate. He challenged the papers with almost identical letters. To George Backer, publisher of the *Post,* he wrote:

Your story . . . is misleading in several respects. First, your headline (on your front page) said that *Time* said that Willkie is "just a fat Alf." *Time* said no such thing. On the contrary, *Time* did say that Willkie is "obviously the hardest-hitting extemporaneous, day-by-day debater of public issues whom Republicans

437

have had for a candidate since Roosevelt I." That is praise indeed—and it is praise which nobody can deny. Second, you state that *Time* was a Willkie backer. . . . *Time* was never and is not now a Willkie "backer.". . . *Time* has found much to commend in Mr. Willkie—so also, over a period of seventeen years, it has found much to commend in Franklin Roosevelt. *Time* thinks just as highly of Wendell Willkie today as it ever did —which is, admittedly, pretty high. . . . He has done more than any man in America to lead this country toward national unity in the vital problems of national defense and foreign affairs. . . .

He wrote the letter, coincidentally, just a few days after the President announced the release of the fifty destroyers to Britain. In his letter Luce argued that Britain owed these destroyers to Willkie more than to any other man, because "Without Willkie's forthright pronouncements on aid to Great Britain in his acceptance speech, no amount of Pershings or Bullitts would have got those destroyers to Britain. . . . When the readers of the New York *Post* go to the polls in November —their votes may go to Roosevelt but some of them should cast at least a little silent vote of thanks to Wendell Willkie. Or so it seems to me." The papers published Luce's letters, although J. David Stern's Philadelphia *Record* accompanied it with an editorial taking issue with Luce on Willkie's part in the destroyer deal. Thanking Stern for his courtesy, Luce wrote, "I do not agree at all with the rebuttal in your editorial but I liked the headline." It read: "While There's *Time* There's Hope."

From the "fat Alf" story onward the campaign was an ordeal for Luce. He felt thwarted by the behavior of the candidate, he groaned over Willkie's blunders and occasional malapropisms, and he was frustrated by the attitude of *Time*. Luce would not give his National Affairs editor, Matthews, any out-and-out orders, and he could not persuade him to see the campaign as Luce saw it—the most important one in history. Matthews thought of himself as the keeper of *Time*'s conscience, defender of fair and detached reporting. Gottfried, who as managing editor had to stand between Luce and Matthews, described Matthews as having "a knack of turning all differences of opinion into issues of conscience. He also found it easy to have a low opinion of other people's motives." Personally, Matthews said, he was for Willkie.

When the Republican candidate left Rushville and began his long train ride across the country, *Time* reported his egregious slips (blurting out "to hell with Chicago" in Chicago; accusing Roosevelt of having urged the Axis leaders "to sell Czechoslovakia down the river" when he had only meant to say that F.D.R. had urged a settlement at Munich). The magazine quoted from a Willkie speech, generally conceded to be the best he had yet made, with no comment except that he had committed another blunder: he had not saved his voice. He spoke "in a voice that scratched, twice almost cracked." On reading this, Luce wrote a furious memo:

We were doing a pretty good job this year—with the War, with National Defense, with "awakening America," with the Conventions, with the Journalism Campaign. . . . A good part of all this, it seems to me, we have thrown away in the last few weeks. And so I feel like crawling into a hole. . . . Now the basis of what I have to say is the proposition that this is an extremely important election. Perhaps some of you don't think it is particularly important. And maybe it isn't. Certainly neither *Time* nor *Life* has given any indication, by its accent or by anything else, that it regards this election as anything but a rather minor circus episode in history. It happens that *Time* is in part a political paper—no political paper could have taken politics less seriously than *Time* has in the last two months. . . . A year and a half ago, Tom [Matthews] and some others came to me asking essentially one question—is *Time* important? Is the news, as *Time* sees it, important? They wanted me to say Yes and I think I satisfactorily said Yes.

So here we come to a Presidential Campaign which I think is vitally important. And *Time* evidently doesn't think so. Anyone who does not think this campaign is important should have nothing to do with the reporting or editing of this campaign— and should report to me accordingly now. I can work with a man

439

who thinks it's important that Roosevelt be elected. I can work with a man who thinks it's important that Willkie be elected. I cannot work with a man who thinks the campaign is not important. . . .

The only question now is whether or not you will accept my leadership in the next few weeks. After this blow-up—the fundamental cause of which is no doubt my own ineptitude—I am willing to trust you. Will you trust me?

Luce then went on to list some ten issues in the campaign ("besides Mr. Willkie's throat") which he felt *Time* should discuss; among these were the third term, the Willkie charge that Roosevelt had been an appeaser, and the handling of national defense. Luce then concluded:

Is Freedom a cause? Is the leadership of the cause of Freedom an issue in the campaign? Is Roosevelt the supremely necessary champion of Freedom? Or doesn't any of it matter?

Matthews sent excerpts from the memorandum to his writers without comment. *Time* began to deal with the issues, but the tenor of its reporting did not change. In its October 7 issue *Time* referred to the Willkie train, then moving east, as a "huge, disorganized cavalcade," and remarked "If [the correspondents] were halfway through one of the greatest political stories in the long record of the U.S., they did not want to hear about it, would have cast a startled eye at any one of their number who had been sophomoric enough to say so." Two weeks later in a Willkie cover story *Time* defined the chief issue of the election as Luce saw it ("For the first time in U.S. history, U.S. citizens were being asked to judge between the State's rights and the citizen's"), but,

The candidates themselves showed the gulf between them most clearly one night last week. In what some men thought his greatest speech, Franklin Roosevelt orated mellowly of hemisphere defense and freedom of the seas, while Wendell Willkie bellowed huskily about plant amortization as a bottleneck in the defense program. Not many . . . U.S. voters can define the word amortization, but even in far-off South America listeners could appreciate the President's vibrant *"Viva la Democracia! . . ."*

The backlash in such stories was what irritated Luce. Matters reached a point where Gottfried suggested that Luce personally take over the editing of the National Affairs section—or stay away and let Matthews do it. "An hour or so after the note was delivered," said Gottfried, "Grover was in my office saying, 'And now you too.' Evidently Harry had been very much tried by Matthews' attitude and my request had hurt him still further." Luce announced that he would exile himself from the editorial floor, but he continued to fulminate from a distance.

Time's readers reacted in a way that must have pleased Matthews. A report on the letters received from them in October noted, "Much of the pro-Willkie sentiment was provoked by what at least 30 readers described as *Time*'s 'smear-Willkie campaign.' And one of our major jobs now is to save the subscriptions of some 60 disappointed Willkie supporters who refuse to support our 'pro-Roosevelt' publication. Criticism from the pro-Roosevelt faction was milder . . . and brought in only 20 cancellation threats."

Although Luce's memo on the campaign coverage had criticized *Life* along with *Time,* he had little reason to complain about the picture magazine. Billings saw the election much as Luce did—or at least the magazine more closely reflected Luce's thinking. Luce was delighted with the last issue of September, which carried Willkie's picture on the cover and said that the coming election was "a great and important referendum the like of which the U.S. had not experienced in its 164 years." He wrote Davenport on the Willkie train that it was "lively and very effective." In fact, the *Life* readers were complaining; according to the letters report covering issues from July 8 through September 30, of 430 letters received about the magazine's coverage of the campaign, 40.4 percent thought *Life* partisan to Willkie, only 1.1 percent saw *Life* as pro-Roosevelt.

In October *Life* reacted to the charges by publishing several pro-Roosevelt articles; in one issue "The Case Against Willkie" by Bruce Bliven, editor of the *New Republic,* offset "The Case Against Roosevelt" by Robert Moses; and in another issue *Life* published "Roosevelt Preferred" by Fiorello La Guardia, Mayor of New York, which Luce personally thought was the most effective piece of propaganda in the entire campaign. The shift in emphasis was noted and resented by some of the more rabid Willkie supporters as *Life's* general manager reminded Luce a year or so afterward: "Many of the Willkie Republicans don't like us because we showed signs of sanity toward the close of the 1940 campaign—which means we withdrew our all-out 'right or wrong' support."

The election figured in only one issue of *Fortune* (October), which printed a pro-Willkie article signed by Russell Davenport and, at the staff's insistence, a counter-balancing article for F.D.R. signed by John Chamberlain. Davenport had at first protested violently against this arrangement, but finally agreed; in the course of the argument Patricia Divver, *Fortune's* head of research, ticked off her former colleague with a wire that may have helped him to see reason: "Who do you think you are—the Editor of *Fortune?*"

Luce kept a continual stream of suggestions, drafts of speeches and wires flowing to the Willkie campaign train. A Willkie speech in San Francisco appears to have been based largely on a draft prepared by Luce. Stillman also, in the early part of the campaign, prepared some memos and drafts intended to help the candidate clarify his views on industrial mobilization. In September, John Martin, who said that he had never even voted in a Presidential election up to that time, devoted his month's vacation to working for Willkie. Willkie's campaign had reached a highly effective stage by October, but his headquarters was still chaotic. A major source of the turbulence was Davenport, who compounded confusion by his insistence on rewriting all the Willkie speeches, often in a style that was ill-suited to Willkie's personality. At one point Luce tried to persuade Davenport to allow other people to draft some of the speeches, writing that he had "no choice but to risk upsetting you . . . because so many people say that they won't or can't tell you 'the truth.'" But Davenport would not listen to Luce either.

In its October 21 issue *Life,* which still had no editorial page, carried a two-page signed article by Luce. In it he advanced his by-now familiar—at least to his editors—thesis that the election was "probably the most important election ever held anywhere in the world under free and unrestricted suffrage"; but he did not come out for either Willkie or Roosevelt. While the response to the Luce article was largely favorable, many readers felt that Luce should have declared himself. To one, Luce replied in a personal letter: "The problem of whether or not to urge the adoption of a certain point of view with respect to public issues or political candidates has been a difficult one for us to decide. . . . We thought it important and for the best interests of our readers that our magazines maintain an impartial attitude. . . ."

In the week preceding the election, *Fortune* made one last Survey, released to the newspapers on November 4, which was extraordinarily accurate. The poll showed that Roosevelt had the support of 55.2 percent of the popular vote. (He actually received 54.6 percent.) The New York *Times* said: ". . . The Editors of *Fortune* can take bows with the best grace of all the predictors. . . ."

Some time after the election Del Paine, who was temporarily in Washington, reported to Luce that he had been informed by a number of New Dealers that no resentment was harbored against Luce and his associates for their parts in the campaign. But there is evidence that Roosevelt and his personal staff were irritated. In its Election Extra *Time* carried a description of the scene at Hyde Park on election night. It was based on the reporting of Felix Belair, who was outside the house and interviewed a number of people who had been with the President as the returns came in.

On reading *Time*'s account, Roosevelt dictated an intemperate letter to Luce ticking off the errors: ". . . There was no row of freshly pointed pencils anywhere on the table or elsewhere. . . . At no time during the evening was his coat off. . . . The tie did not hang low and the collar of the soft shirt was never unbuttoned," etc. On second thought, the President decided not to send his letter; instead, he gave it to his staff with instructions to "(a) Prepare a revised letter from me to Luce" or "(b) You send a letter to Luce. There are some things in life that one should not let certain people get away with."

443

Although Lowell Mellett, an executive assistant to the President, had not been at Hyde Park that night, he chose to sign a letter to Luce: "The description of the scene election night at Hyde Park interested me particularly since I recognized that it was a false picture," he wrote pompously. "No need to tell you how I recognized its falsity, since as you may know I have spent more than thirty years reporting and editing the news. I was offended by this story, as a newspaper man with a fetish for accuracy. . . ." He then recited *Time*'s errors almost word for word as Roosevelt had described them, explaining that he had checked his "instinctive conclusion that the picture of events . . . was one tortured out of all semblance to what probably happened" with a fellow staff member who was "on the scene of the events so colorfully described by *Time*."

It was a curious episode. The story reflected no discredit on the President; the errors were those of minor detail and Belair had done his best to check the facts. Luce, who thought the protest petty and out of all proportion to the alleged offense, contented himself by defending Belair as having done the best job possible under the circumstances. He added that it was obvious Mellett did not like *Time*. He never learned that his critic was in truth the President himself.

In reflecting on the Willkie election many years later, Luce wrote: "Willkie's main trouble was that he didn't know quite what to do about the war issue. Roosevelt had no such trouble. Roosevelt promised the American people—'again and again and again'—to use his own words—that they would never be engaged in 'foreign wars.' He lied and he knew he was lying—he as much as admitted that to me in private conversation. . . .

"The campaign drew to a close, and still the question, on and off the Willkie train, was what should Willkie say about war. He ended up by saying that if the people elected Roosevelt, their boys would be marching on the transports for Europe. Perhaps, by contrast to Roosevelt, Willkie should have told the truth and gone down, with greater honor, in a far greater defeat. Willkie fought well and was defeated. The menace of Hitler helped to nominate him and the menace of

444

Hitler certainly defeated him for the Presidency."

Right after the election the staff received a memorandum from Luce:

> Today and in the days to come we shall be thinking and hearing a great deal about National Unity. Nothing is more important than that we should seek and find the fundamentals of an intelligent patriotism.

He said that Time Inc.'s post-election theme could be taken from *Fortune*'s U.S.A. issue of February 1940 and he acknowledged the debt due Davenport. He paid the tribute, he said, not

> for the purpose of honoring a defeated soldier of a political battle. I do so in order to present a living illustration . . . of the great fact that in the *best* that has been thought and felt by the chief participants on both sides in this campaign there lives an America in which we can be infinitely interested and to which we may be proud to give in any capacity the fullest measure of devotion. . . .

T. S. Matthews offered his resignation as editor of the National Affairs section and asked to be transferred again to the Back-of-the-Book. Luce refused to accept the change, and shortly thereafter, at a company dinner, pointedly praised the National Affairs department as "a great team." In a staff discussion after the election Luce assured those who had disagreed with him during the campaign that they retained his confidence. Paine, who was present, wrote Luce this note: "It was not that I really doubted the position of the loyal opposition within Time Inc.; I wanted it positively reaffirmed. In a world of collapsing faiths one tends to be excessively, indeed belligerently, jealous of the faiths that remain. I feel much better, thank you!"

As the year closed Luce sent Gottfried and Matthews a memorandum which gave a key to his thinking about foreign policy—and which would set the tone for the magazines' coverage in 1941: ". . . There is only one real decision to be made, namely whether or not to accept genuine 'risks of war.' And this decision rests with F.D.R. No other

445

important official seems prepared to make this decision even in his own mind. As one observer put it: 'F.D.R. asked for it and he's got it.' . . . This is no time for beating up the bushes of 'public opinion.' This is a time for leadership—which can come only from one place —from behind the world's most famous cigarette holder."

CHAPTER
29
_____

A Seasoned and Successful Company

In 1941 Charles Stillman, weighing the uncertainties arising from the imminent threat of war, called the attention of the directors to a weakness in the corporation: "Time Inc. is engaged in a highly speculative and competitive business and, as such, its safety depends on having a much larger capital than we now have." He urged that the Board maintain its conservative policy on dividends in order to build up capital. His warning was characteristic of the management's attitude even in the face of affluence; they were still "running scared." As Larsen put it years later, "The fact of success is not easily grasped. We felt there must be something wrong or about to go wrong somewhere. I fear that this was the attitude of both Luce and myself right up to World War II."

This was understandable. From a beginning of $86,000 there had been built one of the most profitable publishing ventures in magazine history. With *Life*'s success the rate of growth became spectacular and unsettling. From 1939 to 1941 the new magazine vastly increased the company's income and more than doubled its profits; in 1939 revenues had been $29,311,057 and before-tax profits $3,893,583; in

447

1941 revenues reached a new record of $45,047,879 and before-tax profits were $8,190,057. It seemed too good to last.

Life added the dollar dimension that enabled what Luce called "a small Big Business" to keep on growing. Its almost explosive growth is explained by the fact that the magazine proved its worth as a prime medium for mass consumer advertising at a strategic moment. Under the stimulus of defense and of war orders from Britain and France, the economy in 1939 quickened after the long stagnation of the Depression. In 1940 the pace picked up and by late 1941 there were already signs of the wartime inflationary pressures to come. The American consumer had money in his pockets once again, and manufacturers eager to catch the surge in buying increased their advertising. *Life*'s pioneer work in merchandising won it support from the retail trade, and many of these new advertising dollars were funneled into the magazine. Although in 1941 *Life* remained second to the *Saturday Evening Post* in dollar volume of advertising, it already led the *Post* in a number of important categories. *Life* was first in advertising of food, clothing, wine and liquor,[1] drugs and toiletries. It was second to the *Post* in automobiles, jewelry and travel.

In 1939, in a bold move, Howard Black had announced an advertising policy designed to emphasize *Life*'s preeminence in the consumer field and maintain high reader interest. He ordered his salesmen deliberately to stop soliciting industrial advertising and other advertisements directed to what he called the "thin market" (i.e., businessmen, wholesalers, industrialists, etc.) and to concentrate on those of personal interest to the consumer. In 1940 he went a step further; the salesmen were told to actively discourage "thin market" orders where they could do so without giving offense. Then in 1941 *Life* announced that it would accept *only* advertisements directed to consumers; Black explained, "We want our readers, men, women and children, to be able to count on the fact that every advertisement in *Life* will feature products for personal use."

As these new advertising orders flooded in, management realized substantial savings in physical costs. In November 1940 Stillman reported that in the first nine months of that year "unit costs of pro-

[1] The *Post* did not accept liquor advertising until 1958.

448

duction and distribution . . . were $1,000,000 less than they would have been on the costs which prevailed in the same period of 1939." He was able to maintain the trend coincident with the rising circulation; in 1941 the average net paid circulation was 3,290,480 (as compared to 3,386,950 for the *Saturday Evening Post*).

While *Life* brought in the greater revenues, *Time* remained a very profitable magazine. Though its profits had been reduced by the 1937–38 recession and by *Life*'s competition, *Time* also benefited substantially in 1939–41 from the general improvement in business. In dollar volume of business *Time* rose to fifth place among magazines. The new advertising policy of *Life* tended to reduce the element of internal competition, and the rising interest in the news had a stimulating effect on *Time*'s circulation: the average net paid circulation for 1941 was just over 850,000, and toward the end of the year it was rising rapidly and well on its way to a million.

One magazine that did not benefit from the prewar boom was *Fortune*. It gained some circulation, but contributed nothing by way of profits in the immediate prewar years. Most of its advertisers—largely in the industrial field—were among the first to benefit from the military build-up, but with allocations and priorities (a new word in the business lexicon) there was little incentive for them to increase their advertising. Thus *Fortune* had a small loss in 1940 and another in 1941.

Neither did *The March of Time* contribute to profits; it did, however, continue to be shown to vast audiences and therefore greatly extended Time Inc.'s editorial influence. The indirect benefit which the company derived from *The March of Time* was thought to wholly justify the effort that went into its production.

Perhaps the most striking characteristic of the company in its nineteenth year continued to be the youth of its staff and responsible executives. Luce, Larsen and Black were in their early forties, Stillman, thirty-seven; the second echelon and the staff were in their twenties and thirties. Of the four top executives of Time Inc. in 1968 in addition to Larsen (chairman of the Executive Committee) and Stillman (chairman of the Finance Committee), three held responsible operating positions in 1941: Andrew Heiskell, chairman, was assistant general manager of *Life;* James Linen, president, was the advertising manager of *Life;* David Brumbaugh, executive vice-president and treasurer, was comptroller and secretary. Hedley Donovan, editor-in-chief, did not join Time Inc. until after the war; in 1941 he was a reporter on the Washington *Post.*

In fact, so dedicated was the management to the idea of youth that one of the issues subject to vigorous debate within the executive was the question of pensions. These were actively opposed by some young men and women who believed an aging staff would be fatal to the enterprise. If men and women were encouraged to grow old in the company's service, argued Mary Fraser, "Time Inc. might as well plan to go out of business on a pension too." She favored retiring men at fifty and women at forty or forty-five. In the end, confronted with the actuarial costs of early retirement, the company was forced to adopt the more conventional retirement age of sixy-five. For a number of years the staff regarded retirement as a purely academic goal.

While growth compelled the company to adopt certain conventional forms of corporate organization, its leadership continued to resist too formal a definition of authority or responsibility, and sought to preserve initiative and freedom of action. For two more decades the enduring combination of Luce, as editor-in chief, and Larsen, as president and chief executive officer, kept up the momentum of the company. While Larsen retained the title of publisher of *Life* until 1946 in addition to being president, he was in fact "manager-in-chief" to those who worked on the business side, just as Luce was editor-in-chief to the editorial staff. In later years, when the publisher system was better defined than in 1941, Luce liked to describe the relations between the editor-in-chief and the president this way: "Each division is led, operationally, by a Publisher and a Managing Editor. The Publisher is the one man who is concerned with all aspects of his magazine—its general well-being. He is responsible for profit and loss . . . *but* he cannot give orders to the Managing Editor. . . . The Publisher reports to the President of the company and the Managing Editor reports to the Editor-in-Chief. What happens between the Editor-in-Chief and the

President is a secret—*all* except the verdict."

In 1941 there was no such clear-cut definition of powers. In fact, to interpret executive titles and to keep track of executive changes in those days required an extraordinary measure of skill. For example, on the business side, under Larsen, two vice-presidents had very large responsibilities that cut across divisional lines. Black was responsible for advertising sales policy and personnel for all the magazines. In addition to finances, Stillman, with Brumbaugh's help, handled production, procurement and planning. He also had the title of general manager of *Time,* which included most of the duties of a publisher, though Luce had assumed that title on the departure of Ingersoll. Vice-President C. D. Jackson, general manager of *Life,* had just completed a year's leave of absence to head the Council for Democracy, which Luce had been instrumental in organizing to promote the democratic spirit.

In March 1941 Pierrie Prentice was named publisher of *Time.* Prentice, also a vice-president, had up to that time been head of the circulation department, which served all the magazines, and had very broad operational responsibilities that extended into public relations and the supervision of all direct-mail solicitations. In 1941 Time Inc. was already one of the nation's largest direct-mail advertisers. In this field, pioneered by Larsen, Prentice had proved himself an innovative and successful operator. Nevertheless he welcomed an opportunity to surrender these activities for the experience of publishing; it brought him back into contact with the editorial operation, which remained his first interest.

It is typical of the casual way in which such matters were handled that Stillman learned of the impending change first from Prentice, who invited him out for a drink one night and asked whether he minded if Prentice applied for his job on *Time.* Prentice had a cheerfully ingenuous way about such things, though such outspoken manners did not always win him friends. On one occasion he told Luce, as one son of the manse to another, that Religion in *Time* was written as if it were "a lot of foolishness" and Gottfried did not see how it could be written in any other way. Prentice felt it should be written by "a first-class journalist with a roving assignment to find out whether God was doing

451

anything worthwhile in our generation and, if so, to report it." Luce agreed with Prentice and gave him the assignment of editing the department while continuing as circulation manager. After becoming publisher, Prentice kept a hand in as an editor for a period by editing the Business section. Notwithstanding their differences on the subject of Religion, Prentice and Gottfried worked together harmoniously and effectively.

Luce's general assumption that men of good will would manage to accommodate themselves to one another without his formal definition of roles and missions did not in all cases work so well as in the transfer of responsibility from Stillman to Prentice. On *Fortune,* Hodgins with tact and sufferance had skillfully handled the publisher's duties during the turbulent regime of Russell Davenport. In 1940, with Davenport's resignation to work for Willkie, Luce had designated Hodgins editor-in-chief as well as publisher of *Fortune,* with Richardson Wood, who had been a staff writer and editor for over three years, succeeding to the title of managing editor. In 1941, the Willkie campaign lost, Luce rehired Davenport and appointed him editor of *Fortune* without making clear his relations to either Hodgins or Wood. This resulted in a first-class foul-up; as Hodgins, who remained a good personal friend of Davenport, explained to Luce and Larsen, the former managing editor immediately began "throwing the joint out into the street . . . trying to move in immediately on the March [1941] issue. When I told Davenport I thought he had made a major diplomatic mistake, his reaction was simple, incredulous surprise. He had run over some six people at a crowded crossing and hadn't even known he had been in an accident."

Hodgins therefore announced he would absent himself until it was decided what should be done. Luce assigned the clean-up job to Del Paine, who came up with what he said was "the perhaps presumptuous suggestion" (in which Wood concurred and which Luce accepted) that he, Paine, be made managing editor. Wood became general manager under Hodgins as publisher, and Davenport remained editor with his duties restricted to writing editorials.

In 1941 Time Inc. launched a new edition of *Time* delivered by air to Latin America, the first of a now world-encircling network of special

452

editions. The idea of delivering *Time* by air had been considered first in 1932 but abandoned because airmail rates were too expensive. Little by little *Time, Life* and *Fortune* acquired a smattering of overseas circulation, but the company's major operations internationally, up until 1941, were confined to *The March of Time,* which in addition to its widely distributed English-language editions produced releases in French, and some in Spanish for showing in Latin America.

In Time Inc.'s offices, it will be recalled (Chapter 27), the decision had been made to foster interest in the hemisphere. Early in 1940 Daniel del Solar, a Chilean and formerly a Latin America editor for the Associated Press, was hired by *Time* to translate an 8,000-word excerpt weekly from the magazine for syndication to Latin American newspapers. Called *"La Marcha del Tiempo,"* it was eventually printed in twenty South American newspapers with a combined circulation of a million. Under Stillman a corporate committee was set up to explore other ventures. Among those considered was a Spanish translation of *Life* (which did come into being after World War II), but this was rejected in favor of a special edition of *Time* printed by offset on rolls (not sheets) of lightweight paper—new technology at the time—to be delivered by air to Latin America. A dummy was prepared by Stillman's assistant James Parton. Luce swiftly approved the project, quoting Shakespeare: " 'Twere well it were done quickly." The new edition was announced as "the world's first plane-delivered magazine," and the company promised that delivery would be extended to other parts of the world as air service became available. Hitherto a few copies had been delivered by air, but at fantastic expense; a Maharajah in India paid $585.60 for the service. The price of $10 a year was made possible by the establishment of new air-express rates by Pan American Airways. The edition was printed in Jersey City, addressed and pre-stamped, then flown to Miami for distribution to local post offices throughout Latin America. The circulation of the new edition soon reached 20,000.

International publishing roiled international sensitivities. To inaugurate the Air Express Edition, the editors had a cover article on Argentina's Acting President Ramón Castillo, who objected to his portrait because, he said, it made him "look like a bandit." In reporting

453

this to the home office Harold Horan, who had been transferred to Buenos Aires from Washington to become the magazine's first full-time Latin American correspondent, suggested special treatment be given to Latin American news. Soon Americans were requesting special treatment of domestic news published in the edition, on the grounds that critical reporting of conditions in the U.S. tended to weaken Latin American confidence in the country; agents of the Rockefeller office for coordinating Latin American affairs argued that *Time*'s criticism of their work undermined their position in Latin America. While Under Secretary of State Sumner Welles opposed the idea of tailoring the edition specially for Latin America, he hoped that the editors might be able "to winnow out" some of the more critical items. But the subscribers to the edition, when polled, strongly objected to any expurgation of the news. Experiments with alterations were tried from time to time, only to be reversed. *Time*'s international editions are on the whole identical in editorial content with the domestic edition. The present Canadian edition is printed and published in Canada, with a Canadian editorial staff preparing a special Canadian news section.

The need of the company for additional capital, to which Stillman referred in the memorandum cited at the beginning of this chapter, became clear soon after the publication of *Life*. The company had been undercapitalized since the day Hadden and Luce decided to go ahead with *Time* without waiting to raise their pre-publication goal of $100,000. There had been no recourse to borrowing, even in launching *Life*. Of great assistance, however, was the increasing amount of deferred income (Chapter 8) resulting from the sale of subscriptions in advance. In 1938, according to the annual report, this reached $4,900,000. Therefore during the period in which *Life* was losing heavily the company's cash position was always somewhat better than the book losses would suggest.

Deferred income as a source of financing has obvious limitations; it is in fact a contingent liability until the subscription has been serviced. As a source of income it is variable, dependent on public acceptance of the editorial product and therefore unpredictable. With an enter-

454

prise the size of *Life* it became desirable to have funds more readily available for large-scale commitments. A situation arose in 1939 in which Stillman thought it wise to contract with the Champion Paper and Fibre Company for long-term delivery of paper made from southern pine. To produce this paper, the Champion management planned to build a new paper mill as an addition to its bleached-pulp mill in Houston. When the company needed assistance in financing construction, it suggested an investment of $1,750,000 in its 6-percent Preferred stock. However, the Time Inc. Board felt that it could prudently invest only $1,000,000, a sum that proved sufficient to assure continuation of the project, and very much to the benefit of Time Inc. Of this investment Stillman said, "Money, sheer gold, was never put to better use by Time Inc. . . . unless it was to foot the 1937 bill on *Life*."

The experience with Champion set Stillman to thinking how Time Inc. might increase its reserves. In 1939 the company was following a very conservative investment policy, keeping most of its funds in cash or government bonds. But in October 1939, when war in Europe raised the specter of inflation, the Executive Committee took under advisement the possibility of investing $2,000,000 "in securities most likely to serve as a hedge against rising prices and unsettled monetary conditions." Stillman, who had successfully championed and carried through profitably such an investment program in 1933–36, was now against such a course. The problems arising from *Life* had altered the company's situation. "I have been of two minds about the wisdom of speculative investments for some time—ever since *Life*," he wrote. "A cash and security position of $12,000,000 is none too much for . . . even our present volume. We are $5,000,000 short as of the end of this year [1939]. So we have no excess funds at all. . . . Consequently, when we speak of investing money today we are not investing surplus funds, we are investing needed funds. . . . Just as soon as something big happens, like *Life*, like war, like inflation, we wish we had more capital. The more I think of the tenacity with which we would hold onto the money if we had it, the closer I come to a serious recommendation that we go out and get it. . . . When *Life* turned the corner I heaved a sigh of relief and figured that we could save our way to a strong capital position. What this discussion of investment policy really highlights is that war has brought uncertainties and problems so perplexing that we scarcely know what to do except to wish that we were better protected with dollars. . . ."

In the past, consideration had been given to selling a new issue of Preferred. The diminution of earnings due to *Life* had made it unlikely there would be a favorable market. Stillman pointed out that a publishing company, unlike an industrial enterprise, could not borrow in anticipation of expansion:

> Our expansions and our temporary difficulties take our cash away but they provide nothing at all as a basis for increased capital or credit. In fact they cripple our ability to get capital because of the "speculative" nature of the business. The principal thing that makes it "speculative" is the complete inability on the part of the money lenders and capitalists generally to appraise the going value of a new publication or an old one that is losing money. That may not make this business a bad or uncertain business but it certainly has a bearing on the financial problems of the company. It means that you have to provide your capital requirements ahead of time. In fact about the only time you can get money cheap is when there is no apparent or prospective need for it.
>
> When a good industrial company builds a new plant they can borrow money or raise money on the new plant. When a publishing company wants money for a new venture, no one cares how good the new venture is. All they really want to know is, can the company still pay if the new venture is a drain on the business. . . .
>
> It is conceivable that the difference between an impregnable capital position and just an average capital position could be the difference between an ability to reassemble a business called Time Inc. after the war and the complete and permanent liquidation of the enterprise.

This line of thinking led to the adoption early in 1940 of a long-range policy to build up capital. The policy represented the conclusions of a committee consisting of Luce, Larsen, Stillman and Luce's brother-in-law Maurice T. Moore,[2] a partner in Cravath and Time Inc.'s counsel, who joined the Board of Directors in 1939. The committee decided there was no substitute "for the old-fashioned saving process," but that it would be desirable to arrange a loan in anticipation of such savings. The loan would provide funds if substantial investments, as in the Champion situation, were required. The committee noted:

> It is no accident that most large companies in our business have substantial investments in printing and paper plants. We are most fortunate to have fifteen million dollars of other people's money working for us. . . . There is no guarantee that we can stay out of paper and printing investments. . . .
>
> In all probability, the company will make $10,000,000 or more in the next three years and . . . $5,000,000 can be added to capital in that preferable way [i.e., savings].
>
> A very happy compromise on capital needs would be to anticipate the probable saving power. . . . It is distinctly not a part of our thinking that this action should be taken to finance the payment of more liberal dividends. . . . Rather the company should set itself resolutely to extinguish this debt out of earnings as fast as a conservative dividend policy will permit. . . .

Accordingly Time Inc. borrowed $2,000,000 from the New York Trust Company and $1,000,000 from the Bank of the Manhattan Company.

The money thus obtained in 1940 enabled Stillman to embark in 1941 on a program destined to strengthen the company against the stress of war. "It is assumed," he wrote, "that the Management . . . is of practically one opinion that this is not the time to turn away like a shrinking violet from some of the problems ahead of us."

Stillman was no shrinking violet. He made the company's first investment in research and development, acquiring the assets and patents of Roy E. Coleman and setting Coleman himself up in a

[2] Moore and Elisabeth Luce were married in 1926.

457

laboratory to continue experiments in developing a new kind of ink from the corn protein, Zein. Though unsuccessful, this established a precedent and a policy that has been followed in the postwar years. Stillman, explaining his investment in the Coleman process, said, "It will not be the cornerstone of our policy to build up a patent situation. . . . We have observed that when research work is being done by one company in a certain field, other alert companies are inclined to follow suit. . . . An important part of the benefit which will flow from this research will not necessarily come from discoveries of our own—it will flow from the work of others done in self-defense." At a later period the company would develop and exploit its own patents; the electronic scanner developed in the company's laboratories from Eastman Kodak's pioneering efforts in this field became the basis for Time Inc.'s wholly owned and successful subsidiary, Printing Developments, Inc.

Stillman also began building up for the first time a substantial inventory in paper. This was made possible by the acquisition of the company's own storage facilities near the Donnelley plant in Chicago. And to facilitate and provide for the economical transportation of paper from the Houston mill to Chicago, the company made a small investment in river barges. Stillman also brought in a third printing contractor to supplement the work done by Donnelley in Chicago and the Cuneo Eastern Press in Philadelphia. The American Colortype Company began printing color inserts for *Life,* and for this work Time Inc. financed a new color press.

In addition to these investments in publishing, a beginning was made on a long-range program of investment in related industries. Stillman recommended the investment of $1,000,000 in the air transport industry, which he believed to be on the threshold of enormous expansion. He felt, on the basis of Time Inc.'s experience with the Air Express edition, that this would play a very great part in the expansion of publishing operations overseas. But by far the most spectacular and successful of Stillman's recommendations was that the company invest $1,000,000 in the stock of the Houston Oil Company. The initial Time Inc. purchases of Houston Oil stock in 1941 led to the formation with Houston Oil in 1952 of the East Texas Pulp and

Paper Company. On the liquidation of the Houston Oil Company in 1956, Time Inc. used the net proceeds of $18,615,000 (after taxes) as the basis for the acquisition of the East Texas Pulp and Paper Company, which is now the wholly owned Time Inc. subsidiary Eastex Incorporated.

As it turned out, the company was unable to invest the whole $2,000,000 as proposed in 1941 or the years immediately following. But from small investments in air transport and Houston Oil Company there developed a coordinated investment policy from which the company derived future benefits. What inhibited large commitments in 1941 was, of course, the continuing uncertainty that made even Stillman hesitate. He summed up the problem for the directors in November 1941: "We do not know just what increase in costs we are going to run into. . . . We have always gone on the theory that in order to protect itself in the purchases of paper, printing and other supplies, it is necessary for the Company to have the ability, from a financial point of view, to go out and do the job for itself. . . . We have often discussed the nature of our business and the fact that so many publications have had periods of great prosperity and then petered out. We are doing our best to try to foresee and meet things which might cause us to follow the same pattern. Certainly, in my opinion, it is necessary to have a strong capital position in order to be able to meet contingencies and take steps, whenever the occasion shall arise, to avoid any such fate." During their stewardship Stillman and his associates were singularly successful in avoiding such a fate.

"*The Day of Wrath*"

T HE STEADILY SUCCESSFUL progress of Time Inc. in 1941 was
in decided contrast to developments in an unsteady world.
Washington's attention was swinging anxiously between the
Atlantic and the far reaches of the Pacific. The British, battered by air
bombardment, were fighting for survival in the Atlantic against the
Nazi U-boats. Japan, in September 1940, by joining Germany and
Italy in the Tripartite Pact, had converted a potential threat into an
imminent one. Washington had declared an embargo on all Japan-
bound shipments of scrap iron and steel, advised Americans to return
home from Japanese-controlled territories and reinforced Hawaii.
Americans were still perplexed as to their ultimate role. In January
Roosevelt asked Congress to lend-lease war matériel to Britain, but
the Administration line remained "methods short of war."

It was in this uncertain climate that Luce developed a proposition
that, so far as he was concerned, gave direction to his country's
history. It evolved in three speeches that he made early in the year—
at Pasadena,[1] Tulsa and Pittsburgh—and which he finally and fully

[1] Before the Association of American Colleges. The Los Angeles *Times* took
the occasion to print a long biographical sketch of Luce, describing him as

defined in an article appearing in the February 17 issue of *Life*. Luce
had come to the conclusion that the U.S. must go to war and he
wanted to say so. But there were probably no more than a dozen political leaders or writers who were prepared to advocate direct intervention and Luce himself hesitated to say flatly what he thought. In
the Pasadena speech he talked around the issue; in Tulsa he was somewhat more forthright and in Pittsburgh he came right out with it:
"Tonight I want first to be honest with you and to say what I really
think. . . . I say that we are already *in* the war. . . . The irony is that
Hitler knows it—and most of the American people don't." In this
speech, and later in the *Life* article, to carry his listeners and readers
over the unpleasant fact that he was urging the U.S. to go to war and
to get into the heart of his proposition, the vision of America's
postwar future, he fell back on a circumlocution.

> We are, for a fact, *in* the war [he wrote in *Life*]. . . .
>
> Of course, we are not technically at war, we are not painfully
> at war, and we may never have to experience the full hell that
> war can be. Nevertheless the simple statement stands: We are *in*
> the war. . . .
>
> Perhaps the best way to show ourselves that we are in the war
> is to consider how we can get out of it. Practically, there's only
> one way to get out of it and that is by a German victory over
> England. . . .
>
> We say we don't want to be in the war. We also say we want
> England to win. . . . So, at the moment, we're in. . . .

He turned to what he called "the larger issue":

> As America enters dynamically upon the world scene, we need
> most of all to seek and to bring forth a vision of America as a
> world power which is authentically American and which can
> inspire us to live and work and fight with vigor and enthusiasm.
> And as we come now to the great test, it may yet turn out that in
> all our trials and tribulations of spirit during the first part of this
> century we as a people have been painfully apprehending the

---

someone "who probably is the most powerful single element in journalism in
the country and an American phenomenon of Horatio Alger proportions in his
own right."

meaning of our time and now in this moment of testing there may come clear at last the vision which will guide us to the authentic creation of the 20th Century—our Century.

He saw "four areas of life and thought" in which Americans might realize such a vision:

First, the economic. It is for America and for America alone to determine whether a system of free economic enterprise—an economic order compatible with freedom and progress—shall or shall not prevail in this century. . . . What then does America have to decide? Some few decisions are quite simple. For example: we have to decide whether or not we shall have for ourselves and our friends freedom of the seas. . . . The vision of America as the principal guarantor of the freedom of the seas, the vision of America as the dynamic leader of world trade, has within it the possibilities of such enormous human progress as to stagger the imagination. . . .

Closely akin to the purely economic area and yet quite different from it, there is the picture of an America which will send out through the world its technical and artistic skills. Engineers, scientists, doctors, movie men, makers of entertainment, developers of airlines, builders of roads, teachers, educators. . . .

But now there is a third thing which our vision must immediately be concerned with. We must undertake now to be the Good Samaritan of the entire world. It is the manifest duty of this country to undertake to feed all the people of the world who as a result of this worldwide collapse of civilization are hungry and destitute—all of them, that is, whom we can from time to time reach consistently with a very tough attitude toward all hostile governments. . . .

But all this is not enough. All this will fail and none of it will happen unless our vision of America as a world power includes a passionate devotion to great American ideals. We have some things in this country which are infinitely precious and especially American—a love of freedom, a feeling for the equality of opportunity, a tradition of self-reliance and independence and also of co-operation. In addition . . . we are the inheritors of all the great principles of Western civilization—above all Justice, the love of Truth, the ideal of Charity. . . . It now becomes our time to be the powerhouse from which the ideals spread throughout the world. . . .

It is in this spirit that all of us are called, each to his own measure of capacity, and each in the widest horizon of his vision, to create the first great American Century.

The immediate response to this article surprised the editors; *Life* received 4,541 letters (of the first 1,271, the letters department reported, 1,196 were favorable, 75 critical). It also provoked considerable discussion, echoes of which are still heard. The columnist Dorothy Thompson pronounced it "an American document," declaring that "This will either be an American century or it will be the beginning of the decline and fall of the American dream." The radio commentator Quincy Howe and the playwright Robert E. Sherwood, an ardent interventionist, were more measured than Miss Thompson but generally approving. Severely critical were Norman Thomas, the head of the Socialist Party, and Freda Kirchwey, editor and publisher of the *Nation,* who wrote: "This program is magnanimous and benevolent, it is large and awe-inspiring. It is also smug, self-righteous, superior, and fatuously lacking in a decent regard for the susceptibilities of the rest of mankind. These particular qualities are the typical stigmata of the Anglo-Saxon in his role as imperialist."

This criticism rankled; all his life Luce had been a critic of British imperialism and an advocate of ending colonialism. Some years later he told an interviewer, purposely using bad English for emphasis, "It has been proposed that I write a redefinition of the American Century and explain that I wasn't no imperialist. I don't know who has taken worse raps than I have for opposition to imperialism. . . . You can't extract imperialism from 'The American Century.' " He was also irritated by those who advocated the same ideas but tried to disassociate themselves from his statement; in 1942 Vice President Wallace declared: "Some have spoken of the 'American Century.' I say that the century on which we are entering—the century which will come out of this war—can be and must be the century of the common man." The vision of the future that Wallace offered differed in few respects

463

from that of Luce, and so he wrote Wallace: "If your disapproving reference to 'The American Century' helped you to gain higher ground, I am of course deeply gratified. But I should not like to think that anything of substance in the essay . . . is inconsistent with your hopes and promises for the increasing freedom and welfare of 'the common man.' " To this Wallace replied, ". . . I do not happen to remember anything that you have written descriptive of your concepts of 'The American Century' of which I disapprove. . . . Nevertheless, it has happened that the phrase 'American Century' did rub the citizens of a number of our sister United Nations the wrong way."

When "The American Century" was reprinted in book form,[2] Luce printed the comments of Miss Thompson, Howe, Sherwood and Robert Spivak along with it. He also included a vigorous essay of objection written by John Chamberlain of *Fortune.* When Chamberlain told Luce he could not agree with his proposition, Luce said, "All right. You write something and I will put it in the book."

Over the years Luce's critics have mocked or sneered at "The American Century"; a recent one, Joseph Epstein, who is also a critic of Time Inc. journalism, wrote in the magazine *Commentary:*

> Although written twenty-six years ago, this program ["The American Century"], moral pretensions and all, constitutes the essence of current American foreign policy—a fact perhaps more widely recognized around the world than in the United States. What it holds out, quite simply, is the promise of American technological and economic resources to any nation which will roughly approximate our economic system, share our political attitudes and adopt our ideology.

Luce would not disagree with this summation; he would most certainly reject the charge that he was morally pretentious.

By the time "The American Century" was published, the Time Inc. publications were being edited on the assumption that it was inevitable that the U.S. would enter the war—and, since it was inevitable, the sooner the better. The magazines supported the Administration moves that entailed "genuine risks of war." Luce felt strongly that the

[2] *The American Century* (Farrar & Rinehart, 1941).

464

President should assert his leadership more emphatically, and during 1941 the magazines frequently reflected the frustration experienced by those who believed that Roosevelt's approach was often devious and hesitant. As British losses in the Battle of the Atlantic mounted, the Time Inc. publications were impatient with the President's reluctance to provide armed convoys for British merchant shipping. If individuals on the editorial staffs were in disagreement with the editorial policy—and some were, of course—there is no evidence in the files of the kind of internal debate that occurred during the Presidential election of the year before.

However, letters to the editors and contemporary newspaper columns leave no doubt that non-interventionists and isolationists thought that the Time Inc. magazines were "warmongering." These groups had no reason to like the Luce publications. When Roosevelt, in the annual message to Congress, warned of those who "with sounding brass and a tinkling cymbal preach the ism of appeasement," *Life* followed up with a two-page spread headed " 'The Ism of Appeasement': Roosevelt Brands Foes of His Foreign Policy." It featured a close-up of Lawrence Dennis, whom *Life* labeled "America's No. 1 intellectual Fascist." Lumped along with Dennis as "foes" of Roosevelt were Charles and Anne Lindbergh, General Hugh Johnson, Mrs. Bennett Champ Clark, of the newly formed America First Committee, and Joseph P. Kennedy, recently returned from his tour of duty as Ambassador to Great Britain; *Life* described him as ". . . defeatist about Britain, in favor of a quick peace."

Missouri's Senator Bennett Champ Clark and his wife were infuriated by this spread and by other assaults on their position by the magazines. When a reporter in the *Time-Life* Washington office called to ask the Senator if he proposed to filibuster the lend-lease bill, he got the full blast of the Clarks' anger. Mrs. Clark asked the reporter if he had seen what *Life* had done to her, and the Senator told him he could expect no help for magazines which were "untrustworthy, despicable, dishonest, insulting and twisted." Then, cooling off, the Senator said he realized that the reporter had little to do with editorial policy, "but you people in mediocre positions are the ones who must suffer." On reading a report of this encounter, Luce sent his regrets to the correspondent "that 'mediocre persons' have to take such raps on behalf

465

of first-class rascals." A subsequent description of the Senator in *Time* was not flattering: "Ruddy-cheeked, merciless in cross-examination, possessed of 'a genius for public rudeness.'"[3]

While the offending issue of *Life* was still on the stands, Kennedy, in a nationwide radio address, denied that he was an isolationist, a defeatist or an appeaser. He said he was for "the utmost aid to England," which would give America time to prepare for eventualities, but he was against entering the war. Luce undoubtedly felt that *Life* had done his friend Kennedy a disservice in linking him with extremists like Dennis. *Life* ran a one-page spread quoting from the Kennedy broadcast and in an editorial comment declared it to be "the most notable utterance of protest yet made against the present trend of national policy. . . . The Editors of *Life* disagree with Mr. Kennedy in that they believe in full-out aid to Britain, without reservations. But they also believe that our national policy is direfully in need of honest and thoughtful clarification."

This theme—the need for clarification—became a familiar threnody to *Time* readers in the spring of 1941. As British defeats multiplied in North Africa, in the Balkans and on the Atlantic, the isolationist opposition to Administration policy intensified. After the passage of the Lend-Lease Act, the editors for weeks running professed to see little but a pall of confusion hanging over the national capital. One of the National Affairs writers of the period recalled: "We tried to assay the general confusion about isolation versus intervention and nearly every week's lead [article] boiled down to the fact that fog settled over Washington." Looking back, *Time*'s managing editor, Gottfried, agreed with him: "Confusion can be established in one word. Perhaps the trouble was that we tried to clarify it and we shouldn't have."[4]

* * *

[3] Two of the Senator's sons work for Time Inc.: Champ Clark is a senior editor of *Time;* his brother Marsh is chief of the Ottawa bureau.

[4] The Harvard *Lampoon* parodied the all too frequent *Time* lead: "Fog settled down over Washington last week. Coming by way of Chesapeake Bay at a mean rate of 10 m.p.h. (according to U.S. Weather Bureauthority Jim Keebling), it crossed over to the Potomac and slowly engulfed the District of Columbia. Only once before had Washingtonians seen its ilk. . . ."

466

From 1938 onward *Time, Life* and *Fortune* had taken a strong line on national defense, supporting every step toward rearming. General Marshall had personally thanked Luce for *Life*'s report in December 1938 on the deficiencies in the armed forces, which he said had been extremely helpful in getting action. In October 1940 Luce had written his editors a cautionary memorandum in which he suggested that in their enthusiasm for the cause of national defense the magazines might have gone too far in underwriting the progress that had been made in U.S. defense:

> If, by any chance, the United States should get into a War which were to present any serious difficulties for us, our publications might become the object of bitter attack—and of justifiable attack in so far as we had led people to believe that adequate progress had been made in National Defense. It is important that the people should not be unduly scared so that they will disapprove the taking of desirable or inevitable risks in pursuit of an intelligent policy. But if their approval of a given policy (a policy which may have our approval) is based on an unduly optimistic notion of our preparedness, we are likely to be lynched. . . . Maybe we did and maybe we didn't underwrite Gamelin and the French Army.[5] But any underwriting we ever gave to Gamelin and the French Army is as nothing compared to our explicit and tacit underwriting of our own entire armed forces. Hitherto our target has been mainly civilians—anti-conscriptionists, pacifists, and generally sluggish civilians. Maybe we better pay a little *critical* attention now to the men whom we have recommended, who are entrusted with so large a part of our fate. . . .

The editors increasingly had the advice and consultation of military experts, with the result that the magazines' coverage became more informed and more sophisticated. A regular contributor to *Life*'s pages was Major George Fielding Eliot, who was retained along with Fletcher Pratt, the naval expert. *Life* was also particularly fortunate in having as one of its principal news editors Edward K. Thompson, who

[5] *Time* and *Life,* like many other publications, rated the French Army high and therefore were surprised by its sudden collapse.

had been a U.S. Army reserve officer since 1928 and who became one of the principal architects of the military reportage. He had started his journalistic career in North Dakota, moved on to the Milwaukee *Journal*, where he became its picture editor and assistant news editor and at the same time served as a stringer for *Life* and *Time*. In 1937 *Life* hired him to be assistant to Wilson Hicks in charge of photographers, but he soon found himself deeply involved in the magazine's news coverage. He was one of those responsible for *Life*'s essay on military deficiencies which won for the magazine the commendation of General Marshall, and he was also editor of the special issue on National Defense in 1941. (In 1942 *Life* lost Thompson to the Army, but he returned to pursue a distinguished career that would carry him to the posts, successively, of managing editor and editor.)

This military and journalistic background was matched on *Time* by one of the writers in the National Defense department, which had been inaugurated in July 1940. Roy Alexander, before joining *Time* in 1939, had been assistant city editor of the St. Louis *Post-Dispatch*. A Stateside marine in World War I, Alexander had continued a part-time military career, flying as a pilot with the 110th Observation Squadron of the Missouri National Guard. He was mustered out as a major and squadron commander when he left St. Louis to join *Time*. Working with Alexander in the National Defense department was John Osborne, who had experience on Southern newspapers and in Washington before coming to *Time*. Together Alexander and Osborne put together a very knowledgeable section that commanded an attentive if not always appreciative readership in defense circles.

During 1941 the magazines were often sharply critical of the defense effort. In a five-page picture report on U.S. industry, published in May, *Life* concluded: "America, whose industrial engine has a horsepower far exceeding any other nation's, is still trying to get out of low gear." *Time*, in the same month, spoke of "the whole civilian defense machinery running without any responsible head, of uncertain policies, of fresh confusions piled on stale confusions." The immediate fault lay, said the magazine, in Roosevelt's War Cabinet, because "For one reason or another each of [its members] has drawbacks. . . ." Most severely criticized was Secretary of War Henry L. Stimson, much revered as an elder statesman and a man whom the press in general treated with enormous respect. *Time* commented:

> With Secretary of War Henry L. Stimson the reason is both age and health. Now no cocktail party passes in the District without a new anecdote about the Secretary's dozing off in some important conference, of his inability to work more than a few hours a day, of his valiant but losing struggle to keep abreast of the demands of war in 1941. No reflections are made on his spirit, his mind, his will: the emphasis is on his years.

Luce was the recipient of the anguished or angry complaints whenever an ox was gored; he heard from Stimson's angry friends and allies. Later in the year *Time* made amends for whatever injustice was done Stimson with a cover story that praised the over-all management of his department, and called him "a cracking good Secretary of War." Luce admonished his editors to continue to be critical but in future to give him some advance warning.

> We have a problem of method to solve. The problem is to apprise me of the attitudes, angles or conclusions which *Time* is going to adopt *in re* controversial matters. Thus, e.g., if you are going to say that the National Defense job is being badly done, as you said brilliantly a month ago, I want to know it—not later than Monday [the day the magazine went to press]. . . . Signal me also on trivial things where you realize you are being unusually bold or blunt—as in calling somebody a really nasty name. I want *Time* should be bold, blunt, etc., but I want to be cut in on the boldness and bluntness before as well as after. . . .

In 1941 Luce was giving as much personal time as he could spare from the magazines to United China Relief, an agency which he had been largely responsible for organizing. In working for it, he was shocked to discover how "large a proportion of Americans thought of China, when they thought of it at all, as a nation of amiable laundrymen who always seemed to be having a tough time, but whose fate had no conceivable connection with the U.S." Luce regarded his native land as an American ally, in the same sense as Britain, long before this was the official position or millions of his fellow countrymen reached the same conclusion. Though throughout 1941 there was steadily increasing concern about Japan's policy in the Pacific, Europe still remained the main focus of U.S. concern. The Time Inc. publications tried to redress this balance by providing American readers with more insight into embattled China.

U.S. news about China came from a handful of reporters in beleaguered Chungking, one of whom was *Time*'s and *Life*'s Theodore H. White. On graduation from Harvard (*summa cum laude,* '38) White had gone to China on a traveling scholarship and landed a job as a writer for the Chinese Ministry of Information. *Time*'s John Hersey, who met him there in 1939, hired him as a correspondent. White was an adventurous and perceptive reporter whose accounts of life in wartime China won him the equivalent of the first "byline" in *Time.* Late in 1940 *Life* sent the photographer-and-reporter, husband-and-wife team of Carl and Shelley Mydans to join White in Chungking. The first pictures that Mydans sent back produced a photo essay in *Life* in March 1941. *Life* had published many picture stories on London under the blitz; Mydans' pictures showed a very different kind of air bombardment which went on daily in a far corner of Asia. Particularly striking were his pictures of the enormous air-raid shelters capable of accommodating the whole population of the city, and *Life* noted: "Chungking is as full of unsung civilian heroes as is London. . . . If possible, the people of Chungking do more laughing and joking, make more cheerful noise and are more completely the same under the bombs than even the Londoners. Death is nothing new here. . . ."

This was a battlefield Luce wanted to see for himself. He and Mrs. Luce flew to Hong Kong by Pan American Clipper, he as the official representative of United China Relief, she as a photographer-correspondent for *Life.* From Hong Kong they flew over Japanese-occupied territory to Chungking. On the day after his arrival Luce, from the American Embassy high on the riverbank opposite the center of the city, watched his first Japanese air raid. Total casualties that day:

forty dead, and as many more wounded. Luce noted, "There is not much sympathy for the victims now because it is felt it is mostly their own fault for not going into the dugouts."

The Luces were received by Generalissimo and Madame Chiang Kai-shek. Luce described the meeting: ". . . You got the feeling that there was no person in the room except the man who had just entered it so quietly. We stood up. A slim wraithlike figure in khaki moved through the shadow and there were a few distinct grunts of encouragement: 'How . . . How . . .' ('Good . . . Good . . .'). The Madame introduced us. . . . He went and stood before his armchair next to where I had been carefully placed . . . motioning us to be seated." The Generalissimo granted the only favor asked, one which Luce had been told would surely be denied: permission to visit the Japanese front. "Now, the second he heard the request," Luce wrote, "his head nodded. *Cui, cui,* can-do–can-do, the Yes-Law of China."

For the better part of two days the Luces flew in a small Beechcraft over the Szechwan plains and the Tsinling Mountains to Sian; from there they went by train, automobile and finally Mongolian ponies to the front and within eyesight of the Japanese guns emplaced on the cliffs of the Yellow River. Luce was much impressed by what he saw of the Chinese Army. On the way home from China, the Luces stopped off in Manila, where they met General MacArthur, field marshal of the Philippine Army. This meeting made as lasting and indelible an impression on Luce as the meeting with Chiang Kai-shek; he remained a lifelong admirer of both men.

On his return to San Francisco, Luce reported on his trip in a speech to the Commonwealth Club. He made the point that Americans as a whole knew little of what was going on in China, saying, "I, as an editor, can only offer profound apologies for the entirely inadequate job which American journalism is doing west of the Golden Gate." His own observations could be summed up in four outstanding impressions:

First, there is the sheer fact of the Chinese people—there are so many of them and to be among them for only an hour is to know that they have qualities which are invincible. Second, Free China

471

is a country at war—bitterly and desperately at war. Thirdly, China is conducting its war under appalling difficulties. . . . Fourthly, there is in China an absolutely magnificent spirit of courage and determination. . . .

Now, if our trip has had any value for me and if it may have any value for others, it will be in correcting this half-truth about Japan being bogged down. Japan is not "bogged down." The Imperial Japanese Army has been stopped cold in its tracks by the soldiers of China. . . .

He was to make the same points in the many speeches which he gave on behalf of United China Relief; they were also the substance of an article, "China: to the Mountains," which appeared in the June 30 issue of *Life* with Mrs. Luce's photographs.

The Luces brought White home with them. When asked why he returned, White told the company house organ, *FYI,* "America is changing so fast, I was getting out of touch and you do get tired of being bombed, particularly when there isn't quite enough to eat. The conversation in Chungking is of the best but the food is poor. . . ." In fact, Luce brought White home because White was full of ideas for articles about China. Shortly after they returned, *Time* had a cover story on Chen Cheng, "Defender of Chungking," which emphasized the importance of the Asian war "to the London-Washington Axis," and called for aid to China: "As for the U.S., a large-scale Chinese success would ease the future tremendously. The Chinese officers of the line think they could achieve that success, if only they had some artillery and some scouting planes. . . ." White contributed four articles to the September *Fortune,* which constituted one of the most comprehensive reports on the Chinese situation published in any U.S. publication prior to Pearl Harbor.

The scope of Time Inc.'s news-gathering services had expanded enormously with the outbreak of the European war. Everywhere photographers and correspondents were on the move; Wilson Hicks, executive editor of *Life,* told the advertising salesmen at their annual convention in June 1941: "[*Life's*] staff photographers and photogra-

472

phers on whose services it has first call total more than those employed by the world's largest news picture agency. Our picture operations are farther flung than those of all the newspapers of the United States combined insofar as use of staff in foreign fields is concerned. In scope of action on the newsfronts of the world there never has been anything in the history of journalism like the picture-getting activity by *Life* so far this year." The company also had correspondents on every war front where accreditation was possible.

In June *Life* published the first interview Hitler had granted to an American press correspondent in a year. Luce had commissioned his host in Brussels, former Ambassador to Belgium John Cudahy, to do a series of articles on German-occupied Europe. The series culminated in Cudahy's reception by Hitler; the interview contained the predictable assurances by the German dictator that he had no aggressive designs on the U.S. In this case the editors were somewhat embarrassed by their own initiative because Cudahy's interview so strongly furthered German propaganda. It was published with a disclaimer, together with a report on the Roosevelt speech of May 27 in which the President proclaimed a state of unlimited national emergency—another step short of war. The editors introduced the Hitler interview with this comment: *"Life* suspects that Hitler chose this particular time for his interview because he hoped it would undercut the President's speech. In *Life*'s opinion the President's speech contained an annihilating answer to Adolf Hitler's 'honeyed words.' This answer is printed immediately following the interview."

The Hitler interview created scarcely a ripple of controversy; a year or two earlier it might have stirred debate, but by this time U.S. opinion had so hardened against the Nazis that even the most rabid isolationist hesitated to cite Hitler's words in support of his position. Hitler had given too many assurances of non-aggression and broken them too often. *Life*'s "scoop" in this instance was merely a footnote to history.

In the course of their worldwide search for news, many *Time* and *Life* editors, reporters and photographers by 1941 shared the experience of baptism by fire; only two, however, had the quite uncommon fate of being taken prisoner on the high seas. *Fortune* writer Charles

473

J. V. Murphy and *Life* photographer David E. Scherman were assigned to South Africa to attempt to get into Dakar, then under the control of the Free French. They flew to Recife, Brazil, there boarded the steamship *Zamzam,* sailing under the neutral flag of Egypt, carrying passengers who included 120 missionaries, 73 women, 35 children. Early one morning, five days out of Capetown, the *Zamzam* was intercepted by the German raider *Atlantis* and shelled. A number were wounded, a few seriously. The captain ordered the sinking ship abandoned and the Germans later, having taken aboard the *Zamzam*'s passengers and crew, sent her to the bottom. The Admiralty announced, after the *Zamzam* was more than thirty days overdue, that she was "presumed lost." Immediately afterward, the Nazi radio announced that everyone, including Murphy and Scherman, was safe.

The *Atlantis,* called at that time *Tamesis,* had transferred the *Zamzam*'s passengers and crew to her supply ship *Dresden,* a cargo vessel in the South American trade which had earlier been a supply vessel for the *Graf Spee.* Conditions aboard the *Zamzam* had been far from ideal. The food was so bad, said Murphy, that the sinking actually came as a relief. But life aboard the *Dresden* was all but intolerable. The male passengers were crowded into forward holds, the women and children into a half-dozen small cabins topside; except for bread, the diet was almost entirely liquid; sanitary conditions were offensive (the prisoners had to build their own privies). The *Zamzam* passengers elected Murphy to be their spokesman and he strenuously protested their being exposed to further danger when the *Dresden* lurked at sea and then decided to run the British blockade. "What we lived and prayed for was a British warship," Murphy wrote. "What we feared was a British submarine."

Scherman had taken pictures of everything, including the sinking of the *Zamzam.* When the passengers were finally put ashore in Occupied France his films were confiscated and sent to Berlin for censorship. Scherman had anticipated that this would happen, and had secreted four undeveloped rolls in some gauze bandages and tubes of toothpaste and shaving cream. With the help of friendly, unnamed emissaries, these arrived on Billings' desk in advance of Murphy's

474

and Scherman's return to New York via Lisbon. Murphy's article and Scherman's remarkable pictures appeared in *Life*'s June 23 issue. The pictures of the German raider were posted in the wardroom of every ship of the line, enabling the H.M.S. *Devonshire* to identify and sink her despite her masquerade as a neutral. German censors miraculously returned the bulk of the film just before Pearl Harbor and a second story appeared in *Life*'s December 15 issue.

In June the Nazi attack on the Soviet Union changed the entire character of the war. It was, to most people, a stunning surprise, though the U.S. commercial attaché in Berlin had an inkling of the German plans and Sumner Welles had transmitted his reports to Stalin through the Soviet Ambassador. Without benefit of such advice, the editors of *Life,* by sheer luck and intuition, were well prepared. Executive Editor Wilson Hicks had a strong hunch that the "all quiet on the Eastern Front" between Germany and the U.S.S.R. would not last. He recalled that ten years earlier Margaret Bourke-White had done an extensive job of photo reportage for *Fortune* on Russia which had been very favorably received by the Soviet Government. He assigned her to do a new portfolio on the Soviet Union, assuming that even if there were no hostilities the investment in time and money would produce a notable set of pictures. The Russians granted visas to Miss Bourke-White and her husband, Erskine Caldwell, and they reached Moscow after first flying to Chungking.

Bourke-White and her husband arrived in Moscow a month before the German attack came, but she learned to her consternation that Stalin had imposed a ban on all photography. "Here was I, facing the biggest scoop of my life: the biggest country enters the biggest war in the world and I was the only photographer on the spot, representing any publication and coming from any foreign country," she wrote.[6] There was a problem too about remaining in Moscow; U.S. Ambassador Laurence Steinhardt warned Bourke-White and Caldwell to leave, offering them the last two tickets on the Trans-Siberian Railway. However, he also told her that if she insisted on staying, he would do what he could to help. Her exclusive pictures of Moscow

[6] *Portrait of Myself* (Simon and Schuster, 1963).

under a German night attack were taken from the roof of the U.S. Embassy and were a world scoop of the first magnitude. In taking them Bourke-White narrowly escaped death; she left the roof a moment before a bomb landed in the street below, shattering the windows of the Embassy. The blast would certainly have blown her off the roof.

Bourke-White remained in Moscow and by her own cajolery managed to continue her photography and produce world exclusives for *Life* for many weeks. With the help of Harry Hopkins, F.D.R.'s personal envoy to Stalin, she received permission to photograph Stalin himself, and Hopkins couriered the films to the United States. She and Caldwell returned to the West via the dangerous convoy route from Archangel around the North Cape.

The Foreign News section of *Time,* only the week before the German attack, had reported a "crisis" in Russo-German relations. The editors did not foresee war. But, just in case, they had on hand four-color engravings of Stalin and Soviet Marshal Timoshenko. On Sunday morning, June 22, 800,000 covers of Emir Abdullah of Trans-Jordan, ready for binding, were scrapped, and the Timoshenko-Stalin cover became the fastest color-printing job ever accomplished up to that time. In Berlin the husband-and-wife reportorial team Stephen and Lael Laird, after months of frustration because the German censorship would let them file few dispatches for *Time* and *Life,* had applied for exit permits. These, too, at first were denied, but after months of argument they were suddenly granted and the Lairds had reached Switzerland en route home when the German-Russian fighting broke out. Swiss regulations forbade correspondents in transit from filing about conditions in Germany. But with the news of the German attack Laird defied the regulations, went on the telephone and succeeded in dictating to New York a story on Berlin as it was just before the Germans opened the new front, and an account from the German side of Rudolf Hess's abortive peace-making flight to Britain. A great deal of Laird's information had not so far appeared in any newspaper.

Prentice took great pride in the magazine's performance. In a talk to the advertising and circulation departments he said, "I have been with *Time* eleven years now. I thought I knew *Time* pretty well. But in the past three months as publisher I have learned that my whole idea of *Time* editorial was four or five years out of date. . . . Ten years ago *Time* was primarily a brilliantly written, clear, condensed, vivid digest of the news in the newspapers. . . . But today not half of the news in *Time* can be found in the newspapers. We use the newspapers as invaluable tip sheets for our guidance in deciding what stories to go look for ourselves—but a *Time* story begins where the newspapers leave off." Even discounting Prentice's natural bias, there was some truth in the statement.

Time Inc.'s commitment to the interventionist argument kept it involved in that great debate right up until Pearl Harbor. Into this debate the German onslaught on the Soviet Union introduced a new and complicating element. *Life* thought it was "a gigantic stroke of luck for hard-pressed Britain and the unprepared U.S." because it "temporarily increased the defenses of the U.S. by the whole Red Army." The comment appeared in *Life*'s July 7 issue.[7]

Time in its lead article also viewed the German attack as possibly "the luckiest military break for the U.S.—outside of an outright defeat for Germany in battle—that the President could have hoped for. . . . He had committed the U.S. to the defeat of Hitler and the nation was still militarily unprepared; now the U.S. had gained at least a few precious days or weeks to push its arming, had found another great power besides Britain to keep Hitler occupied a little longer. . . . But the time gained was no gain unless urgent use was made of it. No good use would be made of it if the U.S., pleased to see Nazism fighting Communism, relaxed its defense efforts. . . ." Among those who felt quite differently about Russia's involvement was former President Herbert Hoover, who cited Stalin's "militant

---

[7] This was another special issue on National Defense, timed to coincide with July 4 and help rouse "the martial spirit." It was perhaps the most impressive of these special issues, with twenty pages of color—more than *Life* had ever used before. It also contained specially commissioned paintings by leading U.S. painters, a forerunner of *Life*'s war-art project leading to the assignment of these painters to battlefronts around the world. To cover the big news from Russia, at the last minute a spread of maps was inserted in the issue.

477

Communist conspiracy" as a plot against the whole democratic world. *Time* quoted Hoover as saying, "It makes the whole argument of our joining the war to bring the four freedoms [8] to mankind a Gargantuan jest." *Time* observed: "From Herbert Hoover down to the smallest hater of Communism, far too many U.S. citizens reacted with an emotional belch."

The former President was offended and protested in a personal note to Luce: "You are still on the masthead of *Time* as Editor. So it is your privilege to get the kicks." Luce replied:

> It is indeed my privilege to receive the kicks—although sometimes they are so good for the soul that I am willing to share them with my colleagues. . . . It was certainly a mistake for *Time* to use your name in the sentence which contained the phrase "emotional belch." . . . May I say [that] your own position is not as clear as it might be. Is it to our interest that Great Britain should win against Hitler? If so, is it possible to put a limitation on the degree of that interest? . . . Or again, in your opinion, should Great Britain sue for peace now? If so, would that be a Hitler victory or wouldn't it? What terms? . . . Perhaps I have not informed myself as to your position as carefully as I should have, but I confess that short of the complete Lindberghian view [absolute isolationism] I don't see how you can set up a doctrine of limited liability in this matter. . . . I said recently that to win a war without fighting is a good trick if you know how to do it. I don't. . . .

The nation still remained divided; on August 12, in the House of Representatives, the resolution extending the service of draftees from twelve to thirty months was saved only by Speaker Sam Rayburn's vote, which broke a 202–202 tie. By this narrow margin the new citizen army of the U.S. was kept in being. The morale in the training camps was low. A reporter for *Life,* who spent a week with a National Guard unit in training, reported that the word among the men was

[8] In the annual message to Congress, January 6, 1941, Roosevelt listed as "the essential freedoms": freedom of speech; freedom of worship; freedom from want; freedom from fear.

478

"OHIO," G.I. code for "Over the Hill in October," meaning a threat to quit when their twelve months' service was up. For this mood *Life* blamed the authorities, concluding: "As far as the men can see, the Army has no goal. It does not know whether it is going to fight, or when or where. If the U.S. political leaders have set any military objective, they have not made it clear to the Army."

The editors appended their own comment: "Whether the morale situation which *Life*'s reporter found is typical of all the new soldiers, *Life* does not attempt to say. His report is published as a sampling of soldier sentiment, with the feeling that the sooner their complaints are honestly faced the sooner they can be dealt with."

Although *Life*'s meritorious purpose was to prod the Army into making training more meaningful, the report provided ammunition for the isolationists. It was picked up eagerly as evidence that the country was still against going to war. The German and Italian press gave it great play. General Marshall, Luce recalled, gave him "a tremendous bawling out" for lending aid and comfort to the enemy. "I found it not always possible to elucidate journalistic motives to soldiers, so I made no great reply," Luce said.

In October *Time* published a cover story on General Robert E. Wood, head of Sears, Roebuck, and chairman of the America First Committee. Respectful of Wood personally, the story castigated the movement, which was described as "a garden [in which] . . . the weeds had gotten out of hand and threatened to choke [it]—Jew-haters, Roosevelt-haters, England-haters, Coughlinites, politicians, demagogues." And the three principal publicists who still supported isolationism—Colonel Robert McCormick, publisher of the Chicago *Tribune,* and his cousins, Captain Joseph Patterson of the New York *Daily News* and Mrs. Eleanor Patterson of the Washington *Times-Herald*—were described as "the Three Furies" who "increased their howls . . . ground out their daily gripes at the risks involved in the Administration's policy of trying to stop Hitler."

This drew an angry riposte in the form of two column-length editorials in the New York *Daily News.* The Scottish-Irish and Mid-western backgrounds of the McCormicks and Pattersons, whose fore-fathers wanted to get "as far away [as possible] from England and English aristocratic ideas" including "lords of the manor and a serv-

479

ant class," were contrasted with Luce's "ancestral background," which, said the *News,* "may help to explain why Mr. Luce is an interventionist." He had been

> born in China, and spent the first 12 or 14 formative years . . . surrounded by servants who at that time could be hired for $4 to $8 a month per servant [which] inevitably gave him an internationalist slant on things. It is therefore natural for Mr. Luce to feel that the United States ought to rescue China from the Japanese and the French, Dutch, Belgians, Russians, etc., etc., from the Germans. The likelihood that these rescue adventures will gut the United States of much of its real wealth . . . does not cut overmuch ice with Mr. Luce. But it is also natural for us, with our Midwestern background, to think first of America. . . .

At this moment when Luce personally and the Time Inc. publications were under attack by some of F.D.R.'s most bitter journalistic critics, the President himself turned on *Time.* Over the years the relations between F.D.R. and Luce had never been close in spite of Roosevelt's cordiality to the magazine in its early days. Luce's identification with the Willkie campaign and the continuing criticism of the Administration's policy undoubtedly rankled with the White House. They do not altogether explain the vehemence with which the President turned on *Time* as a result of an incident in November 1941.

Reporting on the political crisis facing Chile's President Pedro Aguirre Cerda's Popular Front government, *Time* reported that "While the Popular Front swayed, bushy-mustached President Aguirre felt more and more like a man who does not govern but merely presides. He spent more and more time with the red wine he cultivates." There was an immediate, outraged demand from Chile for an official U.S. apology. Adding to the White House's discomfiture, ten days after the article appeared, Aguirre died. On the day of his death, which coincided with Roosevelt's weekly press conference, the President said (and gave a rare authorization to be quoted directly):

> The Government of the United States has been forced to apologize to the Government of Chile for an article written in *Time*

480

magazine—a disgusting lie which appeared in that magazine.
. . . This article was a notable contribution to Nazi propaganda
against the United States. . . . This is another illustration of how
some American papers and writers are stocking the arsenals of
propaganda of the Nazis to be used against us.

The propriety of *Time*'s report was open to question; the facts were
not. Chileans themselves knew that what *Time* had insinuated was
true. The Roosevelt attack went far beyond any diplomatic require-
ment; it was inexplicable except in terms of personal pique or resentment.[9] Luce felt he must answer F.D.R.'s accusation: *"Time* realizes
that the pressure of international politics may explain President Roosevelt's denunciation but believes that the President's words were
unwarranted by the facts and unwise as an attack on a free and honest
press." A letter to this effect was sent to every subscriber in Chile.

While this incident was taking place, Secretary of State Hull was
nearing the end of his protracted negotiations with the special Japanese envoys in Washington. Cables from the Orient told of new
Japanese troop movements in French Indo-China indicating a move
to cut the Burma Road. The U.S. and Japan were on the verge of war.
Luce once said, *"Time* was not nearly as prescient as it ought to have
been and we were totally innocent as to Pearl Harbor." So, of course,
were the nation and its press.

Some years after Pearl Harbor, cautioning one of his correspondents that governments often conceal the risks of war, Luce recalled a
private off-the-record meeting which he had had with Under Secretary
of State Sumner Welles. Welles, he said, "drew a big map of Asia and
ran his finger across a line in South Asia and said, in effect, that if the
Japanese crossed that line there would be war. High officials in the
Government were estimating the chances [of a Japanese war] however
much their calculations may have been concealed from the public.
. . ." That was in the summer of 1941.

By November all serious journalists were openly calculating the
chances of war, and Washington no longer attempted to minimize the

[9] Roosevelt often nurtured resentment against journalistic critics. He once
awarded "an iron cross" to John O'Donnell, of the New York *Daily News,* who
was a bitter-end isolationist.

situation. A *Time* article in the November 24 issue, written by Robert Cantwell, told of the flight of Japan's special envoy, Saburo Kurusu, to the last fateful negotiations in Washington:

Mussolini placed his desk at the end of a huge room so that visitors would have time to grow uncomfortable as they approached it. Last week Saburo Kurusu . . . crossed the U.S. like a man going across a more enormous room.

Nobody tried to make Saburo Kurusu uncomfortable as he made his way across the wide U.S. floor of deserts, mountains, factories, farms, politics, confusion, but at each step he could see reminders of the power of the U.S. . . . . Kurusu flew southward . . . over California's infinitely fertile farmlands, over forests of oil derricks, in fields which alone produce many times as much oil as Japan consumes. . . .

He talked politely to fellow passengers, gave no hint of his thoughts. He must have known that in Washington, at the other end of the enormous room, it was estimated that the chances were 9-to-10 that Japan and the U.S. would go to war.

Two weeks later, in the issue dated December 8, put to press December 1, the lead *Time* story under The Presidency said:

Everything was ready. From Rangoon to Honolulu, every man was at battle stations. And Franklin Roosevelt had to return to his. This was the last act of the drama.

The U.S. position had the simple clarity of a stone wall. One nervous twitch of a Japanese trigger finger, one jump in any direction, one overt act, might be enough. A vast array of armies, of navies, of air fleets were stretched now in the position of track runners, in the tension of the moment before the starter's gun.

A bare chance of peace remained—of a kind of peace very close to war but not quite war. This bare chance was that the Japanese would remain immobile on all fronts but the Chinese. Very few men who were in a position to know thought much of this chance.

* * *

482

The issue of *Life* dated December 8, which appeared on the news-stands December 5, carried a personality sketch of General Douglas MacArthur written by Mrs. Luce, who had flown to Manila in October to interview the newly appointed commander of the U.S. Far Eastern forces. The lead article in the same issue was headlined "The Ancient Imperial Power of Japan Comes to a Showdown with America." It concluded: "The stage was set for war, a distant, dangerous, hard amphibious war for which the American nation was not yet fully prepared." In the Newsfronts section the mood of the American people was described as "extraordinarily complacent. . . . Washington cocked tense ears for the first sounds of shooting on the wide Pacific. Congressional leaders—even isolationists—predicted that a declaration of war on Japan could be shoved through both houses with as little difficulty as a minor appropriation. There was no question that the country was thoroughly aware of the situation. Newspaper headlines loomed heavy with portents. Yet no one worried. . . . Americans were not frightened by the Japanese. . . . The American people felt secure in the belief that America's superb Navy could cope with all difficulties. Americans felt confident, rightly or wrongly, that the Japs were pushovers."

Millions of Americans still remember where they were when the news came on December 7, 1941. Gottfried was lunching with his wife at Longchamps Restaurant, 49th Street and Madison Avenue, when his National Affairs editor, T. S. Matthews, and writer Calvin Fixx came to his table and told him: "The Japs have just bombed Pearl Harbor."

"Matthews may have expected me to jump to my feet and gallop off in all directions," said Gottfried. "He agreed to sit down and have coffee with us while we made new editorial plans for the week's issue. Pearl Harbor was well timed, from *Time*'s point of view. We had thirty-six hours in which to remake the magazine."

The Luces were entertaining guests at Sunday luncheon at their Greenwich, Connecticut, home when the news came over the radio. The editor-in-chief was in his office by mid-afternoon. (His first order was to add a new section to *Time*, "The U.S. at War.") *Life* had gone to press as usual Saturday night. The editorial staff began to reassem-

483

ble, and by 2:30 Sunday afternoon they were remaking the first seven pages of the magazine. In Chicago the production crew had stopped the presses. A new lead article, with pictures of a once serene, formidable-looking Pearl Harbor, appeared in all but the first 125,000 copies (out of 3,400,000) of the December 15 issue, on the stands December 12.

Louis de Rochemont was in New Hampshire. The regular monthly release of *The March of Time*—a film about the Free French—was scheduled to be shown Thursday, December 11, at the Radio City Music Hall and theaters all across the country. He ordered it withdrawn, and between midnight Sunday and Wednesday evening *The March of Time* cut and edited a new release, "Our America at War."

Sometime in the middle of that busy Sunday afternoon Luce took time out from his pressing schedule to telephone his father. They were both deeply moved by what had happened and talked of the new responsibilities the U.S. must now shoulder. The elder Luce, as he hung up the receiver, turned to his wife and said, "I am so glad Harry called. His faith reassures me." That night he died in his sleep. The issue of *Time* which carried the news of Pearl Harbor also printed this item in Milestones:

> *Died.* Dr. Henry Winters Luce, 73, retired Presbyterian Missionary to China, father of *Time* editor Henry R. Luce; in Haverford, Pa. Lifelong friend of China, largely responsible for the establishment of Shantung's first Christian University and Peking's Yenching University, he was a dynamic worker for the political, cultural and religious education of the Chinese. He died in his sleep on the day the U.S. and China became allies against Japan.

The *Time* news service on December 7 had requested correspondents from Portland, Maine, to Portland, Oregon, to report the impact of the news on their fellow citizens. The over-all impression was that after the first shock there was, in very many cases, a sense of relief that the time of indecision was over, that the country was united at last.

484

Luce poured his feelings into perhaps the most emotional of his editorials—a two-page article which led the *Life* issue of December 22. It was written within a few days after the beginning of war and his father's death:

> We have come to the end, now, of as pusillanimous an epoch as there ever was in the history of a great people: the twenty years of American history between 1921 and 1941. It is not even possible to call these years tragic, for tragedy implies at least the dignity of fate. And there was no dignity in these years, and nothing of fate that we did not bring upon ourselves. The epoch that is closing was much less tragic than it was shameful. . . .
>
> This is the day of wrath. It is also the day of hope. . . . For this hour America was made. Uniquely among the nations, America was created out of the hopes of mankind and dedicated to the fulfillment of those hopes. It is for this reason that we accept only two alternatives—either to die in the smoking ruins of a totally destroyed America or else to justify forever the faith of our fathers and the hopes of mankind.

The editorial helps explain why Luce felt that Pearl Harbor, a momentous event in the nation's history, marked a milestone in the company. He was insistent, just before his own death in 1967, that this first volume of the corporation's history end with that "day of wrath." He and Briton Hadden, by creating in *Time* a new and unique form of magazine journalism, had, within a decade, changed the face of all of American journalism; in *Fortune,* then in *Life,* Luce had created still newer media which gave him and his editors an opportunity to raise their voices against the trend of the times. He felt that *Life,* in particular, had done a great deal to restore pride in the American past, and to prepare the U.S. for a new responsibility in the world. When war came, the Time Inc. magazines, *The March of Time* on radio and on the screen were, in his mind, already instruments of a new national purpose.

On December 17 Luce addressed a letter to the President of the United States in which he explained his thinking:

485

. . . You have spoken of the grave responsibilities of the press. They include, we presume, the responsibility of candor and even of criticism within the limits of patriotism, and specifically for the purpose of military victory. That makes our job more difficult perhaps than any other civilian responsibility. We will not flinch it—and we will eagerly welcome guidance and counsel.

During the past two years, we have been in constant touch with various branches of the government and, while assuming full personal responsibility for our own conduct, we have endeavored to be guided by many informal suggestions made to us. And in the days to come—far beyond strict compliance with whatever rules may be laid down for us by the necessities of war —we can think of no greater happiness than to be of service to any branch of our government and to its armed forces. For the dearest wish of all of us is to tell the story of absolute victory under your leadership.

Attached to this formal pledge of support was a note in Luce's own handwriting:

Dear Mr. President,

The enclosed letter is belated because we have been on the job steadily since Dec. 7. I wanted to write it to express to you personally the feelings of my colleagues and myself. May I add a personal word just for myself?

The drubbing you handed out to *Time*—before Dec. 7— was as tough a wallop as I ever had to take. If it will help you any to win the war, I can take worse ones. Go to it! And God bless you.

Faithfully yours,

Harry.

Index

487

ROBERT T. ELSON has worked for Time Inc. for twenty-five years, serving in varying capacities from writer to Deputy Managing Editor and then General Manager of *Life*. His last post before undertaking the writing of this book was that of Chief Correspondent in London for the *Time-Life* News Service.

DUNCAN NORTON-TAYLOR had a distinguished career at Time Inc. extending over nearly thirty years. As a writer and then Senior Editor of *Time* he wrote some sixty "cover stories." After transfer to *Fortune,* where he served on the Board of Editors, he became successively Executive Editor and Managing Editor.

MISS MARGARET QUIMBY has been a senior editorial researcher of *Time;* MRS. ELSA WARDELL was previously a member of the editorial research staff of *Fortune;* MISS MARIE MC CRUM previously was a member of the Corporate staff; and MISS CELIA SUGARMAN lived through a good part of the history here recorded, having joined Time Inc. during the period in which its headquarters were in Cleveland, Ohio.